EUROPE
GOES EAST

EU enlargement, diversity and uncertainty

To Frances and Victoria

EUROPE GOES EAST

EU enlargement, diversity and uncertainty

Edited by **Derek Hall**
Scottish Agricultural College,
Auchincruive, Ayrshire, UK

and **Darrick Danta**
California State University,
Northridge, USA

London: The Stationery Office

© The Stationery Office 2000

The information contained in this publication is believed to be correct at the time of manufacture. Whilst care has been taken to ensure that the information is accurate, the publisher can accept no responsibility for any errors or omissions or for changes to the details given.

Please note that the substance of Chapter 7 on Poland by Andrew Dawson was first published in *The Central and Eastern Europe Handbook: Prospects onto the 21st Century* (Patrick Heenan and Monique Lamontagne, eds). Fitzroy Dearborn, Chicago, 1999.

A CIP catalogue record of this book is available from the British Library
A Library of Congress CIP catalogue record has been applied for

First published 2000

ISBN 0 11 702643 3

Printed in the United Kingdom by Polestar Wheatons Ltd, Exeter
TJ1961 C8 11/00

Published by The Stationery Office and available from:

The Stationery Office
(mail, telephone and fax orders only)
PO Box 29, Norwich NR3 1GN
General enquiries / Telephone orders 0870 600 5522
Fax orders 0870 600 5533

www.thestationeryoffice.com

The Stationery Office Bookshops
123 Kingsway, London, WC2B 6PQ
020 7242 6393 Fax 020 7242 6412
68-69 Bull Street, Birmingham, B4 6AD
0121 236 9696 Fax 0121 236 9699
33 Wine Street, Bristol, BS1 2BQ
0117 926 4306 Fax 0117 929 4515
9–21 Princess Street, Manchester, M60 8AS
0161 834 7201 Fax 0161 833 0634
16 Arthur Street, Belfast, BT1 4GD
028 9023 8451 Fax 028 9023 5401
The Stationery Office Oriel Bookshop
18–19, High Street, Cardiff CF1 2BZ
029 2039 5548 Fax 029 2038 4347
71 Lothian Road, Edinburgh, EH3 9AZ
0870 606 5566 Fax 0870 606 5588

The Stationery Office's Accredited Agents
(see Yellow Pages)

and through good booksellers

CONTENTS

LIST OF TABLES

LIST OF FIGURES

NOTES ON THE CONTRIBUTORS

John Agnew is professor and chairman of the geography department, University of California, Los Angeles (UCLA), USA.

Vladimir Balaz is principal researcher at the Institute of Forecasting, Slovak Academy of Science, Bratislava, and a research fellow in the department of geography at the University of Exeter, England.

Frank Carter is reader in the geography of eastern Europe at the School of Slavonic and East European Studies (SSEES) and University College, London, England.

Darrick Danta is professor of geography at California State University, Northridge (CSUN), USA.

Andrew Dawson is reader in geography at the University of St Andrews, Scotland.

Alan Dingsdale is principal lecturer in geography in the Faculty of Humanities, Nottingham Trent University, England.

Anton Gosar is associate professor in the department of geography, University of Ljubljana, Slovenia.

Deborah L. Gourlay is a rural and regional policy research specialist in the management division of the Scottish Agricultural College (SAC), based in Aberdeen, Scotland.

Derek Hall is professor of regional development at the Scottish Agricultural College (SAC), Auchincruive, Scotland.

David Marples is professor of history and acting director of the Canadian Institute of Ukrainian Studies, University of Alberta, Canada.

Jesus del Río Luelmo is a researcher at the Institut d'Études Politiques de Paris, and previously studied at the Universities of Salamanca (Spain) and Exeter (England).

David Turnock is reader in geography at the University of Leicester, England.

Tim Unwin is reader and head of the geography department, Royal Holloway College, University of London, England.

Allan M. Williams is professor of human geography and European studies at the University of Exeter, England.

PREFACE

This example of transatlantic collaboration represents a timely and, we hope, important contribution to the debate and understanding of the EU enlargement process as it impacts upon the states and citizens of central, eastern and Mediterranean Europe. As editors who have collaborated previously, we are grateful to the distinguished range of contributors who agreed to participate in this venture. The evolution of this volume has not been simple, however. As the EU has itself been evolving policies and attitudes toward the candidate and potential candidate countries of eastern and Mediterranean parts of the continent, so central and eastern Europe itself has been undergoing change and transformation. In the case of parts of the Balkans this process has placed uncomfortable demands upon west Europeans and their allies.

Although the authors of chapters within each section were given similar guidelines, they have been allowed to express the particularly characteristic emphasis of each respective country. Thus the weight given to historical, economic, political and geographical factors varies appropriately in relation to the circumstances of each country. Each, however, is intended to emphasise the relationship between national development and EU enlargement, however apparently minimal that may be in certain cases.

Consistency of treatment and style in such a volume as this inevitably presents editorial problems and ultimately arbitrary decisions. The cartographic style adopted has been to employ anglicised versions of the names of capital cities and of other familiar features regularly anglicised (such as 'Chernobyl'), but otherwise to use local versions of names. Recognising which names fall into the latter group is an arbitrary process which we hope has not produced outrageous inconsistencies. The accuracy and comparability of statistical data continue to pose problems: differences between national and international compilations and between different international compilers inevitably present anomalies. Thus, for example, although the international data employed in Table 1.1 as a means of providing comparative evaluation are derived from a reputable international source, they may differ slightly from the national statistics cited by authors in particular country chapters. We have attempted to keep such disparities to a minimum.

There has been a conscious effort to keep 'Eurospeak' to a minimum. The preceding glossary contains explanations of the acronyms used in this volume and, in particular, highlights some of the terms employed specifically by the European institutions in the enlargement process.

Acknowledgements are due to a wide range of people who have contributed materially and spiritually to this work. In California, to Victoria Martin for her steadfast support and understanding during long evenings and weekends spent in the office rather than at home. In Scotland, to Frances Brown for her sanity and forbearance. To David Fuller in the department of geography, California State University, Northridge, who produced many of the maps for this volume. At the Scottish Agricultural College, Auchincruive, to Linsey Hunter for secretarial and moral support, to David Arnot for computer wizardry with disks in unfamiliar formats, and to numerous other colleagues and friends for their good humour and tolerance. To Hannu Heinilä and colleagues at Häme Polytechnic in Finland, for the time, space and network access out of normal working hours. At The Stationery Office: to Iain Stevenson who encouraged the initial ideas, inaugurated the process and then moved on; to Emma Martin who took over the baton; to Tim Probart, Wendy Lees and Michele Staple who have seen the project to its conclusion, along with the rest of the production team. In particular, Frances Maher should be singled out for her excellent, scrupulous copy-editing. Finally, thanks are due to all the contributors to this volume, and particularly to those for whom its evolution may have seemed a rather protracted affair, as no doubt the EU enlargement process itself will be.

Darrick Danta
Granada Hills, California

Derek Hall
Maidens, Ayrshire

GLOSSARY

$	US dollar
acquis communautaire	the common law of the EU
AD	*anno domini*
ANTREC	Asociata Nationala de Turism Rural, Ecologic i Cultural (Romania)
avis	EU Opinion (on accession applications)
AWS	Solidarity Electoral Action (Poland)
BC	before Christ
BCP	Bulgarian Communist Party
B–H	Bosnia and Hercegovina
bn	billion
BPF	Belarusian Popular Front
BSECC	Black Sea Economic Co-operation Council
BSP	Bulgarian Socialist Party
CAP	Common Agricultural Policy
CCET	Centre for Co-operation with the Economies in Transition
CCT	common customs tariff
CEE	central and eastern Europe(an)
CEECs	central and eastern European countries
CEFTA	Central European Free Trade Agreement
CFCs	chlorofluorocarbons
CFSP	common foreign and security policy
CIA	Central Intelligence Agency (USA)
CIS	Commonwealth of Independent States
CMEA	Council for Mutual Economic Assistance (Comecon)
CPF	Croatian privatisation fund
CSCE	Conference on Security and Co-operation in Europe
CSUN	California State University, Northridge
cu	cubic
DAHR	Democratic Alliance of Hungarians in Romania
DCR	Democratic Convention of Romania

DDT	dichlorodiphenyltrichloroethane
DG	Directorate General
DM	Deutschmark (currency)
DNSF	Democratic National Salvation Front (Romania)
€	euro: European currency unit
EAGGF	European Agricultural Guidance and Guarantee Fund
EBRD	European Bank for Reconstruction and Development
EC	European Commission; European Community
ECB	European Central Bank
ECSC	European Coal and Steel Community
ECU	European currency unit
EEA	European Economic Area
EEC	European Economic Community
EEK	Estonian kroon (currency)
EFF	extended fund facility
EFTA	European Free Trade Association
EIA	Estonian Investment Agency
EIB	European Investment Bank
EID	European Integration Department
EIU	Economist Intelligence Unit
EMEP	Environment Monitoring and Evaluation Programme
EMU	Economic and Monetary Union
EP	European Parliament
ERDF	European Regional Development Fund
ESF	European Social Fund
EU	European Union
EU6	EEC (later EU) founding members (Belgium, France, West Germany, Italy, Luxembourg, the Netherlands)
EU15	current EU members (EU6 plus Austria, Denmark, Finland, Greece, Ireland, Spain, Portugal, Sweden, United Kingdom)
EU20	EU15 plus the Czech Republic, Estonia, Hungary, Poland, Slovenia
Euratom	European Atomic Energy Community
FAO	(United Nations) Food and Agriculture Organization
FDI	foreign direct investment
FIFG	Financial Instrument for Fisheries Guidance
FRY	Federal Republic of Yugoslavia
FSU	former Soviet Union
FYR	former Yugoslav Republic

FYROM	Former Yugoslav Republic of Macedonia
G-7	Group of Seven (Canada, France, Germany, Italy, Japan, UK, USA)
GATT	General Agreement on Tariffs and Trade
GDP	gross domestic product
GDR	German Democratic Republic
GNP	gross national product
GRP	Greater Romania Party
GUAM	Georgia–Ukraine–Azerbaijan–Moldova
GVA	gross value-added
ha	hectare
HDZ	Croatian Democratic Union
HRK	Croatian kuna (currency)
HZDS	Movement for Democratic Slovakia
IBRD	International Bank for Reconstruction and Development (World Bank)
IFOR	NATO-led peacekeeping force in Bosnia and Hercegovina
IGC	Inter-Governmental Conference
IMF	International Monetary Fund
INTERREG	EU assistance programme to develop cross-border co-operation and help areas on the Union's internal and external borders to overcome specific problems arising from their comparatively isolated position
ISPA	Instrument for Structural Policies for Pre-Accession
JNA	Yugoslav National Army
KESH	Albanian energy corporation
kg	kilogram
KGB	Soviet intelligence service
KHF	(UK) Know-How Fund for central and eastern Europe
KLA	Kosova Liberation Army
km	kilometre
LDS	Liberal Democrats (Slovenia)
m	metre
MDF	Hungarian Democratic Forum
MEP	Member of European Parliament
mm	millimetres
mn	million
MOU	Memorandum of Understanding
MSzMP	Hungarian Socialist Workers' Party

MSzP	Hungarian Socialist Party
MW	megawatts
na	not available
NATO	North Atlantic Treaty Organization
NEM	New Economic Mechanism (Hungary, from 1968)
NGO	non-governmental organisation
NIS	newly independent states (the former Soviet Union minus the Baltic states)
NO_2	nitrogen dioxide
NSAA	Nuclear Safety Account Agreement
NSF	National Salvation Front (Romania)
OECD	Organization for Economic Co-operation and Development
OIC	Organization of Islamic Conference
OSCE	Organization for Security and Co-operation in Europe
PCA	partnership and co-operation agreement
PFM	Popular Front of Moldova
PHARE	Poland/Hungary Assistance for Economic Reconstruction (extended to much of the rest of central and eastern Europe)
PKK	Kurdish Workers' Party
PPP	purchasing power parity(ies)
PSDR	Party of Social Democracy of Romania
PSE	producer subsidy equivalents
PSL	Peasants' Party (Poland)
PWR	pressurised-water (nuclear) reactor
R&D	research and development
RBMK	graphite-moderated nuclear reactor
RFE/RL	Radio Free Europe/Radio Liberty
RNUP	Romanian National Unity Party
RS	Republika Srpska
RSS	Agrarian Party of Slovakia
SAC	Scottich Agricultural College
SAPARD	Special Accession Programme for Agriculture and Rural Development
SBA	(British) sovereign base area (Cyprus)
SBDI	South Balkan Development Initiative
SCAs	savings and credit associations (Moldova)
SEB	Skandinaviska Enskilda Banken
SECI	South-east European Co-operation Initiative
SFOR	NATO-led stabilization force (for Bosnia and Hercegovina)

SFRY	Socialist Federal Republic of Yugoslavia
SIDA	Swedish Development Corporation
SIP	Shelter Implementation Project (Ukraine)
SLD	Democratic Left Alliance (Poland)
S–M	Serbia and Montenegro
SMEs	small- and medium-sized enterprises
SO_2	sulphur dioxide
sq	square
SSR	Soviet Socialist Republic
SzDSz	Free Democratic Alliance (Hungary)
TACIS	EU assistance programme for the newly independent states and Mongolia
TALSE	Tallinn Stock Exchange
TB	tuberculosis
TCA	trade and economic co-operation agreement
TD	Transdniestria
TDA	(US) Trade and Development Agency
TEM	Trans-European Motorway
TEMPUS	Trans-European Mobility Programme for University Studies
TER	Trans-European Railway
TEU	Treaty on European Union
TFSC	Turkish Federated State of Cyprus
TINA	Trans-European Infrastructure Needs Assessment
TRACECA	Transport Corridor Europe–Caucasus–Central Asia
TRNC	Turkish Republic of Northern Cyprus
UDF	Union of Democratic Forces (Bulgaria)
UDZ	Croatian Democratic Union
UK	United Kingdom
UN(O)	United Nations (Organization)
UNDP	United Nations Development Programme
UNECE	United Nations Economic Commission for Europe
UNEP	United Nations Environment Programme
UNHCR	United Nations High Commission for Refugees
US(A)	United States (of America)
USSR	Union of Soviet Socialist Republics
Utd DF	Union of Democratic Forces (Bulgaria)
VAT	value-added tax
VMRO	Macedonian Revolutionary Organisation

VPN	Public Against Violence Party (Slovakia)
VVER	Russian acronym for type of PWR
WEU	Western European Union
WHO	World Health Organization
World Bank	International Bank for Reconstruction and Development (IBRD)
WTO	World Trade Organization

Part I

The Context

1

INTRODUCTION

Darrick Danta and Derek Hall

A new European home?

The collapse of socialist politics and central planning of central and eastern European (CEE) countries in the late 1980s created the opportunity, indeed the necessity, of redefining Europe (Heffernan, 1998; Pinder, 1998b: vii; Anon, 2000d) (Figure 1.1). After throwing off the shackles that had bound them since the 1940s, the CEE countries were eager to rejoin the Europe from which they had been estranged by the Iron Curtain and Cold War politics. Like prodigal sons returning from exile, the atmosphere across CEE during mid- to late-1989 was palpable. By the same token, the countries of western Europe appeared all too happy to prepare the welcoming banquet. In particular, countries of CEE saw entrance to the European Union (EU) not just as advantageous and inevitable but as their rightful due. For its part, the EU in the early 1990s was set to embrace the notion of fast expansion eastwards.

A decade has now all but smothered these over-optimistic views held by both sides of the former divide. The countries of CEE soon realised that the Europe they had left some 50 to 60 years before was quite different now; and in the clear light of day the western countries saw just how far behind their brethren had fallen. Euphoria turned to pessimism as the problems of transforming whole economies, dealing with outmoded technology and overcoming entrenched political systems became all too real.

Overview of this volume

This volume seeks to provide insight into the evolving structure of Europe through the lens of the expansion of the European Union. In contrast to other recent works of this nature (Hardy *et al.*, 1995; Mayhew, 1998; Nicoll and Schoenberg, 1998; Dinan, 1999; Henderson, 1999; McCormick, 1999; Stirk and Weigall, 1999) that concentrate on EU legislation and/or topical aspects of integration, this volume presents a series of views on each of the applicant and potential applicant countries of Europe and their evolving relationship with the EU. By viewing the specific circumstances existing in the various nations, a much clearer understanding of the

Figure 1.1: Redefining Europe

context of European integration and EU expansion emerges. This volume thus provides a needed complement to the earlier works and in the process offers an overview of central and eastern Europe at the start of the new millennium.

The volume is organised as follows. The remainder of this introduction sets out a brief synopsis of the European Union in terms of its history, institutions and mechanisms for enlargement. This is followed by an introduction to the group of countries that are in various stages of progress toward EU entry. The majority of Part I comprises chapters intended to provide the context for the process of EU expansion. Allan Williams and Vlad Balaz provide an overview to the CEE applicant countries and details of legislation related to EU expansion. Deborah Gourlay then shifts to a discussion of policy aspects within the EU with respect to enlargement with CEE countries, and John Agnew sounds a particularly critical note in his evaluation of the shifting course of EU sentiments concerning expansion.

Part II is made up of a country-by-country evaluation of the 'first-' and 'second-wave' candidates for EU entry: the Czech Republic, Hungary, Poland, Slovenia, Estonia and Cyprus, symbolically followed by Slovakia, Latvia, Lithuania, Bulgaria, Romania and Malta, and finally Turkey, which although recognised as a candidate at the December 1999 Helsinki EU Summit, is likely to be some way behind most if not all the other 12 countries.

Part III examines those countries of less stable political and economic environments – the Balkans and the former Soviet Union – for whom EU accession, even where sought, is likely to be some considerable way off: Croatia, Bosnia and Hercegovina, Serbia and Montenegro, the Former Yugoslav Republic of Macedonia, Albania, Moldova, Belarus and Ukraine.

The volume concludes with a summary of the major aspects brought out in the various discussions and offers signposts for future developments. Given the nature of the subject matter of this volume, much of the discussion and data closely interrelate. Therefore, the editors have made every effort to cross-reference tables, chapters and other information where appropriate. Each chapter is accompanied by a standard reference map.

An evolving European Union

Much of the rhetoric surrounding the end of the Cold War in 1990 voiced the desire for closer European integration, as had been the case following the end of the Second World War 45 years earlier. For example Mikhail Gorbachev, in a 1989 speech to the Council of Europe, invoked Victor Hugo in a call for a higher union in the 'Common European House' (Mayhew, 1998: 9). This sentiment echoed Winston Churchill's famous 'United States of Europe' speech in September 1946, which helped to focus the collective imagination on a time when all Europeans would see themselves as part of a whole, so that disputes would be settled peacefully rather than through violent means.

The ideas of a united Europe were the inspiration that led, by May 1950, to Jean Monnet and Robert Schuman's plan for an alliance between France and Germany. In particular, the plan established the first instruments of European integration (Dinan, 1999: 1–201; McCormick, 1999: 57–85; Stirk and Weigall, 1999):

- the European Coal and Steel Community (ECSC), established in 1951;

- the European Atomic Energy Community (Euratom), established in 1957; and

- the European Economic Community (EEC), also established in 1957, which came into effect in January 1958.

The Community began to work closely with other European organisations, such as the Organization for European Co-operation (since 1961 the Organization for Economic Co-operation and Development), the North Atlantic Treaty Organization (NATO, founded 1949), the Western European Union (WEU, founded 1954) and the Organization for Security and Co-operation in Europe (OSCE, founded 1973). In addition, the Community established various bodies to further its goals (McCormick, 1999: 87–118):

- The European Commission handles most of the bureaucracy involved in running the institution.

- The Council of Ministers is the main decision-making body with responsibility for broad policy formation and implementation. The presidency of the Council rotates every six months.

- The European Parliament provides a democratic forum for debate and operates as a watchdog.

- The European Court of Justice hears cases involving member states.

- The European Council of heads of states meets at least twice yearly to discuss issues before the Union.

- Finally, the Committee of the Regions brings local concerns to the attention of the Council.

Most EU functions are carried out in Brussels, but Luxembourg and Strasbourg are also important centres of activity.

Since its inception the name of the main institution has changed. Although not made official until 1993, the EEC (also generally known as the 'Common Market' after a customs union came into effect in 1968), Euratom and the ECSC combined during the 1980s to form the 'European Community' (EC). In 1993 the Community underwent a major reorganisation that subsumed, but did not replace, the EC; the new name became the 'European Union' (EU). Currently, the EU is pursuing two broad courses of action: deepening and widening. The first goal involves various mechanisms aimed at bringing member countries into closer economic, political, administrative and security alliances. Important legislation and milestones along these lines include:

- 1951: Treaty of Paris established the ECSC.

- 1957: Treaties of Rome established the EEC and Euratom.

- 1962: Common Agricultural Policy (CAP) launched.

- 1968: Completion of Customs Union.

- 1975: European Council formed.

- 1979: European monetary system begun.

- 1986: Single European Act, which set the goal of creating a single market by 1993.

- 1993: Treaty on European Union (TEU), also known as the Maastricht Treaty, set the goals of achieving monetary union by 1999; new common economic policies; European citizenship; common foreign and security policy; and common policy on internal security.

- 1997: Treaty of Amsterdam covering various aspects of justice and home affairs.

- 1999: Launch of a common monetary policy and single currency, the euro.

Currently, the EU is considering issues of voting and representation, which will form the basis of the next round of treaties (Anon, 1999e).

The second goal of the Union has been that of widening, a process that has been occurring from the organisation's inception. Originally, the EEC consisted of six members: Belgium, France, Germany, Italy, Luxembourg and the Netherlands. However, soon other countries sought membership and the Community underwent a series of expansions:

- first enlargement 1973: Denmark, Ireland and the United Kingdom;

- second enlargement 1981: Greece;

- third enlargement 1986: Spain and Portugal;

- although not officially termed an Enlargement, the former German Democratic Republic was absorbed by virtue of German reunification in 1990; and

- fourth enlargement 1995: Austria, Finland and Sweden.

The latter – the 'EFTA enlargement' – was notable in that all three entrants had higher per capita levels of GDP than the EU average in the early 1990s (Edye and Lintner, 1996: 408).

An important consideration for the future expansion of the EU is the time taken in particular cases for countries to gain membership (McCormick, 1999: 70–74). The United Kingdom first applied for membership in 1961, but was vetoed twice by de Gaulle before finally entering the EU in 1973; a 12-year-period was also required for Denmark and Ireland to join. Greece had shown an interest in joining the Community since the 1950s, was made an associate member in 1961, formally applied in 1975, began negotiations in 1976 and was admitted in 1981. Portugal and Spain both applied in 1977, but political issues prevented them from becoming members until 1986. Austria, Finland and Sweden, members of the European Free Trade Association (EFTA), gained entrance in 1995 after applying in 1991.

Certain 'holdover' countries remain outside the Union. Norway applied for membership in 1962 and negotiations were concluded ten years later; but referenda held in the country in 1972 and 1994 failed to return the sufficient majority in favour of entry. Turkey applied for membership in 1987 (Chapter 17) and Malta applied in 1990 (Chapter 16). The other notable west European country thus far remaining outside the EU is Switzerland, whose desire for neutrality currently outweighs the advantages of membership; the country rejected membership of the European Economic Area (EEA), and thus the possibility of EU entry, in 1995. Iceland has also shown no interest in membership. The only country to actually withdraw from the European Union is Greenland (Kalaallit Nunaat), which did so in 1985 after gaining independence from Denmark in 1979.

Applicants and hopefuls

Several countries in CEE, along with a few others, are currently seeking entry into the European Union. In order to do so countries must meet certain criteria, as specified within three broad categories:

- Political criteria: institutions must be in place to guarantee democratic practice, rule of law and respect for minorities.

- Economic criteria: a functioning market economy must exist and must be able to withstand the competitive pressure of the Union.

- Administrative capacity: instruments must be in place to transpose and implement Community legislation.

These themes – usually referred to as the Copenhagen criteria after the 1993 European Council meeting held there – are supplemented by several other important considerations, such as the state of the environment and the ability to achieve monetary union, fight corruption, assure human rights (Anon, 2000a), provide for common defence (Anon, 1999b) and generally assume other obligations of membership.

The procedure for gaining membership to the EU is long and complicated (European Commission, 1998a, b; Van den Broek, 1998; Gower, 1999; Mayhew, 1998; Phinnemore, 1999). First, a country must begin diplomatic relations with the EU, sign various trade and co-operation agreements and develop a Europe Agreement. After this Agreement comes into force the country can formally apply, which involves submitting a lengthy document for consideration by the European Commission. The Commission then prepares an *Opinion*, or *avis*, on the applicant's characteristics with regard to the criteria, which is issued to the Council. Regular meetings between the Commission and the applicant countries are held and regular reports on progress toward accession are made. When most of the criteria have been met or seem likely to be met in the short term, formal accession negotiations begin with the applicant. At the conclusion of these the country is invited to join. The last step in the process is to hold a referendum in the country on the question of joining the European Union. If this is affirmed by a majority of the voting population, the country can gain access.

During the period 1988–97 ten CEE countries submitted applications to the EU: Hungary, Poland, Czechoslovakia (which divided in 1991 into the Czech Republic and Slovakia), Romania, Bulgaria, Estonia, Latvia, Lithuania and Slovenia; Cyprus, Malta and Turkey were also viable candidates and their applications had been submitted earlier. In 1997 the Council decided to treat the ten candidate countries of CEE in two groups. The 'first-wave' or 'fast-track' of countries was to consist of the Czech Republic, Hungary, Poland, Slovenia and Estonia plus Cyprus; while the 'second-wave' group included the other five CEECs plus Malta. However, in late 1999, at its Helsinki meeting and as an indication of the fluid nature of accession negotiations, the Council reversed its earlier position and elevated Latvia, Lithuania, Slovakia, Bulgaria, Romania and Malta to fast-track status, while Turkey was made a candidate country.

Each of the candidate countries varies widely with respect to size, population, economic performance, political institutions and environmental state (Table 1.1). As will be discussed at length in the individual chapters, these countries are generally much poorer than their west European counterparts, have less experience with democratic and administrative institutions and the state of environmental quality is generally lower (Dawson, 1998; Saiko, 1998; Williams and Bjarnadottir, 1998; Anon, 1999a). To underscore this point, in what is being called the worst

Table 1.1 Central and eastern Europe: key indicators, 1996–1997

Country	Total population (mn)	Area ('000 sq km)	Population density (per sq km)	GDP ($ bn)	GDP per capita ($)	Unemployment (%)	Life expectancy at birth Female	Male	Infant mortality (per 1,000 live births)	% GDP expenditure on Education	Health
Albania	3.32	28.8	116	2.3	680	15.0	74	69	20	3.1	3.0
Belarus	10.22	207.6	49	13.3	1303	2.8	74	63	13	6.2	5.2
Bosnia and Hercegovina	3.74	51.2	73	0.8	502	72.5	na	na	12	na	na
Bulgaria	8.31	111.0	75	10.2	1224	13.7	75	67	18	3.1	3.3
Croatia	4.57	56.5	81	19.5	4268	10.0	77	69	8	na	9.0
Cyprus	0.74	9.3	80	8.5	12023	3.1	80	75	8	6.8	5.1
Czech Republic	10.30	78.9	131	52.0	5050	4.0	77	70	6	5.8	6.7
Estonia	1.46	45.2	32	4.7	3216	10.0	76	65	10	4.7	4.0
Georgia	5.43	69.7	78	0.9	912	2.6	76	69	17	1.5	0.3
Hungary	10.15	93.0	109	44.8	4415	8.7	75	66	10	5.0	6.7
Latvia	2.47	64.6	38	5.5	2237	8.3	76	64	15	5.9	4.0
Lithuania	3.70	65.3	57	9.6	2577	5.9	76	65	10	5.5	5.5
Macedonia, FYR	1.98	25.7	77	3.3	1984	42.5	75	70	15	na	1.5
Malta	0.37	0.3	1186	3.2	8643	4.4	80	75	6	5.8	3.3
Moldova	4.31	33.9	127	1.9	434	1.7	70	63	20	10.4	6.8
Poland	38.65	312.7	124	135.7	3512	11.3	77	68	10	5.4	5.0
Romania	22.57	238.4	95	34.8	1544	6.0	73	65	23	3.5	2.8
Russia	147.14	17075.4	9	462.4	3143	9.0	73	60	17	3.7	2.4
Slovakia	5.38	49.0	110	19.5	3615	11.6	76	68	9	5.7	7.1
Slovenia	1.99	20.3	98	18.0	9055	7.3	78	70	5	6.0	6.8
Turkey	63.75	774.8	82	383.3	2894	5.9	71	66	42	2.6	5.1
Ukraine	50.54	603.7	84	49.7	983	2.8	73	62	14	5.1	4.0
Yugoslavia	10.60	102.2	104	18.1	1711	25.6	75	70	13	4.2	7.4

Source: UNECE, 1999

environmental disaster since the 1986 Chernobyl nuclear accident, an earthen dam containing cyanide and heavy-metal-laced water located near a gold mine in western Romania breached in February 2000, sending toxic materials down the Tisza river and into the Danube. These poisons not only killed virtually all fish and other living things in the waterways, they also pose a long-term threat to the health of the rivers and to the fishing industry that depends on them (Satchell, 2000).

Besides having to contend with difficult economic and underdeveloped political conditions, public attitudes toward the EU in most of the countries are surprisingly low. In surveys carried out over the period 1990–96 by the European Commission in the applicant countries of CEE, only four countries – Romania, Poland, Bulgaria and Hungary – exceeded a 50 per cent rating for any of the years; only Romania averaged over 50 per cent for the whole period (Table 1.2). Furthermore, ratings in several of the countries – notably Hungary, the Czech Republic, Estonia and Latvia – declined during the decade.

Asked how they would vote in a referendum on the question of their country's membership in the EU, only those surveyed in Romania and Poland would vote for entry (Table 1.3). Again, levels in the Baltic nations are surprisingly low, given their security needs and stated desire to rejoin European institutions.

When will enlargement occur?

Ten years ago, amid the light-headedness of the fall of the Berlin Wall, the year 2000 was seen as a reasonable date for new entries to occur; by the mid-1990s, 2005 or 2006 seemed more likely (Anon, 1998). At the time of writing, from the perspective of early 2000, predictions of even longer periods of time being required for accession are being heard through the official silence of the EU on the subject. Indeed, likely entry dates even for the best prepared of the candidate countries are probably in the range 2006–10 and stretch to 2015. For political outcasts such as Serbia the wait will be even longer, perhaps into the third decade of the 21st century.

Many factors have led to a slowdown in the enlargement process. One involves careful examination of the candidate countries. According to most measures, the countries currently on line for accession are significantly poorer and less developed – economically, politically and administratively – than the current members; indeed, the average gross domestic product (GDP) per capita for the applicant countries is only about one-third that of member countries (Pinder, 1998a: 14). However, interesting results were obtained from the development of an index of EU suitability based solely on economic criteria (Anon, 1999c). Using this index, all current and applicant countries were ranked from the strongest or most suitable to be an EU member to the weakest or least suitable. According to the findings, Belgium is the most suitable country, followed by Luxembourg, the Netherlands, Denmark, Portugal, Austria, Ireland, Sweden,

Table 1.2 Trends in positive attitude toward the EU in candidate countries, 1990–1996 (%)

	1990	1991	1992	1993	1994	1995	1996
Romania	na	52	55	45	51	50	65
Poland	46	49	48	37	42	46	58
Bulgaria	47	46	51	42	37	27	42
Slovenia	na	na	45	30	37	35	35
Slovakia	43	37	35	44	37	31	34
Hungary	51	42	34	36	32	30	33
Czech Republic	49	46	45	37	34	36	33
Latvia	na	45	40	40	35	35	26
Estonia	na	38	32	31	29	30	24

Source: *Grabbe and Hughes, 1999: 186*

Table 1.3 Attitude towards membership in the EU among candidate countries, 1997 (%)

Country	For	Against	Undecided
Romania	80	2	8
Poland	70	7	12
Bulgaria	49	4	17
Slovenia	47	15	19
Hungary	47	15	16
Slovakia	46	9	25
Czech Republic	43	11	23
Lithuania	35	6	24
Latvia	34	13	32
Estonia	29	17	35

Source: *Grabbe and Hughes, 1999: 187*

France, Spain, Britain and Finland, with Germany in 13th place. Surprisingly, the next-highest ranked country is Slovenia, followed by the Czech Republic, Poland, Cyprus and EU-founding member Italy. These are followed by Hungary, Malta, Latvia, Estonia, current member Greece, Slovakia, Romania, Lithuania and Turkey, with Bulgaria finishing in the position of least suitability. In some ways this list is unremarkable, serving only to document what keen observers of the European scene already know. What is significant, though, is the relatively high status of countries like Slovenia and the relatively poor showing of Italy and, especially, Greece. These findings point to the large disparities existing not only in the candidate countries, but also among current EU members. They also underline the need to move slowly in any expansion, and to carefully consider the implications of adding new countries and the desirability of selecting criteria for screening applicants that can also be met by existing members.

A further consideration in the enlargement process concerns changes that will occur to EU structure. A major cause for reflection is the potential drain on EU resources, in particular on the European Central Bank (ECB), that enlargement will produce (Anon, 2000b). Another is the inevitable problem of political redefinition, especially in terms of voting regulations in the Council (Anon, 2000c). Still another concern is that the EU may grow so large that it collapses under its own weight, thus heralding a return to nationalism, tariffs and at least trade wars, if not the more deadly variety (Anon, 1999d). EU enlargement means diversity but clearly also uncertainty.

References

Anon, 1998, Widening the Union – but not too fast. *The Economist*, 7 November, pp. 51–52.

Anon, 1999a, Clean up or clear out. *The Economist*, 11 December, p. 47.

Anon, 1999b, Defending Europe. *The Economist*, 4 December, p. 18.

Anon, 1999c, EU enlargement. *The Economist*, 18 December, p. 148.

Anon, 1999d, Free to be European. *The Economist*, 11 September, pp. 21–23.

Anon, 1999e, The Union's tricky treaty. *The Economist*, 13 November, pp. 51–52.

Anon, 2000a, Necessary? *The Economist*, 5 February, p. 46.

Anon, 2000b, The ECB heads for trouble. *The Economist*, 29 January, pp. 81–82.

Anon, 2000c, The Union pauses for breath. *The Economist*, 12 February, pp. 49–50.

Anon, 2000d, What is Europe? *The Economist*, 12 February, pp. 15–16.

Dawson, A. H., 1998, Industrial restructuring in the new democracies. *In* Pinder, D., ed., *The new Europe: economy, society & environment*. Chichester/New York: John Wiley & Sons, pp. 111–126.

Dinan, D., 1999, *Ever closer union: an introduction to European integration*. Boulder/London: Lynne Riener, 2nd edn.

Edye, D., Lintner, V., 1996, Conclusion: prospects for the new Europe. *In* Edye, D., Lintner, V., eds, *Contemporary Europe*. Hemel Hempstead: Prentice Hall, pp. 393–411.

European Commission, 1998a, The European Union's pre-accession strategy for the associated countries of central Europe. *In* Nicoll, W., Schoenberg, R., eds, *Europe beyond 2000*. London: Whurr Publishers, pp. 9–28.

European Commission, 1998b, The challenge of enlargement – the European Commission's opinion, July 1997. *In* Nicoll, W., Schoenberg, R., eds., *Europe beyond 2000*. London: Whurr Publishers, pp. 29–56.

Gower, J., 1999, EU policy to central and eastern Europe. *In* Henderson, K., ed., *Back to Europe: central and eastern Europe and the European Union*. London: UCL Press, pp. 3–19.

Grabbe, H., Hughes, K., 1999, Central and east European views on EU enlargement: political debates and public opinion. *In* Henderson, K., ed., *Back to Europe: central and eastern Europe and the European Union*. London: UCL Press, pp. 185–202.

Hardy, S., Hart, M., Albrechts, L., Katos, A., eds, 1995, *An enlarged Europe: regions in competition?* London: Regional Studies Association.

Heffernan, M., 1998, *The meaning of Europe: geography and geopolitics*. London/New York: Arnold.

Henderson, K., ed., 1999, *Back to Europe: central and eastern Europe and the European Union*. London: UCL Press.

McCormick, J., 1999, *Understanding the European Union: a concise introduction*. New York: St. Martin's Press.

Mayhew, A., 1998, *Recreating Europe: the European Union's policy towards central and eastern Europe*. Cambridge: Cambridge University Press.

Nicoll, W., Schoenberg, R., 1998, *Europe beyond 2000: the enlargement of the European Union towards the east*. London: Whurr Publishers.

Phinnemore, D., 1999, The challenge of EU enlargement: EU and CEE perspectives. *In* Henderson, K., ed., *Back to Europe: central and eastern Europe and the European Union*. London: UCL Press, pp. 71–88.

Pinder, D., 1998a, New Europe or new Europes? east–west development dynamics in the twentieth century. *In* Pinder, D., ed., *The new Europe: economy, society & environment*. Chichester/New York: John Wiley & Sons, pp. 3–21.

Pinder, D., ed., 1998b, *The new Europe: economy, society & environment*. Chichester/New York: John Wiley & Sons.

Saiko, T. A., 1998, Environmental challenges in the new democracies. *In* Pinder, D., ed., *The new Europe: economy, society & environment*. Chichester/New York: John Wiley & Sons, pp. 381–399.

Satchell, M., 2000, Death on the Danube. *U.S. News & World Report*, 128 (8), 42–43.

Stirk, P. M. R., Weigall, D., eds., 1999, *The origins and development of European integration: a reader and commentary*. London/New York: Pinter.

UNECE, 1999, *Trends in Europe and North America*. New York: UNECE.

Van den Broek, H., 1998, Preparing for the enlargement of the European Union. *In* Nicoll, W., Schoenberg, R., eds, *Europe beyond 2000*. London: Whurr Publishers, pp. 3–8.

Williams, R. H., Bjarnadottir, H., 1998, Environmental protection and pollution control in the EU. *In* Pinder, D., ed., *The new Europe: economy, society & environment*. Chichester/New York: John Wiley & Sons, pp. 401–413.

2

WESTERN EUROPE AND THE EASTERN ENLARGEMENT

Allan M. Williams and Vladimir Balaz

The proposed eastern enlargement of the European Union (EU) will be the fifth round of accession to the Union, but it poses markedly different challenges. This is partly because the EU was conceived as an institutional framework in the 1950s, under different circumstances to those in force at the start of the 21st century. It was created in the shadow of the Second World War, was informed by the need to politically rehabilitate the key German economy and was facilitated by the long economic boom of the 1950s and 1960s (Williams, 1998). Integration, subsequently, has been widened (through the enlargements) and deepened (through institutional arrangements, powers and policy remit). The process of deepening was largely driven by the neo-liberal agenda that informed the Treaty of Rome; although stalled in the 1970s, it was revived through the single market project, the Single European Act, and the Maastricht Treaty on European Union (Williams, 1995). The treaty had three main pillars, each of which changed the 'architecture' of the Union in which the eastern countries sought membership. The first pillar included Economic and Monetary Union (EMU); the second outlined a commitment to a common foreign and security policy (CFSP); the third dealt with internal security, including trans-border mobility and crime. Although the Single European Act had marked a decisive shift toward majority voting in the Council, and the Maastricht Treaty transferred some powers to the European Parliament, decision-making remained a cross between intergovernmentalism and co-operative federalism (Kirchner, 1992).

When the prospect of the accession of the central and eastern European (CEE) countries to the EU was first raised in the early 1990s, hopes were expressed that – as in earlier enlargements – 'the benevolent, burgeoning European Community would be ready and able both to succour and to stabilise' (Brown, 1994: 15). However, despite superficial parallels between the eastern and the earlier southern enlargement (Williams *et al.*, 1998), the current negotiations are taking place under very different conditions. First, the economic challenge of transition is far greater in CEE than it was in southern Europe, which had functioning if deformed market economies. Second, the roots of democracy were weaker in most of CEE than had been the case in Portugal,

Spain and Greece. Third, the deepening of integration in the 1980s and 1990s meant that greater adjustments were now required of new members, especially with respect to the single market and the EMU. Fourth, globalisation, international competition, the growth of structural unemployment and the ascendancy of the neo-liberal agenda meant that the eastern enlargement was approached by the existing member states in a less 'benevolent' way. Finally, there were critical strategic defence and security issues, for the ten applicants have borders with Ukraine, Belarus, Moldova and Russia. Moreover, these security issues were faced at a time when the demise of the Cold War had ended the comfortable certainties of the strategic western defence alliance, wherein western Europe was the unquestioning ally of the USA. Further, the ending of the Cold War, described by Douglas Hurd as 'unfriendly but stable' (Budd, 1993: 6), unleashed a wave of nationalism, especially in the Balkans, that threatened the security of the continent.

This chapter reviews the approach of western Europe to integration with CEE. First it outlines the economic challenges, before examining separately the EU's enlargement agenda and the defence and security issues faced by the North Atlantic Treaty Organization (NATO) and the European Union. The chapter mostly focuses on the supranational organisations, but it must be stressed that their approaches have been largely dictated by the interests of the individual member states.

The challenge for European integration

While the debate on integration tends to lump together the CEE countries as members of the former Council for Mutual Economic Assistance (CMEA) and Warsaw Pact, these countries are economically, demographically, politically and culturally different.

The former Czechoslovakia emerged from state socialism with a relatively strong industrial sector, although in common with the rest of CEE it had lagged behind western Europe since the 1960s. The country had been ruled by a rigid communist regime, which was hostile to most of the economic and political reforms initiated during *perestroika*. The former East Germany had a similar industrial character (accounting for a large share of GDP) and relatively high living standards. The hardline government of the German Democratic Republic (GDR) had also been implacably opposed to political and economic reforms before 1989.

In contrast, Hungary had relatively strong agricultural and service sectors, which helped maintain reasonable living standards. Since 1968 the Hungarian government had implemented relatively liberal economic policies and, despite being subject to sharp reverses, had the strongest private sector in CEE. Hungary also had the most liberal political environment, and power was transferred relatively smoothly from the Communist Party to new political formations in 1989. This contrasts with Poland, where the rise of the Solidarity movement had been accompanied by deep political and economic crises, a military coup and the relatively early collapse of state socialism. In the 1980s there was a sharp decline in GDP and shortages of consumer goods. However, relatively strong manufacturing and service sectors helped to maintain living standards at levels similar to those in Hungary and Slovakia (although there was also a large-scale agricultural sector). Political liberalisation was also expressed in a relaxed attitude toward the private sector (agriculture had been collectivised only to a limited extent).

At the end of the 1980s Slovenia was the most developed republic in the former Yugoslavia federation and had strong historical ties to Austria. Its relatively well-developed manufacturing and service sectors provided the highest living standards in central and eastern Europe. Bulgaria and Romania, by contrast, were the least developed European CMEA members. There had been attempts to build strong industrial sectors in these countries but, at the end of the state-socialist period, they still had distinctively rural characters, with low living standards and underdeveloped infrastructures. They also had particularly oppressive and inept political regimes.

The Baltic countries presented special challenges because of their historic economic and cultural ties with Scandinavia, Poland and Germany. Despite Soviet pressures for cultural and economic assimilation, the Baltic republics were able to capitalise on their traditional advantages: favourable locations on the Baltic Sea, higher educational levels, developed infrastructures, a degree of cultural autonomy and a relatively sophisticated economic base. These helped to maintain the highest living standards and the least oppressive governments within the former USSR. After regaining independence they faced a double challenge: losses of traditional markets in the former Soviet Union and difficult political relations with the Russian government, not least over their large Russian populations.

This brief review emphasises that the CEE countries had different economic and political structures in 1989. Therefore, although they were subject to relatively similar challenges in the 1990s – global competition, the loss of former markets and the reorientation of trade to western Europe, privatisation and the construction of democratic institutions and practices – their responses and the outcomes have been different. These transition pathways are explored elsewhere (Pickles and Smith, 1998; Williams *et al.*, 1998), and this chapter comments only briefly on their outcome. In general, there was economic recession until 1993, followed by strong economic growth; yet, in most of the countries, 1989 GDP levels had not been recovered even as late as 1998. The recovery was stronger in Poland and Slovenia, while the Baltic and Balkan countries faced more severe difficulties. In aggregate, by the late 1990s the average per capita GDP in the candidate countries represented only 37 per cent of the EU average (in purchasing power parity terms) but ranged from 68 per cent in Slovenia to 23 per cent in Bulgaria. Per capita GDP levels were a major axis of differentiation among the first and second groups of candidate countries, as defined at the 1997 Luxembourg Summit (Table 2.1), although there were also differences in economic structures, related to the relative weight of services and agriculture. The countries in the first group had higher levels of GDP, larger service sectors and smaller agricultural sectors than the second group, with the exception of Slovakia. These differences are explored further in the next section of the chapter.

Table 2.1 Basic development indicators of the CEE countries applying for EU membership, 1997

1st group of countries	Czech Republic	Estonia	Hungary	Poland	Slovenia
Population (mn)	10.3	1.4	10.2	38.7	2.0
GNP, AM[a]	5 200.0	3 330.0	4 430.0	3 590.0	9 680.0
GNP, PPP[b]	10 380.0	5 090.0	6 970.0	6 510.0	11 880.0
GNP, PPP (% of EU average)	64.0	37.0	49.0	37.0	68.0
Average annual growth, 1987–97	−1.3	−4.8	−0.8	1.0	1.4
Urban population (% of total population)	66.0	74.0	66.0	64.0	52.0
Life expectancy at birth (years)	74.0	70.0	70.0	72.0	74.0
Exports of goods and services (% of GDP)	34.7	77.2	38.9[c]	26.3	57.4
Total debt (% of GDP)	41.5	14.0	53.0	29.4	23.2
Structure of the economy (% of GDP):					
agriculture	na	7.2	6.6[c]	5.1	4.5
industry	na	27.9	30.6[c]	30.7	37.9
services	na	64.8	62.8[c]	64.2	57.7

2nd group of countries	Bulgaria	Latvia	Lithuania	Romania	Slovakia
Population (mn)	8.3	3.7	2.5	22.5	5.7
GNP, AM[a]	1 140.0	2 430.0	2 230.0	1 420.0	3 700.0
GNP, PPP[b]	3 870.0	3 970.0	4 140.0	4 270.0	7 860.0
GNP, PPP (% of EU average)	23.0	27.0	30.0	31.0	46.0
Average annual growth, 1987–97	−3.8	−8.0	−4.9	−2.7	−1.4
Urban population (% of total population)	68.0	73.0	73.0	57.0	60.0
Life expectancy at birth (years)	71.0	70.0	71.0	69.0	73.0
Exports of goods and services (% of GDP)	61.3	50.5	54.6	29.7	56.4
Total debt (% of GDP)	96.7	9.4	16.1	32.6	50.9
Structure of the economy (% of GDP):					
agriculture	23.3	7.4	12.8	22.8	4.8
industry	26.2	30.7	31.8	38.7	33.4
services	50.5	61.9	55.4	38.5	61.7

[a] = US$ per capita (Atlas method). [b] = US$ per capita (purchasing power parities). [c] = 1996.

Sources: *Eurostat, 1999; World Bank, 1999*

The European Union agenda

The Treaty of Rome allows for the accession into the EU of suitable European countries, and both the European Commission and the individual member states have stated that they favour the eastern accession as a way to promote stability and prosperity in Europe. In practice, they have been more reticent when faced with the reality of applications from ten CEE states, which together would add 28 per cent to the Union's population but only 5 per cent to its GDP. While an enlarged market would offer long-term gains in economies of scale and competitiveness, the short-term prospect is for increased costs. The costs are, however, very variable. On the one hand, the Czech and Slovenian GDP levels are close to those of Portugal and Greece, and integration of these countries with relatively small populations need not be too costly. Poland poses a greater challenge because of its large population, its relatively low per capita GDP levels and its underdeveloped agriculture. Even greater problems would be encountered in the integration of Romania and Bulgaria, whose economic development levels are far lower than those of even the first group of candidate countries.

In practice, the support provided by the member states has varied according to their proximity to, and their economic and historical links with, individual CEE countries (Grabbe and Hughes, 1998: 4–6). For example, Scandinavia (for the Baltic states), Germany (for Hungary, the Czech Republic and Poland) and Greece (for Bulgaria and Romania) have all championed neighbouring countries. By contrast, Spain and Portugal have little positive interest in the enlargement, which is viewed in terms of competition for EU structural funds. France has generally been ambivalent about the accession. The last point is critical, for it means that the Franco–German partnership, which has been vital in other integrationist moves such as EMU, has been weak in this instance. In general, therefore, the enlargement discussions have taken place against a background of increasing short-term concerns about labour immigration, the permeability of the proposed new outer boundaries of the Union, higher budgetary contributions, pressures on the Common Agricultural Policy and 'unfair' competition or 'social dumping'.

In these circumstances the enlargement negotiations have already stretched over a number of years, and there is no realistic prospect of their early conclusion. The first formal stage of constructing institutional relationships between the EU and the CEE countries was marked by the bilateral Association Agreements of the early 1990s. These culminated in the 1993 Copenhagen Declaration, which set out an agenda of economic reforms, including trade liberalisation, privatisation, stabilisation and the creation of functioning markets. In practice, the Europe agreements were asymmetrical, reserving significant anti-dumping powers for the EU and excluding so-called sensitive products, such as steel and textiles, in which the CEE countries were most competitive (Gowan, 1995). In return, the Copenhagen agreement held forth the prospect of future membership conditional on the candidate countries fulfilling the political conditions of a European identity:

- democratic status and respect for human rights;

- acceptance of, and ability to implement, the EU's economic and political system (i.e. functioning market economy and associated regulatory systems);

- acceptance of the *acquis communautaire* (including all existing treaties); and

- ability to take on some of the more ambitious goals of economic and political union set out in the Treaty on European Union.

The Essen Summit of December 1994 subsequently extended the Europe agreements to the Baltic states and Slovenia.

During the mid-1990s the European Commission (1997a–j) undertook an assessment of the ten applicants, and their *Agenda 2000* report in 1997 (European Commission, 1997k) provided the basis for the decision to divide the applicants into two sets: the first and second groups (as discussed earlier, see Table 2.1). Each application was subject to relatively detailed scrutiny in terms of the economic and political conditions for membership, although the lack of quantifiable criteria made this a subjective process. The applicants are also subject to annual review (see European Commission, 1998).

In terms of the *political criteria*, several major weaknesses were identified in most of the applicants:

- Democracy and the rule of law: Romania, Bulgaria and Slovakia lacked institutional stability for consolidating democracy. Whilst the first two were considered to have made progress since changes of government in 1997, Slovakia was considered to pose particular problems because the government undermined the rights of the presidency and the courts.

- There were persistent problems in respect of guaranteeing the human and political rights of national minorities, which was especially important in countries with nationally mixed populations. For example, the Baltic states were criticised for denying or delaying naturalisation rights to their significant Russian populations. There were also less serious concerns about the cultural rights afforded to the Hungarian minorities in Romania and Slovakia, although these have been eased by new agreements between the three states. The Roma (Gypsy) minority was a particular source of concern, having been subject to social exclusions and racism, especially in Romania but also in the Czech Republic, Slovakia and Hungary.

There were also concerns about the *economic* readiness of the applicants.

- Questions were raised notably about the functioning of the market economy, including trade liberalisation, prices, removal of barriers to market entry and exit, macroeconomic stability and the efficiency of the financial sector. The Czech Republic, Poland, Estonia, Hungary and Slovenia largely satisfied this criterion, and Slovakia came very close to doing so. The Baltic states, especially Estonia, were making rapid progress, and Latvia was considered likely to meet the criterion in the near future. In contrast, there had been less progress in the Balkan countries, notably in Romania.

- Assessment of the ability to cope with competitive pressures within the EU was more complex. It required satisfactory levels of human capital, infrastructure and education and research, as well as stability and policies to support firms' competitiveness. Most of these could only be effectively evaluated over the medium term, and there were no in-depth studies of the ability of firms to adjust to the single market. In the Commission's opinion, Hungary and Poland had made most progress, followed by the Czech Republic and Slovenia. Slovakia and Estonia were deemed to be in a good position for coping with competitive pressures in EU markets but required more radical economic policies to improve competitiveness. Latvia and Lithuania were taking appropriate steps in their economic policies, but their durability needed to be tested over a longer time. Bulgaria and Romania fared poorly in the economic assessments.

- Integration into the EU requires implementation of the *acquis* – the EU's legal, administrative and regulatory practices – into the regulatory and governance systems of the candidate countries. This task was mainly undertaken by national governments, parliaments and administrative systems and has been exceptionally demanding on time and effort. Progress has been greatest in Hungary and Poland, but the Czech Republic and Slovenia have recently begun to lag behind. There were major challenges in the implementation of harmonised state-aid control, systems of standards and certification, and market surveillance. All the candidates, except Hungary, had failed to develop systems of effective financial control, and there was unsatisfactory enforcement of intellectual property rights.

These assessments were used as a basis for dividing the applicants into two groups. Detailed negotiations were to commence with the first of these: the Czech Republic, Estonia, Hungary, Poland and Slovenia (together with Cyprus). In the second group, Slovakia was unusual in that it failed on political, but not on economic, grounds to meet the membership criteria. These decisions were contested. On the one hand, some member states – for example, Denmark, Finland and Sweden – pressed for negotiations to begin with all ten applicants so as not to exclude any of the Baltic states. In contrast, Germany favoured differentiation, reflecting its priorities in central Europe and its concerns about the costs of enlargement.

Substantive talks with the first group commenced in November 1998, and progress was made in respect of science and research, telecommunications and information technologies, education and training, culture and audio-visual policy, industrial policy, small- and medium-sized enterprises, and common foreign and security policy. There were, of course, some problem areas. For example Hungary was concerned about the positions of the three million Hungarians living in Romania and Slovakia following implementation of the Schengen Agreement. Poland was concerned about the rights of EU citizens to purchase land. In Estonia the key issues were fishing rights, maintenance of trade agreements with other Baltic states and environmental issues, especially related to their energy reliance on open-cast oil shale. At the 1999 Helsinki Summit it was agreed to open negotiations with most of the remaining applicant countries of central and eastern Europe – Slovakia, Bulgaria, Romania, Latvia and Lithuania – as well as with Malta, and Turkey was recognised as a candidate for membership.

Inevitably, the early negotiations have focused on the less controversial issues, and the more difficult ones will probably not be reconciled until the concluding stages. Looking to the future there are five major areas of concern for the EU and the member states.

1 The budget

At present 80 per cent of the budget is allocated to agriculture and the structural/cohesion funds. Any move to reduce this will 'provoke opposition from two of the most powerful lobbying groups in the EU: farmers and the recipients of regional aid' (Grabbe and Hughes, 1998: 91). Yet three competing aims have to be reconciled: maintaining budgetary discipline, especially given the requirements of EMU and the British, German, French and Dutch insistence that there be no increase in the EU's budget ceiling in the period 2000 to 2006; allocation of sufficient funds to the existing members to assuage the concerns of the southern countries; and providing the CEE countries with equitable allocations. The Commission's proposal is that the previously agreed financial ceiling of 1.27 per cent of member states' GDP should be adhered to in 2000–06. This offers some slack over current expenditure which, assuming growth rates of 2.5 per cent in the EU and 4 per cent in the CEE countries, would yield a total budget of 745 bn for 2000–2006, of which 75 bn (16 per cent) would be allocated to CEE. The total aid earmarked for the applicants, especially those in the second group, is limited, both in absolute terms and relative to that received by the southern members. This reflects both the changing economic climate and the way in which earlier enlargements have shifted the balance of interests within the Union.

2 Agriculture

The challenge of CEE is how to integrate currently less efficient agricultural sectors that have considerable potential to improve productivity and output. It is estimated that CEE enlargement could increase the costs of the farm policy by 30–50 per cent, but this will depend on the extent of further EU reforms of the sector, which is under pressure from the USA and other major global producers.

3   **The structural funds**

If the current funding mechanisms for Greece and Portugal were applied to the eastern applicants, they could expect transfers ranging from 6 per cent of GDP in Slovenia to 42 per cent in Lithuania. Apart from the problem of whether this volume of funds could be absorbed, the existing member states are unlikely to contemplate such transfers. Instead, the EU planned a total structural fund of ECU 275 bn for the period 1990–96, with ECU 45 bn being earmarked for new members and applicant countries. This was based on relatively optimistic growth forecasts, on applying a ceiling to the volume of transfers for individual countries and on long transition periods before full membership. The accessions will also cause difficulties for some of the existing member states, for they would reduce average GDP per capita in the EU by 16 per cent and, therefore, make many current recipients ineligible for assistance in future (Grabbe and Hughes, 1998: 100).

4   **Institutional change**

The EU has so far failed to implement the major institutional reforms that most commentators believe are essential before enlargement: increased majority voting and reform of the weighted voting procedures in favour of the larger countries. This has pitted small states against large ones, and the more against the less federalist orientated.

5   **Freedom of movement and rights of residence**

A number of member states have serious concerns as to the possibility of different forms of international mobility in an enlarged EU: labour mobility, movements of Roma and others in search of welfare provision and illegal migration across the relatively porous 'outer' boundaries of the applicant states.

These are all major issues, but by no means the only ones. For example, environmental issues and property purchasing rights also pose difficult challenges. This makes all the more ominous the fact that *Agenda 2000* does not set a firm date for the conclusion of negotiations or for the first round of accessions. This question will be returned to in the conclusions to this chapter.

Defence and security

After an aborted attempt to create a European Defence Community in the 1950s, most subsequent attempts at institution-building in Europe have been concerned with economics rather than with defence and security. The EU only formally committed itself to a common foreign and security policy (CFSP) in the 1991 Treaty on European Union. This constituted little more than a set of aspirations, weakened by the diverse interests of its membership and intergovernmentalist decision-making. There has been only minimalist transfer of power to the Union by member states, who are jealous of national sovereignty in this arena. The only other specifically European defence organisation of note is the Western European Union (WEU), established in 1954, which had been 'in hibernation' for most of its first 30 years of existence (Duke, 1996: 167). Although the WEU was strengthened in the 1990s, it still lacks power and is likely to continue to be subordinate to NATO. Not surprisingly, the main response to the changing opportunities and threats posed by the opening to the East has come from NATO rather than the EU. Overtures have been made toward co-operation with Russia and the former eastern bloc countries. In 1994 the Partnership for Peace was established as a vehicle for intense military co-operation between NATO and its former Cold War enemies and the neutral European states. This was complemented by creation of the NATO–Russia Partnership Council in 1997.

There has been considerable debate amongst the western powers as to the most effective institutional framework for security in post-1989 Europe. The three main options were: an enlarged and stronger pan-European Conference for Security and Co-operation in Europe (CSCE); the division of Europe between the WEU in the West (expanding into CEE) and the Commonwealth of Independent States (CIS) in the East, with NATO fading into the background as the ultimate guarantor of security; and NATO taking the lead, expanding its membership eastwards, but thereby causing Russia to feel even more isolated in a polarised Europe (Gowan, 1999).

Russia had believed that Gorbachev had been given assurance by Germany's Chancellor Kohl that, in return for allowing a reunified Germany to become a NATO member, NATO would not admit former Warsaw Pact countries as members (Granville, 1998). At first, this coincided with the views of Germany and, to a lesser extent, France, both of which had favoured an independent European option. However, by the mid-1990s Germany was beginning to favour the 'dominant NATO' scenario that was promoted by the USA and supported by the UK. The first selective extension of NATO occurred in 1999 when three central European countries were admitted to membership: Poland, the Czech Republic and Hungary.

While the creation of a new institutional framework was the recurrent concern of the western powers, they were faced with more immediate challenges as the former Yugoslavia fragmented. Although intense nationalist pressures were bottled up in the former Yugoslavia – and these were unfettered by the end of the Cold War and exploited by nationalist leaders – the western powers have contributed to and helped shape the crises in the region. Differences among the western powers have also been instrumental in this. On the one hand, the initial priority of most western European countries and the USA was to push an intact Yugoslavia along the road to capitalism. On the other hand, Germany, Austria and Hungary, for different reasons, actively supported the cause of independence for Croatia and Slovenia (Zametica, 1992).

The first critical moment in external intervention came in 1991 when Germany and Austria persuaded the EU (which was anxious to develop its foreign policy role) to mediate in the autonomy disputes between Slovenia and Croatia and the central Yugoslav authorities. The EU did so, with German reassurances that it would not act unilaterally on this issue. However, Germany did unilaterally recognise the independence of Slovenia and, more critically, Croatia. According to Gowan (1999) this was a 'formula for war' because it denied Serbians in Croatia both the sovereign national rights they had under the constitution of the old Yugoslav republic and the CSCE principles for protecting minority rights in the new Croatian constitution. The other member states acceded to this approach, arguably because they had no major stake in the survival of Yugoslavia or in the issue of minority rights. Although this intervention did not cause the ensuing conflict between Croatia and Serbia, it helped to trigger it.

Bosnia was the next arena for western engagement; but now the USA assumed the dominant role. Germany's interests were limited to Croatia and Slovenia, and it had aimed to retain Bosnia within the rump of the former Yugoslavia, recognising the particular problem of the co-existence of three national minorities with sovereign rights. However, the USA wanted to reassert its influence in the region and chose Bosnian independence as the vehicle for this (Gowan, 1999). The USA encouraged a minority Bosnian government to push for independence, even though the Croat and Serb reactions were predictable. The eventual peace settlement, the Dayton Agreement, created a federal rather than a unitary Bosnia and effectively fossilised the territorial division of Bosnia created by the conflict and the vicious processes of 'ethnic cleansing'. The resulting map, which effectively constituted the 'peace settlement', contributed to further ethnic cleansing, most notably the displacement of 600,000 Serb refugees to Serbia. The ineffectiveness of the EU was demonstrated by the fact that the Contact Group, which negotiated the peace settlement, contained representatives from the UK, France and Germany (as well as of the USA and Russia) but not of the European Union itself. National sovereignty still dominated a largely stillborn attempt at pan-European security and foreign policy.

The Kosovo crisis provided the next chapter in the Balkan crisis. While Serb repression of the cultural and political rights of the region's ethnic Albanian population was the underlying cause of the conflict, the western powers initially did not support Kosovar separatism. They feared that Kosovan autonomy would lead to the creation of a 'Greater Albania' and destabilise Macedonia, which also had a substantial Albanian minority. However, the western attempts to keep the crisis in check foundered when Albanian state structures virtually collapsed in 1996 and 1997. The weak Nano government, installed afterwards, could not control the border with

Kosovo and arms flooded across to the KLA (Kosova Liberation Army). This equipped a KLA offensive in 1998, which predictably was met by a Serbian counter-offensive. At first, the USA and Europe acquiesced to Milošević's anti-KLA drive, while encouraging greater autonomy for Kosovo within Yugoslavia. Then in October 1998 American Secretary of State Albright changed tack: she now wanted to establish an effective NATO presence in Kosovo, on the grounds that UN peace monitors could not otherwise function effectively in the region. The argument was steered firmly toward the view that NATO could not back down from its threats to Serbia, and the major European powers acquiesced to this.

Several political lessons can be drawn from the Kosovo crisis. First, although the unity of the alliance held, this was finely balanced at times and demonstrated the diversity of views and interests between Europe and the USA and among the European powers, ranging from the hawkish UK to the hesitant Greece. Second, the key decisions were taken not in the EU, nor even in NATO headquarters in Brussels, but in the USA, which supplied 80 per cent of the air power and most of the sophisticated technology and military intelligence. Third, the crisis worryingly illustrated the chronic instability and weakness of Russia, which was shown to be both ineffective and isolated. Finally, it demonstrated yet again the weakness of collective, and individual, European foreign policy and security. Divergent individual foreign policy goals, the unwillingness of the major military powers – France and Britain – to accept Europeanisation of their defence capabilities, and the ineffectiveness of the Western European Union and of the EU's common foreign and security policy left a lacuna that was filled by the USA acting through NATO.

Future challenges

Europe faces two major challenges at the start of the 21st century. First, it needs to address the weaknesses in foreign and security policy that have been exposed by the Balkan crises, not least because they have only stabilised rather than resolved deep-lying nationalist conflicts in the region. Neither the Kosovan nor the Bosnian crisis has been resolved in the sense that the peace agreements are sustainable without continued external military presence. Meanwhile, further crises may erupt in Macedonia, or in Vojvodina where there is a substantial Hungarian minority population within Serbia, either of which will bring the Balkan crisis to the frontiers of NATO. Of even greater concern is the instability in Russia, where both domestic politics and the economy appear to be increasingly fragile. The 1999 parliamentary elections saw gains for the pro-Kremlin Unity bloc and a decline in support for the Communist Party, but power remained fragmented in the duma. The future role of the USA is also uncertain: whilst it had been strongly interventionist in the Bosnian and Kosovan crises, there is a unilateralist tendency in public opinion and in the legislature in America.

Against this background the future of the 'European security architecture' assumes particular urgency. The first issue is the future membership of NATO. It is widely recognised that the first three eastern members were admitted more on the grounds of politics than on the strategic needs of the alliance. Binnendijk and Kugler (1999: 127) argue that the criteria used:

> *imply that virtually any European country can qualify for admission if it presents its credentials as a budding democracy with a free market economy, civilian control of the military, a responsible foreign policy towards its neighbours and a credible track record in the Partnership for Peace program.*

Membership is seen to offer defence on the cheap, but there are serious doubts as to the capacity and interest of the new and of any future members to contribute to NATO missions. Moreover, it would become increasingly difficult to secure a working consensus in a larger NATO, given its current intergovernmental structure. Would the US be willing to support a weaker NATO that was no longer a reliable instrument of American policy? For these reasons full membership may not be offered to all the applicants. Convincing arguments can be made for the membership of Slovakia and Slovenia, and even for Romania, as 'the Poland of the Balkans', but the accession of the other applicants is more problematic. Some CEE countries will increasingly look to EU membership as a vehicle for their security, as well as a more powerful version of the Partnership for Peace.

The last remarks lead to this chapter's final point: how committed is the EU to opening the door to the East, when will this occur and who will be admitted? Enlargement is essentially a political issue. Although there are long-term economic benefits, in the medium term these appear to be relatively small (estimated at ECU 10 bn by Baldwin *et al.*, 1997) when set against the costs. The essential issue is whether the EU has the political will-power to face challenges: first, to undertake essential institutional reforms, notably streamlining the European Commission, rebalancing power between larger and smaller member states and introducing more majority voting; second, to accept a major redistribution of costs and benefits among the existing member states. These challenges will be overcome as it is now almost inconceivable that enlargement will not occur. However, given the scale of the hurdles to be overcome within the EU – let alone in the applicant countries – a later accession date than the Commission's working hypothesis of 2002 seems likely. Beyond this there are too many issues, both external (World Trade Organization negotiations, the trajectory of the world economy) and internal (the success of EMU, institutional reform, domestic political shifts), to allow any realistic predictions to be made. Certainly it now appears unlikely that enlargement will take place in one step: the emphasis since Helsinki (December 1999) has been upon differentiation and upon each of the 12 candidates involved in accession discussions moving at their own pace. Further, there is the question of the length of the transition periods in some areas, notably the rights to free movement and residence, and the application of the Common Agricultural Policy and the

Structural Funds. All that can be said with certainty is that the 1997 Luxembourg Agreement did not so much define the future architecture of a pan-European Union as set in train a hesitant and contradictory process toward an uncertain future for an enlarged Union.

References

Baldwin, R. E., Francois, J. F., Portes, R., 1997, The costs and benefits of eastern enlargement. *Economic Policy*, 24, 125–176.

Binnendijk, H., Kugler, R. L., 1999, Open NATO's door carefully. *The Washington Quarterly*, 22 (2), 125–138.

Brown, J. F., 1994, *Hopes and shadows: eastern Europe after communism*. Harlow: Longman.

Budd, A., 1993, *The EC and foreign and security policy*. London: University of North London, European Dossier Series, No. 28.

Duke, S., 1996, The second death (or the second coming?) of the WEU. *Journal of Common Market Studies*, 34, 167–190.

European Commission, 1997a, *Commission Opinion on Bulgaria's application for membership of the European Union: The Agenda 2000*. Luxembourg: Office for Official Publications of the European Communities.

European Commission, 1997b, *Commission Opinion on the Czech Republic's application for membership of the European Union: The Agenda 2000*. Luxembourg: Office for Official Publications of the European Communities.

European Commission, 1997c, *Commission Opinion on Estonia's application for membership of the European Union: The Agenda 2000*. Luxembourg: Office for Official Publications of the European Communities.

European Commission, 1997d, *Commission Opinion on Hungary's application for membership of the European Union: The Agenda 2000*. Luxembourg: Office for Official Publications of the European Communities.

European Commission, 1997e, *Commission Opinion on Latvia's application for membership of the European Union: The Agenda 2000*. Luxembourg: Office for Official Publications of the European Communities.

European Commission, 1997f, *Commission Opinion on Lithuania's application for membership of the European Union: The Agenda 2000*. Luxembourg: Office for Official Publications of the European Communities.

European Commission, 1997g, *Commission Opinion on Poland's application for membership of the European Union: The Agenda 2000*. Luxembourg: Office for Official Publications of the European Communities.

European Commission, 1997h, *Commission Opinion on Romania's application for membership of the European Union: The Agenda 2000*. Luxembourg: Office for Official Publications of the European Communities.

European Commission, 1997i, *Commission Opinion on Slovakia's application for membership of the European Union: The Agenda 2000*. Luxembourg: Office for Official Publications of the European Communities.

European Commission, 1997j, *Commission Opinion on Slovenia's application for membership of the European Union: The Agenda 2000*. Luxembourg: Office for Official Publications of the European Communities.

European Commission, 1997k, *For a stronger and wider Union: Agenda 2000*. Strasbourg: European Commission (DOC 97/6).

European Commission, 1998, *Reports on progress towards accession by each of the candidate countries, November 4, 1998: Reports on Bulgaria, the Czech Republic, Estonia, Hungary, Latvia, Lithuania, Poland, Romania, Slovakia, Slovenia.* http://europa.eu.int/comm/dg1a/enlarge/report_11_98_en/index.htm.

Eurostat, 1999, *Key figures No. 4/1999*. Luxembourg: Office for Official Publications of the European Communities.

Gowan, P., 1995, Neo-liberal theory and practice for eastern Europe. *New Left Review*, 213, 3–60.

Gowan, P., 1999, The NATO powers and the Balkan tragedy. *New Left Review*, 234, 83–105.

Grabbe, H., Hughes, K., 1998, *Enlarging the EU eastwards*. London: Royal Institute of International Affairs.

Granville, J., 1998, The many paradoxes of NATO enlargement. *Current History*, 98 (627), 165–170.

Kirchner, E. J., 1992, *Decision-making in the European Community: the Council, Presidency, and European integration*. Manchester: Manchester University Press.

Pickles, J., Smith, A., 1998, *Theorising transition: the political economy of post-communist transformations*. London: Routledge.

Williams, A. M., 1995, *The European Community: the contradictions of integration*. Oxford: Basil Blackwell.

Williams, A. M., 1998, The European Union: cumulative and uneven integration. *In* Unwin, T., ed., *A European geography*. Harlow: Longman, pp. 129–147.

Williams, A. M., Balaz, V., Zajac, S., 1998, The EU and central Europe: the remaking of economic relationships. *Tijdschrift voor Economische en Sociale Geografie*, 89 (2), 131–149.

World Bank, 1999, *World development indicators*. http://www.worldbank.org/html/extdr /data.htm.

Zametica, J., 1992, *The Yugoslav conflict*. London: International Institute for Strategic Studies.

3

THE POLICY CHALLENGE OF NEW EU RELATIONS WITH CENTRAL AND EASTERN EUROPE

Deborah L. Gourlay

In June 1993 the European Council at Copenhagen agreed that those countries of central and eastern Europe (CEE) that had Association Agreements (known as Europe Agreements) with the EU should be eligible to join the EU provided they were able to assume the obligations of membership by satisfying a range of economic and political conditions. Requirements for fulfilling the obligations of membership included a stable and democratic government, respect for human rights and a properly functioning market economy. In addition, applicant countries must be both willing and able to fulfil and implement the laws and regulations of the EU, known as the *acquis communautaire*. The key policy objectives to which countries joining the EU commit themselves include:

- policies to promote economic and social cohesion;

- an internal market without frontiers – i.e. free movement of goods, capital, services and people;

- a range of sectoral policies for industry, agriculture, fisheries, energy, transport and small- and medium-sized enterprises (SMEs); and

- economic and monetary union.

The potential impacts of the accession vary significantly between the five central and eastern European countries (CEECs) currently engaged in detailed discussions on membership. The extent of this impact can be indicated by changes in the average per capita gross domestic product (GDP) of the EU. Poland, with its large population of nearly 40 million and relatively low GDP per capita, will account for the greatest share of the impacts of the next round of enlargement. In contrast, Estonia and Slovenia will have only a marginal impact. Details of impacts by individual candidate country are outlined in Table 3.1.

Table 3.1 The impact of accession of candidate countries

	Increase in population (%)	Increase in total GDP (%)	Change in per capita GDP (%)	Average per capita GDP (EU6 = 100)
EU15	–	–	–	89.0
Hungary	3.0	1.0	–2.0	87.2
Poland	11.0	3.0	–7.0	82.6
Czech Republic	3.0	1.4	–2.0	87.6
Estonia	0.4	0.1	–0.2	88.8
Slovenia	0.5	0.3	–0.2	88.8
EU20	18.0	6.0	–10.0	80.0

Based on 1995 data.

All GDP figures are in purchasing power parities (PPP): as monetary values of GDP do not reflect the domestic purchasing powers of the currencies, data on GDP are given a unit (purchasing power parities) that cancels out differences in price levels (based on price survey data) and the resulting data can then be used to make comparisons in real terms.

Source: *European Commission, 1997a*

With an overall per capita GDP estimated at slightly under 36 per cent of the Community average, the five 'first-round' CEECs lag far behind the four least favoured countries of the present EU, which together stand at 74 per cent of the EU average (European Commission, 1997a). Major differences also exist between the applicant countries, which range from 23 per cent (Estonia) to 59 per cent (Slovenia) of the average for the EU 15 (the current EU members). Within the current member states the range is from 66 per cent to 169 per cent for, respectively, Greece and Luxembourg.

The main impacts of the next round of EU enlargement are likely to be mainly attributable to three of the largest and most westernised applicants, Poland, Hungary and the Czech Republic, and this discussion will focus on these.

EU regional policy

One of the main aims of European Union policy is to ensure that there is a reduction in the economic disparities between the different regions of Europe and encourage the equalisation of overall living standards. In order to achieve this objective, financial assistance is channelled to the less well-off regions through a series of expenditure programmes, which comprise the Structural Funds. These consist of:

- the European Regional Development Fund (ERDF);

- the European Social Fund (ESF);

- the European Agricultural Guidance and Guarantee Fund (EAGGF); and

- the Financial Instrument for Fisheries Guidance (FIFG).

In the pre-accession, 1994–99, period this resulted in programmes for regions where development is lagging behind (Objectives 1 and 6), for declining industrial areas (Objective 2), and for rural areas (Objective 5). In addition, the EU structural policy in the 1994–99 programming period included two training and employment objectives (Objectives 3 and 4), which were not regionally targeted, as outlined in Table 3.2.

Table 3.2 Structural Fund objectives for the 1994–1999 programming period

Objective 1:	Promoting the development and structural adjustment of regions whose development is lagging behind.
Objective 2:	Converting the regions or parts of regions seriously affected by declining industrial regions.
Objective 3:	Combating long-term unemployment and facilitating the integration into working life of young people and of persons exposed to exclusion from the labour market; promotion of equal opportunities for men and women.
Objective 4:	Facilitating the adaptation of workers to industrial changes and changes in production systems.
Objective 5:	Promoting rural development by:
Objective 5a:	speeding up the adjustment of agricultural structures and promoting the modernisation and structural adjustment of the fisheries sector; and
Objective 5b:	facilitating the development and structural adjustment of rural areas.
Objective 6:	Development and structural adjustment of regions with an extremely low population density.

Source: *European Commission, 1996b*

Because the first round of accessions by the CEECs (Hungary, Poland, the Czech Republic, Slovenia and Estonia) involves countries that have low levels of prosperity relative to the Union, the acceding countries will have a strong claim on substantial amounts of Structural Fund payments. Indeed, the successful integration of the CEECs into the EU, particularly into the single market, and the ability of acceding countries to access the benefits of closer integration, will be strongly influenced by the extent of structural actions directed toward these countries. All of the CEEC applicants will thus be net beneficiaries from the Structural Funds. Consequently, their accession will affect the budgetary positions of all the existing member states in relation to the Structural Funds, reducing the positive balances of net beneficiaries and increasing the negative balances of net contributors.

The most important feature that differentiates the forthcoming enlargement from previous expansions is the *extent* of its impact in reducing the average per capita gross domestic product (GDP) for the Community as a whole. This is on a level that is unprecedented within the Community. Table 3.3 shows how the increase in population and total GDP resulting from accession of those CEECs likely to join in the next round of EU enlargement compares with the impacts on population and GDP that occurred during previous enlargements. In particular, the impact on per capita GDP is highlighted. The previous largest impact on per capita GDP was a fall of 6 per cent resulting from the combined effects of the accession of Greece in 1981 and Spain and Portugal in 1986. In comparison, the accession of the three largest CEECs can be expected to result in a 10 per cent decline in the per capita GDP of the EU.

Table 3.3 The impact of successive enlargements of the EU

Acceding countries	Increase in population (%)	Increase in total GDP in PPP (%)	Change in per capita GDP in PPP (%)	Average per capita GDP in PPP (EU6 = 100)
UK, Denmark, Ireland (1973)	32	29	−3	97
Greece (1981); Spain, Portugal (1986)	22	15	−6	91
Austria, Finland, Sweden (1995)	11	8	−3	89
Hungary, Poland, Czech Republic	17	5	−10	80
Hungary, Poland, Czech Republic, Estonia, Slovenia	18	6	−10	80

Based on 1995 data.

Sources: *European Commission, 1997a, additional estimates by the author*

On the basis of the current eligibility criteria, the entire territory of each of the applicant countries could be eligible for assistance under Objective 1 of the Structural Funds. This would represent a substantial increase in 'demand' for Structural Fund expenditure. At the same time, the reduction of the EU average GDP per capita would exclude all but a handful of the EU15 regions that are currently eligible under Objective 1. Assistance under other objectives within the EU15 will also need to be scaled back if the budget is to remain under control. Consequently, the prospect of enlargement was a major factor in the *Agenda 2000* proposals for the reform of EU policies.

It should be noted that in addition to the economic disparities that exist between acceding and existing member states, marked regional differences exist within the applicant countries. Major differences also exist in the growth potential of these within-country regions. In general, the larger urban areas and western regions within the CEECs tend to be more prosperous, typically have a better level of infrastructure provision and attract a higher level of inward investment. The Commission's impact study (1997a) into the effect of enlargement to the applicant countries of central and eastern Europe concluded that:

> *the need for a structural policy to be formulated now and applied as of the next round of accessions is therefore justified both by external factors (reduction of the gap between the CEECs and the Community average) and by the internal necessity of combating increasing disparities within the applicant countries.*

(European Commission, 1997a: 20)

However, in view of the variations in the extent to which different regional economies are dependent on sectors that are likely to be most affected by enlargement, and of differentials in growth potentials between the regions of the CEECs, it will be important to ensure that the adoption of EU policies aimed at promoting national economic development does not contribute to an increase in internal disparities within these countries.

The Commission proposals for reform stated that in order to make the Structural Fund more effective there was a need for simplification of management, greater flexibility and decentralisation in implementation. The number of objectives was therefore to be reduced to three: two regional objectives and a horizontal objective for human resources. The percentage of the population of the Union covered by Objectives 1 and 2 is to be reduced from 51 per cent to around 35–40 per cent. As the acceding countries will all be net recipients of EU funds, these policy reforms were developed within a tight budgetary framework. Limits on the amount allocated to the acceding countries have been set in order to take into account their absorption capacities and the need for efficiency in Structural Fund spending.

For the existing 15 member states the regional impacts of enlargement will be twofold:

- changes to the areas designated under the EU Structural Fund policy, and consequently in the budgetary resources available to those areas; and

- changes in regional competitiveness within an enlarged European Union.

As a consequence of the latter, policies related to the introduction of the single European market will have significant impacts on regional competitiveness and cohesion, and thus on EU regional policy. This interdependence will be particularly strong where industrial sectors most affected by the single market are regionally concentrated.

The single European market

The impact of EU policies related to the single European market on the applicant countries will be dependent on the ability of these countries to respond to the potential opportunities offered by adoption of EU policies and the opening up of EU markets (i.e. their 'response potential'). Their response potential will be determined by two 'types of factors' (European Commission, 1996a; Malecki, 1991, 1995):

- 'environmental conditions' that facilitate or impede trade and economic development (e.g. transport and communications infrastructure, financial sector infrastructure, government policy); and

- their capacity to innovate in order to adapt to changes in the competitive environment ('innovation potential').

These are complex characteristics, dependent on a wide range of factors. For example, relevant environmental conditions include factors such as transport infrastructure, telecommunications infrastructure, institutional environment, labour force productivity, the structure and diversity of the local economy and relative wage levels. Similarly, the innovation potential of a country or region will also depend on a wide range of factors, including expenditure on research and development, skills and education levels, presence of research centres and universities, and cultural factors such as entrepreneurial traditions in the region and any previous history of adapting to change. A brief overview of key factors affecting the ability of Hungary, Poland and the Czech Republic to respond to the challenges and opportunities arising from the single European market and closer integration into the EU is contained in Tables 3.4 and 3.5. This highlights some of the key development needs of the applicant CEECs, which will have to be addressed by EU regional policies, and also some of the factors that will restrict the extent of their integration into the single European market in the short-to-medium term. Major areas of potential impacts of integration of the CEECs into the single market (on both existing and new member states) include: trade effects, foreign direct investment (FDI) effects, the locational decision of firms and the labour market.

Trade effects

Since the beginning of the transition process the introduction of the Europe Agreements has resulted in the removal of EU tariffs on industrial goods and will progressively reduce quantitative trade restrictions. The move toward EU accession has, therefore, led to the progressive dismantling of trade barriers, with a resultant increase in trade between the CEECs and the EU in recent years (Figures 3.1 and 3.2).

Table 3.4 Environmental factors affecting response potential: a summary

Response potential	Poland	Hungary	Czech Republic
Environmental indicators			
Transport infrastructure	Substantial increases in road traffic since 1990 on roads not designed for such heavy traffic. No motorways until 1990. Significant improvements to road and rail infrastructures required.	Road/rail networks have a backlog of maintenance and require substantial improvements to cope with recent increases in traffic and refocusing of trade toward EU.	Around 50% more rail network per km^2 than Poland or Hungary. Road network relatively well developed but unable to cope with increased traffic flows since 1990, including transit traffic.
Telecommunications/ IT infrastructure	Many unsatisfied requests for phone lines. Telecommunications infrastructure ten years behind EU average. Originally lagged well behind Hungary, but has largely closed the gap since 1995. Low digitisation of network. Level of information systems development below the average for the CEECs; hindered by telecommunications system.	Telecommunications network remains the weakest link in the Hungarian infrastructure; around six years behind the EU average. Information system development has now passed the position the average EU country reached two years ago but still lags behind the Czech Republic.	Penetration of phone lines significantly higher than Poland and Hungary but basic telephone services not yet universally available. Rapid modernisation occurring. Information system development most advanced of the three countries, but still hindered by deficiencies in the telecommunications infrastructure.
Institutional environment	Lack of business access to finance. Most bank loans short term (less than one year). Support infrastructure for SMEs needs to be strengthened/better co-ordinated.	Low availability of long-term loans – loans available to business sector generally for less than one year. Government policy on SME development established in 1989. Plans to improve credit arrangements/alleviate tax burden for small companies.	Banking sector not competitive or strong. A number of banks have failed. Main problems include bad debt, lack of transparency, and under-capitalisation. Extensive network of regional advisory centres for SMEs. Funding schemes for SME loans and guarantees exist.
Relative wage levels	Relative wage levels low – c. ECU 250/month in 1997.	Relative wage levels low – c. ECU 230–275/month in 1997.	Relative wage levels low – c. ECU 290/month in 1997. Wage pressure may result from the relatively tight labour market.
Labour force productivity	Productivity low, especially in traditional sectors such as coal and steel/agriculture, but increasing strongly in some sectors, such as in the food processing industry. Manufacturing sector has experienced strong productivity growth.	Productivity low but increasing rapidly in some sectors. Double-digit productivity growth in the industrial sector for a number of years now. Restructuring is at an advanced stage, and a core of Hungarian enterprises are already quite competitive in the EU markets.	Productivity low, and growth in productivity not as high as could be expected in view of low unemployment and low levels of investment, raising questions about the suitability of investments undertaken. More restructuring/productivity gains required.
Structure and diversity of the local economy	Little information available, but reliance on traditional heavy industry and agriculture appears to remain high. There is rapid growth in the services sector. Production of most primary products decreasing.	Significant restructuring has taken place in the industrial sector in recent years. There has been above average growth in machinery manufacture and modern metallurgy, while sectors that are heavy users of energy have declined. Rapid growth in SMEs.	Long-established and diversified industrial sector incorporating traditional industries but also relatively sophisticated engineering products and high-quality glass. Service sector growing rapidly (especially tourism) and absorbing part of the redundant labour force from agriculture and large state firms.

Source: Gourlay et al., 1999; European Commission, 1997b, c, d

Table 3.5 Indicators of innovation potential: a summary

Response potential	Poland	Hungary	Czech Republic
Innovation potential			
R&D	R&D is still regarded as a matter for the state rather than an activity carried out by the enterprise sector.	Strong record in R&D, but declined dramatically in the 1990s. Now expected to increase as economic recovery progresses, and due to participation in EU R&D programmes.	Long-standing tradition of expenditure on R&D, especially in engineering (machinery). Higher expenditure on R&D than Hungary or Poland, mostly by private enterprises. However, research-industry relations are still fragile.
Skills and education levels	Skills/education levels moderate. Number of universities: 11	Skills/education levels moderate. Number of universities: 30	Skills/education levels high. Number of universities: 23
Number of universities/research institutes	Education system suffered before 1989 from the country's isolation and political control, although overall standards were high. Aim to upgrade to EU standards over next 15 years.	Long tradition of excellent education facilities. Now developing vocational training to increase labour mobility and assist economic transition.	Skilled and educated workforce.
Business registration/survival rates	New business formation high. No data on business survival rates. Number of private enterprises has expanded rapidly, mainly through the birth of new enterprises rather than by privatisation.	New business formation high. No data on business survival rates. There has been a huge growth in the number of enterprises in Hungary, almost entirely SMEs, reflecting a dynamic industrial sector.	New business formation moderate. No data on business survival rates. Large firms still dominate, but small enterprises are increasing their share of the market. Growth of the private sector is largely responsible for boosting exports and investment.
Cultural factors	Even under communism, part of the economy was in private hands, especially in agriculture. Pre-1989, roughly one-third of the labour force worked in the private sector. This is one reason why private sector activity expanded so rapidly in the post-communist period. Numbers of private enterprises have increased substantially, mainly through new enterprises rather than from privatisation. The growth of the private sector is largely responsible for the boost to exports and investment.	Hungary has a long-established record of a gradualist approach to economic reform. Rigorous central planning was abolished as long ago as 1968 when the 'New Economic Mechanism' was introduced; more systematic economic reforms began in 1985. Thus some elements of the institutional and legal infrastructure for a market economy have been in place for almost a decade.	Some evidence of resistance to restructuring among workers. Lack of transparency/ accountability in management structures. Weak management capabilities within industry. Achieved successful reorientation of trade toward the West. Quality of exported goods is improving, but value-added is still low. The ability of Czech exports to penetrate new markets suggests that the quality of goods has been improving.

Source: *Gourlay* et al., *1999; European Commission 1997b, c, d*

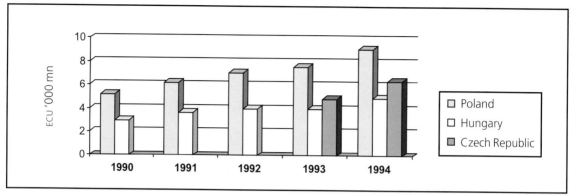

Figure 3.1: Trends in EU imports from Poland, Hungary and the Czech Republic
Data for the Czech Republic not available prior to 1993.

Source: *EUROSTAT, 1996*

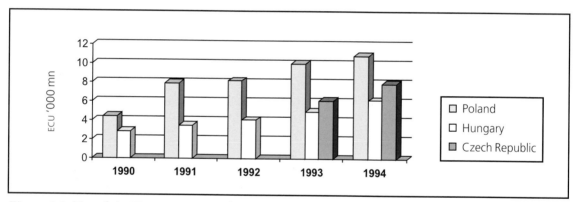

Figure 3.2: Trends in EU exports to Poland, Hungary and the Czech Republic
Data for the Czech Republic not available prior to 1993.

Source: *EUROSTAT, 1996*

In general, the enlarged internal market should create substantial new output and employment opportunities both for the CEECs and for the existing member states. The value of CEEC trade with the Community has more than tripled over the 1989–95 period. As integration proceeds, the rapidly growing incomes in central and eastern European countries should translate into growth opportunities for western European exports. Increased competition from suppliers in eastern Europe may also have a dampening effect on prices for industries and services in the West.

Trade impacts on existing EU member states can be divided into two kinds of effect:

- those arising from direct trade with the acceding countries; and

- displacement of trade relations with third countries (e.g. the fact that Germany is sourcing an increasing proportion of its trade from within the CEECs may in some cases be at the expense of UK trading relationships).

Foreign direct investment effects

In addition to trade implications, increased competition in attracting foreign direct investment (FDI) may be expected to affect existing member states. The flow of FDI into the CEECs has risen significantly as trade has grown. The attraction of the CEECs for FDI is attributable to their proximity to existing EU member states, the availability of a skilled workforce and access to EU markets through the Europe Agreements (European Commission, 1999a). FDI has resulted in the transfer of technology and new management techniques to the CEECs and in the creation of jobs in the area. Hungary has been the largest recipient of FDI, partly due to the early start of economic deregulation and privatisation in that country, which led to many western companies selecting it as their regional base.

Impacts on locational decisions of firms

EU enlargement will, in future, increasingly impact on the locational decisions of firms, primarily as a result of access to new markets but also in the form of relocation due to variations in costs of production. The candidate countries are well placed geographically and may thus be in a good position to profit from their comparative advantages, such as low unit labour costs and low transport costs due to their proximity to the main Community markets. In particular, industries with low sunk costs, and that can achieve a sufficient reduction in transport costs, may be the most inclined to relocate from current member states to acceding countries in which real unit labour costs are lower. (Sunk costs are the historical costs of plant and machinery that have no current resale value. They are thus not recoverable on ceasing operation.)

Labour market impacts

High West–East wage differentials may provide a strong incentive to East–West migration in spite of high unemployment in the West. This could have two consequences. First, it may encourage the development of more flexible labour markets, especially in neighbouring countries (e.g. Germany, Austria, Greece). Second, unemployment rates may increase in the West as there will be limited employment opportunities for those parts of the western labour force that are crowded out (see European Commission, 1997a). Adjustment pressure is likely to be highest at the lower end of the skills/wage scale, but existing member states may also experience an inflow of highly qualified workers. This could, in some cases, have positive effects in terms of alleviating shortages of skilled labour in the existing member states.

Barriers to the operation of the internal market

A number of the environmental factors outlined in Tables 3.4 and 3.5 may be expected to impair considerably the ability of the acceding CEECs to respond to the opportunities opened up by access to EU markets in the short-to-medium term. This will reduce the benefits of EU membership to these countries and will also reduce the potential impacts on existing member states in the short-to-medium term. In particular, major inadequacies in the transport and telecommunications networks of the acceding countries and deficiencies in financial infrastructures are key factors affecting the ability of CEEC firms to exploit the potential opportunities offered by the opening up of EU markets.

Sectoral policies

In terms of sectoral policies, by far the most important element is the Common Agricultural Policy (CAP), which accounts for the single largest share of the EU budget (Table 3.6).

Table 3.6 EU budget appropriations, 2000

	Appropriations for commitments – EU15 € mn (1999 prices)
Agriculture	40 920
Structural measures	32 045
Internal policies	5 900
External operations	4 550
Administration	4 560
Reserves	900
Pre-accession aid	3 120

Source: *European Commission, 1999b*

The acceding countries are more dependent on agriculture than the present member states in terms of area, contribution to GDP and share of employment. EU enlargement will greatly increase the agricultural area of the EU. However, the relatively high workforce and the small average farm size in the CEECs will result in a reduction in the average available area per person employed in the sector. The share of agriculture in employment is particularly high in Poland,

(26.9 per cent in 1995) and considerably exceeds the share of agriculture in gross value-added (GVA; less than 8 per cent) since productivity is low and considerable restructuring is still required if this sector is to become competitive with that of the existing member states (European Commission, 1997a).

The EU is the most important agro-food trade partner for many of the applicant countries. All of the CEECs, with the exception of Hungary, are increasing net importers of agricultural and food products from the EU. In general, agricultural prices are significantly lower in the CEECs than in the EU – although the differences vary between countries and products, the divergence being less for cereals, oilseeds and protein crops than for beef, milk and dairy products. In part these differences in farm-gate prices reflect an inefficient downstream sector (e.g. high transport costs) and quality differences. If significant price differentials between acceding countries and the EU still prevail at the time of accession, the sudden introduction of CAP price levels would result in higher consumer prices in the CEECs, where a relatively large proportion of household budgets is already spent on food. In addition, the food industry in these countries would encounter increased raw material costs at the same time as they had to face increased competition from existing member states.

Extension of the CAP to the CEECs without prior reform of the policy could have been expected to result in increased surpluses in production for most commodity sectors. In addition, constraints on subsidised exports imposed by the World Trade Organization (WTO) would have prevented the EU from disposing of these surpluses on the world markets. Agricultural support policies had therefore to be adapted to allow for the post-accession conditions, with a general reorientation away from price support and toward direct income support as well as an increase in rural development and environmental policy elements within the CAP.

Full implementation of the *acquis* in the agro-food sector will also require the approximation of veterinary, plant health and animal nutrition legislation and marketing standards. This will require investment in public sector inspection and testing facilities in the CEECs, as well as substantial private sector investment in upgrading food industry establishments in order to meet EU requirements.

Economic and monetary union

The acceding countries must endorse the aim of economic and monetary union and will be required to implement the *acquis* in this area, at least to the extent required of non-participant member states. This will involve the adoption of measures to stabilise their economies in the long run, as well as to stabilise nominal exchange rates and co-ordinate economic policies. The new members' ability to participate in the euro area will be judged on the same basis as for existing member states, i.e. on the basis of economic convergence criteria. However, it is unlikely that they will be in a position to participate fully in the euro area at the time of their accession.

Summary and conclusions

EU enlargement to include the CEECs differs from previous enlargements because of the extent of lags in the development of the applicant countries. In particular, characteristics that present major policy challenges related to enlargement are:

- their low per capita income levels;

- their strong dependence on agriculture and so-called sensitive sectors;

- major deficiencies in their transport, telecommunications and energy infrastructures and networks; and

- their weak administrative capacities.

In spite of the rapid economic growth and the pace of structural adjustment in some of the applicant countries in recent years, the scale of the task and the extent of the investment required means that these features are likely to persist over the medium term. In addition, high unemployment both in the EU and in most of the applicants' economies will make it more difficult for those sectors and regions that are potential 'losers' in the adjustment process to find alternative employment.

The accession of such a group of relatively poor countries will present a real challenge to Community policies aimed at increasing economic and social cohesion and reducing disparities between the regions. This challenge will be all the greater as a result of adjustment strains arising from the opening up of the acceding countries to competitive pressures within the European single market. Adjustment strains are likely to be regionally concentrated, with the greatest strains occurring in those regions that are heavily dependent on agriculture, or in industrial sectors that are most sensitive to the effects of enlargement. Care will have to be taken to ensure that policies aimed at economic development on a national level do not increase existing within-country disparities in the CEECs.

The opening up of eastern European markets should lead to a further intensification of cross-border transactions. EU enlargement should increase trade for two reasons. First, closer integration will mean that a greater share of CEEC trade will be with the Union. Second, accession will stimulate economic growth in the applicants and thus raise their import demand. In addition, policies aimed at increasing economic and social cohesion may assist these countries to undertake the investment necessary to enable them to expand their production potential.

Implementation of the Europe Agreements will, to a large extent, have resulted in extensive integration of the markets of the EU countries and of the candidate countries prior to accession. However, in those sectors where trade liberalisation under the Europe Agreements has been limited, considerable change is likely to occur on accession. In general, the effect of the pre-accession process will be to bring forward some of the adjustments required, thereby making the transition process more gradual.

In spite of these caveats, the CEECs involved in the first round of enlargement are well placed geographically and may thus be in a good position to profit from their comparative advantages, such as low unit labour costs and low transport costs, due to their proximity to the main Community markets. Their location should also prove an asset in relation to the upgrading of energy, transit and communications infrastructures. The integration of the CEECs into the EU can be expected to provide a strong boost to their economic development. The resulting economic growth in the CEECs should, in turn, result in a general increase in demand within the EU, creating opportunities for both existing and new member states.

References

European Commission, 1996a, *The impact of the development of the countries of central and eastern Europe on the Community territory*. Brussels: European Commission.

European Commission, 1996b, *Structural Funds and Cohesion Fund: regulations and commentary*. Brussels: European Commission.

European Commission, 1997a, *The effects on the Union's policies of enlargement to the applicant countries of central and eastern Europe*. Brussels: European Commission. http://europe.eu.int/comm/dgla/agenda2000/en/impact/contents.htm.

European Commission, 1997b, *Commission Opinion on Hungary's application for membership of the European Union*. Brussels: European Commission (DOC 97/13).

European Commission, 1997c *Commission Opinion on the Czech Republic's application for membership of the European Union*. Brussels: European Commission (DOC 97/17).

European Commission, 1997d *Commission Opinion on Poland's application for membership of the European Union*. Brussels: European Commission (DOC 97/16).

European Commission, 1999a, *Sixth periodic report on the regions*. Luxembourg: European Commission (DG XVI : Regional Policy and Cohesion, Inforegio).

European Commission, 1999b, *Presidency conclusions – Berlin European Council, 24th and 25th March 1999*. Luxembourg: European Commission (D/99/1).

EUROSTAT, 1996, *Country profile: central and eastern European countries, 1994*. Luxembourg: Office for Official Publications of the European Communities.

Gourlay, D. L., Copus, A. K., Petrie, S., 1999, *Implications of EU enlargement for structural policy in Scotland*. Unpublished SAC research report to the Scottish Executive. Aberdeen: Scottish Agricultural College.

Malecki, E. J., 1991, *Technology and economic development: the dynamics of local, regional and national change*. London: Longman.

Malecki, E., 1995, *Entrepreneurs, networks and economic development: a review of recent research*. Gainesville: University of Florida, Department of Geography.

4

HOW MANY EUROPES?

The changed terms of debate in the 1990s over EU enlargement into central and eastern Europe and the acceptance of uneven development in Europe's future

John Agnew

In the immediate aftermath of the surprising collapse of Soviet domination in central and eastern Europe (CEE) and the disintegration of the Soviet Union itself there was considerable euphoria over the possibility of incorporating the newly liberated region into a revived project of European unification. After years of drift and immediately before the end of the Cold War the European Community, as it then was, underwent a renewed lease on life that had already led to the goal of the single market and was shortly to lead to the Maastricht Treaty of 1993 (Moravcsik, 1998). The new developments were mainly about 'deepening' the linkages and mutual dependence among existing members. But they were also about rejuvenating the 'idea' of Europe as an integrated entity; so the real possibility of carrying on the established pattern of admitting new members once they meet certain criteria for joining was not discounted at the time. Indeed, there had long been a broader vision of 'Europe' as expressed, for example, in French president de Gaulle's image of an integrated Europe extending from 'the Atlantic to the Urals'.

The difficulties and dilemmas experienced in CEE during the 'transition' from authoritarian politics and planned economies to more democratic and liberal regimes, however, seemed to sour western élite and academic discussion on both the ease and the appropriateness of extending the 'European project' to the east. As accession became less abstract, the potential costs to existing members of admitting relatively poor states also loomed larger – particularly at a time of persisting recession throughout western Europe. Together these created doubts that found expression in a new discourse about EU enlargement that is sceptical about the previously self-evident claims of CEE to full membership in the EU. The terms of debate about EU enlargement have thus shifted from arguing the political-economic necessity of including large swathes of CEE in the European 'homeland' to a much more selective discussion involving the application of a range of criteria for membership, of which macroeconomic ones have become increasingly important. At the same time and to a large degree, admission into the North Atlantic Treaty Organization (NATO) and other security groupings and the largely symbolic issue of membership in the Council of Europe rather than paths on 'the road to Europe' are seen as substitutes for full EU membership. Paths to membership through other arrangements (such as the European Free Trade Association) are also on offer.

The changed approach to CEE, however, augurs a fundamental reorientation of the European project as a whole away from a single Europe to a multi-tier, patchwork Europe with various 'degrees' of actual membership. To anticipate the main conclusion, this chapter argues that this trend in public discussion about EU enlargement to the east represents a full-fledged victory for a neo-liberal vision of Europe. In this vision uneven economic development across the continent is not seen as a temporary state of affairs to be corrected by policies from Brussels, but is accepted as an inherent feature of the future of Europe. Indeed, it is viewed implicitly as an attractive feature of an 'integrated Europe' in which common rules of property and capital mobility prevail everywhere, and in which differences in incomes and standards of living between a core area, a peripheral Europe and an external Europe are institutionalised. Thus at least three Europes replace the two of the Cold War and the one of the original post-Second World War visionaries of a united Europe.

EU enlargement and central and eastern Europe

Debate over enlargement of the European Union has had two interrelated themes that have undergone subtle but important transformations during the course of the 1990s. The first theme concerns the qualifications of applicants for full membership. The drift here has been from an emphasis on broadly political criteria to relatively narrow economic criteria, with NATO and membership of other organisations held up as 'alternatives' to full membership in the EU. At the same time, a geopolitical line has been more firmly drawn between a 'central' Europe in tune with the European project and an 'eastern' periphery 'beyond the pale' of integration into the 'new' Europe. The Cold-War-era division of Europe into two has given way to a threefold division based on a political-economic 'fault line' dividing a potentially 'European' central zone from a more distant, despotic East.

The second theme involves the increasing tension between the official EU position that eastern expansion can simply follow the model of previous enlargements and the practical need to reform the objectives and organisation of the EU in response to the 'widening' of the membership. Initially, the focus was on incorporating new members into the framework of existing Euro-agreements in much the same way that previous expansions brought in new members. Of course, the collapse of the existing regimes in CEE came as a great surprise, so the lack of a specific policy about how the accession of non-western European states to the EU might be dealt with is not that remarkable. But with its 15 members straining to meet current tasks, increased by the last round of reforms associated with the Maastricht Treaty, expansion is now seen as requiring a revision of the structures and policies – from voting procedures in the Commission to the Common Agricultural Policy – that were devised more than 40 years ago for the original Community of six members. Implicit in many of the proposed reforms is the idea of a Europe at various 'speeds', in terms of conformity to central norms governing economic growth, population mobility, regional development and social welfare, and with the possibility of 'opting out' of policies that are either too or insufficiently rigorous for local standards (e.g. EU environmental controls are insufficient for Denmark; Britain resists common passport controls and membership in currency union) (Laurent and Maresceau, 1998).

Beginning in the mid-1980s the European Community, as it then was, began negotiating a series of bilateral trade agreements with various countries in CEE – Hungary in 1988, Poland in 1989, the Soviet Union in April 1990, Czechoslovakia and Bulgaria in December 1990 and Romania in 1991 – although ties went back further (Shlaim and Yannopoulos, 1978). The rapid pace of political change in central and eastern Europe in 1989 and 1990 called for a more proactive response from the European Community to the region. The prospect of German unification gave particular impetus to securing a degree of regional political-economic stability. As a result the EC established the PHARE programme, designed to support reform in recipient states. Targeted initially at Poland and Hungary, the programme was later extended to include Romania, Bulgaria and Yugoslavia in 1991 and Slovenia in 1992. As early as 1990, however, the scale of the transformation process made a more comprehensive response from the EC, in the form of renegotiated trade agreements, an urgent requirement (Kramer, 1993). Underpinning these new agreements, first focused on Poland, Hungary and Czechoslovakia, was a mental map of Europe divided into concentric circles, with increasing distance to the east, each circle or belt seen as conforming less to reform possibilities, and hence prospective integration into the EC (Preston, 1997: 198). This view emerged slowly during the early 1990s, but by 1995 was at the centre of negotiations over applications for membership. In the Copenhagen Declaration of 1993 the Czech and Slovak Republics (following the 'velvet divorce'), Poland and Hungary stated their intent to become full members in the 'new' European Union (named as such also in 1993). The EU heads of government agreed that the associated countries in CEE should become members of the EU once they satisfied the political and economic criteria for membership. By and large, EU member governments had lost some of their earlier enthusiasm about extending full membership eastwards; nevertheless the 'classical principles' of enlargement were restated by the Copenhagen Council of 1993:

Membership requires that the candidate country has achieved stability of institutions guaranteeing democracy, the rule of law, human rights and respect for and protection of minorities, the existence of a functioning market economy as well as the capacity to cope with competitive pressures and market forces within the Union. Membership presupposes the candidate's ability to take on the obligations of membership including adherence to the aims of political, economic and monetary union.

(European Council, 1993)

This was to prove an impossible task. Although it provided a clear set of goals to aim at, and an externally imposed discipline on reform, it also imposed major obligations on the EU itself. In the white paper presented to the Cannes European Council (June 1995) a more specific but much narrower approach to phased adoption of the internal market *acquis* of the EU was outlined. The onus for 'making the grade' was placed firmly on the applicants and no timetable for aligning applicants with the EU was put forward. Rather, the document focused on three elements of adaptation to the internal market required of applicants: legislation, administrative and technical structures and technical assistance from the EU. The overall thrust, however, was upon the role of establishing the market mechanism as a prerequisite for accession to the EU. Partly this reflected the sense that many political changes, such as the goal of electoral democracy, had been achieved. But it also represented a substantial narrowing of the criteria. The dilemma for the EU has been twofold. First, there is a lack of consensus among EU members about expansion (e.g. Britain favours rapid expansion as a barrier to 'deepening' of the EU; Portugal, Greece and Spain worry about the impact of CEE entrants on their benefits from the common agricultural and cohesion policies). Second, there is the difficulty of employing the same criteria as in previous enlargements because of (a) the greater complexity of the post-Maastricht and post-EMU EU and (b) the lower economic base from which the new applicants, compared to the poorest previous ones, must move in a much shorter period of time if accession was to occur during the 1990s or early in the new millennium (Preston, 1997: 204).

In its *Agenda 2000* statement of 1997 the European Commission proposed that five CEE countries had satisfied the criteria for *opening* membership negotiations: the Czech Republic, Estonia, Hungary, Poland and Slovenia (European Commission, 1997). This was endorsed by the European Council in December 1997. Negotiations were to be on a bilateral basis, even though this elicited opposition from some members who prefered multilateral negotiations. What was most remarkable about *Agenda 2000* was the degree to which 'transition to a market economy' became the single mantra for success, closely followed by a variety of macroeconomic indicators, not dissimilar to those associated with accession to the EMU and the euro (small government budget deficits, low inflation, etc.). According to the *Agenda 2000*, Hungary and Poland were the most advanced in the process of transition to a market economy, with the Czech and Slovak Republics not far behind. Estonia was seen as equally advanced but weak with respect to its ability to withstand competitive pressure. Poland, Hungary and the Czech Republic were seen to be capable of adopting a large part of EU legislation (the *acquis communautaire*) in the medium term with 'effort'.

Although 'it is a taboo … to deny ultimate membership to the applicant states … there are many who would quietly rejoice were enlargement to be almost indefinitely postponed' (Spencer, 1998: 61). This sentiment has been reflected in the increasingly selective approach to membership and has been paralleled by increased debate inside and outside the European Commission about alternatives to full membership in the EU, even for those countries with whom negotiations for entry have been pursued for some time (e.g. see Fritsch and Hansen, 1997; Croft *et al.*, 1999). Such 'alternatives' included integration at the level of EFTA (the European Free Trade Association) as a path toward 'eventual' full membership in the EU (a path followed by many previous new members such as Sweden, Austria and Finland) or integration at the level of the EEA (European Economic Area), in which the Internal Market Programme would be extended to the prospective members but the Common Agricultural Policy and Cohesion Policy, etc. would not apply.

Expansion of NATO has taken on a symbolic role as a partial substitute for EU membership, indicative of a 'welcome' from 'the West' irrespective of its actual security relevance for the countries in question (Brown, 1999). Czech, Polish and Hungarian membership of NATO since 1998 is widely seen as giving them recognition as favoured candidates for membership in the other, and more important, European 'club': the EU. The widespread adoption of the term central Europe, to distinguish those more qualified for NATO and EU memberships from the others, represents a clear demarcation between those who can look forward to some sort of integration into 'Europe' and those who cannot (e.g. see European Commission, 1998). For countries such as Romania and Bulgaria not even the possibility of EFTA or NATO membership was raised. Prior to 1999 they were rarely if ever mentioned in Commission documents. They appeared to have fallen off the map of potential entrants, as had most of the Balkans and the whole of Europe to the east of Poland and Hungary – save tiny Estonia, championed by its Finno-Ugric brothers/sisters in Finland (Steil and Woodward, 1999).

If enlargement of the EU to the east has been increasingly defined in terms of economic criteria and limited to an ever-shortening list of acceptable supplicants, at least part of the answer lies in the deferring of reform of the EU as it exists that would be mandated by rapid eastern expansion. The official position was that the eastern expansion of the EU could follow the path of previous expansions. Unfortunately, this became more and more untenable across the course of the 1990s. There thus arose a profound tension between the official Commission point of view and the practical realities facing the EU in preparing for the accession of new eastern members (Price *et al.*, 1999). The major problem has been that of dealing with a possible quantum leap in political-economic diversity among members at the same time that other projects, particularly monetary unification, not only require large amounts of political capital from existing members but also complicate the adhesion of new members without a recent history of sophisticated monetary and financial organisation.

The possibility of nearly doubling its membership over a short span of years raises troubling questions for the goals and organisation of the EU. One is the legitimisation crisis associated with the lack of popular control over the Commission and its organs (Mann, 1998; Banchoff and Smith, 1999). This is exacerbated by the addition of new members. Another question, directly opposed to the first, is the relative efficiency of EU organs when all members have fairly equal representation. A third is the strong disparity in incomes and standard of living between the prospective eastern members and even the poorest regions and population segments of western states. This will introduce a contrast in wage rates and living conditions into the EU that will make the objectives of Cohesion Policy extremely difficult to implement without reducing or eliminating regional development funds for existing members. Moreover, without significant reform of the Common Agricultural Policy (CAP), extending current levels of price supports to new eastern members will put an enormous strain on the total EU budget (Redmond and Rosenthal, 1998). Finally, to receive support for expansion from some existing members, side-payments or policy allowances will also have to be made, thus further fragmenting what is already a fragile set of 'core' principles governing common policies at the heart of the European integration process. The official position had been deaf to these practicalities, yet the existing members were not, leading to heightened discussion in the late-1990s of a Europe *à la carte*, irrespective of official pronouncements that only 'full' membership was possible for new members or allowable for existing ones (Laurent and Maresceau, 1998).

Rapid and comprehensive incorporation of the countries of CEE into the EU, so enthusiastically predicted in many circles in the early 1990s, has faded away. By 1999 not only was the list of prospective members much reduced to a limited number of central European states, but the main criteria for admittance had become economic ones, particularly the neo-liberal one of 'transition to a market economy'. Without far-reaching reforms of the EU itself it is not clear that the adhesion of new members will do anything other than exacerbate already wide disparities in economic and social well-being between parts of Europe. Yet there are significant political barriers to building a more solidly institutionalised and democratic EU. The vision of a single Europe may be increasingly sacrificed to one of three: a core Europe, itself increasingly divided in its degrees of conformity to common policies; a peripheral Europe, perpetually 'on the road' to membership but shunted into various half-way houses for an extended period of time; and an external Europe, excluded even from discussion of the merits of membership, desperately searching for some way of demonstrating its European 'credentials'.

The EU and uneven development

The EU project can be seen historically as an effort by western European élites to overcome their divisions in order to regain their power in relation to the rest of Europe and thus their centrality in world affairs (e.g. see Delors, 1991). From the outset, two sets of objectives have been in delicate balance. On one side, a European-scale entity provides a gigantic market in which the most efficient producers can emerge to go head-to-head with those from the United States and Japan. But, on the other side, this process must be insured by a territorial compact in which those places and people that suffer the consequences, in loss of jobs and decreased incomes, will be compensated through new investments and pay-offs of one kind or another. Reorganising uneven development from a national to a Europe-wide scale, therefore, has always been a major part of the 'European project'. It has rested, however, on a continuing commitment to those countries and localities that would inevitably lose as this process took its course.

As long as membership remained largely available to countries with histories of industrial and financial development at a world standard, this trade-off remained resolvable. Each could gain some competitive advantage even as it lost elsewhere. The previous accession to membership of Ireland, Portugal and Greece, however, illustrates the problems and possibilities associated with a larger expansion to CEE. The main advantage each had was lower wage rates, rather than much in the way of existing industrial plant or expertise in particular services. Through massive infrastructure investments, however, the EU has helped to develop each of these economies toward a European norm. The difficulty is that these investments cannot be made on the same scale in CEE without bankrupting the EU and creating resentments among existing members.

But something else has happened to the 'European project' over recent years beyond increased demands on the central budget from poorer members. It has become increasingly dominated by a neo-liberal vision in which the mere adhesion to 'market principles' is seen as miraculously leading to large increases in economic growth. This is signalled by the way in which the debate over accession by eastern countries into the EU is increasingly dominated by fairly narrow economic considerations. Meantime, the political goal of the EU – to compensate and ameliorate for losses by means of redistribution – is increasingly downplayed relative to the overall economic 'success' of the Union in the world economy (e.g. see Jacquemin and Pench, 1997). Enlargement of the EU to the east, therefore, has come at a particularly inauspicious time in the evolution of the EU.

Trends within the existing EU point to the increased polarisation between members and regions within countries across a range of economic indicators (Hardy et al., 1995; Croft et al., 1999). Although the Maastricht Treaty significantly upgraded the role of regional policies, available funds are still relatively small. At the same time the single European market has tended to work very much against this, exacerbating core-periphery differences within countries and across the

EU countries as a whole. Enhanced competition following from the revitalisation of the EU due to the Maastricht Treaty has had two effects. One is to select between 'superior' and 'inferior' locations according to existing potential. The second is to build up economies of scale in the superior locations, institutionalising initial advantages into permanent ones. MacKay (1995: 162) puts it well: 'To a certain degree, success and failure are self-perpetuating.' But only if nothing is done to counter the market process. In theory, market assumptions may produce spatial equilibria; in practice, markets rarely seem to.

To the extent, therefore, that the EU is dominated by adoption of a neo-liberal image of development and less committed to redistribution among countries and across regions, the expansion to the east will enhance rather than reduce country-by-country and inter-regional differences. This will represent a true departure from the original 'compact' upon which the project of European unification was based and abandonment of the idea of creating a single Europe. In its place will be a Europe of institutionalised uneven development. Not only the potential new members will be affected. Even 'core' Europe will be subject to the new project, one closer to the American model of dramatic regional differences in incomes and unemployment but much more competitive globally as a result of the 'shake out' possible in the larger market provided by the reduction in barriers to trade and capital mobility.

This 'Brussels' Europe (Emerson, 1998: 227) of the present EU, and perhaps some new central European members, will be flanked to the east by a tier of excluded states available as sites for low-cost assembly by EU-headquartered firms. Justified in cultural-political terms as a fault line between two 'civilisations', rending the geographical Europe (as in Huntington (1993) and other accounts, e.g. Emerson (1998)), this offers a larger-scale vision of uneven development beyond that already emerging within the confines of the EU itself. The new EU, however, is probably not the one that the countries of CEE have wanted to join. Their current enthusiasm should be tempered by what might well be in store for them if they succeed. Indeed, instead of lining up to join and reorienting their economies according to EU directives they might be well advised to trade more with one another and re-establish the organisational linkages with one another that they rashly abolished in the immediate euphoria of the end of the Cold War. Such a 'half-way house' might prove to be a better destination, at least until the EU reassesses its current neo-liberal vision of spatial economic logic.

Conclusion

It is a commonplace of discussions about the EU that it represents a novel type of institution based on an 'alternative means of organising human beings' (Linklater, 1998: 218) than existing states. It is a great ideological hope and organisational prototype for the whole of humanity. If Europeans can sink their differences after what they did to one another in the 20th century then there is hope for all. It is partly in this spirit, and in the hope also of economic salvation, that most of the countries of CEE have applied to join the EU. This claim on behalf of the EU, however, rests on the view that the space it contains is in the process of reconfiguration, such that where you are within its limits does not matter. Akin to the most romanticised and misleading versions of globalisation, this signifies that 'the identification of boundaries – and associated notions of "here" and "there", "far" and "near", "outside" and "inside", "home" and "away", "them" and "us" – is more problematic than ever' (Scholte, 1996: 49). Yet, within the EU and in relation to its expansion to the east, this is anything but true (Ross, 1998). National identities and national differences on EU policies remain strong. If anything, country-by-country and inter-regional economic differences are becoming *more* not less important. In this context, the goal of a single Europe begins to retreat from the horizon, replaced by a vision of multiple Europes stratified by the roles they can perform in turning European firms on the whole into a global economic force.

References

Banchoff, T., Smith, M. P., eds, 1999, *Legitimacy and the European Union: the contested polity*. London: Routledge.

Brown, M. E., 1999, Minimalist NATO: a wise alliance knows when to retrench. *Foreign Affairs*, 78 (3), 204–218.

Croft, S., Redmond, J., Rees, G. W., Webber, M., eds, 1999, *The enlargement of Europe*. New York: St Martin's Press.

Delors, J., 1991, *Le nouveau concert européen*. Paris: Odile Jacob.

Emerson, M., 1998, *Redrawing the map of Europe*. London: Macmillan.

European Commission, 1997, *For a stronger and wider Union: Agenda 2000*. Strasbourg: European Commission (DOC 97/6).

European Commission, 1998, The challenge of enlargement – the European Commission's opinion, July 1997. *In* Nicoll, W., Schoenberg, R., eds, *Europe beyond 2000: the enlargement of the European Union towards the east*. London: Whurr Publishers, pp. 29–56.

European Council, 1993, *Conclusions of the presidency*. Copenhagen: The European Council.

Fritsch, M., Hansen, H., eds, 1997, *Rules of competition and east–west integration*. Dordrecht: Kluwer.

Hardy, S., Hart, M., Albrechts, L., Katos, A., eds, 1995, *An enlarged Europe: regions in competition?* London: Jessica Kingsley.

Huntington, S. P., 1993, The clash of civilizations? *Foreign Affairs*, 72 (1), 22–49.

Jacquemin, A., Pench, L. R., eds, 1997, *Europe competing in the global economy: reports of the Competitiveness Advisory Group*. Cheltenham: Edward Elgar.

Kramer, H., 1993, The EC's response to the new eastern Europe. *Journal of Common Market Studies*, 31, 213–225.

Laurent, P.-H., Maresceau, M., eds, 1998, *The state of the European Union, vol. 4: deepening and widening*. Boulder: Lynne Rienner.

Linklater, A., 1998, *The transformation of political community*. Cambridge: Polity Press.

MacKay, R. R., 1995, European integration and public finance: the political economy of regional support. *In* Hardy, S., Hart, M., Albrechts, L., Katos, A., eds, *An enlarged Europe: regions in competition?* London: Jessica Kingsley, pp. 159–179.

Mann, M., 1998, Is there a society called Euro? *In* Axtmann, R., ed., *Globalization and Europe: theoretical and empirical investigations*. London: Pinter, pp. 184–207.

Moravcsik, A., 1998, Europe's integration at century's end. *In* Moravcsik, A., ed., *Centralization or fragmentation? Europe facing the challenges of deepening, diversity, and democracy*. New York: Council on Foreign Relations Press, pp. 1–28.

Preston, C., 1997, *Enlargement and integration in the European Union*. London: Routledge.

Price, V. C., Landau, A., Whitman, R., eds, 1999, *The enlargement of the European Union: issues and strategies*. London: Routledge.

Redmond, J., Rosenthal, G. G., eds, 1998, *The expanding European Union: past, present, future*. Boulder: Lynne Rienner.

Ross, G., 1998, European integration and globalization. *In* Axtmann, R., ed., *Globalization and Europe: theoretical and empirical investigations*. London: Pinter, pp. 164–183.

Scholte, J. A., 1996, Beyond the buzzword: towards a critical theory of globalization. *In* Youngs, G., Kofman, E., eds, *Globalization: theory and practice*. London: Pinter, pp. 43–57.

Shlaim, A., Yannopoulos, G. N., eds, 1978, *The EEC and eastern Europe*. Cambridge: Cambridge University Press.

Spencer, T., 1998, Enlargement – a parliamentary practitioner's perspective. *In* Nicoll, W., Schoenberg, R., eds, *Europe beyond 2000: the enlargement of the European Union towards the east*. London: Whurr Publishers, pp. 57–61.

Steil, B., Woodward, S. L., 1999, A European 'New Deal' for the Balkans. *Foreign Affairs*, 78 (6), 95–105.

Part II

The Candidates

INTRODUCTION

Darrick Danta and Derek Hall

This section of the book presents discussions of the 13 candidate countries of central, eastern and Mediterranean Europe that are actively seeking entry to the European Union. As explained in Part I, this means that the countries have formally applied to the EU, have signed a Europe Agreement, have had an *Opinion* prepared by the European Commission concerning progress made toward accession, and are in the process of meeting the varied requirements of membership. For much of the latter 1990s the countries of central and eastern Europe were differentiated into two groups: the so-called first-wave countries (the Czech Republic, Hungary, Poland, Slovenia, Estonia and Cyprus) and the second-wave countries (Slovakia, Latvia, Lithuania, Bulgaria and Romania). In addition, Malta and Turkey had applications pending, but for various reasons were treated in a separate category. At its Helsinki Summit in December 1999, however, the EU decided to move all 13 countries to applicant status.

If admitted, the candidate countries would significantly alter the current composition of the EU. In terms of population, although the candidate countries are on average 52 per cent smaller than the EU15 (13.06 million against 24.89 million), adding all 13 countries would swell the total population of the EU by 45.5 per cent, from 373.30 million to 543.14 million (Table II.1). Likewise, the addition of the countries would add 1,863 sq km to the EU, which represents an increase of 59 per cent to 5,006 sq km. However, much of the increase in both population and area is accounted for by Turkey, which holds 63.75 million individuals on 775 sq km.

Table II.1 EU15 and candidate country comparisons, 1996–1997

Group	Population (mn)	Area ('000 sq km)	GNP/GDP ($ bn)	Per capita GNP/GDP ($)
EU15 countries				
Total	373.30	3 143.00	7 979	
Average	24.89	209.53		21 400
Candidate countries				
Total	169.84	1 862.77	730	
Average	13.06	143.29		4 616

Sources: *McCormick, 1999: 44; authors' calculations from data in Table 1.1*

In terms of economic structure, the candidate countries are much poorer than their EU neighbours. At nearly $8,000 bn the total output of the EU totally dwarfs that of the candidate countries' $729.8 bn. Comparing per capita figures, EU citizens enjoy an average level that is 464 per cent higher than those living in the candidate countries, $21,400 against $4,616. Clearly, the contemplated expansion represents a very significant undertaking that is without precedent in the annals of EU history.

Each of the chapters that follows represents a view of the key characteristics of the candidate countries prior to EU enlargement. These are set within a brief historical context and an evaluation of evolving relations with the EU, particularly during the 1990s. In each case, authors have tried to evaluate the fitness of their country to join the EU and to highlight issues that may pose problems for, and may hinder, the candidate country achieving accession.

References

McCormick, J., 1999, *Understanding the European Union: a concise introduction*. New York: St Martin's Press.

5

THE CZECH REPUBLIC

Frank Carter

The Czech Republic lies at the heart of Europe (Figure 5.1). Like many other states in central and eastern Europe, over recent years it has experienced rapid change, where free elections and a democratic system have replaced a former strict, one-party political system. It is also one of Europe's newest states, created in January 1993 after the break-up of the former Czechoslovakia into two separate countries as a result of the 'velvet divorce'.

Figure 5.1: The Czech Republic

Again, like many other European states in the 20th century, the republic has undergone the impact of wars, foreign occupation, political instability, dictatorship and economic decline. Even so, it possesses a long heritage of industrialisation supported by a diligent and enterprising population. This image has attracted many foreign companies to invest in the country's growing economy in recent years. Nevertheless, the country does face serious problems, partly as a result of the closure of unprofitable factories as a consequence of embracing a market economy. Whilst unemployment has remained low, prices have risen, especially for basic goods and food. Pollution continues to degrade the country's air, water, soil and vegetation, partly an inheritance from former communist times. Nevertheless, there is belief among the Czech people that these problems can be overcome and that their country will rapidly adjust to the vagaries of the new economy (Pick, 1997). Their republic could become a model for all those central and east European states that have emerged from four decades of communist control, should they happen to be successful.

The statistical background

The Czech Republic is a landlocked country, lying in the central part of Europe, with an area of 78,866 sq km. In January 1997 its population totalled 10,309,137, or 131 people per sq km (Český Statistický Úřad, 1997). In European terms this placed the country in 21st place (for area), 12th (for population) and 13th (for density of population). After the partition with Slovakia in January 1993 the Czech Republic was no longer part of a country that maintained a border with former lands of the Soviet Union, a situation that had existed for much of this century. Its new borders were with the neighbouring states of Poland (761.8 km), Germany (810.3 km), Austria (466.3 km) and Slovakia (251.8 km).

The territory of the Czech Republic lies on a major European watershed, which separates the basins of the North, Baltic and Black Seas and is centred on the mountain of Králický Sněžník (1,423 m). Major rivers include the Labe (Elbe; 370 km) and Vltava (433 km) in Bohemia, the Morava (246 km) and Dyje (306 km) in Moravia, and the Odra (Oder; 135 km) and Opava (131 km) in Silesia and northern Moravia.

The Czech Republic is located on the borders of two mountain systems, each of which had its own geological development. In the western and central parts of the republic the physical landscape consists of the Česka vysočina uplands, largely dating from the late Palaeozoic period. In contrast, ranges of Mesozoic age form the Šumava, Český les, Krušné hory, Krkonoše, Orlické hory and Jesiniký mountains. The Beskydy mountains in the east appeared during the Tertiary period as part of the western Carpathian system. A series of river valleys are located between the two mountain systems.

The country experiences the influence of both oceanic and continental climates, typified by prevailing westerly winds, intensive cyclonic activity and ample precipitation. Bohemia is mainly under the sway of maritime conditions, while Moravia and Silesia are more affected by continental influences. Overall, these conditions produce a humid continental climate, with warm summers and cold winters. Rainfall is usually more frequent in summer, often accompanied by thunderstorms. Dry, clear autumns and damp springs are both of short duration. In Prague, the average January temperature is −1 °C and in July, 19 °C. The capital city receives an average annual rainfall of 485 mm, which in winter months often falls as snow. Just over half the land (53 per cent) is under agriculture, and forests (largely coniferous) cover a third of the country. Brown soils are most common. Unfortunately, some parts of the country's land suffer from pollution damage.

Population growth over the last 250 years on the territory now occupied by the Czech Republic is shown in Table 5.1.

Table 5.1 The Czech Republic: population, 1750–1997

Year	Population ('000s)
1750	3.3
1800	4.7
1850	6.7
1870	7.5
1900	9.4
1920	10.0
1930	10.7
1950	8.9
1970	9.8
1980	10.3
1990	10.3
1997	10.3

Source: *Holoček, 1993: 27*

Clearly, a population peak was reached in the inter-war years and has not yet been surpassed. Under communism there was a steady growth up to 1990 (to 10,362,740) but then, with the demise of communism, population dropped in 1991 (to 10,308,682) and fluctuated toward a renewed peak in 1994 (10,336,162). Since then it has declined to its 1997 level of 10,309,137.

Females account for 51 per cent of the total population; some 25.7 per cent of the population is 15 years of age or under, and 19 per cent are over retirement age, which is 60 for men and 57 for women. Vital population statistics for 1996 reveal that births totalled 90,763 (11.8 per thousand population), deaths 56,709 (5.5), marriages 53,896 (5.2), and divorces 33,113 (3.2). Infant deaths were 5.47 per thousand live births (Český Statistický Úřad, 1997).

There are eight administrative regions (*kraj*), one of which is the capital, Prague (Table 5.2). It is noticeable that some two-fifths of the population live in the administrative districts of Moravia. Approximately 85 per cent of the inhabitants reside in towns of more than 2,000 people. As is indicative of an industrialised economy, more than half the population live in cities of over 10,000 inhabitants and a third in cities with over 50,000 persons. Table 5.3 gives the country's seven largest cities with more than 100,000 inhabitants (i.e. 23 per cent of the urban population).

Table 5.2 The Czech Republic: administrative regions by area and population, 1997

Region	Chief city	Area		Population	
		sq km	%	No.	%
Prague	–	496	0.63	1 204 953	11.69
Central Bohemia	Prague (Praha)	11 014	13.97	1 105 234	10.72
South Bohemia	České Budějovice	11 346	14.39	700 595	6.80
West Bohemia	Plzeň (Pilsen)	10 875	3.79	859 306	8.34
North Bohemia	Ústí nad Labem	7 799	9.89	1 178 977	11.44
East Bohemia	Hradec Králové	11 240	14.25	1 234 781	11.98
South Moravia	Brno	15 028	19.06	2 054 989	19.93
North Moravia	Ostrava	11 068	14.03	1 970 302	19.11

Source: *Český Statistický Úřad, 1997: 54, 56–57*

Table 5.3 The Czech Republic: population of cities with more than 100,000 inhabitants, 1997

City	No. of inhabitants
Prague	1 204 953
Brno	387 570
Ostrava	323 870
Plzeň	170 449
Olomouc	104 380
Liberec	100 356
Hradec Králové	100 280

Source: *Český Statistický Úřad, 1997: 58*

Ethnically, according to the population census of March 1991, four-fifths (81.2 per cent) of the population were Czechs, 13.2 per cent claimed they were Moravians, 3.1 per cent Slovaks and 0.6 per cent Silesians; 2.5 per cent were of other nationalities, including small communities of Poles, Roma (Gypsies) and Germans. Minority ethnic groups still use their own language, but the official state language is Czech, a member of the west Slavonic group. From a religious viewpoint, Christianity remains the dominant religion. In the 1991 census two-fifths of the country were members of the Roman Catholic Church. A further 15 per cent nominally declared themselves Protestant, most belonging to the Evangelical, Czech (Reformed) and Hussite churches. The latter has the largest Protestant denomination with about 400,000 members. A number of smaller religious communities have their own churches, including the Old Catholics, the Czech and Moravian Brethren and the Baptists. An Eastern Orthodox Church also exists. The Czech Republic also has a small Jewish community with their own synagogues, mostly located in Prague. Significantly, nearly a third of the population – mainly among the younger generation – stated in the census that they had no religious beliefs. Church membership remains higher in older age groups.

Under communism, the former Czechoslovakian economy was depicted as that of a developed industrialised country with intensive agriculture (Slepička et al., 1989; Renner, 1994). Soon after the fall of communism, the Czech economy experienced rapid advances. Gross domestic product rose by 2.3 per cent in 1994 and increased a further 9.1 per cent in 1995. By 1996 privatisation was all but complete, with 98.5 per cent of the economy in private hands. The private sector expanded and foreign investment grew. Unfortunately, large sectors of industry still remained outdated and required restructuring. It has been estimated that failure to respond to this situation will mean up to one-third of heavy industrial plants going into liquidation over the next few years. In order that essential industrial modernisation of these plants can take place, more foreign investment is needed. The tourist industry is one sector of the economy that continues to prosper; in 1995 it earned a revenue equivalent to $2,875 mn. Such activity stimulates private sector growth and augments foreign currency reserves.

Even after partition the Czech Republic is still ranked among the most industrialised states in the world. This position has been based on solid foundations, for during the communist period production rose more than tenfold. Minerals provided a solid base, particularly through the reserves of hard coal and lignite. The main sources were located in the Most, Chomutov, Kladno, Ostrava and Sokolov coalfields. Uranium ore is also exploited and in 1985 gold deposits were found near Prague. Industry provides about three-fifths of the country's GNP and employs about one-third (32 per cent) of the workforce. The manufacture of machinery, chemicals and rubber, food and beverages and iron metallurgy provide the major industrial branches. Unfortunately, as the Czech Republic seeks new trade areas to replace those traditional markets that have gradually faded with the demise of Comecon (CMEA) these industrial branches will possibly decline in significance. They will probably be superseded in importance by service sector industries, especially tourism, and by those manufacturing companies producing glass and porcelain items, for example to satisfy export demand.

Compared with west European countries, Czech agriculture is rather labour intensive and remains the most state-subsidised sector of the economy. The main crops grown are sugar beet, wheat, maize and potatoes. In 1996 most farming was undertaken by private enterprise, which cultivated 56 per cent of all arable land; in contrast agricultural co-operatives tilled only two-fifths (41 per cent). Private-plot farming was insignificant, totalling only 3 per cent of both agricultural land and output. For agricultural enterprises, it is still difficult to venture into long-term planning, mainly as a result of the rapidly changing economic climate. Nevertheless, given more favourable conditions in future, the Czech Republic could be a stimulating new presence in Europe's agricultural market-place.

With reference to transport and communications, in 1996 the Czech Republic had 55,489 km of roads and motorways (423 km). There were also 9,435 km of railway tracks, of which less than a fifth (2,859 km) had been electrified. The Labe (Elbe) and Vltava are the country's major navigable rivers, with Děčín and Prague, respectively, their chief ports. In addition, the Oder river allows access to the Baltic Sea via the Polish port of Szczecin. River transport has declined considerably since 1990 when goods carried totalled 6,370 million tonnes, compared with 2,879 million tonnes in 1996; tonne-kilometres also dropped, from 1,405,000 to 901,000 over the same period. Air transport provides domestic links between Prague and Ostrava, Plzeň and other regional centres, and the capital city is also a major international air terminus. In 1996, 91 per cent of the total number of flights were for abroad (25,232 out of 27,854). Foreign destinations accounted for 97 per cent (1,916,000 out of 1,982,000) of all passengers carried, while goods transported abroad reached nearly 98 per cent (13,665 out of 13,959 tonnes). Czech telephone and fax communications need to be improved. Data reveal only 29 telephone connections were made for every 100 inhabitants; the waiting period for installation is still far too long, with about 597,000 telephone lines awaiting installation in 1996.

The historical legacy

The present territory of the Czech Republic has been inhabited since prehistoric times. Habitation by hunter-gatherers can be traced back to the Upper Palaeolithic period in Moravia and was based on important Pleistocene sites at Dolní Věstonice, Pavlov, Předmostí, Stránská skála and Pekárna (Svoboda et al., 1996). In the Neolithic period the Moravian river valleys were inhabited by hunting tribes, which eventually colonised Bohemia. These invaders from the east brought with them a knowledge of using metals; after 2000 BC Bronze Age culture was evident in central Bohemia and named after the village of Únetice. Two different groups of inhabitants existed in Bohemia by 1500 BC, one cremating their dead, the other using mound burials.

In the 5th century BC two major nomadic Celtic tribes, the Boii and Cottini, entered present-day Czech territory from northern and eastern Europe. Among their legacies were a number of place names, most significant of which was the early appellation for Bohemia. Their territory ranged from Bavaria into southern Bohemia and as far north as Prague; the Romans later named this area 'Boiohaemia'. Other Celtic place names include the rivers Labe (Celtic Albis; becoming the Elbe in Germany) and Jizera (the same origin as the Ysère in France). The Celts also created a system of urban habitation, with an economy based on trade and industry, centred on their largest settlement Boiohemum; some settlements were located in forested areas near ore deposits, such as Stradonice in Bohemia and Hradisko in Moravia, while others were sited along main river routeways (Polišenský, 1991).

With the demise of the Celts in central Europe, following clashes with the Thracians, Germanic tribes began to penetrate their territory from the west. This led to skirmishes between the Boio and Teutons, with the latter slowly occupying part of the Boio's territory. By 12 BC a Teutonic group, the Marcomans (Marcomanni), had conquered much of the Boio's land, and former Celtic settlements were abandoned and left in ruins. During the ensuing centuries Bohemia and Moravia were to witness much disturbance as nomadic tribes battled with each other over trade and land. The Marcomans were eventually defeated by other Teutonic groups, who colonised the southern valleys, while the Avars and Slavs migrated in from the east. By the early years AD the Roman legions were expanding northwards toward the Danube, but they never managed to cross the basins of the Morava and Dyje rivers in any number. They did succeed in building a few fortifications in southern Moravia, which were linked to the 'limes Romanus' located along the Danube; however the Romans, like the Marcomans, left few traces of their presence on present-day Czech Republic territory.

After the Gothic invasions of the 5th century and the resulting 'migration of peoples', numbers of Slavs moved into Bohemia and Moravia from the north-east, while the Avars came into central Europe from the south-east. Legend has it that sometime during the 5th century AD one of the chiefs (a 'Father Cech') of a Slavonic tribe entered Bohemia; he surveyed the surrounding landscape, found it agreeable and decided to settle there with his tribe, called Czechs after him. They were already well established by the 6th century AD in what is today Bohemia.

However, the first state of any significance was founded in Moravia, namely the Great Moravian Empire, which developed in the early 9th century (Poulík, 1985). It is frequently associated with the arrival of Christianity to the region. Two Byzantine monks, Cyril and Methodius, arrived in 863 and taught the Slavs Christian prayers and rituals in their own language. After the death of the last prominent Moravian ruler (Svatopluk, AD 870–894) the empire suffered internal weaknesses and yielded to Magyar attacks. Given these changed geopolitical conditions the political centre moved from Moravia to Bohemia, now ruled by the Přemyslids. These were Czech princes who were determined to rule over Bohemia. In AD 929, one of their number, Prince Václav (Wenceslas), swore allegiance to a German ruler, King Henry I, which aroused anger among his fellow princes and led to his murder in AD 935; he eventually became patron saint of the Czech nation. The Přemyslids were deposed in the early 11th century and Vladislav (Władisław), king of Poland, was invited to become their ruler. His most significant act, based on an alliance with the German king, was to bring Bohemia into the Holy Roman Empire as a fiefdom paying a tribute to the emperor.

The Přemyslids returned to power with the death of King Vladislav in 1037. In the hope of creating a powerful merchant/artisans class his successor, King Břetislav, encouraged Germans to immigrate to Bohemia's urban centres. His idea was to use them to weaken the disloyal rural nobility. As a result the German settlers established urban centres covering much of western and northern Bohemia, a German law code was adopted and there was increased trade with German cities. In order to reinforce German influence there, an element that was to remain throughout Bohemia's history, German clergy were dispatched to Bohemia by ensuing Holy Roman emperors.

In the 13th century the rule of Přemysl Otakář II was a period of great expansion for the Czech kingdom. Several new towns were built, many of which retain their medieval appearance to this day, and numerous strong castle fortresses were constructed to maintain royal power. The reign of Charles (Karel) I of Bohemia between 1346 and 1378 (from 1355 as the Holy Roman Emperor Charles IV) is considered to be the most famous period in Czech history. Charles encouraged the cultural and commercial development of the Czech Lands, and Prague was converted into an imperial capital; new edifices were built, including the development of Nové Mesto (New Town), as well as churches and state monuments. In 1348 he founded Charles University, the oldest in central Europe, renovated the city's castle and constructed the now famous Charles Bridge in the city.

During the mid-1300s the immense wealth and strength of the Roman Catholic Church was beginning to be questioned in Bohemia. Czechs favoured reform, but the German Bohemians remained faithful to the pope. After the death of Charles IV religious quarrels inevitably arose between the Czechs and the Germans. The Czech reformists were led by the rector of Charles University, Jan Hus (White, 1995; Fudge, 1998). He became a figurehead in the struggle of the Czech people for freedom from the Holy Roman Empire and liberation from German control. The martyrdom of Jan Hus in Constance (1415) encouraged his followers, the Hussites, to rebel against German rule. In 1419 Jan Žižka a Czech nobleman, led a Hussite army that ransacked German urban centres and razed Catholic monasteries and churches to the ground. Forces loyal to the emperor attempted to quell the rebellion in a struggle that was to develop into the Hussite

Wars (1420–1433). This conflict ended with religious compromise; the greatest long-term effect on Europe was the influence it had on the importance of an individual's right to freedom of thought.

In 1526 Louis, king of Bohemia and Hungary, was killed in battle against the Ottoman Turks at Mohács (Hungary). The Czech nobles elected a member of the Habsburg family, Archduke Ferdinand I, to occupy their throne in the hope of averting an Ottoman conquest of their country. They believed that a central European federation of Austria, Hungary and the Czech Lands would be better equipped to deter further Turkish expansion. Not only was this ploy successful, it also led to Habsburg rule of their country from 1526 until 1918. Prague was, once again, to become a centre of Europe science and culture during the reign of the Habsburg Emperor Rudolph II (1576–1611).

However, the old enmity between Czech and German remained. In Bohemia German Catholics continued their loyalty to the Habsburgs; but in Bohemia and Moravia the nobility, clergy and ordinary people opposed Habsburg rule. The situation deteriorated in 1617 when the Habsburg throne was occupied by Ferdinand II, a man determined to erase Protestantism from his territory. A year later Czech nobles, in protest at his policy, ejected three of Ferdinand's advisers from a window in Prague Castle, an event that became known as the 'Defenestration of Prague'. Circumstance worsened when the Czechs enlisted an army to confront the Habsburgs, a confrontation that ended in their defeat at the Battle of White Mountain in November 1620. The defiant Czech nobles were chased out of their country, and their defeat signalled the origin of the Thirty Years War between the Protestant and Catholic states of Europe. Its conclusion in 1648 (Treaty of Westphalia) meant that Bohemia and Moravia remained Habsburg territory. German Catholics appropriated Czech property and lands, all teaching and publishing in Czech was outlawed and German became the country's official language.

In 1740 a new era of more liberal reform was ushered in when Maria Theresa became empress of the Habsburg lands. This milestone was to bring Austria and Bohemia closer together and led to a more efficient approach to government rule. The reform process was continued by Maria Theresa's successor, Joseph II (1780–1790); his most notable achievement was the abolition of serfdom (1781–1785), thus allowing Czech peasants to leave their rural abodes for the rapidly expanding urban centres and the opportunity for factory employment. Events in Paris during his reign (the French Revolution), were to inspire the Czechs to create a nationalist revival half a century later (Agnew, 1993). The movement, headed by František Palacký, demanded an end to German power in the country and the foundation of an autonomous Czech state that would include Bohemia, Moravia and Silesia. During 1848 an unsuccessful uprising took place in Prague against the Habsburgs, and this proved the death-knell of the Czech independence movement. The victors imposed strict marshal law throughout Bohemia and Moravia, thus fuelling the long-standing friction between Czechs and Germans in the country.

With the demise of the Habsburg monarchy in 1918 Bohemia and Moravia (with Slovakia and Ruthenia) emerged as part of the new Czechoslovakian state under the presidency of Tomáš Garrigue Masaryk (Teichová, 1988). Politically, the inter-war period was characterised by a coalition government: the Agrarian Party supported farmers, the National Democratic Party promoted industry and business and the Communist Party (after 1921) encouraged state ownership for all forms of production. Following Masaryk's resignation in November 1935, the new president, Eduard Beneš, had to face the rise of Hitler in the neighbouring state of Germany. Since its inception Czechoslovakia had been plagued by various ethnic problems. In the Czech Lands one of the largest groups was that of the ethnic Germans, who began agitating for closer ties with Germany. Many of them resided in the Sudetenland border region and wished to see this area united with Germany. In September 1938 the situation was clarified by the Munich Conference, which permitted the secession of Sudetenland to Germany. This event gave Hitler the pretext in March 1939 to successfully invade the Czech Lands, resulting in Bohemia and Moravia becoming a German Protectorate and remaining so throughout the Second World War.

Beneš and his government-in-exile returned to Czechoslovakia in April 1945, and in the following month Soviet troops entered Prague; Germany capitulated and peace in Europe was restored. Elections took place in Czechoslovakia during 1946 and the Czechoslovak Communist Party won a disputed victory, with 38 per cent of the votes; their leader, Klement Gottwald, became prime minister. Two years later, following the resignation of 12 non-communist government ministers, the Communists seized power. A new constitution declared the country a 'people's democracy'; in future only communist-approved candidates were nominated for the national elections. Beneš resigned and the country came under the aegis of the Soviet Union. Thus began four decades of Soviet domination, highlighted from a western viewpoint by the short-lived Prague Spring of 1968. Alexander Dubček and his colleagues made attempts to give the country 'socialism with a human face' through new reforming zeal, but this was abruptly ended in August of that year with the occupation of Czechoslovakia by Warsaw Pact troops. All this was to change in 1989 with the fall of communist rule, and in 1990 the Civic Forum opposition party was officially registered as a legal organisation (Holý, 1996). The 'velvet revolution' had taken place and Václav Havel was elected president of a new, short-lived, Czech and Slovak Federative Republic. From the outset tensions were apparent between the two regions; these were resolved through the 'velvet divorce' of the two participants, and on 1 January 1993 Bohemia and Moravia formed the new independent Czech Republic.

Developments after 1989

Many observers were surprised by the speed of the communist collapse and the end of central planning in Czechoslovakia, in spite of the increasing amount of popular political unrest. What was to become known as the 'velvet revolution' started with a student demonstration in

November 1989. That same month a successor to the old Charter 77 organisation, Civic Forum (Občanské fórum), was founded to represent all democratic groups in the Czech Republic. Civic Forum's leading representative, Václav Havel, was elected president of Czechoslovakia a month later.

The post-communist Czech Republic began with an almost entirely new political administration; free elections were proclaimed in June 1990, seven months after the velvet revolution. The result was an overall majority for the Civic Forum Party, confirming the desire for a pluralist parliamentary democracy by the Czech people. The new government now had the authority to execute radical reforms to supplement the limited number of reform measures introduced in the last years of communist rule. Already in 1990 new macroeconomic policies were starting to take shape with the activation of a radical transition/austerity plan. However, it was not until January 1991 that a complete package of policies became effective (OECD, 1991; Kupka *et al.*, 1993). Included in the main economic measures were restrictive monetary and fiscal policies, a privatisation programme, price liberalisation affiliated with limited controls, internal convertibility linked with a sharp currency devaluation and protectionism by means of import surcharges (Charap and Dyba, 1992; Schwartz *et al.*, 1994). Most Czechs supported these changes, but were surprised by the swift method of application and the breadth of recommendations conceded. The motivator behind these reforms was Václav Klaus, minister of finance and a supporter of strict monetarist policies. His strategies, however, incited considerable resistance from the Civic Movement (formerly the Civic Forum); Klaus took umbrage to this reaction and in March 1991 fashioned his own Civic Democratic Party. The move to the right in Czech politics was now clearly confirmed.

If macroeconomic policy was to work, according to Klaus, it had to be moulded by a very prolonged and cautious monetary growth accompanied by balanced budgets. Great emphasis was placed on the operation of the exchange rate, which had to be both workable and protected, even at the cost of purchasing power parity. Klaus believed that if it was to be successful, the notion of privatisation required a combination of both conventional and unorthodox methods (Svejnar, 1995; Myant *et al.*, 1996; Chvojka, 1997). This stance was part of the logic behind his famous voucher privatisation scheme. Klaus's philosophy not only hastened the fulfilment of the voucher scheme but assisted in the success of the whole privatisation process (Takla, 1994). For example, by the end of 1992, voucher sales had contributed to the sale of 21,400 small businesses and the privatisation of some 900 state enterprises (Benáček, 1995). In October–November 1993 vouchers were again on sale to Czech citizens in the second and final stage, and this resulted in a further 770 enterprises being privatised (Bilsen, 1994).

In June 1992 new elections confirmed the country's political swing to the right. Klaus's party won nearly a third of the vote, which permitted him to constitute a coalition government with other allied parties. In contrast, the centre Civic Movement party was overthrown, polarising parliament into left and right political wings. Klaus's ability to mould together a viable political party supported by branch headquarters at grass-root level proved the basis for this election success. In sharp contrast, the Civic Movement had remained phlegmatic, resting on its laurels following the achievements of the velvet revolution.

National revivalism and separatism was another spin-off from the 1992 election (Skalnik Leff, 1995). In some sections of Czech society there was dissatisfaction with the organisation of the Czechoslovakian state; eventually this was to lead to a split between the Czech and Slovak federal republics. Demand for independence, from a Czech viewpoint, was based on persistent disagreements between the two republics. There was continued doubt about the political future, contributing to the uneasiness felt by the Czechs regarding a successful transition to democracy. In fact, after the 1992 elections Havel resigned as president of Czechoslovakia because of his inability to prevent the rise of nationalism in the two federal republics.

The scene was set for a division of Czechoslovakia. Negotiations between the Czech (Klaus) and Slovakian (Mečiar) leaders, led to an agreed 'velvet divorce', with 1 January 1993 set as the formal separation date. Some of the citizens in both republics believed there should have been a referendum. If this had taken place it would not have resolved the many altercations that existed between the Czech and Slovak peoples; however, a referendum would have given the people of Czechoslovakia an option over their country's future. Separation had been masterminded by a few senior politicians rather than the nation as a whole. In reality this implied that any future problems arising from the split into two independent republics could be blamed on the two leaders and their senior political advisers, rather than on the federal government or the rank and file.

For the new Czech Republic, the division of Czechoslovakia in 1993 represented a far more constructive way of conserving its economy than any previous government's domestic policy could have achieved. It now enjoyed the relative security of economic expansion, which could not have been achieved by the former federal administration. Yet the Czech economy, in spite of its innate geographical and historical advantages, had to confront a situation of newly found freedom from the Soviet bloc. This brought with it the strain of privatisation and led to a spectacular short-term increase in prices and unemployment (Marcinien and Wijnbergen, 1997). As a result, the government had to initiate a system of value-added tax in order to adjust its economy to western markets.

Furthermore, even by late 1993, state-owned firms still produced over four-fifths (85 per cent) of industrial output, in spite of the achievements in industrial restructuring within the extensive privatisation programme. The delay suffered by some enterprises waiting to privatise during the restructuring process was part of the problem. This had placed some enterprise managers in a quandary, not knowing whether or not to improve production performances, increase investment or prepare for new markets. There also remained the uncertainty associated with state subsidies for covering operating costs (Souček, 1997; Myant, 1997). The outcome in some enterprises led to the dismissal of employees, especially in textiles and mining where dismissals reached between 25 and 40 per cent. For example, as a result of dwindling sales between 1990 and 1993, production in the Ostrava coal mines dropped from 18 to 13 million tonnes and employment was halved (from 100,000 to 49,500). At the Kladno steel works a comparable employment pattern appeared, with the workforce plunging from 20,000 to 9,000 over the same period. Due to the loss of east European markets some large enterprises were sold to western firms. A typical example was the Škoda engineering complex at Plzeň: its 'AutoŠkoda' section was bought by Volkswagen and 'Škoda Energo' (turbines) went to Siemens (Germany) and Westinghouse (USA).

Czech agriculture, in contrast, was more successful despite an employment decline from 600,000 to 222,000 between 1991 and 1996. This three-fifths loss of employees meant that agriculture engaged only 5 per cent of the state's economically active population by 1996 (Bičík and Götz, 1998). Moreover, considerable changes in farm ownership have occurred since 1990 (Kraus *et al.*, 1994). In 1990 a quarter (25.9 per cent) of all agricultural holdings were state farms, two-thirds were co-operatives (66.5 per cent) and private farms represented a mere 1.3 per cent of the rest (OECD, 1995). By 1994 the country's 310 state farms were under restitution, being claimed by former owners or converted into joint-stock companies. In contrast, the 1,300 co-operatives remained more or less intact, and there was a constant increase in private farms. The latter totalled over 60,000 by the end of 1994 and covered 23 per cent of agricultural land (20.6 per cent arable). However, size differential was significant: only 1,100 of privately owned farms had more than 100 ha; the average size was just 16 ha (Ptáček, 1996).

Czech foreign trade patterns shifted in the early 1990s, in keeping with changes throughout eastern Europe. Exports to western countries increased, while those to former Comecon members declined. Together with Poland and Hungary, the Czech Republic signed its associate membership status with the EC in December 1992, when still part of the former Czechoslovakia. This agreement involved a phased suspension of export tariff barriers over the next eight years. Unfortunately, about a third of Czech exports to the EC were negatively affected by quotas set on steel, textiles and food. In 1993 poor Czech export performances to the EU could be directly ascribed to a cap on steel exports. Further sufferance was felt in April 1993, when Czech meat exports suffered from a general ban on all east European imports to the EU due to an outbreak of foot-and-mouth disease in Croatia.

Prior to 1989 there was a total ban on foreign investment in the country, but only a year later the Czech Republic had become an attractive area for investors due to its political stability and successful stabilisation programme. In 1990 Klaus pushed through parliament a series of laws encouraging foreign investment (Dobosiewicz, 1992). The result showed that between 1990 and

1992 direct investment in Czechoslovakia totalled $1,898 mn, mainly to the Czech Republic; a third of the funding came from Germany (32.2 per cent), 29.5 per cent from the USA and 13.8 per cent from France.

Unfortunately, in 1993 several major contracts collapsed, providing much less direct foreign investment than the Czechs had anticipated. Nevertheless, the overall situation in the Czech Republic remained attractive for would-be foreign investors, thanks to lower wages, a highly skilled work force, an economic infrastructure and a supportive government, topped off by proximity to German markets (Rutland, 1994; Zemplinerová, 1997).

During the second half of the 1990s it was hoped that earlier transition successes would continue. Everything on the surface seemed quite positive. Of all the former east European communist countries, the Czech Republic appeared the most stable by 1995. According to most opinion polls Klaus's party commanded the greatest popularity; this was based on the smooth progression to capitalism without any significant social unrest, as well as on the culmination of the government's successful mass privatisation programme. The economy had grown by 4 per cent annually since the introduction of capitalism, and inflation dropped to 10 per cent; the unemployment rate remained at an exceptionally low 3 per cent and there was a budget surplus (Anon, 1995).

Deeper down, however, problems were emerging on the Czech horizon. Two-fifths of the population, according to a government poll, were not convinced they had a better standard of living and they remained poor despite all the transition success (Mareš and Možný, 1995). Moreover, the government still had thousands of businesses for sale. The new economy also meant that, through a failure to compete successfully, outdated enterprises went into liquidation, leading to increased unemployment. The postponement of privatisation of gas and electricity utilities was also a source of consternation. Furthermore, living costs rose sharply due to the lifting of price controls. Another issue was corruption in high places, when opposition leader Miloš Zeman accused the government of sleaze. In the public sector tough spending policies led to discontent, especially in the health service, and there was a failure to devolve power to local authorities (Pavlinek, 1992). All this led to a growing criticism of Klaus's government strategy and boded unfavourably for the future.

By 1997 the picture was becoming much clearer. The Czechs' earlier optimistic mood was beginning to sour. Polls conducted by the Institute of Public Opinion in Prague confirmed this perception: less than half (44 per cent) of those interviewed approved of post-1989 developments. Over three-quarters (78 per cent) of the pollsters recognised some of the benefits of communism, including free education, the national health service and subsidies for farmers and public transport. However, most pollsters now approved of the better travel opportunities abroad and the freedom of expression. The major causes of discontent were the breakdown of

Klaus's strict monetary policy and weaknesses in a free-market economy. His government had failed to furnish the expected level of overall prosperity. During 1996 a loss of confidence in the Czech economy occurred, exacerbated by corruption in business affairs and decline in foreign investment. The latter had halved, from its 1995 peak of $2,526 mn to $1,275 mn in 1997 (EBRD, 1998). Klaus's inevitable resignation came in December 1997, fuelled by poor economic growth, inflation over 10 per cent, growing unemployment, lower wages and monetary devaluation. Even so, his errors should not be blamed on strategy but on the execution of policy. Klaus's departure did not signal the eclipse of a free-market economy in the Czech Republic, rather the urgent need for a cleansing of public life.

The way ahead

In the Czech Republic it is recognised that much work is still needed to prepare for EU entry. Earlier, the EU viewed associate membership positively, the only cautions relating to the lustration law (a ban on public service employment for previous Communist Party members, collaborators and secret police), the lack of free access for the press to administrative documents and discrimination against the Roma population (Anderson, 1997). An updated freedom of information law came into force from January 2000, although by mid-2000 a new civil service law to replace the lustration law was still in preparation. A series of suggestions to ameliorate the situation for the Roma population is under review.

The obligations associated with EU membership are proving more difficult for the Czech Republic. First, there is the problem of converting legislation on paper into reality, authenticated by an effective administrative organisation. Success will involve updating a disorganised political bureaucracy, purging the courts of incompetence and a speedy improvement in regional government. Second, the Czechs must create a functioning market economy, which, within the EU, is able to cope with competitive pressures and market forces. To obtain this goal the Czechs must turn around deficiencies in the banking and financial system, provide better corporate management, make more progress in enterprise restructuring and correct trade deficiencies.

The brunt of these improvements has fallen on the government elected in the June 1998 elections. The debatable result has given power to a Social Democratic minority government (74 out of 200 parliamentary seats) under the leadership of Miloš Zeman. In July 1998 the Czech Republic's first centre-left government since the collapse of communist rule was appointed by President Havel. It has since emerged that victory occurred only through a controversial pact with Klaus; his Civic Democratic Party agreed not to introduce or promote a vote of no confidence in Zeman's minority cabinet.

There are signs of economic recovery but difficulties remain (Myant, 1998). The good news is that Czech inflation slowed down during the second half of 1998 as the economy teetered on recession. There is a belief, however, that after about two years growth policies and foreign investment plans could potentially boost real growth to 5 or 6 per cent (Djankov and Hoekman, 1998). Attempts have been made to accelerate economic growth and restructuring through a partly revised tax structure. This would encourage investment through a lowering of corporate tax from 35 to 20 per cent and through clearer rules on depreciation. Personal taxes would have to remain steady, while social security taxes and consumption taxes would have to be raised to EU levels through an adjustment of the value-added tax system. The Czech parliament is also hoping to allow more involvement in a tax-holiday scheme. The idea is to attract investors from abroad to a country that is still dragging behind Poland and Hungary in luring post-communist foreign direct investment. A more inviting lower threshold for direct investment (down from $35 mn to $10 mn) is being considered for those interested in qualifying for the scheme (Mastrini, 1998).

Other more positive evidence has emerged. The European Investment Bank has offered 30 mn to finance small projects in the Czech Republic on the environment, energy conservation, the infrastructure, industry and tourism. This is part of the EU's co-operation policy of dispensing loan finance for capital investment toward third countries. Moreover, the largest Czech commercial bank (Komerční) predicted that GDP would rise and that in 1999 there would be a 2–3 per cent growth in the economy. Furthermore, in 1998 it predicted that the trade deficit would drop by a third over the previous year and that inflation would be between 5.8 and 6.2 per cent. Unfortunately, unemployment rose from 5.2 per cent in 1997 to 6.2 per cent a year later. Employment has been handicapped by restrictive policies, but a rise in the economy would encourage growth and produce only a moderate jobless rate (Anon, 1998).

According to the 1991 population census some 33,500 Romas lived in the Czech Republic. Many of the Roma population have become strangers in their own land since the introduction of a Citizenship Law, which instantly designated them as foreigners through disenfranchisement. In order to become a Czech citizen a Roma inhabitant has to meet several difficult stipulations, including proof of registered residency and a criminal-free record. This affects the Roma population in several ways, including the right to employment opportunities, access to public housing and access to schooling and welfare benefits. Essential flaws in the law still remain, although some aspects have been modified. Criticism of the attitude toward the Roma population by the Czech Republic has been made by the United Nations Commission on Human Rights, especially relating to the surprisingly large number of Roma children located in schools for the mentally handicapped. Furthermore, extremist attacks on Romas continue. The local authorities in some Czech townships have fenced Romas into 'ghetto style' settlements, on the basis that they are a nuisance to society (Gledhill, 1997; Boyes, 1998). Clearly, acceptance of basic human rights for the Roma population has to happen before the Czech Republic can expect to obtain full EU membership.

The environment is another burdensome issue. Much has yet to be done to reverse four decades of communist environmental legacy (Tickle and Vavroušek, 1998). Admittedly, crucial environmental improvements in the Czech Republic have been made since 1990, especially regarding airborne pollutants. Initially this was thanks mainly to the passive consequences of economic restructuring and to restrictions on the use of artificial fertilisers and on coal mining activity. Investment in desulphurisation methods at industrial enterprises has also led to an improvement in air quality. On the other hand, there has been a rise in municipal waste, a spin-off from the market economy, and the previous importance placed on public transport, especially non-polluting trams, has declined with the increase of car ownership. In 1996 Czech financial input into environmental protection was two to four times higher than in many EU countries, but it is apparent that considerably more is needed before EU levels can be achieved (Braniš, 1996).

In seeking admittance to the EU, the Czech Republic is going to find it expensive to achieve EU environmental standards. The cost has been calculated at 3–5 per cent of Czech GDP over the next decade. On a more positive note, the European Commission has praised the Czech Republic for its adoption of a rigorous policy for reducing air pollution by 1998, partly through the closure of most polluting enterprises, but there is still much to be done. On a European scale, by the mid-1990s the Czech Republic had the second highest per capita emission of sulphur dioxide (106 kg SO_2 annually) on the continent (after Bulgaria); it was seventh highest for nitrogen oxides (40 kg NO_2 annually) (Johannesson, 1998). Much has yet to be done to make sure of a successful EU membership application, in spite of the adoption of 31 new environmental laws by 1996 (Anon, 1992; Kruh, 1996).

In reality the country's environment still seems far from being protected (Tickle and Walsh, 1998). The future may be linked to the competence of environmental groups, either politically or as a social movement, but so far these have had little success. An alternative, though less satisfactory, possibility is the EU recommendation for reaching its environmental standards. According to European Commission suggestions, for high-cost countries like the Czech Republic to obtain potential full membership status, they only need only to achieve priority environmental standards before being accepted. Part of their accession treaty would be an agreement to fulfil EU environment levels at specific dates in the future. This could prove a saving grace for the Czech Republic's contemporary environmental problems.

Conclusion

Located in the heart of Europe, the territory of the present Czech Republic has played a critical role in the history of the continent. The early independent rulers gave way to the ambitions of neighbouring states, and the country spent considerable time as a member of the Austro-Hungarian Empire. After the First World War it became part of the new Czechoslovakian successor state. Its independence was to last a mere two decades before German and then Soviet domination plunged the country once more into subjection for another half century. In the early 1990s it survived a peaceful separation from its Slovak neighbour and embarked upon a programme of change and modernisation, which gave hope for the future.

Success was dependent upon a thriving, dynamic economy. In the early 1990s the country had the advantages of low unemployment – a rarity amongst the new transition states – a strong pro-western leader in Václav Klaus, a well-respected president in Václav Havel and state boundaries adjoining two EU member states. The Czech capital Prague blossomed as an attractive centre for foreign business and a popular tourist destination. Yet by the end of the decade these advantages had soured, failing to fulfil the early promise.

While political life during most of the 1990s appeared to be exceptionally stable, cracks have subsequently appeared. The election of a minority coalition government under Prime Minister Miloš Zeman has failed to address the country's basic problem of economic stagnation as a result of being dogged by two years of recession. Clearly, the emphasis must be on attracting more foreign direct investment (FDI) to supplement the $12.8 bn in stock by mid-1999. There is also a need to ratify essential legislation more quickly and to avoid the long delays often associated with the passage through parliament. The political situation has been further tainted by a November 1999 opinion poll, which revealed that, a decade after the country's democratic revolution, the communists – still committed to a command economy – were the most popular Czech party.

Stronger government action is certainly needed to reverse the legacy of a misled economic policy in the early 1990s and rapidly to restructure Czech industry. Such moves are vital if early EU membership is to be secured. Yet the Czech accession bid received a jolt in October 1999 with the publication of a scathing EU report (European Commission, 1999), which criticised not only the country's economy but also its minority rights situation. The EU attitude was clearly coloured by early 1999 events in Ústí nad Labem, where a wall had been erected to physically separate the Roma community from the Czech residents.

Overall, perhaps the deepest contemporary problem is Czech 'provincialism' – a legacy from the past. This is linked to understandable Czech wariness of foreign influence and loss of national individuality. This perception has to be overcome, however, if the country is to be successful in the globalised and restructured world of the 21st century.

References

Agnew, H. L., 1993, *Origins of the Czech national renascence*. Pittsburgh: University of Pittsburgh Press.

Anderson, R., 1997, EU membership: preparation comes but slowly. *Financial Times*, 1 December, p. II.

Anon, 1992, Zákon České národní řády ze dne 19 unora 1992 o ochrané přirody a krajiny. *Zpravodaj Ministerstva životního Prostředí ČR, Čislo 4*. Prague: Příloha.

Anon, 1995, Czech Republic: odd man out. *The Economist*, 4 November, p. 58.

Anon, 1998, Komerčni Bank sees GDP up 1.3–1.7 % in 1998. *New Europe*, 26 July, p. 11.

Benáček, V., 1995 *The transition of small businesses and private entrepreneurship in the Czech Republic*. Colchester: University of Essex, Centre for European Studies, Occasional Papers in European Studies No. 5.

Bičík, I., Götz, A., 1998, Czech Republic. *In* Turnock, D., ed., *Privatization in rural eastern Europe: the process of restitution and restructuring*. Cheltenham/Northampton MA: Edward Elgar, pp. 93–119.

Bilsen, V., 1994, Privatization, company management and performance: a comparative study of privatization methods in the Czech Republic, Hungary, Poland and Slovakia. *In* Jackson, M., Bilsen, V., eds, *Company management and capital market development in the transition*. Aldershot: Avebury, pp. 35–56.

Boyes, R., 1998, Czech towns put Gypsies into 'ghetto'. *The Times*, 26 May, p. 6.

Braniš, M., 1996, Environment in the Czech Republic: state of the art and recent development under economic and political transition. *Sborník České Geografické Společnosti*, 101/102, 169–179.

Český Statistický Úřad, 1997, *Statistická Ročenka České Republiky '97*. Prague: Scientia.

Charap, J., Dyba, J., 1992, The reform process in Czechoslovakia: an assessment of recent developments and prospects for the future. *Communist Economies and Economic Transformations*, 4 (1), 3–22.

Chvojka, P., 1997, Banking sector's role in restructuring of CEEC economies: case study of the Czech Republic. *Ekonomický Časopis*, 45 (6–7), 511–545.

Djankov, S., Hoekman, B., 1998, *Avenues of technology transfer: foreign investment and productivity change in the Czech Republic*. Colchester: University of Essex, Centre for Economic Policy Research, Discussion Paper Series No. 183.

Dobosiewicz, Z., 1992, *Foreign investment in eastern Europe*. London/New York: Routledge.

EBRD, 1998, *Transition report update 1998*. London: EBRD.

European Commission, 1999, *Regular report from the Commission on progress towards accession: Czech Republic – October 13, 1999*. Brussels: European Commission. http://www.europa.eu.int/comm/enlargement/czech/rep_10_99/.

Fudge, T. A., 1998, *The magnificent ride: the first Reformation in Hussite Bohemia*. Aldershot: Ashgate.

Gledhill, R., 1997, Romany refugees head for Britain after Canada closes the door. *The Times*, 20 October, p. 5.

Holoček, M., ed., 1993, *Česká republika*. Prague: Nakladatelství České geografické společnosti.

Holý, L., 1996, *The little Czech and the great Czech nation: national identity and the post-communist social transformation*. Cambridge: Cambridge University Press.

Johannesson, M., 1998, Environmental space: making pollution personal. *Acid News* (Stockholm), 2, p. 20.

Kraus, J., Doucha, T., Sokol, Z., Prouza, B., 1994, Agricultural reform and transformation in the Czech Republic. *In* Swinnen, J. F. M., ed., *Policy and institutional reform in central European agriculture*. Aldershot: Avebury, pp. 107–133.

Kruh, Z., 1996, *Povez mi, kdo je nejkrasnejši: politické strany a životní prostředí*. Prague: Academia.

Kupka, M., Tuma, Z., Zieleniec, J., 1993, Czecho–Slovak survey. *In* Winiecki, J., Kondratowicz, A., eds, *The macroeconomics of transition: developments in east central Europe*. London/New York: Routledge, pp. 43–61.

Marcinien, A., Wijnbergen, V., 1997, The impact of Czech privatisation. *Economies in Transition*, 5 (2), 289–304.

Mareš, P., Možný, I., 1995, *Status for the poor: the institutionalisation of poverty in post-communist Czech society*. Colchester: University of Essex, Occasional Papers in European Studies No. 7.

Mastrini, J., 1998, Economics czar says rate cuts could restore growth. *New Europe*, 2 August, p. 10.

Myant, M., 1997, Enterprise restructuring and policies for competitiveness in the Czech Republic. *Ekonomický Časopis*, 45 (6–7), 546–567.

Myant, M., 1998, Transition in the Czech Republic. *Proceedings from the Scottish Society for Russia and East European Studies*. Glasgow: University of Glasgow, pp. 5–14.

Myant, M., Fleischer, F., Hornshilde, K., Vintrová, R., Zeman, K., Souček, Z., 1996, *Successful transformations? The creation of market economies in eastern Germany and the Czech Republic*. Cheltenham/Northampton MA: Edward Elgar.

OECD, 1991, *Czech and Slovak Federal Republic 1991*. Paris: OECD.

OECD, 1995, *Review of agricultural policies: Czech Republic*. Paris: OECD.

Pavlinek, P., 1992, Regional transformation in Czechoslovakia: towards a market economy. *Tijdschrift voor Economische en Sociale Geografie*, 83 (4), 361–371.

Pick, O., 1997, The Czech Republic in the world. *Perspectives: Review of Central European Affairs* (Prague), 8, 5–11.

Polišenský, J. V., 1991, *History of Czechoslovakia in outline*. Prague: Bohemia International.

Poulík, J., 1985, *Great Moravia and the mission of Cyril and Methodius*. Prague: Orbis Press Agency.

Ptáček, J., 1996, Czech agriculture in transition. *Sborník České Geografické Společnosti*, 101 (2), 110–127.

Renner, H., 1994, *A history of Czechoslovakia since 1945*. London: Routledge.

Rutland, P., 1994, The economy: Czech Republic. *In* Anon, *Eastern Europe and the Commonwealth of Independent States 1994*. London: Europa Publications, 2nd edn, p. 266.

Schwartz, G., Stone, M., van der Willigen, T., 1994, Beyond stabilisation: the economic transformation of Czechoslovakia, Hungary and Poland. *Communist Economies and Economic Transformation*, 6 (3), 291–313.

Skalnik Leff, C., 1995, *The Czech and Slovak Republics: nation versus state*. London: Westview.

Slepička, A., Hošková, E., Ronnås, P., Sjöberg, Ö., 1989, *Rural Czechoslovakia: patterns of change under socialism*. Stockholm: Studies of Institute of Economics and Geography, Report No. 7.

Souček, Z., 1997, Changing strategy of Czech enterprises. *Ekonomický Časopis*, 45 (6–7), 584–600.

Svejnar, J., 1995, *The Czech Republic and economic transformation in eastern Europe*. London: Academic Press.

Svoboda, J., Lozek, V., Vlček, E., 1996, *Hunters between east and west: the Paleolithic of Moravia*. New York: Plenum.

Takla, L., 1994, The relationship between privatization and the reform of the banking sector: the case of the Czech Republic and Slovakia. *In* Estrin, S., ed., *Privatization in central and eastern Europe*. London/New York: Longman, pp. 154–175.

Teichová, A., 1988, *The Czechoslovak economy 1918–1980*. London/New York: Routledge.

Tickle, A., Vavroušek, J., 1998, Environmental politics in the former Czechoslovakia. *In* Tickle, A., Walsh, I., eds., *Environment and society in eastern Europe*. London/New York: Longman, pp. 114–145.

Tickle, A., Walsh, I., eds, 1998, *Environment and society in eastern Europe*. London/New York: Longman.

White, E. G., 1995, *The great controversy: between Christ and Satan*. Grantham: Stanborough Press.

Zemplinerová, A., 1997, Small enterprises and foreign investors – key players in enterprise restructuring and structural change. *Ekonomický Časopis*, 45 (10), 810–850.

6

HUNGARY

Alan Dingsdale

A brief history

Hungary is a small country situated in the middle of continental Europe (Figure 6.1). It has a population of 10.16 million and a territory of 93,000 sq km. It has few natural resources and must rely on the inventiveness of its people.

Figure 6.1: Hungary

The Hungarian tribes conquered the Carpathian Basin in 895–96 and established settlements across Transylvania, the Great Plain and Transdanubia. For the next 100 years the Magyar chieftains fought for consolidation of their position between the Holy Roman Empire and Catholic Christianity from the west, and the Byzantine Empire and Orthodox Christianity from the east. Prince Bulcsú, seeking to secure his south-eastern border, went to Byzantium and was converted to Christianity there in 948. The Holy Roman Emperor Otto I defeated the Hungarian princes Bulcsú and Lehel at the Battle of Augsburg in 955 and executed them both. Prince Géza (955–970) developed close contacts with the Holy Roman Empire, invited the pope to send missionaries to his territories, converted to Christianity and had his son István (Stephen) baptised a Catholic. Domestically, he promoted the resettlement of warriors who left their tribal loyalties behind and entered his service, and thus challenged the military basis of the clan chieftains. In this way he began the task of constructing a feudal state, a task that his son István was to complete.

István, Hungary's first king, founded the state in 998. István established the institutional framework for societal transformation to western style feudalism, breaking the power of the tribal chieftains and enlisting the assistance of the Catholic Church. He appropriated tribal lands and redistributed them to consolidate his secular and spiritual power. The church was endowed with huge landed property and István was canonised. Every ten villages were required to build and maintain a local church. Italian, German and Czech monks spread western Christian culture. István rejected missionaries from the Orthodox Christian Church and in so doing turned the traditions of Hungary to the West.

István established a new territorial administrative division of the kingdom and a new aristocratic élite to govern the counties that were formed. Church and civil administration roughly corresponded territorially. He encountered resistance from traditional and conservative forces, most notably from Koppány, the military leader of Transylvania.

The policies and choices of Géza and István brought Hungary into western European civilisation. Hungary subsequently experienced all the great periods of culture and conflict that marked the epochs of western European history.

King Matthias and the Renaissance

In the 'Castle District' of Buda and overlooking the Danube stands the Matthias Church. In the Budapest landscape it is a prominent reminder of Hungary's greatest king. In the late 15th century Matthias strengthened royal control against the powerful nobles, established a royal army and reformed taxation and the law to place his reign on a firm foundation. He attacked and then made peace with the Turks, whose power had grown as their armies advanced from the south-east borderlands of Europe, spreading Islamic civilisation into Christian Europe. He realised that without western allies Hungary could not resist the Turkish advance and so he sought to construct a Danubian empire incorporating Bohemia, Moravia and Silesia.

Matthias was a renowned patron of the arts. His wife, Beatrice of Aragon, introduced Italian Renaissance culture into the court. Matthias soon took the initiative in replacing Gothic styles with Renaissance styles; the minor fabric of royal palaces was remodelled from the Gothic and Gothic-form statues and ornaments were replaced. He founded a library, the *Biblioteca Corviniana,* which displayed magnificent illuminated codices. Foreign experts and craftsmen, especially Italians, were invited to Buda, and Hungarian craftsmen and artists perfected the new techniques. Humanist scholars advanced the secular spirit in literature and sciences, though not without church opposition.

The rule of the Habsburgs

In 1526 the Turks defeated the Hungarians at the Battle of Mohács, and Archduke Ferdinand of Habsburg became king of Hungary. However, the territory of the state founded by István was divided into three parts: the west and the north, known as Royal Hungary, was ruled by the Habsburgs; Transylvania was ruled by elected Hungarian princes under Turkish suzerainty; and Transdanubia and the area of the Great Plain were ruled directly by the Ottoman Turkish Sultan. For nearly 200 years there was conflict between the rulers of these three territories. Hungary was a battlefield reflecting the dynastic, religious and national rivalries that afflicted Europe.

The defeat of the Turkish siege of Vienna in 1683 signalled the beginning of the Habsburg reconquest of Turkish Islamic territory for Christian Europe, the final act of which was to precipitate the First World War in 1914. In 1699, by the Treaty of Karlowitz, the Habsburgs expelled the Turks from Hungary. From the Hungarian point of view one oppressive regime was replaced by another and Hungary was brought into the Habsburg hereditary territories. The Habsburgs installed a new nobility and endowed it and the Catholic Church with vast landed estates in Transdanubia and the Great Plain, which had been depopulated under Turkish rule. This association of church and state was reminiscent of the policy of István. Catholic Germans, known locally as Swabian, were settled on the land in newly built villages. Croatian and Serbian settlers moved into Hungary. The Orthodox Christian Serbs were granted freedom of worship and wide autonomy. The Protestant Hungarian villagers were denied religious freedom and there was forced conversion to Catholicism in the period of the Counter-Reformation. Some districts of the Great Plain were recolonised by smallholders whose farms were known as *tanya*. They created a distinctive landscape in contrast to the *puszta* of noble estates. The *tanya* was a very special form of rural settlement, because the legal and administrative control of these farmsteads was vested in the towns from which the colonists originated. Thus towns such as Debrecen and Kecskemét in the Great Plain came to rule very large administrative territories.

The creation of *tanya* farmsteads continued throughout the 18th and 19th centuries and into the 1920s.

The Empress Maria Theresa, in a spirit of Enlightenment, strengthened the central power of the Habsburg state and initiated policies to develop the economic strength of Hungary. The restoration of ancient privileges won the remnant of the old Hungarian nobility over to the Habsburgs. The church, endowed with new landed estates, retained enormous power. Church control of education, literature and the arts ensured adherence to Catholic and Habsburg dominance, despite the presence of a substantial Protestant community in Hungary. In 1848 the wind of nationalist revolution swept across Europe. The Hungarian middle class, formed mostly from the lower gentry, rebelled against Habsburg rule. Though the revolution was suppressed it led in 1867 to 'the compromise', gaining Hungary some independence from Austria within the 'dual monarchy'. Following 'the compromise' the Hungarian economy expanded rapidly, but some Hungarians thought 'the compromise' an act of shame, which sacrificed national identity and history for material transience (Forgács, 1994).

The Treaty of Trianon and the dismemberment of 'Great Hungary'

The Treaty of Trianon, part of the Versailles settlement that followed the First World War, destroyed Hungary territorially. Two-thirds of the territory of István's kingdom was lost to successor states. The loss of Transylvania, annexed by Romania, was a particular blow to Hungarians, who saw it as a cradle of Hungarian culture. Two million Hungarians found themselves as minorities within new states, many were expelled and practically all were discriminated against. After a short-lived communist state under Béla Kun, the aristocracy regained power in the new territorial state of Hungary and, hoping for a Habsburg restoration, established a regency under Admiral Miklós Horthy. Horthy's authoritarian rule strengthened Hungarian revisionist policies and led to a degree of wartime protection from the worst excesses of Nazi German policies. During the Second World War Hungary regained some territory in Transylvania, but this was again lost at the end of the war. Including its final phase as a regency, Habsburg rule had endured in Hungary for 420 years.

The period between the wars was, for Hungarians, overshadowed by the 'dismemberment' of Great Hungary. Successor states were forcefully nationalist in political and economic affairs. A powerful sense of grievance predominated in Hungary. But at the same time there was a conflict between aristocratic nationalist sentiment and the spread of modernity in the cultural and material worlds of Hungarian society. The clash of ideas and lifestyles was strongest in Budapest.

Budapest was a modern city. Formed by the amalgamation of Buda, Pest and Óbuda in 1873, it grew very rapidly before the First World War and dominated Hungarian cultural, social and economic life. The planning and regulation of the city initiated at that time laid the foundation for its eclectic architecture and rich urban fabric. Dynamic businessmen and artists promoted new ideas in the arts, commerce and society. These groups created a new nationalist modernity, but were unable to displace the entrenched predominance of the aristocracy. After the First World War, the pace of Budapest's transformation to metropolitan and cosmopolitan status slowed down in comparison to other central European capitals such as Berlin and Vienna, where, until 1933, more liberal political regimes allowed experimentation in arts and cultural expression.

Communist rule after the Second World War

Communist rule was established in Hungary following the Second World War. The new communist rulers were determined to overthrow all the institutions and ideas of the past and to create a vision of a socialist future filled with equality and modern ideas. The application of a Stalinist economic and political regime in Hungary had a mixed reception. In 1956 Hungarians made a stand against Soviet Russian domination. After initial successes their popular revolt was crushed by Soviet military action. The regime established under János Kádár was to prove one of the most distinctive and independent thinking in the eastern bloc. Kádár remained in power until 1984 and gave an important stability and continuity to Hungary's reformist style.

In 1968 the Kádár government introduced the New Economic Mechanism (NEM) that set Hungary on to one of the most liberal paths toward communism experienced in eastern Europe. The NEM was intended to introduce 'market socialism' by combining microeconomic efficiency with indirect government regulation and socialist ethical principles. It involved important changes of strategy. It removed obligatory plan targets, incentives based on quantity of production and centrally controlled resource allocation and investment. These were replaced by market forces, price and wage flexibility, incentives based on efficiency and quality of production and devolution of decision-making about business strategy and investment to company managers. Thus two of the pillars of the communist economic system, central decision-making and planning, were modified. State ownership of enterprise was not touched at all.

The NEM was a purely economic strategy. No attempt was made to modify the political system. The Hungarian Socialist Workers (Communist) Party (MSzMP) remained in complete control of government. In 1971 the new local government law made some changes in the relationship between central and local government. Earlier local government had simply been the local representative of central government and had little or no opportunity to initiate projects of its own. By the new law, local governments were given some responsibility and the opportunity to raise some of their own revenue.

Hungary in the 1980s

The New Economic Mechanism of 1968 and the local government law of 1971, together with other broad changes, had been the basis of an attempt to introduce 'market socialism' into Hungary, mainly by reducing the extent of direct central government control over decision-making. As a result, Hungary had emerged as the most economically liberal country in the communist bloc. In the 1980s there was further progress toward a market socialist economy, which in some ways redefined the boundaries of socialist organisational practice.

By the early 1980s the government realised that if economic growth was to be sustained, radical reform must continue and greater efficiency allied to greater added-value output must be achieved. As a small country with few natural resources participating in international trade, Hungary could not afford the wastefulness that characterised communist production methods. Solutions to the problems were seen in the promotion of small- and medium-sized enterprises with (in effect) private financial inputs; in restructuring large-scale state enterprise; and in encouraging joint ventures with foreign companies (Dingsdale, 1991).

Small- and medium-sized enterprises

New laws of 1982 permitted the establishment of small-scale 'economic partnerships'. Individuals could join together to produce all manner of manufactures and commercial services as, to all intents and purposes, private ventures. Certainly they encouraged private individual initiative. Hungarian ministers were supportive of entrepreneurs wishing to set up a small business, ranging from a textile factory to a grocery shop, and viewed the role of profit and exports as priorities for the efficient functioning of the economy. Several different sorts of business association came into being, but all were regarded by ministers as small co-operatives. This allowed the government to present them as socialist forms of enterprise organisation. Regulations permitted such firms to employ as many as 500 workers. The government saw these new firms as providing goods and services that state-owned, large-scale companies could not produce. The number of such small firms rose rapidly from 6,593 in 1982 to 49,763 in 1987, and the number of workers they employed rose from 67,576 to 530,270 during the same period (Dingsdale, 1991). Small firms were able to produce different goods and services from the large-scale enterprises and to do so more efficiently. They were paralleled in agricultural production by the shifting of the balance between co-operative farming and private-plot production. The former was more efficient at producing extensive crops and raising animals, for which large-scale mechanised farming was needed. The latter was regarded as more efficient in producing intensive, often market garden, crops, for which small-scale methods were seen as more appropriate.

Many of the new firms grew out of the 'second economy' that had flourished since 1968. Because much of this activity had bordered on illegality, and the status of those working in it was unclear, it was sometimes called 'the shadow economy'. Its growth and the wealth it created was untapped by the government as a source of revenue. The new laws enabled the government to regulate and to tax this informal sector in order to harness its innovative and entrepreneurial skills for the national economy. The government's encouragement of these new forms of personal enterprise was tempered by its insistence on charging higher rates of tax than for state-owned companies.

Restructuring state enterprise

New laws of 1985 introduced a new environment for economic activity. There was to be less direct government involvement in economic structural change and there would be further decentralisation of economic and political power. Full employment was to be maintained, but changing employment demands would be met by redeploying workers in local labour markets. Firms would no longer be protected from bankruptcy.

While these laws further encouraged small-scale enterprise, their greater impact came in the ailing state sector. First to be affected were the heavy industrial branches that had been the backbone of early communist industrialisation and were now preventing structural change. Large state subsidies for coal mining and iron and steel production were removed by stages in a planned contraction, restructuring and rehabilitation programme. This inevitably involved job losses and greater financial pressures on coal and iron and steel consumers, and it consequently met with resistance. Despite this anti-trust policy some monopolistic trusts were maintained because they were regarded as efficient. One example of survival was the vertically integrated aluminium industry. It was dominated by Hunglu, the state-owned trust consisting of 16 enterprises engaged in all aspects of aluminium production, from bauxite mining, through smelting to fabrication, research and foreign trade.

It was not only the industrial sector that came under consideration for restructuring. In fact de-industrialisation had already set in, in so far as jobs in industrial enterprises had been falling and those in the tertiary sector had been growing. The balance of the occupational structure of the country had been moving toward the service and financial sector. The financial sector, previously neglected for reasons of ideology, came under scrutiny with a view to reorganisation that would promote efficiency and competition. The National Bank created commercial credit departments that competed with each other in an almost western style. The plans of 1988 contained a wide range of measures to introduce real capital, money and commodity markets in Hungary.

Encouraging joint ventures

The Hungarian economy had been increasingly opened up to western business in order to secure western finance, advanced technology and expertise. These features, it was hoped, would smooth the path from an emphasis on quantity to one on quality of outputs. Joint ventures with foreign corporations were possible from 1972, but progress had been hampered by high taxes on profits and stifling regulations. Amendments to the laws in 1982 had little effect, with the result that four years later considerable liberalisation and a relaxation of restrictions were introduced. The second half of the 1980s saw an increase in the pace of joint-venture formation between foreign and Hungarian companies. West German and Austrian corporations were most active, but Italian, Dutch, Swedish, Japanese and even Greek, Portuguese and Indian companies also participated (Dingsdale, 1991).

Political development

The decade or more of economic reform following the introduction of the NEM had no parallel in the political arena until the 1980s. The relationship between the central and the local government had changed, weakly placing obligations on local government but not transferring much real power. During the 1980s political development was to become a major dimension of change. As political unrest began to be felt in parts of central and eastern Europe during the early 1980s, the Hungarian government was quick to respond. It recognised 'soft' opposition groups and modified electoral rules to pave the way for a reduction in the dominance of the Communist Party. The 1985 election gave the first multi-candidate choice since 1947, voters being given the chance to nominate and vote for their own candidates. Even so, the parliament elected in 1985 was predominantly composed of communist deputies. However, the first signs of independent thinking among those deputies were visible. Some members were willing to hold discussions with non-parliamentary opposition groups. Toward the end of the 1980s a negotiated agreement was reached between the government and the opposition groups that legalised other parties and withdrew the sole right of the Hungarian Socialist Workers Party to form the government. In 1989 a new electoral law passed by parliament set up multi-party elections for 1990 (Kovács and Dingsdale, 1998).

The Gabčikovo–Nagymáros 'water steps' Danube dam project

The story of the Gabčikovo–Nagymáros 'water steps' dam project on the river Danube is a good example of the way that political change occurred in Hungary during the 1980s. The purpose of the project was to generate electricity, regulate river floods and improve navigation on the Danube. When the Danube flows eastwards from Austria it forms the border between Slovakia and Hungary. The river in this stretch was always a natural hazard, and flood-control measures had been undertaken since the 17th century. The idea for the Gabčikovo–Nagymáros project was formed in the 1950s between the communist Czechoslovak and Hungarian governments. Early preparatory progress was very slow, but in 1977 an agreement was signed to go ahead with the building work. Despite Hungarian government claims that the project would not have a major impact on the local environment, independent reports forecast environmental disaster.

The Danube Circle and the Nagymáros Committee, consisting of independent intellectuals, were formed to protest against the project's environmental effects, such as the destruction of forests and farmland. Ethnic conflict was also a factor as Hungarian-inhabited villages in Slovakia were to be flooded by the lake. At first, protest meetings were broken up by the police. But after the Hungarian government agreed with the Austrian state electricity company to supply Austria with electricity in return for a loan from the Austrian government, the Austrian Green Party accused its government of exporting its environmental problems. The Austrian Greens gave support to Hungarian opposition groups, who also gained the support of communist MPs and mobilised popular anti-government feeling. The Hungarian government changed its stance; environmentalist protest meetings were permitted. Environmentalists were joined by the forerunners of new political parties such as the Hungarian Democratic Forum. The government even proposed a referendum on abandoning the project under pressure of popular protest. However, in 1989 the Hungarian government decided for itself to withdraw from the project. Whilst work on the Czechoslovak side continued, work at Nagymáros, entirely within Hungary, ceased. However, the Czechoslovak – and subsequently the Slovak – government continued the project, and the dispute with Hungary. It is still not fully resolved, despite efforts made by the EU and hearings in the International Court of Justice. Following a change of government in Slovakia in late 1998, the new government was more conciliatory in its approach, perhaps influenced by its more general aim of gaining entry to the EU.

Thus the actions of the Hungarian government, at first typical of the communist past, changed over the decade. Protest was allowed and contributed to the organisation of opposition political groups. Popular opinion began to have an influence on government policy, and radically new forms of opinion testing were contemplated. The general public, led by intellectual and scientific opinion, played a major role in affecting government policy.

Social change

Political and economic change were accompanied by social changes. Under the early communist system individuality had been suppressed in a spirit of collectivism; individual expression was regarded as subversive; all social organisations had been within the auspices of the Communist Party. The political and economic changes of the 1980s brought back a sense of individuality, but required the development of new skills. In an economy that saw wage levels and prices determined by the state, the idea of income tax had been unnecessary. With the loosening of control and the emergence of private enterprise, personal accountability for income tax became necessary. At the same time taxes such as VAT were introduced.

Personal mobility also became much freer. Hungary was the first Soviet bloc country to open its border to the West. Not surprisingly, given the historical context, it was with Austria. This action permitting greater individual freedom of international movement complemented increased internal freedom. It also had an important international consequence in its impact on the migration of east Germans to west Germany. In the summer of 1989 east Germans who enjoyed unrestricted travel to Hungary, were able to cross, unmolested, into Austria and thence to west Germany.

Post-communist developments in Hungary

In 1990, in the first multi-party election since 1947, the Hungarian electorate gave its judgement on the period of communist rule. To nobody's surprise the MSzMP was defeated and a centre-right coalition, led by the Hungarian Democratic Forum (MDF), with Joszef Antal as prime minister came into government with policies to democratise political institutions and establish a market economy. Despite the progress made in political and economic changes in the 1980s, the country was ill-prepared for the new world into which it was thrust. The decade since 1990 has been a difficult one. The ministers of the new government had no previous experience and, as it turned out, little skill in designing and presenting policies that were effective in managing a market economy and supervising the introduction of a plural political culture.

The picture was not totally bleak in either the political or economic arenas, especially when compared with the performance of other former socialist countries. Perhaps the most important of all the achievements of the first post-communist government was that it stayed in office for its full term. This was not replicated in other newly independent countries. The political stability that this represented was continued after the 1994 election. The reformed wing of the MSzMP, under its new name of Hungarian Socialist Party (MSzP), won that election. It, too, ran its full term until defeated in the election of May 1998.

Furthermore, the MSzP government continued the general thrust toward a market economy and political plurality. Despite winning a landslide victory in 1994, it governed in coalition with the right wing Free Democratic Alliance (SzDSz). Its domestic policies continued the drive toward privatisation of state assets, the encouragement of private small- and medium-sized enterprises and stable monetary policy. The austerity package introduced by Finance Minister Bokros in 1996 showed how far the government had moved from its former ideological position. Laws were enacted to encourage foreign direct investment, foreign government assistance and the transfer of expertise and technical skills. Whilst these processes were far from smooth, the performance compared well with other former socialist countries.

The overall policy stance of the MSzP, like that of its predecessor, placed great stress on gaining access to the European Union. It worked with its immediate neighbours to promote the central European co-operation embarked upon by the Antal government. It actively pursued membership of the North Atlantic Treaty Organization (NATO), joined the World Bank, the Organization for Economic Co-operation and Development (OECD), the International

Monetary Fund (IMF) and the Council of Europe. It signed treaties of friendship with its immediate neighbours. These treaties were of great importance in maintaining political stability in the area because the treatment of the Hungarian minorities in the surrounding countries was an emotive issue for Hungarian nationalist parties at home, as well as for the foreign governments who feared Hungarian revanchism.

The new government elected in March 1998, a coalition led by Viktor Orbán's Young Democrats Alliance (Fidesz), adopted a similar overall policy position, but with a contrasting emphasis. Privatisation and marketisation received greater attention than in the later years of the Horn government. Membership of the EU remained a top priority, and friendship with immediate neighbours was also seen as important. Subsequently, however, while civil and political liberties are regarded as higher in Hungary than anywhere else in CEE, questions have begun to be raised about the government's attitude toward and adherence to democratic procedures (e.g. see Bush, 1999).

All post-1990 governments have supported trans-border co-operation between historic regions and the fostering of close relations between neighbouring border counties. Western Hungarian counties have participated in the Alp-Adria working group since 1986. This group includes 19 provinces from Slovenia, Croatia, Austria, Italy, Germany and the Czech Republic. The Hungarian counties of Hajdu-Bihar and Szabolcs-Szatmár-Bireg participate in the Carpathian Euroregion that links them with border counties in Romania, Slovakia and Ukraine. In October 1998 the West Pannonian Euro-region was established, building on existing co-operative agreements with the Austrian Burgenland province and Hungary's western counties. These organisations engage in a very wide range of co-operative ventures, often stressing civic co-operation and including environmental protection, links between ethnic minorities, infrastructure projects and educational activities. Hungarian counties also participate in the much looser Working Community of Danube Provinces, which encompasses 24 provinces whose populations speak eight different languages. There are also plans to upgrade the Slovenian–Hungarian Regional Council, which was founded in 1996.

Hungary and refugees from Romania and Yugoslavia

Between 1988 and 1993 some 233,000 asylum seekers were registered as entering Hungary (Dingsdale, 1996). They came in two waves, the first from Romania, the second from Yugoslavia. The first were fleeing discrimination; the second were fleeing war and 'ethnic cleansing'. When the first groups began to arrive there was no legal or organisational framework to deal with them. Hungary signed the Geneva Convention on Refugees in 1989 and established a refugee department in the ministry of the interior, but not until 1994 was a law promulgated to create a framework of policy for refugees. These refugees, especially those from Yugoslavia, were dealt with in a spirit of humanitarian crisis management (Dingsdale, 1996).

From 1987 onwards increasing numbers of refugees were entering Hungary from Romania. There was a heightened sense of discrimination and fear among the ethnic Hungarians living in Romania as the Ceauşescu regime intensified its policy of *sistematizare* to reorganise rural settlement by moving villagers into agro-industrial complexes and destroying some villages (Turnock, 1991). Those leaving Romania were, therefore, primarily ethnic Hungarians.

The collapse of Yugoslavia was a sad and graphic example of the consequences of ethnic national enmity. Despite a direct interest in Yugoslavia, the Hungarian government resisted partisan involvement. Some 350,000 Hungarians lived in Vojvodina, the northern province of Serbia. Under the Yugoslav Federal Constitution of 1974, Vojvodina enjoyed autonomous status, but one of the first acts of Milošović after he came to power was to remove this autonomy and impose direct rule from Belgrade. At the same time Hungary played an important humanitarian role, acting as a place of refuge for all ethnic groups displaced by the fighting in the disintegrating Yugoslavia. Between 1991 and 1993 some 70,000 refugees from Yugoslavia were registered in Hungary (Dingsdale, 1996). The United Nations High Commission for Refugees (UNHCR) in Budapest reckoned this was about half the actual number who fled temporarily from Yugoslavia to Hungary. As no visa was required to enter Hungary from Yugoslavia, the actual number of refugees was difficult to count.

In 1991 Hungary placed restrictions on Romanians entering Hungary, but kept the border open for refugees from the former Yugoslavia until July 1992. Since the end of the war in Bosnia–Hercegovina the situation has become normalised between these countries. Hungary does, however, have a serious problem in dealing with illegal migrants from further east in Europe and from outside the continent. Whilst it pursues EU membership, Hungary is acting as an absorber of migrants from numerous regions of the world, thus protecting the EU countries because many migrants have the EU as their ultimate destination. Hungary has signed repatriation agreements with the EU to add a second line of defence for EU member states.

Foreign direct investment

Foreign direct investment (FDI) has been associated with the successful privatisation programmes. Hungary in general and Budapest in particular have done exceptionally well in attracting FDI. Between 1989 and the end of 1996 Hungary attracted $15 bn of foreign investment. This was 29.8 per cent of the total foreign investment in the former socialist countries (excluding Russia), the highest in any of those countries, and represented $1,450 per capita. Budapest is seen as a gateway into central and eastern Europe. Between 1989 and 1992 Budapest localised 30 per cent of all foreign investment in the former socialist countries. Approximately $10 bn of foreign capital had been invested in Budapest by the end of 1996. Fifteen of the world's largest 20 transnational corporations have opened offices in this city, which has the most advanced telecommunications system and the best-educated population (Enyedi, 1994).

Outside Budapest the impact of FDI has been much less marked, but contrasting regional and local patterns can be recognised. An east/west regional contrast is particularly marked, and a north/south dimension is also noticeable. Some regions have fared badly because of their association with socialist heavy industry. Foreign investors have been unwilling to buy the assets of declining sector companies and have also shied away from 'greenfield' investments in these regions. For example, the north-east region has not been successful in interesting foreign corporations to invest in new ventures or take over existing companies. Whilst Budapest has been spectacularly successful, investment has also been attracted by towns lower down the urban hierarchy where local governments and local entrepreneurs have been particularly active. Székesfehévár, in western Hungary, is one such example. As a result of local initiatives in western Hungary, infrastructure was improved, a training centre was established and the local specialist skills base promoted. Soon Siemens, Phillips, IBM, Cannon, Akai, Emerson Electric, Shell-Gas Hungary, Alcoa and Ford were persuaded to set up on the city's new industrial estates and invest $2 bn. Nyíregyháza, in the most easterly district, was at first slow in attracting investment, but since it received special Hungarian government regional policy assistance it has also attracted support from some little-known western sources. The Flemish government supported the development of an enterprise park on a former Soviet army base, and corporate FDI is now being increasingly placed in the town.

Alongside foreign investment, the Hungarian government has recognised that it has a role to play in fostering a new industrial base. At the end of the 1990s it introduced two new initiatives:

- encouraging local companies to become multinationals' suppliers, adding further depth to FDI; and

- offering the country's smaller companies subsidised finance, thus ending the crippling cash shortages that had rendered local companies increasingly uncompetitive (Kapoor, 1999).

Assistance from the EU for economic recovery and development

In 1989 the EEC set up the PHARE programme. Initially intended to support Poland and Hungary with a view to helping them free themselves from communist control, it was rapidly extended to other former socialist countries. By 1993 Hungary had received ECU 450 mn from PHARE, 17 per cent of the total; only Poland did better. Hungary also received bilateral assistance from several western European countries. The British government's Know-How Fund (KHF) was instrumental in providing Hungary with expertise in a wide range of technically specialised areas, ranging from environmental protection through education initiatives to administrative training.

Hungary and the idea of central Europe

The idea of central Europe was revived in intellectual circles in the mid-1980s and arguably played a part in the shift from communism (Garton Ash, 1986). It had a distinctly anti-Russian character and also sought to separate Poland, Czechoslovakia and Hungary from south-east Europe. After the collapse of communism, the new governments of these three countries formed the Višegrád Group and the Central European Free Trade Agreement (CEFTA) (Dingsdale, 1999). The former is a loosely arranged political grouping; the latter is designed to boost trade and economic co-operation between central European countries. Whilst neither of these organisations appears to be particularly strong, they are contributing to a consolidation of stability in political and economic progress. Slovenia joined them in 1994, Romania became a member of CEFTA in 1997 and most of the other former communist countries are keen to become members. It is perhaps not without significance that Poland, Hungary, the Czech Republic and Slovenia, the leading members of these groups, made up two-thirds of the 'fast-track' candidates for EU membership until the December 1999 Helsinki Summit.

Prospects for Hungary's successful incorporation into the European Union

Three questions are central to the enlargement of the European Union:

- Can the candidate countries cope with the technical – economic, political and administrative/legal – aspects of membership?

- Can the Union cope with the task of incorporating the candidate members?

- Can the candidate countries cope with the cultural aspects of membership?

Judged against each of these questions, Hungary stands a good chance of making a successful transition into the EU. With regard to the first question Hungary has made good progress in each aspect. The country is democratic and politically stable. Although there are more than 100 registered political parties, only six have gained parliamentary seats and they have done so at each election since 1990. This stability results from a complex but effective electoral system adapted from the German and Austrian models. The system incorporates single-member constituencies, county and national lists of party candidates, proportional representation, and two rounds of voting. It is a thorough test of public opinion. Turnouts in each election, though not matching western European figures, have been more than 56 per cent of the electorate in all cases. Although extremist parties exist they have little support among the Hungarian electorate.

Economic progress has been considerable, though not without difficulty. The so-called Bokros package of austerity measures in 1995 was perhaps a key achievement in economic transition. By 1998 Hungary had a fully functioning market economy, but the regulatory system for monopolies and the financial system was in need of strengthening (Meth-Cohn, 1998). Real GDP growth was consistently strong from 1996 (Table 6.1) and was anticipated, by the government, to continue to rise into the early years of the next decade. By 1998 gross industrial production had returned to 1989 levels. Forecasts in 1999 of a short-term slowdown in economic growth were regarded as a positive sign by the EBRD. The forecasts were taken to indicate that the Hungarian economy was responding to the general European business cycle instead of to local factors related to the transition. The task for Hungary over the next two decades is to maintain a growth rate 3 per cent per annum above that of the EU as a whole in order to ensure a rise in GDP per capita that is comparable with EU countries. This can only be achieved if the quality of products is improved and new investment is vigorous. This will not be easy for Hungary, a country with limited mineral resources. It emphasises the importance of trade and the need for significant value-added production activities. Hungary is on the point of sustainable economic growth, but it will be a demanding task to achieve it.

Table 6.1 Hungary: major economic indicators, 1994–1998

	1994	1995	1996	1997	1998
Population	10.2	10.2	10.2	10.1	10.1
GDP per capita ($)	4 052	4 374	4 441	4 513	4 730
% share of industry in GDP	27.4	23.1	23.5	25.0	na
% share of agriculture in GDP	6.0	5.9	6.1	5.8	na
Exports ($ bn)	7.6	12.8	14.2	19.6	20.7
Imports ($ bn)	11.2	15.3	16.8	21.4	22.9
GDP % change in real terms	2.9	1.5	1.3	4.6	5.1

Source: *EBRD, 1999: 229*

By 2002, when Hungary hopes to join the EU, it is confidently expected that the bulk of the EU legal framework – the *aquis communautaire* – will be in place in Hungary. The government elected in 1998 is determined to achieve this with only a few exceptions. One difficult area has been the 'greening' of Hungarian legislation. Despite great strides in changing environmental laws, setting more demanding standards and implementing a National Environmental Programme, there is still much to do. Successive governments took the view that when economic and environmental considerations were in conflict, economic development should take priority. Sustainable economic development was a stated goal, but in practice was not the first priority. The present government signalled its good intentions in the environmental field by announcing soon after it came into office that there would be greater funding for environmental protection. It was seen as the one weak link in Hungarian progress to EU entry. However, it has also declared its belief that the need for derogations and for a period of grace in some specific details of the environmental *acquis* should not delay entry into the Union. The Hungarian parliamentary environmental committee echoed these sentiments. EU officials, too, have expressed such hopes, but have also made it clear that real progress must be demonstrated.

EU monitoring reports are very favourable to Hungary in these technical aspects (European Commission, 1999). The EU's assessment of Hungarian progress toward acceptability is measured against three general criteria of progress: adopting the *acquis*; political plurality and civil rights; and economic competitiveness and a functioning market economy. In all these areas the EU Commission's assessment of Hungary has been very favourable. In 1997 and 1998, although there is no actual ranking, the implicit ranking gave Hungary top marks in each category according to the three Copenhagen criteria (Meth-Cohn, 1998).

Some major problems remain, however, from the EU point of view. The political stance of different member states plays a part in the enlargement process. More important are the Union's major 'internal' objectives – Economic and Monetary Union (EMU) and the Common Agricultural Policy (CAP). Hungary could not be admitted to these programmes: it does not meet the criteria for membership of EMU, and the cost of subsidising Hungarian agriculture is more than the Union could stand even in a reformed CAP. These issues affect the question of the whole future configuration and the nature of the Union. What will membership of the Union actually mean for Hungary? What kind of a Union will it be after Hungary is a member?

The EU promotes a particular idea of Europe. This derives from the western European cultural and historical experience, a sense of a western European civilisation. Hungary is part of this western European civilisation. It is Roman Catholic and Calvinist and traces its traditions through the great periods of western European history, as Europe emerged from Christendom. The Renaissance, the Reformation, the Counter-Reformation, the Enlightenment and the secularisation of the state are all historical experiences recorded in the formation of Hungarian national identity. Hungarians saw themselves as the bulwark of these traditions against powerful eastern 'barbaric' influences. However, Hungary was only lightly brushed by the series of 'revolutions', beginning in the late 18th and the 19th century, that combined these cultural antecedents into a practical transformation of societal and cultural relationships to create modern Europe. Western European civilisation acquired its modern trajectory through the French Revolution, the capitalist urban/industrial revolution, the demographic transition, the nationalist revolution and the technological revolutions. These 'modern' features, spreading from the west made only a relatively weak impact on Hungary before eastern influences overran the country in the post-Second World War imposition of Soviet Russian domination. Hungary made an unsuccessful effort to throw off these eastern influences in 1956, but without immediate western help was not able to do so. During the 1990s Hungary's adoption of the new modernisation from the West reflects a widespread belief among Hungarians that the country is embarked upon a 'return to Europe', its natural home.

Hungary seems set to become a successful new member of 'Europe'.

References

Bush, J., 1999, The other deficit. *Business Central Europe*, 6 (67), 39–40.

Dingsdale, A., 1991, Socialist industrialisation in Hungary. *In* Slater, F., ed., *Societies, choices and environments*. London: Collins, pp. 441–475.

Dingsdale, A., 1996, Hungary as a place of refuge. *In* Hall, D., Danta, D., eds, *Reconstructing the Balkans: a geography of the new southeast Europe*. Chichester/New York: John Wiley and Sons, pp. 197–208.

Dingsdale, A., 1999, Redefining eastern Europe: a new regional geography of post-socialist Europe? *Geography*, 84 (3), 204–221.

EBRD, 1999, *Transition report 1999*. London: EBRD.

Enyedi, G., 1994, Budapest and the European metropolitan integration. *GeoJournal*, 32 (4), 399–402.

European Commission, 1999, *Regular report from the Commission on progress towards accession: Hungary – October 13, 1999*. Brussels: European Commission. http://europa.eu.int/comm/enlargement/hungary/rep_10_99/.

Forgács, E., 1994, Avant-garde and conservatism in the Budapest art world: 1910–1932. *In* Bender, T., Schorske, C., eds, *Budapest and New York: studies in metropolitan transformation, 1870–1930*. New York: Russell Sage Foundation, pp. 309–322 .

Garton Ash, T., 1986, Does central Europe exist? *New York Review of Books*.

Kapoor, M., 1999, Forget the past. *Business Central Europe*, 6 (60), 18–21.

Kovács, Z., Dingsdale, A., 1998, Whither east European democracies: the Hungarian general election of 1994. *Political Geography*, 17 (4), 437–458.

Meth-Cohn, D., 1998, The new bogeymen. *Business Central Europe*, 5 (57), 46–47.

Turnock, D., 1991, The planning of rural settlement in Romania. *Geographical Journal*, 157 (3), 251–264.

7

POLAND

Andrew Dawson

There are many reasons why Poland should not already have been admitted to the European Union (EU), but no good ones. On the morrow of the fall of socialism there in 1989, the EU might have responded to the evident wish of the Polish people and those of several other countries in central and eastern Europe to 'rejoin' Europe after 50 years of invasion, occupation and colonialism. However, it did not do so, preferring to raise yet further the barriers to entry by agreeing to implement monetary union in the Treaty of Maastricht of 1993. Ten years after the fall of the Berlin Wall, the EU's budgetary arrangements appeared to make no provision for Polish accession until 2006, at the earliest. The contrast with the rapid reincorporation of western Germany into western Europe's collective structures, including the forerunner of the EU, the European Coal and Steel Community, after the Second World War is shaming. There is no question that post-socialist Poland has faced serious transition problems or that the impact of entry into the EU upon it and the Union would be considerable. However, neither matter is of such weight as to merit the cautious, not to say foot-dragging, approach adopted by Brussels. This chapter will provide a brief history of Poland's relations with western Europe; it will assess some of the principal developments since the fall of socialism; and it will evaluate the country's fitness to join the EU and the likely significance of its accession.

A brief history

Poland occupies a pivotal location in the geography of Europe (Figure 7.1). Lying at the interface between the continent's Slavonic and Teutonic areas of settlement, its history has been one of migration – often forced – and shifting frontiers. Similarly on the fault line between Catholic and Orthodox Christianity, and therefore between the Roman and the Cyrillic script, it has felt the pull, not so much of its Slavonic roots, but of western European culture. As the largest of the peoples and states which occupy this intermediary position – the true 'central Europe' – Poland has, indeed, been the pivot of Europe ever since the state's foundation in AD 966.

In modern times Poland has found itself sandwiched between the major industrial states of north-west Europe, on the one hand, and Russia, on the other. As such, its economic

Figure 7.1: Poland

development has owed much to its changing relations with its neighbours. In the 19th century, when Poland did not exist as a state, some areas that were inhabited by Poles and form part of present-day Poland, enjoyed considerable economic development as a result of their location. Warsaw, Łódź and the extreme east of the Upper Silesian coalfield, in particular, attracted western European entrepreneurs and skilled workers, seeking to exploit opportunities to supply the Russian Empire, in which those places lay, while retaining the closest possible links with their home areas. High import tariffs, especially after the mid-1870s, led to substantial capital investment in all three places, but especially in and around the textile town of Łódź, by Belgian, British, French and, especially, German firms. Notwithstanding an absence of local fuel and a shortage of water, by 1914 the 'Polish Manchester', as it had become known, was a town of 500,000, dominated by mills and made filthy by their chimneys. Its cloth was sold throughout the Russian Empire.

The economic history of the rest of what is now Poland was very different. Outwith the three places mentioned above, little of what was known as the Congress Kingdom had any significant industrial or urban development. Feudalism, which was only abolished in the Russian Empire in the 1860s, left a mass of peasant farmers, few of whom owned land, working chiefly to supply their immediate needs, using primitive means of husbandry and with little commercial outlet for their products. Even worse, however, was the situation in Galicia: those parts of southern Poland that at that time belonged to the Austro–Hungarian Empire. Starved of industrial development, both population pressure and rural poverty were intense, giving rise to substantial emigration to the industrial cities of western Europe and North America.

It was the 'western and northern territories' – areas then within Germany – that experienced the greatest economic development before 1914. Along with the Ruhr, the Upper Silesian coalfield was one of the two great German powerhouses providing not only fuel, but also a variety of metallic ores (including that of iron) and other minerals, upon which a range of heavy industries grew up in the second half of the 19th century. However, few parts of what is now western Poland were untouched by the effects of the Industrial Revolution. By the late 19th century a majority of people lived in urban settlements, and the network of towns was both dense and well developed. In addition to the area's many small market towns, the cities of Gdańsk (Danzig), Poznań (Posen), Szczecin (Stettin) and Wrocław (Breslau) were major foci of the economy, with a wide range of manufacturing industries and commercial services. All were linked together and with the rest of Germany by a dense railway network. Agriculture, freed from feudalism at the start of the 19th century, was conducted mostly on large estates or medium-sized holdings and was commercially oriented. However, only part of the western and northern territories was inhabited by Poles at that time, and the majority of the population was German. Only in such cities as Katowice (Kattowitz) and Poznań, and in the area around Poznań, was there a substantial Polish presence. It was these areas that were incorporated in the re-established Poland after the First World War.

Inter-war relations between Poland and western Europe were mixed. Although Germany was the dominant trading partner, political links with France were always stronger. During the 1930s the Polish government, conscious of the fact that the country's strategic industries lay close to the German border, sought to develop a central industrial region much further east, around the confluence of the Wisła and San rivers. Difficulties over the export of Polish coal through the so-called Free Port of Danzig led to the construction of a dedicated rail link between Katowice and the Baltic and the building of a new port on Polish territory at Gdynia. Meanwhile, relations with Czechoslovakia and Lithuania, with whom there had been territorial disputes in the early 1920s, were strained; those with the Soviet Union, from which Poland had seized a large part of Belorussia and the Ukraine in the Polish–Russian war of 1920, and which had retreated into hostile isolation, were minimal.

The Second World War overturned this situation. Poland lost the territory that it had taken from the Soviet Union, but acquired most of the German lands to the east of the Odra (Oder) and Nysa (Neisse) rivers. Huge shifts of population followed as Germans fled westward from the advancing Russian army, to be replaced by Poles from those areas taken by the Soviet Union. The onset of the Cold War in the late 1940s confirmed Poland's domination by the USSR, and the subsequent political and economic development of the country was linked closely to that of the whole Soviet bloc. Contact with western Europe was limited; international migration ceased; and Polish political and economic systems diverged markedly from those in the West. However, many Poles were opposed to Soviet control and its particular form of economic management, expressing their opposition in the Poznań riots of 1956 and the Gdańsk revolt of 1970, in further troubles in 1976 and in the Solidarity uprising of 1980. Notwithstanding several changes of leader over that period, the communist authorities lost much of their credibility. The imposition of martial law in 1981, and the murder of a troublesome priest, Father Popiełuszko, by military police in 1984, destroyed what was left. The economy stagnated. Eventually, in June 1989, the regime was obliged to concede a free election for the Upper Chamber of parliament and a minority of the seats in the Lower Chamber. It was trounced. The principal opposition party, Solidarity (*Solidarność*), won 99 of the 100 seats contested in the Upper Chamber and almost all those open to free election in the Lower. Eastern Europe's first post-communist government was formed. It was only later in the year that the Berlin Wall fell, taking the rest of central Europe's communist governments with it.

Post-socialist development

Polish aspirations in 1989 were clear. The vast majority of the population wished to replace the system of communist control and central planning with a plural parliamentary democracy, an independent judiciary, a more market-based economy and the right of private citizens to engage in business. Poles also wanted to join the North Atlantic Treaty Organization (NATO) and the European Economic Community (later, the European Union). However, at that time no country had made the transition from Soviet central planning to the free market, and concern was expressed as to whether it would be possible. In particular, doubt was cast on the ability of the people of central and eastern Europe to cope with the social dislocation that economic transition was likely to cause. Doubts were also expressed as to whether countries in the region could develop the legal and financial infrastructure necessary for the establishment of an economy based on the rule of law and the private ownership of property.

Much, however, has been achieved, especially in Poland. Indeed, Poland has become something of a model for other former communist countries. In particular, the constitution has been reformed, macroeconomic stability was quickly established, the private sector of the economy soon surpassed the public sector in importance, and social stability has been maintained in the face of such substantial change, notwithstanding a great deal of individual hardship.

The constitutional settlement

Fundamental to the changes that have occurred has been the successful establishment of a plural democracy, achieved in the face of considerable difficulty. As one of their final acts, the communists attempted to undermine reform by enacting an electoral law that instituted proportional representation in its purest form. The first fully free, post-communist election produced a parliament composed of a large number of political parties, few of which had many seats, which created severe problems for the formation and survival of governments. There have been several administrations since 1989, all of which have been coalitions or minorities. However, the threshold of votes for representation in parliament has since been raised to 5 per cent, and the number of parties has shrunk drastically: after the 1997 election there were only five. Moreover, the electoral process has worked smoothly, leading to changes in administration that have generally reflected the wishes of the electorate. The election of 1993 brought to power a left-of-centre government, led by the Democratic Left Alliance (SLD), a party composed largely of former communists, whereas that of 1997 produced a more right-wing administration, dominated by Solidarity Electoral Action (AWS). Similarly, the first presidential election by universal suffrage, in 1990, installed Lech Wałęsa, the Solidarity leader; the second, in 1995, saw his defeat and replacement by Aleksander Kwasniewski, a former communist. Furthermore, although administrations have varied in their enthusiasm for the post-socialist transformation of Poland, there has been no wish to return to communist practices and there has been much common ground between the major parties. This fundamental constitutional stability has rested in no small part upon the maturity of the electorate, which has 'drawn a line' under events in the communist era and accepted that most of those who were members of the Communist Party, but who now espouse social democracy, are not thereby debarred from public office.

Reform of local government

Another example of the rapid maturing of Poland's plural democracy since the overthrow of communism has been the reform of local government. As part of its transition, the country has been reorganising the constitutional relationship between its tiers of government and redrawing the map of local authorities. During the communist period local authorities were legally branches of central government, possessing few, if any, independent powers. That arrangement was overturned in 1990, when elected communal (*gmina*) councils were empowered to raise revenue and undertake actions not reserved to other authorities. However, it was acknowledged that one, and perhaps two, further tiers of directly elected local authorities would be needed if the principle of subsidiarity was to be effected. Nevertheless, little progress was made between 1993 and 1997, when the Democractic Left Alliance (SLD) and its coalition partner, the Peasants' Party (PSL), could not find a structure that would favour both of them. Following the 1997 election, in contrast, a new, more united administration made proposals for the completion of the reform.

Those proposals involved a return to something similar to the traditional pattern of local authorities. Prior to 1975 the country had been divided into a small number of regions (*województwa*), accompanied by a lower tier of about 300 counties (*powiaty*). However, both these 'large' regions and counties were replaced in 1975 by a single tier of 49 much smaller regions. By 1998 all the major political parties had agreed to return, at least in principle, to the earlier model. They were also agreed that the financial relationship between the centre and the regions should become more transparent. Under the communists there was much scope for individual politicians to influence the flow of funds from central government to regions and a widespread belief that the system was corrupt. It was, therefore, decided that regions should initially receive the same, fixed, proportion of the national taxes on income and value-added that are raised within them, and only a limited equalisation of revenues after that, on the ground that more elaborate systems of central-government grants, related to the particular needs of individual regions, would be more difficult to understand and more open to manipulation by interested parties. However, it followed that each region should be sufficiently large to generate the income that would be required to provide such services as police and economic development. It was doubtful that the smaller of the 49 regions – some 15 had populations of less than 500,000 – would have been able to do this.

Initially, the AWS (Solidarity Electoral Action) government proposed that there should be 12 regions and about 320 counties, a structure that would have gone far to meeting those requirements. However, that proposal ran into stiff opposition, founded in the country's political geography. The principal opposition party, the SLD, which has strong support in many of the middle-sized towns that might have served as foci of regions, wished to see a much larger number of them. Some of those living in regions that would have disappeared under the government's proposals objected to the possibility that they would be incorporated into larger units which were suffering from severe social and economic problems or are likely to do so; they feared that they would be called upon to subsidise such areas. Others pointed out that their regions were well-established and widely recognised entities, underpinned by a significant historical or cultural status. The Catholic Church supported the city of Częstochowa, which is the country's most important site of pilgrimage, in this regard. All were concerned that the loss of regional authority headquarters from their towns would inhibit attempts to attract custom and investment. During the spring and summer of 1998 there was much public protest, but eventually a compromise was reached in which the major parties agreed to 16 regions. Elections for the new authorities passed off smoothly in October 1998, and the new bodies took office in January 1999.

Economic restructuring

Poland's constitutional settlement has been accompanied by an equally successful macroeconomic one. Post-communist Poland inherited a large monetary 'overhang' of personal savings, accumulated by households that had earned money but could find little within the highly regulated economy to spend it on. The country had also incurred substantial hard-currency debts to governments and banks in the West during the 1970s and 1980s. The currency was not convertible. Drastic action – called 'shock therapy' by some – was taken by the first post-communist government to solve these problems. In 1990 trade was freed from most central controls, and the majority of price controls were scrapped. Prices rose rapidly, thus destroying the 'overhang'. Negotiations were launched with the country's foreign creditors, as a result of which its debts were either rescheduled or cancelled. The International Monetary Fund (IMF) provided a large standby fund to underwrite the value of the złoty on world currency markets, and the currency became convertible at a rate in line with the country's underlying economic conditions. Speculators did not attack, and the government did not need to draw on the IMF guarantee. What is more, these early achievements have been sustained. Despite considerable economic disruption within the country in the early 1990s, and a substantial unrecorded element within the economy, the government has been able to collect most of the taxes it has levied and maintain its budgetary discipline. Inflation has fallen rapidly, from the extraordinary levels of that period to about 6 per cent per annum in 1999, while the value of the currency, which has declined slowly, has proved to be more stable than many of those of supposedly more soundly based market economies. This stability has been recognised by foreigners: Poland has been one of the most successful of the former communist countries in attracting foreign direct investment.

The effect of shock therapy on the domestic economy was also dramatic. The replacement of central planning by the free market exposed enterprises to the discipline of paying the real costs of their activities, while obliging them to produce goods at a price that customers could afford and of a quality that would persuade them to buy. There were sharp falls in demand for all except essential products. Industry was also affected by the reform of the arrangements governing international trade. The restoration of the right of individuals and firms to own and run their own businesses was accompanied by the restoration of their right to import and export; many people took the opportunity to import western brand-name products, thus undermining the demand for locally produced goods. At the same time the government, which had, in effect, been a major customer – especially of the industries supplying armaments and infrastructural goods – reduced its demand substantially. The Council for Mutual Economic Assistance (CMEA) – which had managed trade between communist countries and which, like their internal economies, was conducted according to the principles of central planning rather than the market – collapsed, taking with it much of the previous trade between Poland and other countries in central and eastern Europe. Levels of output fell sharply in many industries. Some publicly owned enterprises, facing rapidly mounting debts, were liquidated. Employment fell from 17 million in 1989 to just over 14 million. Unemployment – an unheard of phenomenon under central planning – reached almost three million, or about 17 per cent of the workforce.

The structural impact of these changes was marked. In 1989 about 30 per cent of Polish employment was in manufacturing and mining. By 1993, at the nadir of economic decline, that had fallen to about a quarter. The proportion in trade – the most buoyant of the services – had, however, grown from 9 per cent to 14 per cent. There was also a substantial change in the relative sizes of the public and private sectors, brought about by a sharp decline in the number of jobs in all parts of the public sector (other than education and health) and an increase in those in private ownership, especially retailing, construction, transport and manufacturing (Table 7.1). By 1993 only 43 per cent of employment was in the public sector; by 1997 it had fallen yet further, to 32 per cent.

Table 7.1 Poland: employment, 1989–1997

	Changes 1989–93 (%)			Total in 1997 (%)
	Private sector	Public sector	Total	
Agriculture	–8	–66	–17	27
Mining and manufacturing	+10	–40	–26	24
Construction	+51	–75	–35	6
Transport	+23	–39	–30	5
Trade	+77	–69	+34	13
Education	–42	–2	–3	6
Health care and social welfare	+32	–3	–1	6
Total (%)	+9	–35	–16	
Total ('000)	+687	–3 463	–2 776	15 941

Sources: *GUS, 1994a, b, 1998d*

These changes affected the country very unevenly, and there have been wide variations in unemployment between regions, ranging from Warsaw, Poznań and Kraków, where the rate has been less than half the national average, to some of the more rural areas in the north and the former mining area of Wałbrzych, where between a quarter and a third of the labour force was out of work in 1993 and between 15 and 20 per cent were still unemployed in 1998 (GUS, 1998e). This pattern reflects the structural changes. The growth in services appears to have bolstered the largest cities. On the other hand, the slump in manufacturing and mining seems to have affected some towns, and especially those in Upper Silesia, much less severely than others: it may be that these areas, in which the socialist sector of the economy remains large, will prove to be particularly vulnerable to any new wave of reform. It should also be noted that there has been a significant shake-out in agriculture, affecting not only the relatively small public sector, but also the sector in private ownership. It is, perhaps, for this reason that unemployment appears to have struck some of the regions in which the proportion of jobs in the private sector in the late 1980s was relatively high just as severely as some of those regions that depended heavily upon the public sector.

Changes of such magnitude and rapidity, involving considerable individual hardship, tend to destabilise societies, but there has been little public unrest. The economy, which began to grow again in 1993, has continued to do so at a pace that has led to a steady decline of unemployment, to about 9 per cent in 1998, and to a return to the standard of living of the late 1980s. However, the process of transition is not yet complete. The pace of reform was checked in 1993, following the election of a left-of-centre government; although some of the public sector had been privatised, about 3,000 enterprises, including many of the so-called industrial dinosaurs, remained in public ownership. In 1995 the government transferred 500 of the largest – though not the coalmines – to 15 national investment funds, each managed by groups of Polish and foreign banks, in the hope that such arm's-length organisations would be able to achieve the restructuring that has proved to be so difficult for politicians. Some have survived, but others have been broken up and sold to the private sector.

Coalmining

Under the communist model of development, the highest priority was accorded to increasing the output of fuel. Many new mines were sunk in Upper Silesia to supply coal for coking, and several huge opencast workings were developed in central Poland in conjunction with purpose-built electricity generating stations. Poland also built up a large export market in bituminous coal, not only to other CMEA members but also to western Europe. The country's 450,000 miners were among its highest paid workers. However, labour productivity was abysmal. Furthermore, several of the mines, including those which were being sunk in the 1970s and 1980s in the newly discovered Lublin coalfield, faced such difficult geological conditions that they could never have covered their costs in a market economy. The removal of government subsidies to the industry, the fall in demand from the country's heavy industries, the more efficient use of fuel brought about by economic reform, and the disruption of the industry's markets in the Soviet bloc, led to the closure of all the pits in the small Lublin and Wałbrzych fields, a sharp fall in employment in the industry in general and the promise of closures in Upper Silesia (Table 7.2).

By the mid-1990s, however, few had occurred, even though three-quarters of the Upper Silesian mines had been losing money, the industry's debts had soared and its taxes remained largely unpaid. In 1990 the government was advised by the American consultants, Arthur Andersen, to close up to 15 pits; and in 1993 the World Bank offered to meet some of the social costs, if at least nine were shut. There has been talk of halving the workforce over a period of ten years. In 1996 the government announced a further cut of 18 per cent in the output of coal and the closure of 20 mines by the end of the century. However, it proved incapable of action on such a scale, let alone privatisation. Instead, it fell back on attempts to introduce some sort of internal market within the industry – attempts that failed to balance the books – and indicated that it did not intend to privatise industries, such as coal, which it considered to be 'strategic' (Riley and Tkocz, 1998). In short, for much of the 1990s Polish governments appear to have had no realistic answer to the problems that the reform of the economy has created for the industry, and have proved politically unable to choose between the radical restructuring that will be necessary before substantial amounts of private capital can be attracted and a return to overt public subsidy. However, spurred on by the need to make changes in order to gain entry to the EU, it has now been acknowledged that the number of coalminers must fall to 130,000 by 2002.

Table 7.2 Poland: coalmining, 1986–1997

	1986	1993	1997
Number of mines	95	90	72
Employment	452 000	352 000	279 000
Output of black coal (mn tons)	192	130	138
Output of brown coal (mn tons)	67	68	63

Sources: *GUS, 1987, 1994b, 1998d*

Health

In some parts of central and eastern Europe, the collapse of communism has led to killing, the destruction of housing, the expulsion of people from their homes, shortages of food, and war, whilst in others there has been inadequate institutional reform and economic stagnation.

Fortunately, Poland has avoided these extremes. Nevertheless, the stresses of transition have been very great and, writing in 1997, one commentator claimed that:

The health of Polish society is constantly deteriorating, which can be exemplified, among others, by a growing rate of psychophysical disabilities (to a large extent connected with social and professional insecurity, high death rates caused by circulatory disorders and cancer, and a high rate of health disorders among children and youth).

(European Council, 1993)

There is some evidence to support this claim. Male life expectancy at birth fell sharply during the first two years of the transition, as to a lesser extent did life expectancy for women (GUS, 1998c). However, the longer picture is quite different. Whilst the early communist years produced a marked improvement in life expectancy for both men and women – that for men rose from about 59 years in 1952 to 67 in the mid-1970s – no further improvement was achieved during the last 15 years of communist rule. By 1996, in contrast, it had risen to 68 years. Similarly, women's life expectancy, which also declined slightly in the 1980s, has been improving again since the early 1990s and reached 77 years in 1996.

More particularly, since 1991 there have been some marked falls in the standardised death-rates associated with some of the more common diseases. Deaths from circulatory diseases for men, which had risen from 722 per 100,000 in 1989 to 759 per 100,000 in 1991, and from 731 to 752 for women, had fallen by 1996 to historic lows of respectively, 636 and 670. Similarly, deaths from accidents and other external causes, which had risen from 122 per 100,000 for men in 1989 to 139 per 100,000 in 1991, had also fallen: to 114 by 1996. The steep decline in infant mortality, which was occurring before 1989, has continued; the rate has more than halved since 1980, dropping from 255 per 10,000 live births to 191 per 10,000 in 1989 and 122 in 1996. Similarly, after a period between 1990 and 1993 in which no improvement was achieved, the steep reduction in tuberculosis has been resumed. In contrast, death-rates from cancer have continued their climb of the 1980s.

However, there are exceptions. Although care must be taken in the use of non-standardised death-rates at the regional level, the industrial city of Łódź – which has faced severe problems of economic and social adjustment – and its environs appear to be one of the least healthy places in the country. The 1996 death-rate, at 13.5 per 1,000, was far in excess of the national average of ten. The city has had the highest death-rate since the mid-1980s, and the gap between it and the national average has been widening. More particularly, for both men and women there was a much higher recorded incidence of deaths from circulatory diseases and cancer in the city than in Poland as a whole.

Population

The improvements in health have affected the country's demographic development. During the Second World War about six million people in Poland were killed, much of the population was incorporated into the Soviet Union, and the country emerged from the war with a population of only about 24 million. However, the falling death-rates and, especially, the country's high birth-rate led to rapid growth thereafter, so that by 1980 the population had risen to 36 million. Since then, in contrast, growth has slowed, and there has been little increase since 1989. In 1998 there were almost 39 million people in Poland.

This slowdown has been caused in large part by the falling birth-rate. Whereas in 1950 there were 109 live births per 1,000 women aged between 15 and 49, by the late 1980s the figure had fallen to about 70 per 1,000, and to 41 in 1997. Natural increase, which had been 530,000 a year in the mid-1950s, had sunk by 1997 to 32,000, all of which was in rural areas. The net reproduction rate has been below one throughout the period since 1989, and a fall in the population has only been avoided by its increasing longevity. As a result of these changes the Polish population has been ageing. In 1950, 5 per cent was aged 65 or more, but by 1990 this had doubled, and by 1997 the figure had risen to almost 12 per cent. Official Polish statistics indicate that 14 per cent of the population is now classed as being of post-working age (GUS, 1998d).

There have also been other important demographic changes since 1989. First, whereas throughout the period of central planning – and notwithstanding serious problems of accommodation in urban areas – there was a net movement of more than 100,000 each year to urban areas, that trend has been weakening. In 1997 the figure was only 15,000. In the late 1940s only about a third of Poles lived in towns, but by 1989 the proportion had risen to 62 per cent, where it has stayed. Second, since the Second World War the population had included only one significant minority, Germans, but it has become increasingly homogeneous. During the 1970s and 1980s the communist authorities allowed Germans of pensionable age to return to west Germany, and much of the net emigration of about 20,000 each year from Poland was accounted for by such people. There are now only about 300,000 members of German cultural organisations in Poland, largely in Upper Silesia. Two of the 460 seats in the Lower House of the Polish parliament are reserved for the country's German minority.

EU entry

One of the principal Polish aspirations in 1989 was to become more firmly connected with western Europe, and the country was relieved when two of the more important organisations binding it to other communist countries – the CMEA and the Warsaw Pact – collapsed in the early 1990s. It was also relieved to see some further waning of Russian power, exemplified by the break-up of the Soviet Union in 1991, though it has been alarmed by the subsequent instability of Russia, the Ukraine and Belarus. All Poland's post-communist governments have sought to strengthen the country's ties with western Europe, and in this they have had some success. In 1992 an association agreement was signed with the EU. However, it was not generous (Messerlin, 1993). Access to EU markets for a range of so-called sensitive goods – food, chemicals, steel and textiles – was severely restricted, and Polish workers were not allowed to participate in the EU's single labour market. Some technical and other aid was offered, but the substantial resources associated with the EU's common agricultural and regional policies were not made available. In spite of Polish pressure, it was not until the autumn of 1998 that the EU began serious negotiations with a view to admitting Poland, and even so it is unlikely to gain entry before 2006.

Trade

Nevertheless, by the mid-1990s Poland had achieved a spectacular turnaround in its pattern of international trade, especially with the EU. In 1985 Polish trade amounted to 31 per cent of the country's gross domestic product (GDP) (GUS, 1998b). Trade in primary and simply processed goods accounted for about 36 per cent of the total, and manufactures for the rest. Mineral fuels were by far the most important item of both exports and imports. The most important trading partner was the Soviet Union, with whom 27 per cent of trade was conducted, followed by west Germany, east Germany and Czechoslovakia. Trade with the communist bloc in Europe as a whole accounted for 48 per cent of the total.

Between 1985 and 1990 Polish trade fell sharply, but recovered, and amounted to 44 per cent of the country's GDP by 1995. By that date trade in primary and simply processed goods had sunk to 23 per cent, whilst manufactures had risen to 77 per cent. Mineral fuels had been displaced as the most important item in both imports and exports. There has also been a marked reorientation of trade. The united Germany's share of the total rose from 13 per cent in 1985 to 32 per cent in 1995, whilst that with the EU as a whole now accounts for about two-thirds of the total. Trade with the former communist countries of central and eastern Europe declined sharply, to 17 per cent.

Much of this change has been associated with the regrowth of the private sector in Poland. Private trade, which had been illegal before 1990, accounted for 64 per cent of the total in 1995, and a higher proportion of it has been with other market economies than with former communist countries. However, the private sector has been responsible for much of the increase in imports and has accounted for the whole of the country's large trade deficit. In contrast, the public sector has continued to trade extensively with central and eastern Europe, and particularly with Russia, where it accounted for 62 per cent of Poland's total trade with that country. Moreover, trade by the public sector has been largely in balance, though the worsening economic problems in Russia and the Ukraine since the mid-1990s have undermined that position.

The environment

In 1997 the European Commission published its assessment of the progress made by each of the applicant countries toward meeting the criteria for entry (European Commission, 1997). In many respects the Commission foresaw no major difficulty for Poland. However, there were several areas in which it considered that the country will only be able to meet EU requirements 'in the medium term', and a few areas require either very substantial action or are only likely to be met in the long term. The Commission reserved its strongest language for comment on the environment: 'very substantial efforts will be needed, including massive investment and strengthening of administrative capacity to enforce legislation. Full compliance with the *acquis* could be expected only in the long term, and would require increased levels of public expenditure' (European Commission, 1997: C3) especially in relation to waste water and air pollution.

In so saying, it is doubtful whether the Commission has been entirely fair. The first post-communist governments instituted new and effective systems of environmental protection and increased expenditure on pollution control and the cleansing of waste. Furthermore, the sharp increase in the price of energy and minerals in the early 1990s and the substantial falls in the output of many of the country's heavy industries have done much to reduce emissions. Moreover, the imminent privatisation of the country's steel mills and the further rationalisation of its coalmines are likely to lead to further reductions in pollution.

Pollution

It has been claimed that, at the end of the 1980s, Poland was one of the dirtiest countries in Europe (Nowicki, 1997). However, the country is now somewhat cleaner (Table 7.3). Between 1985 and 1997 industry, farming and domestic users all used less water, and aggregate demand fell by 24 per cent. Discharges also declined. However, discharges of untreated waste-water fell even faster – by 74 per cent – while untreated discharges of industrial waste-water fell by 87 per cent. Between 1993 and 1997 the length of rivers with excessive levels of inorganic pollution fell from 54 to 31 per cent. In contrast, progress with regard to other forms of water pollution has been slower. The proportion of rivers with excessive levels of organic pollution declined only from 89 to 85 per cent, and the levels of pollution of many Polish lakes and of groundwater remain high. The quality of water supplied through the public mains also improved only slowly during the 1990s. Deposits from Poland's rivers in the Baltic Sea of no less than 15 out of 25 harmful substances, including chlorides, nitrates, phosphates and sulphates, were higher in 1996 than in 1990; however, those of such heavy metals as cadmium, copper, lead and zinc, and also DDT, were substantially lower.

Some progress has also been made in reducing atmospheric pollution (Table 7.4). Between the late 1980s and 1992 there were steep falls in the emissions of carbon, nitrogen and sulphur dioxide, and of ammonia, methane, particulates and heavy metals. There has been a further decline in some of these since then. Much of this improvement has resulted from substantial falls in emissions from the manufacturing industry. On the other hand, emissions of greenhouse gases from road vehicles have been rising, although at only about half the rate of the increase in the number of vehicles.

Not surprisingly, it is some, but by no means all, of the larger cities that are the most serious sources of pollution. The greatest discharges of untreated industrial and domestic waste-water in 1997 occurred in Warsaw, Łódź, Bydgoszcz, Szczecin, Kraków and Toruń, in that order. As a result, substantial stretches of the Wisła and Odra, and many of their principal tributaries, were excessively polluted in that year, though it should be noted that the quality of water in some of the rivers entering Poland from neighbouring states, and in particular the Bug, Nysa and Odra, was also poor. Voivodships with the worst atmospheric pollution in 1996, as defined by nitrogen and sulphur dioxides and particulates, were led by Katowice, followed by Piotrków, Konin, Warsaw, Jelenia Góra, Szczecin and Tarnobrzeg, in that order – all of these have substantial coal or lignite-burning and/or metallurgical or chemical industries – whilst those with the highest emissions of greenhouse gases were Katowice and Warsaw. Katowice, Legnica, Częstochowa and Kraków had the highest atmospheric emissions of heavy metals. Among towns with populations of 100,000 or more, deposits of particulates were highest in some of the more industrial suburbs of Warsaw – Ursus and Wilanów – and in Kalisz, Rzeszow and parts of Łódź. There are also problems in rural areas. Few houses are connected to main sewers, and there is much pollution of surface and groundwater from farms (GUS, 1998a).

International comparisons indicate the progress that Poland has made. Although, in 1995, the proportion of the population served by communal sewerage, at 42 per cent, was well below that in most western European countries, it was above that for both Belgium and Greece. Moreover, the country's rivers compared well with those in several EU states. Polish emissions of carbon dioxide per capita were below those in no less than 8 of the 15 current members of the EU, and emissions of nitrogen dioxide were below those in no less than 10. Many of the principal cities of the EU suffered from higher levels of nitrogen dioxide than Warsaw or Łódź in the mid-1990s. Among a range of measures, only in per capita emissions of sulphur dioxide and the use of chlorofluorocarbons (CFCs) was the Polish performance in the mid-1990s worse than that in western European countries. Average levels of sulphur dioxide in Warsaw and Łódź were higher than in many of the principal cities of the EU. Similarly, Poland remains one of the principal producers of sulphur-based pollutants in Europe and is a considerable net exporter, being responsible for much deposition of such material in the Ukraine, Russia, Belarus and the Baltic Sea, but for little of that in the EU (GUS, 1998a).

However, levels of pollution must be set against standards of living. As Poland is a relatively poor country, few houses were connected to main sewers and many factories released untreated waste into rivers or the atmosphere. In the late 1970s, only 0.3 per cent of the country's GDP was spent on environmental protection. Since then, in contrast, economic growth and some foreign assistance have enabled much to be done: by 1997 expenditure had risen to 2 per cent of GDP, one of the highest figures in Europe; the State Inspectorate of Environmental Protection had closed down or curtailed the emissions of most of the most serious sources of industrial pollution; more than 300 new communal waste-water treatment plants had been built; and desulphurisation equipment had been installed in many of the coal-fired power stations (Nowicki, 1997). Set against these improvements, the Commission's judgement of Polish environmental protection would appear to be grudging, and its call for yet further massive expenditure by a country whose GDP per capita is approximately one-third of that in the EU would appear to be harsh.

Table 7.3 Poland: water use, 1985–1997 (mn cu m)

	1985	1995	1997
Water use – total	15 453	12 066	11 799
by industry	10 921	8 431	8 424
by agriculture	1 606	1 177	1 083
by domestic users	2 926	2 457	2 292
Water discharges	12 903	9 981	9 961
Of which:			
requiring treatment	4 624	3 020	2 849
untreated	2 000	700	520
Industrial waste – water discharged directly to surface water	10 485	8 129	8 269
Of which:			
requiring treatment	2 205	1 167	1 157
untreated	755	105	103

Source: *GUS, 1998a*

Table 7.4 Poland: air pollution, 1990–1996 ('000 tonnes)

	1990	1995	1996
Carbon dioxide	384 000	330 000	373 200
Nitrogen dioxide	1 280	1 120	1 154
Sulphur dioxide	3 210	2 376	2 368
Particulates	1 980	1 308	1 250
From vehicles			
carbon dioxide	27 641[a]	32 280	35 800
carbon monoxide	1 253[a]	1 219	1 290
nitrogen oxides	446[a]	450	483
lead	0.67[a]	0.42	0.42

[a] Figures for 1991.   Source: *GUS, 1998a*

Agriculture

However, the most intriguing aspect of the Commission's 1997 report was its failure to acknowledge the significance of what may prove to be the single most serious problem for Polish entry: farming. Among the CEE countries only Poland and Yugoslavia failed to collectivise their farms under communism; Poland abandoned the attempt in the aftermath of the Poznań riots. However, the communist authorities showed little sympathy for farmers, subjecting them to discriminatory charges and obliging them to obtain equipment and fertiliser from, and to sell much of their output through, state-owned enterprises. After a series of land reforms between the wars and in the immediate aftermath of the Second World War, the industry was dominated by small peasant-holdings. Although many people left the land during the communist period to take up jobs in towns, this structure changed little. Difficulties were placed in the way of farmers who wished to enlarge their holdings, and the opportunities for investment were limited. Only in the north and west of the country, in areas that had belonged to Germany before the war and where large estates had been seized by the government at the end of that conflict, were there many large holdings.

As a result of the economic reforms of 1990, many of the – hitherto heavily subsidised – state farms collapsed. At the same time the market for farm products was disrupted by the sharp reduction in trade with other CEE countries and an influx of imports of much higher-quality food from the rest of the world. However, faced with high levels of unemployment in the towns, indigent farmers found that they were unable to leave the land. Whilst western investors were willing, and in some cases eager, to invest in other parts of the economy, there was no significant inflow of foreign capital to agriculture. There was considerable distress in some rural areas.

Since then the government has provided some protection for farmers, but little else has changed. Agriculture continues to employ one of the largest proportions of the workforce in any European country – about 27 per cent – but to produce only about 7 per cent of the country's GDP. Only about 8 per cent of Poland's two million farms are of 15 ha or more. If the economy continues to grow rapidly, there will be some opportunity for people to seek other livelihoods, allowing the enlargement and intensification of holdings and improvements in the standard of farm hygiene and the quality of products. However, very great changes will be needed, probably requiring many years, before the gap between farm employment and agricultural productivity can be bridged.

The implications of all this for EU accession are considerable. If Poland were to be admitted, the number of farms in the EU would increase by about 30 per cent, and the application of the Common Agricultural Policy, as it now stands, to Poland would require either an increase of about 15 per cent in the contributions of member states to the EU's budget or a substantial redistribution of agricultural support away from existing members. Given the past reluctance of the current members to face down their agricultural lobbies, it is difficult to see how such changes could be achieved.

The effects of entry

It is difficult to forecast what changes admission to the EU would make to Poland, not least because much may change, not only in Poland and the EU, but also in the wider economic, political and social context in which both must operate up to 2006 and beyond. However, some indication can be given as to what might happen if Poland were to enter in the very near future, that is, under present arrangements. The removal of barriers to trade would benefit some of the larger and better organised farmers. It would also benefit some sectors of the manufacturing industry. On the other hand, many farmers and some manufacturers might find that customers preferred products of higher quality from western Europe, much as happened immediately after the freeing of trade in the early 1990s. In short, structural economic change would probably accelerate after admission, and some Poles would lose their jobs. The completion of privatisation would facilitate such restructuring: the European Commission reports that productivity is twice as high in firms that have received foreign direct investment as in the economy as a whole (European Commission, 1998). However, the extension to Poland of the Common Agricultural Policy's system of farm support would increase the incomes of many farmers, and the whole country would be eligible for support from the EU's Regional Fund. Many new jobs might be created in construction and related industries following the application of Regional Fund money to the improvement of the country's modest infrastructure. Meanwhile, the EU's labour markets would be opened to Polish workers: large numbers of well-educated, younger Poles might seek work in other EU countries.

Some parts of the country would benefit from these changes (Figure 7.2). Those metropolitan regions that have already been successful in attracting both Polish and foreign investment, such as Warsaw, Kraków and Poznań, would continue to grow. However, the relative disadvantage of other areas might become even more obvious. Old industrial areas and those suffering severe pollution, and in particular the Upper Silesian coalfield – once exposed to the full effects of western European competition and takeover – would face the effects of even more rapid rationalisation. Meanwhile, the more rural, eastern parts of the country, which are already the poorest, would find themselves on the periphery, not only of Poland but also of the EU; the European Commission has drawn attention to the need to impose more stringent controls over trade and migration across the country's eastern frontiers.

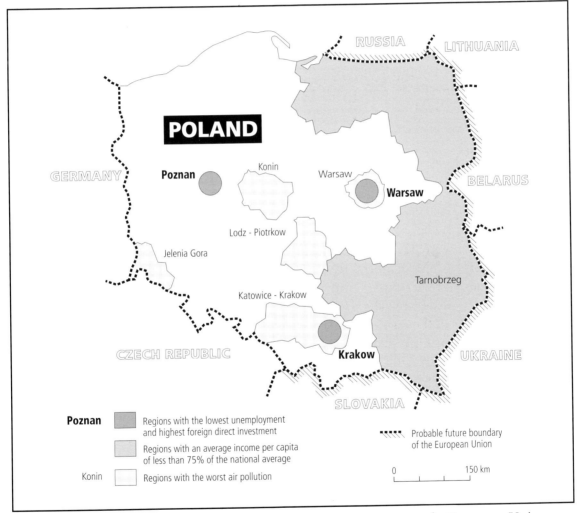

Figure 7.2: Poland: areas that may be affected by the country's entry to the European Union

Conclusion

In several important regards Poland has 'set the pace' for post-communist institutional and economic reform in central and eastern Europe. There has been a substantial restructuring of the Polish economy, but the process is far from complete in either the primary or secondary sectors. Nevertheless, economic growth has been robust, standards of living have been rising, environmental protection has been strengthened and the health of Poles has begun to improve again. Unlike the 1980s, when Polish society was in disarray and its economy stagnant, the post-communist future would seem to be bright. However, the country's entry to the EU remains distant. Western Europe, having failed to defend Poland in 1939 or to prevent its takeover by the Soviet Union at the end of the Second World War, would seem to be failing yet again to respond adequately to the aspirations and achievements of the Polish nation.

References

European Commission, 1997, *For a stronger and wider Union: Agenda 2000*. Brussels: European Commission (DOC 97/6).

European Commission, 1998, *Regular report from the Commission on progress towards accession: Poland (November 4, 1998)*. Brussels: European Commission.

Firlit-Fesnak, G., 1997, What about social policy? Social effects of system transformation in Poland. *In* Wojtaszczyk, K. A., ed., *Poland: government and politics*. Warsaw: Elipsa, pp. 35–46.

GUS (Glowny Urzad Statystyczny), 1987, *Rocznik statystyczny 1987*. Warsaw: GUS.

GUS (Glowny Urzad Statystyczny), 1994a, *Poland: quarterly statistics*. Warsaw: GUS.

GUS (Glowny Urzad Statystyczny), 1994b, *Rocznik statystyczny 1994*. Warsaw: GUS.

GUS (Glowny Urzad Statystyczny), 1998a, *Ochrona srodowiska 1998*. Warsaw: GUS.

GUS (Glowny Urzad Statystyczny), 1998b, *Rocznik statystyczny handlu zagraniczego 1998*. Warsaw: GUS.

GUS (Glowny Urzad Statystyczny), 1998c, *Rocznik statystyczny ochrony zdrowia 1997*. Warsaw: GUS.

GUS (Glowny Urzad Statystyczny), 1998d, *Rocznik statystyczny 1998*. Warsaw: GUS.

GUS (Glowny Urzad Statystyczny), 1998e, *Rocznik statystyczny Województw 1998*. Warsaw: GUS.

Mess erlin, P. A., 1993, The EC and central Europe: the missed rendez-vous of 1992? *Economics of Transition*, 1, 89–109.

Nowicki, M., 1997, Poland. *In* Klarer, J., Moldan, B., eds, *The environmental challenge for central European economies in transition*. Chichester/New York: John Wiley & Sons, pp. 193–227.

Riley, R., Tkocz, M., 1998, Coal mining in Upper Silesia under communism and capitalism. *European Urban and Regional Studies*, 5 (3), 217–235.

8

SLOVENIA

Anton Gosar

Slovenia is one of Europe's youngest states, located between the Danubian lowland, the Mediterranean (Adriatic) and the Alps. It borders Austria to the north, Italy to the west, and Hungary and Croatia to the east and south, and has a pleasant climate. In terms of size (20,296 sq km) and population (1.97 million) the nation-state of Slovenia is relatively small. Even the longest diagonal route between Italy and Hungary – better known as Europe's 'Sun Belt Traffic Axis' (highway E–57/E70, lately used heavily by trucks travelling from and toward central Europe's Danubian Basin) – can easily be managed in four hours' driving time. The air space of Slovenia is crossed by planes using the air-corridor Upper Blue 5 (Frankfurt – (Villach – Zagreb) – Athens), which links Austria and Croatia in 3.48 minutes. The state of Slovenia is placed between the Romance peoples in the west, the German nation to the north, the Ugric Magyars in the east and the South Slavic Croats and Serbs and Bosnian Muslims in the south (Klemenčič and Gosar, 1994). Given its central location and excellent connectivity, Slovenia can rightfully be called 'the gateway of central Europe'.

The first state of the Slavic Slovenes, Karantania, which existed at the turn of the first millennium, was short-lived. During the next couple of centuries Catholic Slovenes (and neighbouring Croats and Hungarians) fought 'on the outer glacis' of the Holy Roman (Austrian) Empire against non-Christian Muslim intruders. South Slavic peoples, oppressed and exploited by both empires – Habsburg's Austria in the case of the Slovenes and Croats; Turkish Ottoman for the Serbs, Montenegrins and Macedonians – took the opportunity to unite after the First World War. The Slovene became one of the three constituting nations of the new state (the Kingdom of Serbs, Croats and Slovenes). Both the Yugoslavian kingdom and Tito's post-Second World War communist Yugoslavia could not survive for long. The diverse state arrangements of the past, distinctive cultural traits and the progressively divergent development levels have made it difficult for the south Slavic peoples to remain together. Yugoslavia disintegrated in 1991, after 72 years of existence; shortly thereafter Slovenia established its statehood sovereignty. On 15 January 1992 Slovenia was recognised by the states of the European Union, and in May 1992 it became the 172nd member of the United Nations. Slovenia became a regular member of the Conference of Security and Co-operation in Europe (Rupel,

Figure 8.1: Slovenia

1992). On 7 April 1992 the United States recognised the new nation-state – along with those of Croatia and Bosnia and Hercegovina. The process of recognition was concluded with the forming of a diplomatic relationship with the USA on 27 August 1992. In 1996 Slovenia began negotiations to join the European Union, but was unsuccessful in its 1997 attempt to join the North Atlantic Treaty Organization (NATO). In 1998 Slovenia became a member of the Security Council of the UN. As a member of NATO's Partnership for Peace programme, Slovenian police and military forces joined colleagues of the western alliance in Bosnia and Hercegovina (1996) and in Kosovo (1999).

The geographic location of Slovenia within Europe has always been of outstanding importance: it served as a transitional filtering zone for peoples, goods and ideas. Slovenia's role today is of a similar nature. By the 1980s, when political, societal and economic changes were taking place in what was communist eastern Europe, Slovenia was already a transit zone of major social and commercial importance. Traffic flows between EC member Greece (and non-member Turkey) and western Europe (Germany) were particularly heavy. The devolution of south-eastern

Europe's centrally positioned state has to a large extent stemmed the flow toward the destinations mentioned. Interested businesses, in particular Austrian, German, Italian and French, did not forget Slovenia's geopolitical advantage. Austrian banks are located in the capital city of Ljubljana; Renault has its largest central European factory in Novo Mesto. Since it remains peaceful – despite the ongoing instability in the Balkan neighbourhood – the region is in the process of becoming a gateway area of central and eastern Europe (CEE). Traffic and goods from Europe's Mediterranean EU member states – Spain, France and Italy – already criss-cross Slovenian territory on their way to the landlocked CEE countries, including Ukraine and Russia, and vice versa. Traditionally, the northern Adriatic and the harbours of Venice and Trieste in Italy, Rijeka in Croatia, and Koper-Capodistria in Slovenia have served as import and export points for landlocked countries such as Austria and the German federal state of Bavaria (Vrišer, 1994). Due to exports of BMWs, the Slovenian port of Koper-Capodistria was nicknamed 'the Bavarian Hong Kong' by Italian newspaper editors. In fact, along with Durrës, Albania, this is the fastest-growing port facility in the Mediterranean.

Following independence a major goal was to improve the country's highways on the Barcelona–Marseille–Milan–Venice–Trieste/Koper–Ljubljana–Maribor–Budapest–Kiev/Mosc-ow route. For the year 2000, 318 km of four-lane highways were scheduled for completion. But, much to the disappointment of Croatia, this does not contribute to that country's links with western Europe (Rijeka–Trieste; Zagreb/Rijeka–Graz/Vienna–Salzburg/Munich). The completion of the south-east–north-west axis (Athens/Istanbul–(Belgrade– Zagreb)–Hamburg) was postponed until the year 2010. The 8 km Karawanken Tunnel (highway E–70: Munich–Salzburg–Ljubljana) was opened for traffic in 1992. Although it eliminated the obstacle of the alpine range, on average less than 3,000 of the expected 8,000 vehicles per day pass through the tunnel, due to the discontinuation of traffic flows to and from the Balkans in 1991. Major companies use other routes and detours (via Hungary and Romania) or have introduced other ways of getting their shipments to reach destinations in Greece, Turkey and the Middle East.

The nation-state's evolution

Until 1918 Slovenes were residents of the Habsburg monarchy. They lived within six administrative units or provinces of Austro–Hungary (also known as the Slovenian Historic Provinces): Carinthia, Styria, Carniola, Gorizia, Trieste, Istria. These were located in the western part of the dual monarchy and in the Transmureland in its eastern (Magyar) part. With the exception of Carniola, Slovenes did not constitute an ethnic majority in any of the named administrative units. In 1848 the Slovenes formulated a programme for the unification of all their ethnic territories. In this area, Slovenian would become the official language in education and government and Slovenes would constitute their own parliament. The programme of 'The United Slovenia' (Zedinjena Slovenija) foresaw no change in statehood: (a unified) Slovenia would remain a part of the Habsburg monarchy (Vodopivec, 1993). In the aftermath of the First World War Slovenia became a single administrative unit (Dravska banovina) of the Kingdom of Serbs, Croats and Slovenes (later called the Kingdom of Yugoslavia). Some peripheral areas contiguously settled by Slovenes remained in Austria (Carinthia) and Hungary or were annexed by Italy (Gorizia, Trieste and Istria). The Slovenian presence in Yugoslavia was to a large part beneficial for the multi-ethnic federation, the region and the citizens of Slovenia. Slovenia was the most industrialised area and able to accommodate the needs of the 20-million-strong market of the south Slavic state. The occupation and divisions of Yugoslavia by Germany, Italy, Hungary and Bulgaria during the Second World War affected Slovenia as well. Areas settled by Slovenes were incorporated into the Third Reich (Styria, Upper Carniola), Hungary (Transmureland) and Italy (Lower Carniola). The uprising and resistance of the local population resulted in casualties, migrations and general destruction.

After the Second World War and until 1991, Slovenia was a republic of the Tito-communist led Socialist Federative Republic of Yugoslavia. The new multi-ethnic state gained areas in the west in accordance with post-war peace accords. Best known are the London (1954) and Osimo (1972) Agreements dealing with the Italo–Yugoslavian border. With the exception of Trieste and several coastal cities, former Italian provinces with a predominantly Slavic population were to a large extent incorporated into Slovenia and Croatia. Slovenia received, among predominantly karstic lands, a window to the Mediterranean in the form of a 47 km coastal strip along the Adriatic, to the south of the city of Trieste (region of Koper-Capodistria). Slovenes still inhabit, as a minority, the provinces of Friuli-Venezia Giulia in Italy and Carinthia and Styria in Austria, and are present in the borderlands of Hungary (the Rába region). Slovenia was autonomous in most of the development decisions within the Yugoslav federation. Slovene know-how, its transitional and geopolitical character (along western borders of the state) and its industrial tradition were important binding factors of the federation. Slovene businesses invested and were heavily involved in mining operations, industrial production, transportation, and trade and tourism, also in other parts of the federation. Slovenian products were famous for their quality and durability (Klemenčič and Genorio, 1993). Slovenia was the richest of the Yugoslav republics and generally outpaced the others, also in employment structure (Table 8.1).

There are a number of reasons why Slovenes wanted to separate from Yugoslavia. Already during the period of the kingdom and later under communism, their survival was endangered by the increased centralisation of the state. After the Second World War, and in particular after 1980, the Slovenian economy had to adjust to the interests of the less prosperous parts of what was then Yugoslavia. Serb leaders were eager to change the constitutional arrangements of 1974, which gave republics veto power before the implementation of laws. Slovenes feared a proposed change in the electoral system through which Serb representatives – in accordance with the number of ethnic residents – would easily gain a relative majority in the parliament. By the end

Table 8.1 Slovenia: within Yugoslavia, 1989

Socialist Republic/ Autonomous Province	Population ('000)	Employment (1981 census) (%)			Illiteracy (1981 census) (%)	GNP index[a]
		Agriculture	Industry	Unemployed		
Serbia proper	5 840	34.5	20.9	12.0	11	100
AP Vojvodina	2 051	32.0	25.6	12.5	6	117
AP Kosovo	1 939	42.2	20.7	35.6	18	28
Montenegro	639	26.0	21.9	26.6	9	77
Macedonia	2 111	28.9	23.7	22.1	11	67
Bosnia and Hercegovina	4 479	28.5	26.2	20.1	15	69
Croatia	4 683	24.1	26.1	7.4	6	127
Slovenia	**1 948**	**12.5**	**36.9**	**3.2**	**1**	**204**

[a]Serbia = 100.

Source: *Savezni zavod za statistiku SFRJ, 1990: 442–445*

of 1990 Serb ethnic nationalism, Belgrade's economic centralism and the arrogance of the Yugoslav army reached a point that was no longer tolerable for the Slovenes (Nečak, 1993). April 1990 saw Slovenia's first democratic elections since the Second World War. They were organised in accordance with the new electoral law, which was passed by the then communist-led Slovenian parliament. With 55 per cent of the seats, a coalition of six non-communist parties won the chamber of political affairs. In all, 24 political parties participated in the elections. Political ideologies within the coalition ranged from Christian Democrat to Socialist and also incorporated several ecological movements. On the basis of the 1990 election results, the first freely elected Slovenian government was formed, led by Christian Democrat Lojze Peterle – a geographer. Among the members of the new government were eight university professors as well as several members of the previous Slovenian communist governments.

Eight months later, on 23 December 1990, the citizens of Slovenia voted by a vast majority (88 per cent) for an independent state. In 1991 Slovene politicians started to negotiate a peaceful separation of Slovenia from the body of the five remaining Yugoslav republics, though without success. On 25 June 1991 Slovenia unilaterally declared independence, an act that was followed by an attack on Slovenia of the (then still) Yugoslav National Army (JNA). The principal goal of the JNA was to occupy border crossings and detain political leaders. With the help of EU mediators, on 8 July 1991 an accord among warring factions was reached, the so-called 'Brioni Declaration', and fighting ceased. The agreement froze the implementation of Slovenia's independence until October 1991. Slovenia resumed implementation of its independence by introducing its own currency, the tolar. By the end of December 1991 the Slovenian government had gained control over the territory of the state, established a viable economy and clearly defined its borders. By then it had met all conditions for international recognition, including the protection of rights of two national minorities (Italian, Hungarian) and the Roma (Gypsy) ethnic group. Disappointment was expressed in Austria and Germany that the once strong German minority was not included in these rights. After a long parliamentary debate the new constitution was adopted by the Slovenian parliament in the spring of 1992. The constitution derived many of its ideas from western Europe, particularly Austria. In accordance with the constitution, the state assembly, the congress, comprises 90 members, and the council of the state, the senate, 40 members. Elections for the president of the state were held in December 1992. Milan Kučan, the former president of the former League of Communists, was unquestionably the favourite: from among eight presidential candidates, he gained 64 per cent of the vote. Elections to the congress and the senate also took place, and the centrist Liberal Democrats (LDS) became the strongest party in the parliament. Dr Janez Drnovšek, the president of the LDS and a long-time member of the 1981–91 post-Tito Yugoslav presidency, was named prime minister. The leading roles were not changed in the 1996–97 elections.

Geopolitics of the economy

The departure of Slovenia from Yugoslavia deeply affected the Slovene economy through the final loss of a market that had already contracted by the end of the 1980s. The Serbian authorities at that time called upon their citizens to boycott Slovenian products, due to disagreements with Slovenia over the handling of Kosovo's Albanian population. The war and general instability on the territory of the former Yugoslavia in the period 1991–99 hindered all forms of communication with former trade partners. Between 1995 and 1999 Slovenia signed trade agreements with the nation-states of Croatia, Macedonia and Bosnia and Hercegovina (again). But the dissolution of Yugoslavia also brought some economic advantages for Slovenia. In 1995 Slovenia joined a (partly) tax-free zone of the Višegrád states, establishing the Central European Free Trade Agreement (CEFTA). But matters in Slovenia were, at the beginning of national independence, hardly prosperous or flourishing. The inflation rate in Slovenia in June 1992 was 26.2 per cent, although it had declined to 18 per cent by 1996. Due to EU fiscal policies affecting states seeking Union membership, Slovenia's inflation had dropped to 8 per cent by 1999. In June 1991 the average monthly salary in Slovenia was $628, in 1995 $710 and in 1998 $805 (Statistical Office, 1999: 248). The opening of Slovenian markets to the West also had some negative effects on the Slovenian economy, particularly on unemployment rates, which rose until 1996 to reach about 23 per cent of the Slovenian workforce. By 1998 the unemployment rate was down to 7.7 per cent (Table 8.2) (Statistical Office, 1999: 234–235). Unemployment primarily affected the lesser-developed regions of the Slovenian north-east (Maribor) and the mono-structured industrial centres (mining, heavy metal production) of central Slovenia. In

1986 there were about 392,000 people working in different branches of industry. In 1991 this number sank to 321,000, and in 1996 to 252,000.

Table 8.2 Slovenia: major economic indicators, 1998

Economic activity	GNP (%)	Employment (%)[a]
Agriculture, forestry and fishing	5.0	1.8
Mining, industry and manufacturing	29.5	39.1
Construction	5.6	5.1
State related services	2.8	2.0
Transport and communication	7.5	5.1
Trade and tourism	15.4	12.2
Finances and other business services	16.5	6.6
Public administration and defence	5.5	7.2
Social and personal services	12.1	20.9

[a] Unemployment total: 126,625.

Source: *Statistical Office, 1999: 245–250*

Ljubljana and Koper-Capodistria: major gateway cities

The economies of Ljubljana (capital city) and Koper (major oceanic port) are based on their outstanding geostrategic positions (Table 8.3). They are located on both sides of the lowest crossing point of the Alps (Postojna Gate, 612 m), connecting the Mediterranean and the Danubian basins. Ljubljana is, in addition, on the intersection of railways and roads linking Germany (Munich) with south-eastern Europe (Athens, Istanbul). Koper-Capodistria has an excellent port facility, with rail and highway connections into the hinterland, thereby linking landlocked countries of central Europe with global maritime trade. One of the advantages of Koper-Capodistria (and other Northern Adriatic ports) is that the voyage to the Near and Far East usually takes a week less than from the European North Sea ports.

The administrative function of Ljubljana (350,000 inhabitants), as the capital of the new nation-state, attracted many official state (e.g. consular) and economic activities to the city. Ljubljana was never considered an industrial centre. In the 1970s, at the peak of the communist-planned economy, industry provided jobs for fewer than 50,000 people. Trade and finance are a traditional function of Ljubljana. A university town (42,000 students) since 1919, this is also an educational and cultural centre of the nation-state. In the 1990s tertiary activities increased at the expense of the secondary sector. The number of jobs in industry declined by almost a half, and the share of the active industrial population fell from 23.8 per cent to 19.2 per cent. The

Table 8.3 Slovenia: traffic on major road transport routes, 1988 and 1998

| Direction | Average annual number of vehicles[a] | | | | | |
| | All vehicles ('000s) | | Lorries (%) | | Foreign (%) | |
	1988	1998	1988	1998	1988	1998
Trieste/Koper–Ljubljana/Maribor–Budapest and v.v.	393	2 805	9.5	28.0	71.5	52.0
Zagreb–Ljubljana–Koper/Trieste and v.v.	3 460	4 807	18.2	25.4	47.4	20.2
Zagreb–Maribor–Vienna and v.v.	5 787	4 551	16.0	10.1	61.6	21.7
Ljubljana–Maribor–Vienna and v.v.	6 227	15 696	11.2	16.5	66.9	54.6
Ljubljana–Salzburg–Munich and v.v.	2 322	3 224	5.9	11.7	50.3	46.4

[a] Measurements at or close to border posts.

Source: *Ministry of Transport and Communications, 1999*

proportion of the population employed in other branches of the economy has increased: in transport from 4.7 per cent to 9.5 per cent, in trade from 13.8 per cent to 20.1 per cent, in financial, technical and business services from 8.2 per cent to 19.9 per cent. The number of companies in the tertiary sector increased threefold and the share of Ljubljana in the Slovenian average increased from 32 per cent to close to 48 per cent (Rebernik, 1999).

With the establishment of peace in Croatia in 1995 and the implementation of the Dayton Agreement in Bosnia and Hercegovina a year later, the situation has become more favourable to both Slovenian gateway towns. The road toward south-eastern Europe (Zagreb–Belgrade) has been reopened and both transalpine crossings (Austria–Ljubljana; Italy/Koper-Capodistria–Ljubljana) are regaining European priority. Koper-Capodistria is directly connected by rail and road with Hungary, the Czech Republic, Slovakia, Austria, southern Germany, northern Italy and Switzerland. Unfortunately neither the railway nor the road is suited to the needs. The majority of cargo (60–75 per cent) entering or leaving is transferred via rail on a single-track, steep ascent (up to 20 per cent). Current capacity of the section is 22 pairs of trains a day, which is not sufficient: port shipments in 1999 required at least 30 pairs of trains a day. The European Bank and Brussels have promised financial assistance for the construction of a second track by 2005. The geostrategic position of the port of Koper is diminished also by the fact that there is no direct railway connection between Slovenia and Hungary. Railway transports have to pass through Croatia (30 km), which raises the cost and thus diminishes the competitive position, especially in comparison with neighbouring ports. This obstacle should be overcome by the 25 km rail track under construction between Puconci-Hodoš (Slovenia) and Zalalovo (Hungary), which should be finished by the year 2002. Interestingly, this railway section, crossing the once Hungaro–Yugoslav border, was discontinued during the peak years of the Cold War (Jurinčič, 1996).

Disregarding the fact that only a smaller amount of cargo arriving at or leaving Koper port is transported by land (less than 30 per cent, mostly perishables), good road connections are important for any harbour. The 'Sun Belt' motorways are still under construction on the territory of Slovenia, although at 1994 conferences in Vienna and Crete European transport ministers confirmed priority for the Koper-Capodistria–Hungary/Austria highway route. The reason for the delay in construction can partly be explained by the increase in traffic on the Balkan axis in 1998–99. Consequently, the Slovenian government decided to begin construction of a 27 km link in the Ljubljana–Zagreb motorway. In 1995 Koper became the premier 'Austrian' port, as Austria imported or exported 35 per cent of its cargo coming or leaving by ship through Koper-Capodistria. Out of 8,337 tonnes of trans-shipment in 1999, just 34 per cent began or ended in Slovenia. Some 5,470 tonnes were exchanged in 1999 with countries of central Europe (Table 8.4). The ending of hostilities in the Balkans has also opened the Croatian port of Rijeka for Hungary, the Czech Republic and Slovakia.

People on the move

Italians and Hungarians live in the newly established nation-state of Slovenia as autochthonous minorities. These minorities, although very small, enjoy all the privileges of citizenship and special minority rights: bilingual schools, bilingual inscriptions on road signs and office buildings, and financial support for their cultural activities (Gosar, 1993). From a historical viewpoint, Germans are autochtonous peoples of Slovenia as well. Their disappearance after the Second World War and the dispersed distribution of just 750 members do not justify their claims for similar rights.

Table 8.4 Slovenia: the port of Koper – national trans-shipment of goods, 1980–1999

('000 tonnes)	Austria	Czech Republic	Slovakia	Hungary	Other	Total
1980	206	131	131	210	484	1 162
1990	1 557	266	266	529	317	2 936
1995	1 712	527	437	1 039	343	4 059
1999	1 951	372	234	619	2 294	5 471

Source: *Luka Koper, 2000*

Throughout most of the 20th century Slovenia was a country of emigration. The situation changed in the 1960s as the number of incoming migrants from other Yugoslav republics exceeded the number of Slovenes migrating abroad. Such migration trends were perhaps not in Slovenia's best interest, but were the consequence of increased job opportunities. Metal manufacturing (Jesenice) and coalmining (Velenje) towns are typical environments of south Slavic immigrant communities (Klemenčič, 1993). These processes of labour migration had a strong impact on the ethnic structure of Slovenia's population. Thus the proportion of Slovenes, which was 97 per cent in 1948, fell to 90.5 per cent in 1981 and to 87.8 per cent in 1991. Most immigrants were Croats, Serbs or Bosnian Muslims who came from ethnically mixed communities of Croatia and Bosnia and Hercegovina. In the 1981 and 1991 censuses there were also several thousand who, in accordance with Article 170 of the then Yugoslav constitution, declared themselves as 'Yugoslavs', identified themselves with the region, or did not state their nationality (Table 8.5).

Slovenia's first freely elected government passed a very liberal law on citizenship in 1991. According to this law, all immigrants who had permanent residence and employment in Slovenia for at least six months prior to independence could apply for Slovenian citizenship. As a result, in 1993 there were 169,500 inhabitants of Slovenia with dual citizenship: 78,000 citizens had their roots in Bosnia-Hercegovina, 61,000 in Croatia, 25,000 in Serbia (including Kosovo) and around 5,000 in Macedonia and Montenegro (Lanjšček, 1993). The passing of such a law proved

Table 8.5 Slovenia: ethnic structure, 1953–1991

Nationality	1953		1971		1991	
	No.	%	No.	%	No.	%
Slovene	1 415 448	96.50	1 624 029	94.10	1 727 018	87.80
Italian	854	0.06	3 001	0.17	3 064	0.16
Hungarian	11 019	0.75	9 785	0.57	8 503	0.43
Roma	1 663	0.12	977	0.06	2 293	0.12
German	1 617	0.11	422	0.02	546	0.03
Croat	17 978	1.23	42 657	2.47	54 212	2.76
Serb	11 225	0.77	20 521	1.19	47 911	2.44
Muslim	1 617	0.11	3 231	0.19	26 842	1.36
Albanian	169	0.01	1 281	0.07	3 629	0.18
Yugoslav	na	na	6 744	0.39	12 307	0.63
Other	4 835	0.33	14 489	0.84	79 661	4.05
Total	1 466 425	100.00	1 727 137	100.00	1 965 986	100.00

Source: *Statistical Office, 1999: 78*

to be a wise political move as it contributed to Slovenia's swift international recognition. During the wars in Croatia and Bosnia and Hercegovina many refugees lived in Slovenia legally and illegally; around 14,000 shelters were established for their use in abandoned Yugoslav army barracks. A similar number of non-Slovene citizens have become guests in homes of their relatives and friends. However, continued immigration pressures forced Slovenia to close its borders permanently to the citizens of the war-torn parts of the Balkans in 1994, to close several shelters in 1996 and repatriate migrants to their independent states. Around 7,000 remained, being housed in six refugee centres. The 1999 Kosovo NATO bombing campaign introduced Albanians, and later Serbs and Gypsies, to the refuge communities. During the 'Yugoslavia campaign' less than 5,000 refugees were officially registered, most of whom were sent back to Kosovo in September/October 1999.

Since gaining independence the constant problem of the Slovenian government has been the porous border with Hungary and Croatia. On average around 50 illegal immigrants are caught daily by the border police. Estimates are that at least a similar number of immigrants freely pass from Slovenian territory to find jobs in countries of the European Union, in particular in Austria and Italy. Peoples of Asian origin (Kurds, Vietnamese) and from states of eastern Europe (Ukraine) and south-eastern Europe (Romania, Yugoslavia) are most often on the move. In 2000 Slovenia introduced visa requirements for most of the above countries, thereby harmonising its own law with the Schengen laws of the European Union.

Slovenia and the European Union

Slovenia signed the first co-operation agreement with the European Union (EU) in 1993. Subsequently work started toward signing an accession contract. This had previously been vetoed by Italy over the question of liberalising the real estate market for ethnic Italian, former Yugoslav citizens. Based on a Spanish compromise in 1996 the accession contract was signed and the starting date of relationship preferences was set for 1 February 1999. Following its Luxembourg *Agenda 2000* decision regarding enlargement, in 1997 the EU invited Slovenia to join the first round of candidates in the relevant negotiations. Screening of the Slovenian laws began soon after, and in June 1999 18 out of 31 topics were reported as successfully co-ordinated (with the basic *acquis communautaire* regulations). At the dawn of the new millenium Slovenia is considered to be among the three best-suited candidates for accession. In accordance with the bilateral agreement, a free-trade agreement between the EU and Slovenia will come into effect in 2005.

Financial and know-how assistance of the EU is primarily oriented toward legislation (29 per cent), infrastructure (18 per cent) and regional development (12 per cent). PHARE funds are allocated to support these sectors of the economy and societal organisation. In particular, border regions with EU countries gain from this arrangement. PHARE funds contribute between $25 mn and $100 mn (in 1999: $31 mn) annually to the national budget, approximately one-fifth of the average support received by accession candidates. Slovenia is considered to be on a similar development path to some exisiting EU member states. *Eurostat*, the European Statistical Office Report 1999, acknowledges that the GNP of Slovenia ($12,169 per citizen) is just 1 per cent less than the Greek figure and 3 per cent less than that of Portugal. General development and accession efforts of the government are justified through the annual increase of the Slovenian GNP (currently $20 bn), which between 1993 and 1998 varied from 2.8 to 5.4 per cent (Deutsch-Slowenische Gesellschaft NRW, 1999). For countries participating in the 1999 Stability Pact for South-eastern Europe, Slovenia is ranked among donor countries and institutions. Trade with EU member nations is fairly well established (Table 8.6).

Table 8.6 Slovenia: trade partners and major products, 1999

Country	Exports		Imports		Products			
	Value ($ mn)	Growth rate (%)	Value ($ mn)	Growth rate (%)	Exports (in value) (%)		Imports (in value) (%)	
Germany	2 570	+4.5	2 086	+7.7	Cars and parts	14	Cars and parts	12
Italy	1 255	+0.5	1 696	+8.8	Pharmaceuticals	4	Petroleum	5
Croatia	815	−2.6	431	−7.5	Furniture	6	Electronics	5
France	747	+61.4	1 258	+28.3	Electronics	6	Pharmaceuticals	2
Austria	621	+9.9	801	+1.6	Textile products	4	Aluminium	1
Total (world) trade	9 049	+8.1	10 098	+7.8		100		100

Source: *Chamber of Commerce, 2000*

The Commission has reported favourably on the progress of Slovenia's efforts to join the EU (European Commission, 1999). However, while it acknowledged that Slovenia fulfils the Copenhagen political criteria and has to maintain macroeconomic stability, reforms in several areas of the economy (agriculture) and administration/legislation were seen as too slow and insufficient. Only partially have accession priorities been met in the areas of banking and finance, insurance, overall administrative and judicial capacity (land registration). Alignment in the areas of free movement of persons, capital and services is still due. Investment in the Slovenian economy is considered too low, and the measures to attract it not sufficiently stimulating. Improvement is needed in several infrastructure sectors. Continuing attention needs to be paid to border control, drug trafficking and improving the environment (European Commission, 1999). At the Krško nuclear power plant and in several conventional plants

(Trbovlje, Šoštanj) environmental measures are required to be taken. The relations between neighbouring states have to be ameliorated, in particular with Croatia (regarding the border disputes, in particular in the Pirano Bay; the pre-independence savings of Croatian citizens in Slovenian banks; the real estate reciprocity adjustment, etc.). This, and the unresolved matters with neighbouring Italy (the opening of the real estate market and mutual compensations, due to historical injustice) and Austria (regarding the (non-)autochthonous German minority (Old-Austrians) in Slovenia, and cross-border pollution problems), are considered to be bilateral problems to be solved on the basis of mutual co-operation and should not affect EU accession.

Conclusion

The recent Balkan wars have impacted on Slovenia through refugee immigration and the loss of the 20 million-strong former Yugoslav market, trade relations and tourism. The rupture of communications at several levels has changed the character of the economy and development policies, and has reoriented imports and exports. As the situation in the Balkan neighbourhood is resolved, Slovene companies will play an important role in restoring areas devastated by war. As a member of the Stability Pact for South-eastern Europe, the donor country Slovenia looks confidently towards the future. In the forefront of Slovenia's ambitions to play an important role in the region is the development of a trade–finance–research triangle, based on the gateway character of Koper-Capodistria, Ljubljana and Maribor.

References

Chamber of Commerce (and Industry of Slovenia), 2000, *Main economic indicators 1999*. Ljubljana: Chamber of Commerce.

Deutsch-Slowenische Gesellschaft NRW, 1999, *Slowenien in Europa*. Dortmund: Deutsch-Slowenische Gesellschaft NRW.

European Commission, 1999, *Regular report from the Commission on progress towards accession: Slovenia – October 13, 1999*. Brussels: European Commission. http://europe.eu.int/comm/enlargement/slovenia/rep_10_99/index.htm.

Gosar, A., 1993, Nationalities of Slovenia – changing ethnic structures in central Europe. *GeoJournal*, 30 (3), 218–223.

Jurinčič, A., 1996, Koper – maritime gateway to central Europe. *In* Gosar, A., ed., *Slovenia – a gateway to central Europe*. Ljubljana: The Association of the Geographical Societies of Slovenia, pp. 33–42.

Klemenčič, V., 1993, Jugoslawien – Zerfall und Bildung neuer Staaten. *In* Karl Ruppert, ed., *Europa: Neue Konturen eines Kontinents*. Munich: Oldenbourg, pp. 213–224.

Klemenčič, V., Genorio, R., 1993, The new state of Slovenia and its function within the frame of Europe. *GeoJournal*, 30 (3), 323–335.

Klemenčič, V., Gosar, A., 1994, The European integration viewed from the Slovenian perspective. *In*

Hajdu, Z., Horvath, G., eds, *European challenges and Hungarian responses in regional policy*. Pecs: Centre for Regional Studies, Hungarian Academy of Sciences, pp. 67–79.

Lanjšček M., 1993, Poslanci Državnega zbora za odpravo dvojnega državljanstva v Sloveniji. *Slovenec*, Ljubljana, 1 December, p. 1.

Luka Koper, 2000, *Letno poročilo 1999*. Koper-Capodistria: Luka Koper.

Ministry of Transport and Communications, 1999, *National roads in Slovenia*. Ljubljana: Ministry of Transport and Communications.

Nečak, D., 1993, A chronology: voices from the Slovenia nation. *Nationalities Papers*, 21 (1), 173–189.

Rebernik, D., 1999, Prebivalstveni razvoj Ljubljane po 1. *Geografski Vestnik*, 71, 41–60.

Rupel, D, 1992, Skrivnost države. *In Spomini na domače in zunanje zadeve 1989–1992*. Ljubljana: Cankarjeva založba, pp. 158–182.

Savezni zavod za statistiku SFRJ, 1990, *Statistički godišnjak 1989*. Beograd: Savezni zavod za statistiku SFRJ.

Statistical Office (of the Republic of Slovenia), 1999, *Letopis RS*. Ljubljana: Statistical Office.

Vodopivec, P., 1993, Slovenes in the Hapsburg Empire or Monarchy. *Nationalities Papers*, 21 (1), 159–172.

Vrišer, I., 1994, Einige wirtschaftsgeographische Überlengungen über die möglichen Beziehungen der Nachfolgestaaten Jugoslawiens zur Europäischen Gemeinschaft. *In* Wolff, H., ed., *Südosteuropa Aktuell 18: Südosteuropa und die europäische Integration*. Munich: Südosteurope Gesellschaft, pp. 65–85.

9

ESTONIA

Tim Unwin

Estonia is widely seen as being among the most successful of the countries of eastern Europe and the former Soviet Union in making the transition to a liberal democracy and a free market (Figure 9.1). However, much depends on the criteria by which such success is measured. As an editorial in *Business Central Europe* in June 1998 suggests, Estonia's 'success presents a powerful argument for liberal economics: by ruthlessly clearing away the past and liberalising markets it has become far wealthier than the other Baltic countries, and will almost certainly get into the EU before them' (Anon, 1998: 5). Kapoor (1998: 9) comments in a similar vein: 'By following the most radical free market course in the region, it has cleared out old Soviet industry, achieved soaring growth and become the only part of the former Soviet Union to be on the fast track to the EU.'

Such success, measured in purely economic terms, is indeed remarkable and reflects not only the relative strengths of Estonia's economy during the Soviet period, but also the energy and determination of the Estonian people. Not all Estonians, though, have benefited equally from this transformation. Also, the spatial implications of the macroeconomic policy instruments by which the transformation has been implemented have been largely ignored, as governments have sought to align Estonia's economy ever more closely with the requirements of accession to the European Union (Harter and Jaakson, 1997; Unwin, 1998; Valdes *et al.*, 1998). Moreover, even advocates of Estonia's success, such as Kapoor (1998), highlight the collapse of the republic's agriculture and point to the difficulties still facing the industrial sector.

This chapter explores the context against which Estonia has been able to achieve such success, but also notes the problems that closer integration with the EU has brought. It begins with a historical overview of Estonia's struggle for independent nationhood, and then traces the political and economic structures that have emerged since 1991. The conclusion explores some of the implications that Estonia's planned accession to the EU might have for the future.

Much of the literature on the transformations taking place in eastern Europe has been written from a positive perspective, unashamedly advocating the benefits of liberal democracy and

Figure 9.1: Estonia

applauding the ways in which governments have sought to move from the rhetoric of planning to that of the market (World Bank, 1996). As Smith and Pickles (1998: 2) suggest: 'Mainstream transition theory has, then, largely been written in terms of the discourses and practices of liberalisation.' However, since the mid-1990s and particularly following the economic crises in eastern Asia and Russia, there has been a growing recognition that the market mechanism may well not provide optimum solutions, and that so-called liberal democracy comes in many different guises, not all of which are as benign as some would suggest (Gowan, 1995; Held, 1995). Importantly, there has been enormous variation in the practice of transition, as governments across eastern Europe have sought to graft the principles of the free market and liberal democracy on to the vestiges of the command economy and communism. Moreover, as earlier chapters in this book have highlighted, the EU's expansion eastwards is far from innocent, and can be interpreted largely as a response to the interests of particular sections of western European society. Whilst achieving political stability in central and eastern Europe can be claimed as a desirable goal in its own right, the economic opportunities that 'Europe's new members' provide for their older partners in terms of cheap labour, an expanded market and low-cost raw materials are the key factors in driving forward ever-closer integration. As Habermas (1994) has stressed, it is crucial to understand and distinguish the differences between economic and political processes and interests. There is no guarantee that liberal democracy, in any of its forms, need accompany the emergence of a free market, nor that either of these should *necessarily* be in the interests of the majority of the population in any given state.

Historical context

For most of its history the land now within the boundaries of the Republic of Estonia (Figure 9.1) was ruled by outsiders: in the 13th century Danes; then Germans until the 16th century; Swedes from 1561 until the early 18th century; and finally Russians from the Great Northern War of 1700–21 until the end of the the First World War in Europe (Raun, 1991; Taagepera, 1993; Lieven, 1994). Throughout much of the latter part of this period Estonians served mainly as labour on the extensive estates of the German Baltic barons who formed the ruling class. As Kahk (1994: 11) has summarised, 'For over six hundred years, Estonian life as such was almost wholly the life of the countryside and village people.'

As elsewhere in Europe (Hooson, 1994) the 19th century witnessed the emergence of strong nationalist sentiments in Estonia. In part this reflected the long-established opposition between the peasantry and alien landlords. The link between the Estonian people and the land is crucial to understanding the subsequent history of Estonian national identity. However, the Estonian national awakening of the 1860s was also very much a middle-class affair, involving the creation of a standardised literary language, the publication of a national epic (*Kalevipoeg*), the establishment of a national theatrical society, and the holding of song festivals (Kurman, 1968; Loit, 1985; Taagepera, 1993; Unwin, 1999).

In the 1880s this efflorescence of Estonian identity was increasingly thwarted by a rising tide of Russification following the accession of Alexander III as tsar in 1881. This led not only to a shift of power away from the Baltic Germans to Russian administrators, but also to the use of Russian as the main language of education. Following the attempted revolution of 1905, though, the moves toward Estonian independence gradually quickened (Raun, 1984), and with the 1917 revolution in Russia and the end of the 1914–1918 war in Europe, a Salvation Committee declared Estonia independent on 24 February 1918. One of the first acts of the new constitutional assembly was to pass a radical land reform law in 1919, which led to the redistribution of over 2.3 million ha of land, mainly to the Estonian peasantry. By the 1930s, despite considerable land reclamation, around three-quarters of all farms in Estonia remained less than 20 ha in size, and this emphasis on independent small-scale farming provided a highly significant element in the emerging identity of what it meant to be Estonian (White, 1994). Whilst Estonia had been among the more industrialised parts of the Russian empire in the early

20th century – the Kreenholm textile mills at Narva, for example, being one of the largest in the world – it proved difficult to expand the republic's industrial base, in large part because the Soviet market remained closed. Estonia's economy, therefore, remained heavily reliant on agriculture, with butter and bacon providing the country's main exports, and Germany and Britain being the main markets.

The territorial advances and retreats of the Second World War initiated waves of Soviet and then German conquest of Estonia, each with its associated violence, terror and destruction. The final Soviet invasion of Estonia in September 1944 led to the incorporation of the republic into the Soviet Union, and involved considerable brutality and oppression, with many Estonians being either killed or deported (Laar, 1992; Abrahams and Kahk, 1994). The imposition of a command economy, with centralised decision-making from Moscow, gave rise to forced industrialisation and agricultural collectivisation policies. Oil-shale production and electricity generation expanded rapidly, and substantial numbers of Russian-speaking people migrated to the industrialising urban centres of the north coast of Estonia. In the agricultural sector just under 3,000 collective farms had been created by 1950, but subsequent reforms led to a diminution in their number, so that by 1960 there were only 648 collective farms and 154 state farms. By 1975 the former had been aggregated still further to only 188 in number, at which date there were also 166 state farms (Abrahams and Kahk, 1994; Unwin, 1994).

By the 1980s Estonia's industry was based mainly on light manufacturing and food production, each of which accounted for about one-quarter of industrial output in 1991 (Jõeste, 1993). Machine building and metalwork contributed approximately one-eighth of industrial output, with timber, wood processing, paper and cellulose accounting for a further 10 per cent. Oil-shale provided the basis of energy production as well as raw material for a chemical industry, which also exploited the republic's phosphorite deposits. In agriculture, there was considerable specialisation in livestock production, which depended heavily on imported fodder from other parts of the Soviet Union and which provided substantial meat and milk supplies for cities elsewhere in the Soviet Union (Table 9.1). During the last decade of Soviet rule, Estonia's foreign trade balance was characterised by large net imports, with some 95 per cent of Estonia's exports and between 80 and 85 per cent of its imports being from and to other Soviet republics (Jõeste, 1993).

The political framework of transition and European accession

The attempted restructuring of the Soviet Union under Gorbachev, with his twin pillars of *glasnost* and *perestroika* (Kaiser, 1994), provided the context within which Estonians proclaimed an increasingly separatist nationalism during the latter part of the 1980s (Taagepera, 1993; Lieven, 1994). This was built not only on memories among the elderly of the republic's former

Table 9.1 Estonia: selected economic indicators, 1980–1995

	1980	1985	1990	1995
Total population on 1 January	1 469 217	1 513 083	1 571 648	1 491 583
Urban population as % of total population	69.83	71.28	71.47	70.01
Physicians per 10,000 population	na	35.6	35.0	31.1
Employed labour force	na	na	826 400	663 200
Unemployed labour force	na	na	5 300	63 500
Inactive	na	na	270 500	334 900
Total sown area of field crops (ha)	1 087 600	1 077 600	1 116 300	850 700
Number of cattle	818 700	840 200	757 800	370 400
Number of poultry	6 842 700	6 911 500	6 536 500	2 911 300
Sawn timber manufacture (cu m)	637 000	668 000	500 000	348 900
Paper (tonnes)	93 100	90 300	77 300	5 900
Cotton fabric ('000 sq m)	178 438	197 846	169 153	90 346
Cement (tonnes)	1 213 000	1 094 000	938 000	417 600
Beer (hectolitres)	889 000	923 000	769 000	492 000
Production of oil-shale primary energy (terajoules)	296 441	250 542	209 596	122 370
Passenger cars	126 500	177 000	240 900	383 400

Sources: *Statistikaamet, 1994, 1997*

independence, but also on growing concern about the economic malaise affecting the everyday lives of Estonians as well as on increasing opposition to the environmental degradation caused by phosphorite exploitation. By the end of the decade formal political parties had resurfaced, and in November 1989 the supreme council of the Estonian SSR declared the 1940 resolution by which Estonian joined the USSR to be null and void. During 1990 Estonia moved ever closer to full independence, which was eventually achieved in August 1991 and recognised by the Soviet Union a month later. Whilst there was great diversity among the various political leaders of the independent republic, two central aspirations dominated most of their rhetoric, namely a free market and liberal democracy. The main legal instruments through which these were to be achieved were introduced in 1992: monetary reform and departure from the rouble zone; the approval of a new democratic constitution; and presidential and parliamentary elections (Unwin, 1998). One of the first major pieces of legislation introduced as early as October 1991, though, was the land reform law, which sought to return to former landowners or their heirs the land that they had held before the Soviet occupation. This had significant symbolic as well as economic ramifications, in that rather than forging a new landholding structure based on social and economic conditions prevailing elsewhere in Europe in the late 20th century, it looked back to a past period of Estonian national identity, where small independent farmsteads had been both the norm and the ideal.

A central political problem following independence was the need to establish a new constitution. According to the 1989 census there were people of some 121 different nationalities living in Estonia, and only 61.5 per cent of the population was Estonian. The remainder were mainly Russian speakers, who had settled or been born in the republic since 1945, most of whom lived in the urban industrial centres along the northern coast or were in the military. Whilst some of these people wished to leave Estonia, the majority chose to stay, having nowhere else to turn to and wanting to continue to benefit from the relative affluence of life in Estonia. While the 1992 constitution did indeed state that rights, duties and liberties of citizens of foreign states and stateless persons would be the same as for Estonian citizens, article 57 expressly stated that voting rights would belong only to Estonian citizens (Unwin, 1998). For those who were not citizens during the inter-war period and for their descendants, a period of residency, competence in the Estonian language and an oath of loyalty were required before Estonian citizenship could be obtained. Consequently, many of the Russian-speaking population, together with external human rights groups, complained vociferously about the particular character of Estonia's newly created 'ethnic democracy' (Smith, 1996). Concerns in the European Union and the Council of Europe over this situation eventually led to the passing of a new law on citizenship (January 1995), which was designed to make it easier for Russian speakers to become Estonian citizens should they so wish. This removed an important stumbling block to closer relations with the European Union. However, in July 1999 both Russia and the EU once again voiced criticism over Estonia; this time with respect to the 1998 language act, which requires elected municipal and parliamentary representatives to demonstrate competence in the Estonian language, and for Estonian to be the language of business.

The dominant forces in Estonian politics since independence have been parties or coalitions broadly interested in liberal reform, the creation of a free market and closer integration with the EU (Lauristin and Vihalemm, 1997). The victory of the Fatherland Party (*Isamaa*) in the first elections in 1992, campaigning on a platform of moderate nationalism, free-market economics and restitutionalism (Lieven, 1994), proved highly significant in shaping the future direction of the republic's economy. While the 1995 elections saw a slight shift away from such policies, with the coming to power of the Coalition Party and Rural Union (*Koonderakond ja Maarahva Ühendus*), these proved to be short-lived, and the collapse of the government in October of that year led to a new coalition agreement in which free-market economic principles, such as a balanced budget, a stable currency, privatisation and an open economy, were once again to the fore. The resignation of prime minister Tiit Vähi in February 1997 following a property scandal did little to change the political consensus, as the new prime minister, Mart Siimann, retained most of the previous cabinet. In the 1999 elections, although the Centre Party led by Edgar Savisaar had the highest share of the vote, Mart Laar once again returned as prime minister, this time of a government coalition between the Pro Patria, Moderates and Reform Party.

A central political aspiration of successive Estonian governments has been initially to gain recognition by, and then integration into, international bodies, particularly the Council of Europe, the North Atlantic Treaty Organization (NATO) and the European Union (Table 9.2). While Estonia joined NATO's Partnership for Peace programme in 1994, vehement opposition from Russia meant that it was not nominated as one of the first CEE states fully to join an expanded NATO. Progress with accession to the EU has, nevertheless, been much smoother, with a free-trade agreement being signed in July 1994 and an association agreement in 1995 (Berg, 1997). Indeed, as the quotations that opened this chapter indicate, Estonia is one of the furthest advanced countries of eastern Europe and the former Soviet Union in the progress that it is making toward joining the EU. While the agreement reached with the EU clearly begins by stating that it is intended to provide an appropriate framework for political dialogue between the two parties, the central tenor of the document is economic integration, and it is therefore to the economics of transition that the next section of this chapter now turns.

Table 9.2   Estonia: key dates in EU relations, 1991–1998

August 1991	Direct relations established between Estonia and the EU, following the latter's recognition of Estonian independence.
January 1992	Estonian ambassador accredited to the European Commission in Brussels.
14 May 1993	Estonia becomes a member of the Council of Europe.
February 1994	Estonia signs the Partnership for Peace programme framework document with NATO.
November 1994	Estonia becomes an associated partner with the Western European Union.
1 January 1995	Free trade agreement (signed 18 July 1994) between Estonia and the EU becomes fully operational.
12 June 1995	Estonia signs Association Agreement with the EU.
26 April 1996	Estonia receives the European Commission's *Opinion* (*avis*) designed to assess whether Estonia is ready for membership negotiations.
October 1997	Publication by Estonia of *Road to reform* outlining the republic's future plans for integration.
13 December 1997	European Council summit in Luxembourg agrees to begin EU accession negotiations with Estonia in April 1998.
1 February 1998	Estonia's Association Agreement with the EU comes into force.
31 March 1998	Formal beginning of Estonia's accession negotiations with the EU.

Source: *Derived from Foreign Ministry, Estonia, 1998a*

The economics of transition

Estonia's declaration of political independence shattered the extensive network of economic integration that had previously lain at the heart of the command economy (Bradshaw, 1997). Gone almost overnight were guaranteed markets for manufactured products and food produced in Estonia at prices that were globally uncompetitive. Likewise, subsidies on a range of goods from energy to animal feed were reduced or removed altogether, leaving Estonian farmers in particular claiming that they were the least supported of any in the whole of Europe. But Estonia faced very serious structural problems in the immediate aftermath of independence. With a population of only around 1.5 million, on a land surface of just over 45,000 sq km, and with limited physical resources other than timber and oil-shale, few options were really available to the government, whose position was in any case becoming increasingly constrained as European and North American agencies sought to ensure that it followed the stringent requirements of shock therapy (see, for example, Van Arkadie and Karlsson, 1992; Odling-Smee, 1992). Nevertheless, Estonia also had some advantages that set it aside from its neighbours. Prime among these were its well-educated labour force, the relatively high standard of living of its inhabitants, linguistic contacts with neighbouring Finland and close cultural links with Sweden.

Macroeconomic policy instruments

As in most other so-called transition economies, Estonia has sought to transform its command economy to that of a free market through the application of a limited number of key macroeconomic policy instruments (Lugus and Hachey, 1995). Four fundamental principles have thus underlain Estonia's economic restructuring: a stable currency, a balanced budget, liberal foreign trade (Eesti Pank, 1996) and privatisation.

Currency reform

Estonia was the first of the countries in the rouble zone to implement currency reform, introducing its new kroon in June 1992 at a fixed exchange rate of EEK 8 to 1 Deutschmark (Leimus, 1993; Kelder, 1997). Significantly, this rate has never been changed. As Siim Kallas and Mart Sõrg (1995: 52) have argued: 'The need to introduce its own currency resulted from the re-establishment of political independence in Estonia that had to be supported by economic sovereignty. But a groundwork of economic independence is an independent monetary system.'

For Estonia to make a successful transition to a market economy, it was essential that a stable currency be created as a medium of exchange and a unit of account. In order to meet the estimated $120 mn gold and foreign currency reserves necessary for currency reform, Estonia concluded agreements with Britain, Sweden and Switzerland for the return of the 11 tonnes of gold which it had abroad before it was occupied in 1940. Furthermore, the Estonian supreme council committed reserve areas of the state forest worth an estimated $150 mn to the Bank of

Estonia as an additional guarantee for foreign currency reserves. Some 4 million cubic metres of forest was thus made available for sale should it be necessary to support the Estonian kroon (Kallas and Sôrg, 1995). In effecting currency reform the government also introduced a foreign exchange law, which was designed to ensure that foreign currency could only be used in clearing accounts with foreign banks, and that all such banks had to have a licence from the Central Bank. In the immediate aftermath of currency reform, the Bank of Estonia fought hard to retain its independence from government control. Thus, although the Estonian parliament sought to combine the bank's budget with that of the state in December 1993 (Kallas and Sôrg, 1995), lobbying by the bank enabled this resolution to be cancelled. By building up sufficient gold and foreign currency reserves, the bank has been able to carry out effective monetary policies, which have provided a fundamental platform of stability for Estonia's economic development.

A balanced budget

Budgetary reform was also an essential element of Estonia's macroeconomic policy framework, and this involved the entire reorganisation of the state's revenue and expenditure arrangements as well as the separation of state and local budgets. Its key success has been in achieving a balanced budget, which in 1997 was set at EEK 12.5 bn and in 1998 at EEK 14.96 bn. Toward the end of Estonia's first period of independence, in the 1938–39 fiscal year, indirect taxation accounted for 49.5 per cent of state revenue, direct taxes for 11.5 per cent, customs duties for 7 per cent, and income from state property for 32 per cent (Tang and Nilgo, 1995). Under the Soviet regime the budget of the Estonian Soviet Socialist Republic was closely determined from Moscow, but in the late 1980s turnover tax provided more than 50 per cent of revenue, with taxes on the profits of state enterprises accounting for about 30 per cent. New budget and tax laws were introduced as early as 1989, although they were subsequently modified and revised. Whilst the main source of revenue was initially a value-added tax – which accounted for between 40 and 50 per cent of central government revenue in 1992 and 1993 – and enterprise income tax contributed a further 20–25 per cent, new social and medical insurance taxes to be paid by employers were also introduced to support the government's social fund. Initially both personal and enterprise taxes were progressive, but the relatively high top rates of taxation and the novelty of the system led to many arrears.

In June 1993 a new law on the state budget provided a clear framework for the structure of revenues and expenditure, as well as mechanisms for its implementation, and from January 1994 a single rate of 26 per cent was introduced for both personal and enterprise taxation. Currently, VAT is set at 18 per cent, and the social tax paid by employers is set at 33 per cent. A central element of budget reform has been a dramatic reduction in subsidies. By the mid-1990s some stability in budget structure had been achieved, and corporate income tax was due to be abolished from 2000.

A key problem that has proved difficult to resolve is the relative balance between local and state revenue-raising and expenditure. In 1992 local budgets received all of the personal income tax and 35 per cent of the enterprise income tax, as well as the natural resources tax and other local taxes, but this led to very great spatial inequalities in revenue (Tang and Nilgo, 1995). Consequently, new legislation in 1993 sought to reshape the balance between state and local budgets. This aimed to devise principles upon which money would be assigned from the state budget to municipal budgets, and through which subsidies could be granted to municipalities. Theoretically, these principles should have ensured that budget income per capita in local governments was equal, but many municipalities were nevertheless left with insufficient revenue, and debates still continue as to how best to solve this problem.

Liberal foreign trade

The third basic element of Estonia's macroeconomic transition policy was to implement a liberal foreign trade regime, designed to reduce the importance of trade with the former Soviet Union and to integrate Estonia more closely into the global economy (Table 9.3). In seeking to achieve this, the state has restricted its activity to the issuing of licences, quotas, a new customs regime and the development of trade agreements with foreign states. Immediately on independence, exports were temporarily limited by quotas and licences, but by 1992 price liberalisation, the ending of rationing and currency reform all enabled most such restrictions to be lifted. Thus, while 38 quota restrictions were in force at the beginning of 1992, only two, those on gravel and fire-clay, remained at the start of 1994 (Kala, 1995). Customs duties have been kept very low, and although these were planned to contribute 2 per cent of the state budget in 1993, their contribution had fallen to zero by 1996. Free-trade agreements were signed with Sweden to take effect from 1 July 1992, Norway from 1 September 1993, Switzerland from 2 March 1994, Lithuania and Latvia from 1 April 1994 and the European Union with effect from 1 January 1995 (Table 9.2). Substantial trade problems, expressed in part through high customs tariffs, nevertheless remain with Russia, and these will need to be resolved before Estonia can fully benefit from its policy of liberal trade arrangements. Structurally, there is a growing imbalance between exports and imports. Thus while exports accounted for 52 per cent of total foreign trade in 1992, they only accounted for 39.3 per cent in 1996 and 39.7 per cent in 1997. This meant that Estonia had a trade deficit of EEK 20.9 bn in 1997 (Purju, 1998). A substantial part of Estonia's exports consist of subcontracting and re-export from customs warehouses, and this applies particularly to the machinery and textiles sectors (which together accounted for 26 per cent of the state's exports in 1997) as well as to some processed foodstuffs. Machinery and equipment, again largely associated with reprocessing, accounted for 22 per cent of imports in 1997, followed by vehicles and transport equipment at 12.1 per cent and processed foodstuffs at 9.2 per cent. In an effort to resolve the growing trade imbalance, in October 1999 the government eventually approved an act to introduce import tariffs, which will permit duties to

Table 9.3 Estonia: major trading partners, 1996–1997

Country	Exports (%)		Country	Imports (%)	
	1996	1997		1996	1997
Russia	16.5	18.7	Finland	29.1	23.4
Finland	18.3	15.7	Russia	13.6	14.4
Sweden	11.6	13.5	Germany	10.0	10.1
Latvia	8.3	8.7	Sweden	8.2	9.1
Lithuania	5.7	6.1	USA	2.3	3.8
Germany	7.0	5.6	Japan	2.0	3.3
Ukraine	5.0	4.9	United Kingdom	3.3	3.1
United Kingdom	3.5	3.7	Italy	3.2	3.0

Source: *Derived from Purju, 1998*

be charged on goods imported from countries outside the EU apart from those with which there is a free-trade agreement.

Privatisation

The final dimension of macroeconomic transition has been privatisation. The earliest privatisations of state enterprises took place in 1991, but proceeded more rapidly after currency reform in 1992. Following the law on privatisation in June 1993, which laid out the details of four different types of privatisation, an increased number of privatisations took place by both international and domestic tender, leading to 54 contracts with a total value of EEK 353.2 mn being signed during that year. The next two years saw the peak of privatisation, with 215 contracts worth EEK 1,340 mn being signed in 1994, and 142 contracts worth EEK 919 mn being signed in 1995 (CCET, 1996a; Purju, 1998). Although privatisation of state enterprises in Estonia has generally been seen as a success, Kein and Tali (1995) note that it has not been without its problems. They thus identify six key issues that have hampered its progress: the slow process of restitution to former owners; the disincentives inherent in privatising leased property; the difficulty of selling leftovers when assets of a former enterprise were split for privatisation; the effects of deterioration and underinvestment during the pre-privatisation period; uncertainties with regard to the legal status of land; and difficulties in resolving basic questions concerning the relative balance between the interests of core investors and minority stakeholders. As well as state enterprises, the 34.3 million sq m of living space that existed in January 1992 has also been subject to privatisation, a process that has been both slow and complex. The main law on the privatisation of dwellings was passed in May 1993 (although it has subsequently been amended several times) and provided for tenants to have pre-emptive rights to buy their living space, but only until 1 December 1994 (Kein and Tali, 1995). Dwelling privatisation was meant to be carried out through the use of national capital vouchers, with one year's employment providing vouchers equivalent to the base price of one square metre of general floor space in a standard panel dwelling. Many problems have been encountered in this privatisation of housing, including the low quality of the buildings, the complexities of forming housing associations and the high costs of heating, and it is thus still an ongoing and incomplete process.

The sectoral influence of reform

The results of the above macroeconomic policy instruments have varied considerably, both sectorally and spatially. Whilst the urban, commercial and financial sectors have benefited considerably, many rural areas of the republic, far from the capital Tallinn, have suffered decline and relative deprivation (Harter and Jaakson, 1997). This section of the chapter addresses the fortunes of the financial, industrial and agricultural sectors of the economy since 1991, but first presents an overview of foreign direct investment in Estonia during this period.

Foreign direct investment (FDI)

The success of Estonia's macroeconomic policies has been directly reflected in the amount of FDI that the republic has attracted: for 1998 Estonia had the highest FDI per capita of all the transition countries – with $407 per person, compared, for example, with $132 for Poland. The implementation of a commercial code in September 1995, extended in July 1996, has brought Estonian commercial legislation fully into accord with that of the EU, and by the end of 1997 some EEK 16,456 mn from more than 100 countries had been invested in Estonia. The largest amounts have been from Finland (28.8 per cent) and Sweden (20.7 per cent), followed by the USA (5.8 per cent), Russia (5.7 per cent), Denmark (4.7 per cent), Norway (4.7 per cent) and Singapore (4.2 per cent). By mid-1997 most of this investment had gone into industry (37.8 per cent) or the wholesale and retail trade (22.9 per cent). Finance accounted for only 14.2 per cent of FDI, with transport, warehousing and communications accounting for 13.1 per cent; real estate and leasing made up a further 4.2 per cent. This left only 7.8 per cent accounted for by all other sectors of the economy (Purju, 1998; and unpublished statistics provided by the Estonian Investment Agency). Not only is such investment sector specific, it is also highly spatially selective (see for example Phare, 1998). Tallinn thus has 79 per cent of all companies with foreign investments in them, with a further 11 per cent being found in the surrounding county of Harju and 8 per cent in the county of Tartu, Estonia's second city. That leaves only 2 per cent of enterprises with foreign investments located in Estonia's other counties. Initially, most FDI was from neighbouring Nordic and Baltic countries, but one of Estonia's great advantages for foreign investors is its tariff-free access to the European customs area, while at the same time providing cheaper labour, raw material and operating costs. This has now begun to attract investors from further afield, such as the USA. One of Estonia's major overseas investors is the Singapore-based Tolaram Group, which has acquired both a textile mill and a pulp and paper plant. After substantial investment, Baltex 2000 is now a modern producer and exporter of yarn and fabric, while Horizon Pulp and Paper produces kraft paper and sacks for the Asian, Scandinavian and western European markets. The Tolaram Group has also invested in 300,000 sq ft of real estate in Tallinn, and from here it is making forays into other Baltic countries, with, for example, the purchase in 1997 of the Latvian fibre enterprise formerly known as Dauteks.

The financial sector

In the immediate aftermath of independence and currency reform, a plethora of new banks emerged in Estonia. By the end of 1992 there were thus some 42 different banks in operation, but with the Central Bank specifically allowing the weakest of these to fail, their number had halved by the end of 1993. In 1994 electronic banking services and bank cards were introduced, and several banks also established subsidiary leasing companies. Later that year the first banking licences were issued to foreign banks, and Hansapank became the first Estonian bank to have a share issue floated on the international market. By September 1997 there were 12 Estonian commercial banks and one Finnish bank licensed to undertake full banking operations in the country (EIA, 1998).

The most serious threat to Estonia's financial sector came in late 1997 and early 1998. A stock exchange had been established in Tallinn in May 1996, and the rapid expansion of the economy in the mid-1990s, with GDP growth rates rising from -2.7 per cent in 1994 to +2.9 per cent in 1995, +4.0 per cent in 1996 and +9.0 per cent in 1997, caused considerable over-optimism, particularly among many of the younger, inexperienced Estonian bankers. Consequently, the stock market crash of September–October 1997 led to serious difficulties, particularly for those banks with high stock assets. From a high of almost 500 points in late August 1997, Tallinn's TALSE index a year later was hovering around the 100-point mark. The key bank to suffer initially from the crash was the Maapank, in which many small rural investors had their savings. With a very large stock portfolio, the bank ceased operations in June 1998 and the government had to intervene to compensate investors for their losses, the money required being taken from the state budget. Soon afterwards the government approved two important bank mergers: the first between Hansapank and Hoiupank, to create the largest bank in the Baltics with assets of EEK 24.1 bn; the second between Ühispank and Tallinna Pank, creating an institution with assets of more than EEK 16 bn. By the first half of 1999 this restructuring appeared to have revitalised the banking sector, with the profits of Estonia's three largest banks, accounting for around 90 per cent of the sector, totalling some EEK 99 mn.

These mergers indicate the future direction in which Estonian banking is likely to develop: seeking increasingly to develop an international profile, and with it fewer large banks dominating the market. It also seems likely that the largest Estonian banks will in turn be taken over by even bigger international banks, interested in gaining a foothold in Estonia and the wider Baltic region. The first signs of this process happening occurred in November 1998 when the Swedish Swedbank gained a 60 per cent stake in Hansapank and Skandinaviska Enskilda Banken (SEB) announced its intention to take a 32 per cent stake in Ühispank. This followed increasing financial difficulties for Estonian banks throughout the autumn of 1998, exemplified in early October by the Central Bank beginning bankruptcy proceedings against Estonia's sixth largest bank, the EVEA bank, and the securities administration halting the trading of eight investment funds because the net value of their funds had fallen below the minimum requirement of EEK 5 mn.

Industrial restructuring

Table 9.1 provides some broad indicators of the dramatic restructuring that has taken place in Estonian industry (see also Kilvits, 1995). At a very general level, total industrial production at constant prices declined to a low of 50.8 per cent of its 1991 level in 1994, but then began to rise to 51.8 per cent in 1995 (Statistikaamet, 1997). Subsequently, industrial output rose 1.1 per cent in 1996, and then by a remarkable 13.0 per cent in 1997 (Purju, 1998). This trend, however, has not been sustained, and Estonia's industrial output fell by 11 per cent in the first quarter of 1999. In 1995 manufacturing of food products, beverages and tobacco products contributed 28.9 per cent of industrial production, energy 13.5 per cent, chemicals and chemical products 8.1 per cent, wood manufacture 6.7 per cent and textiles 5.9 per cent. This industrial restructuring has been associated with a considerable increase in unemployment, with employment in manufacturing, for example, falling from 214,900 in 1989 to 143,200 in 1994 (Statistikaamet, 1997) and then to 86,600 by the end of 1997 (Purju, 1998). Whilst this has had considerable social effects (see, for example, Statistikaamet, 1998), looked at more positively, it also indicates an appreciable increase in labour productivity.

The maintenance of a stable energy sector was crucial to Estonian industrial development during the 1990s. Whilst the Estonian electricity system is integrated with those of Latvia and Lithuania, Estonia is unique in the contribution of oil-shale to its energy production (Laur and Tenno, 1997). In 1990 oil-shale thus contributed 94 per cent of Estonia's total primary energy production, and although the contribution of firewood and peat has increased over the last decade, some 86 per cent of all Estonia's primary energy is still produced from oil-shale (Statistikaamet, 1997). A key issue in the energy sector has been the reconstruction of the district heating systems throughout the country, but particularly in the major towns, and the World Bank as well as the Swedish Development Corporation (SIDA) and the European Bank for Reconstruction and Development (EBRD) are contributing significantly to these projects. World Bank funding is also being used to implement an ambitious energy conservation programme, but it is a very major task to reconstruct in a more energy efficient manner the housing stock that was initially built during the Soviet period.

Food processing remains the dominant manufacturing sector, with more than 50 per cent of total sales volume being accounted for by milk and fish processing alone. However, textiles, clothing, leather and footwear are all increasing in production, following their nadir in the mid-1990s (Purju, 1998). New investments in forestry and paper production, such as those by the Tolaram Group (noted above), are also beginning to have an impact following dramatic declines in the early 1990s (see Table 9.1). While there is therefore a visible turnround in industrial production, it remains very fragile. In the third quarter of 1997 the largest 669 enterprises only employed 97,000 people, at an average of 145 employees per enterprise (Purju, 1998), and many of these companies are simply subcontracting work for larger foreign companies interested primarily in Estonia's cheap labour and raw materials. There is relatively little indigenous funding of research and development activities in Estonia, and the official ministry of economic affairs' annual report for 1997–98 readily acknowledges this, commenting that: 'Estonia lags behind the EU as well as most of the Central and East European countries in the financial volume of R & D' (Purju, 1998: 64).

It is crucial for the future development of Estonian industry that indigenous companies shift away from providing cheap exports, and instead invest in basic manufacturing that will produce additional value for the Estonian economy. During the 1990s Estonia's cheap labour force made it a desirable location for foreign investment, but as wage rates increase this competitive advantage will rapidly disappear. Instead of simply exporting timber, for example, Estonian companies need to invest in modern mills that will enable them, rather than their Scandinavian competitors, to benefit from the greater profits to be made from selling processed products such as paper or furniture. Despite these problems, though, managers of small- and medium-sized enterprises in Estonia remain generally optimistic about the future, particularly in the wood processing, tourism, food processing and trade sectors (EIM, 1997; Venesaar and Smallbone, 1997; Phare, 1998).

Agriculture

Estonian agriculture has suffered even more dramatically from 'transition' than the industrial sector (Unwin, 1994, 1997). Table 9.1 illustrates the very large decline in both livestock numbers and the sown area of field crops that occurred between 1990 and 1995. Whilst there is some evidence that the downward plunge of production has ceased, and that output in 1997 was slightly higher than that of 1996 (Purju, 1998; see also Telliskivi, 1998), the situation for the majority of Estonia's farmers remains bleak. Driven by its free-market ideology, and determined to ensure that Estonia would be among the first countries of eastern Europe to join the EU, the Estonian government initially cut all agricultural subsidies in the early 1990s. This had catastrophic effects, and meant that subsidised EU agricultural produce could flood the Estonian market at prices far below those that would even cover the costs of production in Estonia. Witnessing the collapse of the agricultural sector by the middle of the decade, the government relented somewhat on its harsh policies, but even in 1996 the rate of agricultural subsidies in terms of producer subsidy equivalents (PSE) was only 7 per cent, compared with an average PSE in OECD countries of 36 per cent (Purju, 1998).

Two structural processes have been central to the reorganisation of Estonian agriculture: land reform and farm reform (Unwin, 1997; Alanen, 1999). As noted above, one of the first pieces of legislation following independence was the implementation of a land reform policy in 1991, designed to return land to those who owned it prior to the 1939–1945 war. There was initially enormous optimism among those seeking to develop farms on their family land, with some estimates suggesting that there would be as many as 60,000 private farms by the year 2000 (Danish Agricultural Advisory Centre, 1992). Despite the existence of accurate land registers dating from the 1930s, the process of land privatisation has been painfully slow, and by 1997 there were only some 22,722 private farms and 854 agricultural enterprises (limited liability companies, joint stock companies or state farms) in existence (Purju, 1998). In large part this reflects the disillusionment of people in rural areas and their lack of optimism concerning the future viability of agriculture. In contrast to the centralisation of land reform, the restructuring of the 150 collective farms and 152 state farms that existed in 1985 (Unwin, 1994; Alanen, 1999) was left to local negotiation. By 1996 only some 28 per cent of former collective farms had fully completed their reform, and even by 1998 around 10 per cent of collectives had yet to finalise their restructuring (Purju, 1998). This delay in effecting comprehensive farm reform has meant that almost a decade has passed in uncertainty and ambiguity, and this, alongside the lack of farming subsidies, goes a long way to explaining the collapse of the agricultural sector.

Before independence Estonia's agriculture was essentially geared to providing meat and dairy produce for the urban centres of the Soviet Union; wheat for human consumption was imported. With the collapse of the Russian market, and the aspiration to provide a wider diversity of production for domestic consumption, there has been a considerable reorientation of agricultural production toward wheat, fodder and legumes (CCET, 1996b). According to Purju (1998), domestic production thus now accounts for 60 per cent of the demand for wheat for human consumption, and 75 per cent of that for rye. Meat production, however, also only accounts for about 60 per cent of domestic consumption, and there is therefore still a need for Estonia to import a considerable amount of its food requirements. Rural unemployment is high, with the share of the labour force in agriculture, hunting and forestry falling from 18 per cent in 1989 to 11.1 per cent in 1995 (Statistikaamet, 1997).

The social and spatial implications of reform

The benefits of 'transition' in Estonia have not been equally distributed, either socially or spatially. This is not merely a matter of the differences between urban and rural life, but it lies deep in the nature of the 'transition' process. Almost all economic indicators illustrate that the majority of the benefits of transition have been concentrated in Tallinn and the surrounding county of Harjumaa, where some 90 per cent of foreign investment has been made. 'Transition' has benefited the young, the better educated and the affluent, to the detriment of the poor and the elderly. Differences in where these contrasting groups of people live mean that regional inequalities have also increased considerably since independence. To take but one indicator: pensioners account for only between 22.3 per cent and 24 per cent of the population in Harjumaa, Raplamaa and Järvamaa, whereas they comprise over 28 per cent of the population in the southern counties of Võrumaa, Põlvemaa, Valgamaa and Viljandimaa. As the Ministry of Internal Affairs (1998) notes, one of the main characteristics of Estonia's development in the 1990s was a dramatic widening in centre–periphery differences in economic growth, incomes and unemployment.

One key indicator of increasing social inequality has been the rise in the prevalence rates of diseases, particularly those related to conditions of poverty. The incidence rate of active tuberculosis has thus increased from 21 per 100,000 in 1990 to 40.4 per 100,000 in 1996, and the rates of diseases of the circulatory system as well as mental and behavioural disorders have also more than doubled between 1991 and 1996 (Statistikaamet, 1997). Another indicator of social change is that the crude birth-rate has plummeted from 16.16 in 1987 to only 9.05 in 1996, giving rise to a negative natural increase in population every year since independence. While a tourist, or visiting foreign 'expert', in central Tallinn would thus see enormous 'positive' changes over the last decade – great improvements in the standard of living of many people, a complete transformation of the retailing system, the construction of impressive new buildings, and flourishing hotels, restaurants and bars – a short bus journey to some of the peripheral housing blocks or the port area around Kopli, let alone a longer journey to rural areas far from the capital, would indicate that all is not well with Estonia's economic transformation. Much of Tallinn's apparent progress has also been based on a boom in consumer credit, with banks lending nearly twice as much money in 1997 as they did in 1996. Even the gloss of success is therefore extremely fragile, and were foreign employers to reduce their presence in Estonia, or banks to cut back on their lending, the veneer of vitality would rapidly crack.

As a result of these growing regional and social inequalities, the government has sought to implement a regional development strategy, with an Advisory Council of Regional Policy being established in 1995 and the Estonian Regional Development Agency being formed in 1997. However, given the very limited financial resources of local governments, and the small size of the budget available to the Regional Development Agency, there has as yet been very little

147

evidence of a reduction in regional inequalities. Indeed, the main principles of Estonia's national regional policy – including the fostering of 'local self-reliance rather than reliance on redistribution of resources by the central government', 'avoiding permanent subsidies', 'requiring local initiatives', and an emphasis on the use of sectoral policies to influence regional development (Ministry of Internal Affairs, 1998: 8) – seem unlikely to benefit the people and places most in need of assistance.

The implications of accession

Estonia's economic, political and social restructuring during the 1990s has been fundamentally tied to successive governments' aspirations to join the EU. Indeed, this has been the driving force behind many of the harshest economic policies which have been specifically designed to put Estonia on the fast track to EC accession. Despite the adverse social and spatial implications of such policies, there still seems to be widespread support within the republic for accession (Berg, 1997; Lauristin and Vihalemm, 1997; Raudjärv, 1998). In large part, such support appears to be dominated by the belief that accession will enhance Estonia's national security and the stability of society (Liuhto, 1996), while also providing a wider market for Estonian produce. This was clearly reflected in a speech by President Meri at the French Institute of Foreign Relations in February 1997, when he stated:

> Once the European Union has set the applicants for membership a definite threshold, it is in the interest of Estonia like any other European country to meet those criteria in all respects. We do not need concessions, which would dilute the essence of the Union and make it similar to many impotent world organisations. Estonia, even though she has a taste of blood in her mouth, already meets a lot of legislative and economic requirements set by the European Union. According to an EBRD assessment Estonia is one of the fastest and most successful reformers among the post-communist states ... And it is not only economic criteria I am talking about. In the year 1997 we can again enjoy a sweet privilege in Estonia that we were deprived of for such a long time: we live in an open society where there is constitutionally guaranteed freedom, where the military are strictly under civilian control and where a viable non-governmental sector prospers. Democracy functions in Estonia.

(European Commission, 1997: 8)

The most important date so far in Estonia's progress toward accession was 12 June 1995 when the association agreement was signed, bringing Estonia into a qualitatively different relationship with the EU (see Table 9.2). From that date, co-operation was begun in almost all spheres of life (Berg, 1997), and the agreement was unprecedented in that it included no transition period. This was in marked contrast to its neighbours, Latvia and Lithuania, which sought a more gradual approach to accession. In order to facilitate integration with the EU, the government has established four interrelated groups: the Commission of Ministers, the Council of Civil Servants, Expert Groups in each ministry, and an Office for European Integration (Foreign Ministry, Estonia, 1998a).

In July 1997 the European Commission published its detailed *Opinion* on Estonia's application for membership (1997), and this highlighted the strides that had already been made to satisfy the three conditions of membership: the stability of institutions guaranteeing democracy; the existence of a functioning market economy; and the ability to take on the obligations of membership, including political, economic and monetary union. The Commission thus commented:

> *Estonia can be regarded as a functioning market economy. The good macroeconomic performance observed over the past few years is the result of rapid progress in economic liberalisation and privatisation. A new and rigorous policy framework has been enshrined in law, and any loopholes tend to be closed off rather quickly. The currency board system and the generally prudent stance on fiscal policy have helped to maintain internal equilibrium and to attract large capital inflows.*

> (European Commission, 1997: 33)

It went on to note:

> *Estonia should be able to make the progress necessary to cope with competitive pressures and market forces within the Union in the medium term, provided in particular that the export base is broadened. The setting of a low exchange rate and low unit labour costs have facilitated the switch to light manufacturing industry as a source of foreign reserves. The banking sector is healthy and expanding strongly. Estonia has been a major recipient of foreign direct investment, although the inflow has decreased recently. However, the export base is rather narrow, and the need to finance the rising trade and current account deficits is a matter of concern.*

> (European Commission, 1997: 39)

With hindsight, this seems to have been an over-optimistic picture of the Estonian economy, particularly given the stock market crash and the difficulties facing the banking sector in 1998. Moreover, throughout the Commission's opinion there is remarkably little acknowledgement of any of the problems and contradictions involved in accession. As with the other countries seeking to join the EU, accession is very much on the EU's terms, with Estonia being given very little say in the negotiations. This is especially so in the agricultural sector where the language of the EU's recommendations makes clear that Estonia *must* satisfy certain requirements before accession:

Substantial efforts must be made to ensure the alignment of Estonian legislation with EU requirements. With regard to veterinary and phytosanitary requirements, special attention must be paid to the upgrading of establishments and the inspection and control arrangements for protecting the EU's external borders. Administrative structures must be strengthened to ensure the implementation and enforcement of the policy instruments of the CAP including import arrangements. The agri-food sector must be further restructured to ensure its competitive capacity.

(European Commission, 1998a)

Furthermore, there is a very real tension in the agricultural sector, because of the conflicts within the EU itself over exactly what rural strategy should be adopted in the future (although for a more positive view from the World Bank, see Valdes *et al.*, 1998). While the Commission insists that applicants approximate their legislation to that of the EU, at the same time it recognises that the Common Agricultural Policy (CAP) has had a number of negative effects in the past, including the distribution of support to areas which are not among the most disadvantaged, and that it has in some places actually led to rural decline rather than enhance the quality of rural life (European Commission, 1998b). The real problem, though, is that some member countries of the EU, particularly France and Germany, are very reluctant to see the Commission's *Agenda 2000* proposals accepted, and are therefore stridently fighting them. Consequently, countries such as Estonia, which are eager to enter the EU, are having to implement agricultural policies that the Commission itself knows are flawed.

By September 1998 Estonia was nevertheless able to present its position papers on the 12 chapters of the *acquis* that had already been screened, and only in the three areas of company law, fisheries and statistics was the government seeking to negotiate further or to apply for a short transition period (Foreign Ministry, Estonia, 1998b). It does, therefore, appear that Estonia is continuing to make good progress toward accession. Given the high stakes for which Estonian governments have decided to play – choosing to focus exclusively on rapid privatisation, minimum government intervention, the freest of free markets and strict financial regulation – the risks, though, are also high. The stock market crash of 1997–98 and the shaking out of the banking sector might be seen as reflecting the beginnings of the unravelling of Estonia's economic success story, but they can also be interpreted as a much-needed step on the way to growing economic maturity. All European countries have faced difficulties in the late 1990s with the downturn in the south-east Asian, Japanese and Russian economies, and Estonia is no exception. However, the confidence placed in the banking sector by SEB and Swedbank indicates that they at least envisage Estonia pulling through this difficult period.

Conclusions

Accession to the EU is very much on the EU's terms, and these have to date primarily served the interests of the rich and powerful. The EU is above all a body designed to promote the capitalist relations of production that underlie the neo-liberal agendas of the free market. Despite policies such as the social agreement appended to the Treaty on European Union (Williams, 1998), the EU has done little really to prevent increasing social and spatial inequality within its borders. Moreover, its policies are specifically designed to benefit its members and to enhance their competitive advantage over external countries. Consequently, there is a fundamental tension facing states such as Estonia that are eager to join. For the last decade companies within the EU have overtly exploited Estonia's low labour rates, cheap raw materials, and opening markets. Yet, at the same time, Estonia has had to merge its economic and political structures ever closer to those of the EU, thus contributing even further to such exploitation. The government and people still believe that the resultant social and spatial inequalities that have emerged in Estonia have been worth this sacrifice. Indeed, it is difficult to see what alternative options there were, given that the whole emphasis of political and economic change in Europe during the 1990s has been on ever closer integration; it would have been very hard to have swum successfully against such a tide.

The future for a country as small as Estonia must, therefore, lie within the context of its relations with the EU. Unless there are very dramatic changes in EU policy, it seems inevitable that further social and spatial inequalities will emerge both within Estonia itself, and between Estonia and the present members of the EU. While moving toward ever closer integration with the EU, Estonian governments also need to identify ways of enhancing the republic's basic productive economy, in both the agricultural and the manufacturing sectors. At the same time, a greater share of government revenue needs to be invested in sound regional development policies, in order to bring the benefits of accession and economic restructuring to people living in all parts of the country.

Acknowledgements

The research upon which this chapter is based has been generously funded by The British Academy and the Estonian Academy of Sciences for which I am most thankful. I am also very grateful to my many colleagues in Estonia for their advice and hospitality, and particularly to Anton Laur and Reet Karukäpp.

References

Abrahams, R., Kahk, J., 1994, *Barons and farmers: continuity and transformation in rural Estonia (1816–1994)*. Göteborg: Faculty of Arts Europaprogrammet, University of Göteborg.

Alanen, I., 1999, Agricultural policy and the struggle over the destiny of collective farms in Estonia. *Sociologia Ruralis*, 39 (3), 431–458.

Anon, 1998, Editorial. *Business Central Europe*, 6 (52), 5.

Berg, B., ed., 1997, *Estonian economy and European integration*. Helsinki: ETLA, The Research Institute of the Finnish Economy.

Bradshaw, M., ed., 1997, *Geography and transition in the post-Soviet republics*. Chichester/New York: John Wiley and Sons.

CCET, 1996a, *Investment guide for Estonia*. Paris: OECD.

CCET, 1996b, *Review of agricultural policies: Estonia*. Paris: OECD.

Danish Agricultural Advisory Centre, 1992, *The National Advisory and Training Centre in Jäneda, Estonia*. Skejby: Danish Agricultural Advisory Centre.

Eesti Pank, 1996, *Eesti Pank bulletin*, 2. Tallinn: Eesti Pank.

EIA, 1998, *Invest in Estonia fact sheets*. Tallinn: EIA.

EIM, 1997, *Small and medium-sized enterprises in Estonia: a survey amongst 1500 SME-entrepreneurs*. Zoetermeer: EIM Small Business Research and Consultancy.

European Commission, 1997, *Agenda 2000 – Commission opinion on Estonia's application for membership of the European Union*. Brussels: European Commission (DOC 97/12 15 July).

European Commission, 1998a, *Enlarging the European Union. Accession Partnership – Estonia*. Brussels: European Commission. http://europa.eu.int/comm/dg1a/enlarge/access-partnership/estonia-ap.htm.

European Commission, 1998b, *Agenda 2000 Commission proposals*. Brussels: European Commission. http://europa.eu.int/en/comm/dg06/ag2000/agprop/mot-en.htm.

Foreign Ministry, Estonia, 1998a, *Estonia and the European Union*. Tallinn: Foreign Ministry. http://www.vm.ee/eng/policy/eu/estoeu.html.

Foreign Ministry, Estonia, 1998b, *Estonia's position papers on twelve chapters of the EU acquis*. Tallinn: Foreign Ministry. http://www.vm.ee/eng/policy/eu/0909pos.htm.

Gowan, P., 1995, Neo-liberal theory and practice for eastern Europe. *New Left Review*, 213, 3–60.

Habermas, J., 1994, Europe's second change. *In* Pensky, M., ed., *The past as future: Jürgen Habermas interviewed by Michael Haller*. Cambridge: Polity Press, pp. 73–98.

Harter, M., Jaakson, R., 1997, Economic success in Estonia: the centre versus periphery pattern of regional inequality. *Communist Economies and Economic Transformation*, 9 (4), 469–490.

Held, D., 1995, *Democracy and global order*. Cambridge: Polity Press.

Hooson, D., ed., 1994, *Geography and national identity*. Oxford: Blackwell.

Jõeste, M., ed., 1993, *Estonia: a reference book*. Tallinn: Estonia Encyclopedia Publishers.

Kahk, J., 1994, Historical roots. *In* Abrahams, R., Kahk, J., *Barons and farmers: continuity and transformation in rural Estonia (1816–1994)*. Göteborg: Faculty of Arts Europaprogrammet, University of Göteborg, pp. 9–49.

Kaiser, R., 1994, *The geography of nationalism in Russia and the USSR*. Princeton: Princeton University Press.

Kala, A., 1995, Foreign trade. *In* Lugus, O., Hachey, G. A., eds, *Transforming the Estonian economy*. Tallinn: International Centre for Economic Growth, pp. 280–308.

Kallas, S., Sôrg, M., 1995, Currency reform. *In* Lugus, O., Hachey, G. A., eds, *Transforming the Estonian economy*. Tallinn: International Centre for Economic Growth, pp. 52–70.

Kapoor, M., 1998, The flawed miracle. *Business Central Europe.* 6 (52), 9–11.

Kein, A., Tali, V., 1995, The process of ownership reform and privatization. *In* Lugus, O., Hachey, G. A., eds, *Transforming the Estonian economy*. Tallinn: International Centre for Economic Growth, pp. 140–168.

Kelder, J., ed., 1997, *Eesti rahareform 1992*. Tartu: Postimees.

Kilvits, K., 1995, *Industrial restructuring in Estonia*. Tallinn: Institute of Economics, Estonian Academy of Sciences.

Kurman, G., 1968, *The development of written Estonian*. The Hague: Mouton.

Laar, M., 1992, *War in the woods: Estonia's struggle for survival 1944–56*. Washington: Compass Press.

Laur, A., Tenno, K., 1997, Development strategy of the oil-shale energetics. *In* Ruhr-Universität, ed., *Probleme und Strategien der Umstrukturierung von Industrieregionen – Mit Blick auf Isa-Viru in Estland*. Bochum: Institut für Berg- und Energierecht der Ruhr-Universität, pp. 195–207.

Lauristin, M., Vihalemm, P., eds, 1997, *Return to the western world: cultural and political perspectives on the Estonian post-communist transition*. Tartu: Tartu University Press.

Leimus, I., 1993, *Eesti Vabariigi rahad 1918–1992*. Tallinn: Olion.

Lieven, A., 1994, *The Baltic revolution: Estonia, Latvia, Lithuania and the path to independence*. New Haven/London: Yale University Press.

Liuhto, K., 1996, *Estonian enterprise managers' opinions on the impact of the European Union on Estonia*. Turku: Turku School of Economics and Business Administration.

Loit, A., ed., 1985, *National movements in the Baltic countries during the 19th century*. Stockholm: University of Stockholm Centre for Baltic Studies.

Lugus, O., Hachey, G. A., eds, 1995, *Transforming the Estonian economy*. Tallinn: International Centre for Economic Growth.

Ministry of Internal Affairs, 1998, *Regional policy in Estonia*. Tallinn: Ministry of Internal Affairs and Estonian Regional Development Agency.

Odling-Smee, J., ed., 1992, *Economic review: Estonia*. Washington: International Monetary Fund.

Phare, 1998, *The Phare Estonia regional development project survey of regional investment climate report July 9, 1998*. Tallinn: Phare.

Purju, A., 1998, *Estonian economy 1997–1998*. Tallinn: Ministry of Economic Affairs.

Raudjärv, M., ed., 1998, *Eesti Vabariigi integreerumine Euroopa liiduga – majanduspoliitika eesmärgid ja abinõud*. Tallinn: Mattimar OÜ, Tallinna Tehnikaülikool, Tartu Ülikool.

Raun, T., 1984, The Estonians and the Russian empire, 1905–1917. *Journal of Baltic Studies*, 15 (2), 130–140.

Raun, T. O., 1991, *Estonia and the Estonians*. Stanford: Hoover Institution.

Smith, A., Pickles, J., 1998, Introduction: theorising transition and the political economy of transformation. *In* Pickles, J., Smith, A., eds, *Theorising transition: the political economy of post-communist transformations*. London/New York: Routledge, pp. 1–22.

Smith, G., 1996, When nations challenge and nations rule: Estonia and Latvia as ethnic democracies. *Coexistence*, 33, 25–41.

Statistikaamet, 1994, *Eesti Statistika Aastaraamat 1994*. Tallinn: Statistikaamet.

Statistikaamet, 1997, *Eesti Statistika Aastaraamat 1997*. Tallinn: Statistikaamet.

Taagepera, R., 1993, *Estonia: return to independence*. Boulder: Westview.

Tang, P., Nilgo, H., 1995, Budget reform. *In* Lugus, O., Hachey, G. A., eds, *Transforming the Estonian economy*. Tallinn: International Centre for Economic Growth, pp. 92–111.

Telliskivi, V., ed., 1998, *Põllumajandus ja maaelu, Ülevaade 1997*. Tallinn: Eesti Vabariigi Põlumajandusministeerium.

Unwin, T., 1994, Structural change in Estonian agriculture: from command economy to privatisation. *Geography*. 79 (3), 246–261.

Unwin, T., 1997, Agricultural restructuring and integrated rural development in Estonia. *Journal of Rural Studies*, 13 (1), 93–112.

Unwin, T., 1998, Rurality and the construction of nation in Estonia. *In* Pickles, J., Smith, A., eds, *Theorising transition: the political economy of post-communist transformations*. London/New York: Routledge, pp. 284–306.

Unwin, T., 1999, Place, territory and national identity: an interpretation of Estonia. *In* Herb, G. H., Kaplan, D. H., eds, *Nested identities: nationalism, territory, and scale*. Lanham: Rowman and Littlefield, pp. 151–173.

Valdes, A., Csaki, C., Fock, A., 1998, Estonian agriculture in efforts to accede to the European Union. *Post-Soviet Geography and Economics*, 39 (9), 518–548.

Van Arkadie, B., Karlsson, M., 1992, *Economic survey of the Baltic states: the reform process in Estonia, Latvia and Lithuania*. London: Pinter.

Venesaar, U., Smallbone, D., 1997, *Eesti tootvate väike – ja keskettevõtete arenguprobleemid*. Tallinn: Eesti Majanduse Instituut.

White, J. D., 1994, Nationalism and socialism in historical perspective. *In* Smith, G., ed., *The Baltic States: the national self-determination of Estonia, Latvia and Lithuania*. Basingstoke: Macmillan, pp. 13–40.

Williams, A. M., 1998, The European Union: cumulative and uneven integration. *In* Unwin, T., ed., *A European geography*. London: Addison Wesley Longman, pp. 129–148.

World Bank, 1996, *From plan to market: world development report 1996*. Oxford: Oxford University Press.

10

CYPRUS

Derek Hall

A brief history

The island of Cyprus covers a land area of 9,250 sq km and is the third largest Mediterranean island after Sicily and Sardinia (Figure 10.1). Its population was approximately 740,000 in 1998, of which 78 per cent were Greek and 18 per cent Turkish. The numbers professing the Greek Orthodox and Muslim faiths were identical in their proportions to the Greek and Turkish populations. English is spoken alongside Greek and Turkish. The capital is Nicosia. Cyprus lies some 800 km from the mainland of Greece and less than 100 km from Turkey. Greeks have inhabited Cyprus since ancient times, and the Greek Orthodox Church remains strong. Conquered by the Turks in 1571, the island remained under Turkey until 1878, when it was ceded to Britain for administrative purposes. At the outbreak of the First World War the British formally annexed it. Political problems in Cyprus, especially following the Second World War, have been symptomatic of the nature of wider Turkish–Hellenic relations and are ingrained in the island's ethnic imbalance. Civil violence began in 1955 with Greek demands for *enosis* – union with Greece – for which Archbishop Makarios emerged as a leading proponent. The Turkish population resisted any move for incorporation within the Greek state, and as a counter to *enosis* pressed for partition of Cyprus into Turkish and Greek sectors. Britain had two military bases on the island, reflecting Cyprus's role as a last remaining British defence garrison in the eastern Mediterranean.

The disorders in Cyprus lasted for four years and cost over 600 lives before agreement was reached on the island's future (Panayiotopoulos, 1999). In 1959 it was decided that Cyprus would be prepared for independence, to be guaranteed by Britain, Greece and Turkey under agreements signed in Zurich and London. Such status would prohibit union with another state, or partition of the island into two or more parts. The president of Cyprus would be Greek and the vice-president Turkish. British sovereignty would be retained over the two areas used as bases. The Republic of Cyprus was constituted as an independent state in August 1960, and in March 1961 was admitted to the British Commonwealth.

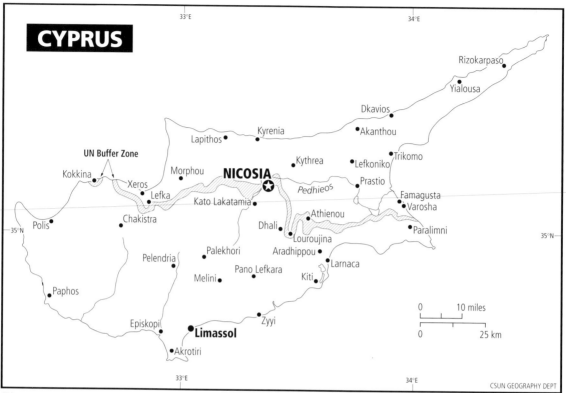

Figure 10.1: Cyprus

Independence for Cyprus did not end its problems, however. There developed little concept of Cypriot nationhood: citizens continued to think of themselves as Greek or Turkish Cypriots (but see, for example, Mavratsas, 1997; Papadakis, 1998). Further, the economy was not strong, with chronic unemployment. Agriculture was the mainstay of the island, with some mining and export of copper. Here was a country that had statehood thrust upon it largely as a compromise among foreign powers which quarrelled over its political future. Cyprus had no army but was garrisoned by British, Greek and Turkish forces. Its supreme constitutional court consisted of a neutral president and two judges, one Greek and one Turkish. As an area of balance between the interests of three countries, Cyprus faced a difficult task in working out the intricate problems of representative self-government and the development of a national consciousness.

Turks argue that Greek Cypriots started to unpick the constitutional power-sharing arrangements within three years of independence (Boulton, 1999). Triggered by a coup backed by military rulers in Athens, designed to annex the island to Greece, Turkish military intervention in 1974 saw the invasion and occupation of 37 per cent of Cyprus's territory and the expulsion of 200,000 Greeks from that northern 'half' (Zetter, 1994). United Nations sanctions were subsequently imposed against the Turkish 'occupation'.

This division has persisted (Kliot and Mansfeld, 1997), with the Republic of Cyprus government representing the Greek Cypriot 'south', and the Turkish Republic of Northern Cyprus (TRNC), declared in 1983 but recognised only by Turkey, acting on behalf of the 'north'. The Turkish Cypriots want a confederation of Cyprus recognising two states, but no return of Greeks to homes in Kyrenia or Famagusta. The Greek Cypriots want a reunified island with the return of all refugees. They certainly want unity of their country, but not necessarily of its people (Fisk, 1998).

The island's partition focused economic attention on the role of tourism, which, in the 1970s and 1980s, took on a prime economic importance in the south (e.g. see Gilmor, 1989; Kammas and Salehiesfahani, 1992; Clements and Georgiou, 1998). With a UN economic boycott of Turkish Cyprus, however, precluding direct access except from Turkey, tourism in the north has remained largely muted – only around 10 per cent of the island's total – and fluctuating (Lockhart, 1994; Scott, 1995; Warner, 1999).

In education, however, northern establishments are recognised internationally, and students receive, for example, British Council grants and Fulbright awards. The 1960 constitution, which established Cypriot independence, gave separate responsibility for education to both communities. In the Turkish 'north', the Eastern Mediterranean University, which was founded in 1979, has well over 11,000 students, with English as the medium of instruction. Turkish Cypriot academics have calculated that in 1994–95 overseas students, and their visiting relatives, were responsible for expenditure equivalent to 11.6 per cent of GNP, with a multiplier estimated to be the equivalent of nearly 20 per cent. Higher education has a significant impact on the northern Cyprus economy, whilst in the south the private colleges still await government recognition (Hughes, 1999).

Economic growth in the Republic of Cyprus since the early 1990s has ranged around an annual average of 4 per cent, a figure set as the objective for GDP growth in the government's 1999–2003 strategic development plan. In 1998 unemployment was 3.3 per cent of the labour force. A trade deficit of 28 per cent of GDP is partially offset by a surplus on invisibles of 21 per cent of GDP, in tourism, offshore business and other services. Total FDI (foreign direct investment) flows are estimated to be in the range of 1–1.5 per cent of GDP (European Commission, 1999a).

Cyprus–EU relations

Cyprus was among the first countries to sign an association agreement with the then European Economic Community and has been included with five CEE countries in the 'fast-track six'

(Table 10.1). Initial interest to conclude such an agreement was expressed in the early 1960s in parallel with the British application for membership to the Community.

In 1971 the government of Cyprus entered into negotiations with the EEC, and in December 1972 an association agreement was signed between the two parties, aiming to establish a customs

Table 10.1 Cyprus: chronology of EU relations, 1972–1999

1972
December Cyprus and the EEC sign an association agreement providing for the gradual elimination of all trade barriers and the creation in two stages (first until 1977) of a customs union. The agreement comes into force on 1 June 1973.

1974
August Turkish military occupation of 37 per cent of the island.

1975
February Turkey unilaterally declares a Turkish Federated State of Cyprus (TFSC).

1977
September The first stage of the customs union is extended until 1979. Its provisions are later extended until 1983, 1985 and 1987.

1978
November First EEC–Cyprus financial protocol is signed, worth ECU 30 mn.

1983
November Turkish Republic of Northern Cyprus (TRNC) unilaterally declared; only recognised by Turkey.

December Second financial protocol signed for ECU 44 mn.

1987
October Protocol to the association agreement is signed for the transition into the second stage of the agreement; to be implemented in two phases 1988–97 and 1998–2002/03.

1990
May The delegation of the European Commission opens in Nicosia.

June Third financial protocol takes effect, worth ECU 62 mn.

July Cyprus submits to the European Council formal application for membership to the Community.

1993
June European Commission issues *Opinion* on Cyprus application. Considers Cyprus eligible, undertakes to familiarise government with *acquis communautaire* and sets January 1995 for the reassessment of the situation pending the UN Secretary General's efforts for a political settlement. Council adopts *Opinion* in October 1993.

1994
February Council appoints EU observer to the Cyprus peace process in the light of the review of Cyprus's application.

June and December European Councils in Corfu and Essen note that the next phase of the Union's enlargement will involve Cyprus (and Malta). This is confirmed in June 1995 by the European Council in Cannes.

1995
March The Council of Ministers agrees on the general policy framework for the development of a structured dialogue with Cyprus with a view to opening membership negotiations six months after the end of intergovernmental conference. The Council invites the Commission to submit proposals for a pre-accession strategy for Cyprus and calls upon the Commission to organise, in consultation with the government of Cyprus, the requisite contacts with the Turkish Cypriot community, to inform it of the advantages of EU accession and allay its concerns about the prospect.

1995 continued

June Fourth financial protocol signed for ECU 74 mn.

July Council adopts procedures for the structured dialogue between Cyprus and the EU.

November Republic of Cyprus participates in First Euro-Mediterranean Conference and signs the Barcelona Declaration.

1997

February Commissioner van den Broek pays official visit to Cyprus to meet leaders of both communities. Calls on both sides to seize the opportunity for a settlement offered by the prospect of accession.

June The president of the Republic of Cyprus is briefed by the Dutch presidency and the European Commission on the results of the Amsterdam European Summit.

July The Commission in its *Agenda 2000* confirms the start of accession negotiations with Cyprus.

1997 continued

December Luxembourg European Council conclusions state the opening of accession negotiations on 31 March 1998.

1998

March Opening of the accession negotiations.

October European Commission progress report toward accession.

1999

October European Commission progress report toward accession.

December Helsinki Summit: 'second-wave six' invited to join accession negotiations alongside the 'fast-track six', of which Cyprus is one.

Sources: *Various*

union in two stages and within a period of ten years. The agreement came into force in June 1973 and contained arrangements on trade, financial and technical co-operation which were intended to benefit the population of the whole island. The first stage provided for the phased reduction of tariffs on industrial goods and agricultural products. The political and economic consequences of the 1974 Turkish occupation delayed the implementation of the second stage. As a result, this first stage was extended until the end of 1987.

A protocol for the second stage of the association agreement was signed in Luxembourg in October 1987, with provisions for a customs union between 'Cyprus' and the EU to be completed by the year 2002, or 2003 at the latest. This provided for the elimination of all tariffs and quantitative restrictions on all manufactured goods and on a number of agricultural products (mainly potatoes, citrus fruit, other fruit and vegetables and wine). In parallel, 'Cyprus' would adopt progressively the EU's Common Customs Tariff (CCT) to bring its own customs tariffs in line with those of the Union by the end of 1997.

In July 1990 the (Greek) Republic of Cyprus applied to join the European Community. The European Commission in its *Opinion* on the application, issued in June 1993 and endorsed by the European Council in October, considered Cyprus eligible for membership, and *in expectation of progress on the political problem* confirmed that the EC was ready to start the process with Cyprus that should lead to its eventual accession. The *Opinion*:

- recognised the European identity and character of Cyprus and its vocation to belong to the Community; and

- confirmed that Cyprus satisfied the criteria for membership and was suitable to become a member (European Commission, 1997).

Substantive accession negotiations began in November 1998.

Pre-accession strategy

In 1995 the European Council began a structured dialogue with the Republic of Cyprus as part of its pre-accession strategy. Other elements of this strategy included the negotiation of agreements for participation in programmes on education and training (Socrates, Leonardo, Youth for Europe), audio-visual media (Media II), scientific research and technological development, cultural co-operation (the Ariane, Kaleidoscope and Raphael programmes), and energy (Save II). There was also continued harmonisation of Cyprus's legislation with the *acquis*. In March 1995 the EU General Affairs Council considered also that the accession of Cyprus to the EU should bring increased security and prosperity to both communities on the island. In particular it should allow the 'north' to catch up economically and should improve the

Table 10.2 Cyprus: EU financial and technical assistance, 1979–1999

Periods of financial protocols	Grants (€ mn)	Loans (€ mn)	Special loans/ risk capital (€ mn)	Total (€ mn)	Objectives
1st 1979–83	6	20	4	30	Infrastructure development projects: Nicosia sewage system; Vassilikos–Pentaskinos water development and supply; the Dhekelia power project; the Southern
2nd 1984–88	10	28	6	44	conveyor project; Nicosia master plan. Resources of both first and second protocols were used in projects of a bi-communal nature.
3nd 1989–93	13	44	5	62	To promote the transition of Cyprus's economy toward EU integration, emphasising SME development in tourism and manufacturing, and the establishment of a European Institute on the island.
4th 1995–99	22	50	2	74	To promote economic development and association agreement objectives; to assist economic transition to accession; to promote a settlement of the Cyprus political problem.
Total				210	

Sources: *Republic of Cyprus, 1998: 5–6; European Commission, 1999b*

outlook for growth and employment particularly for the Turkish Cypriot community. The Council considered that the latter must perceive the advantages of EU accession more clearly and that its concerns at the prospect must be allayed. The Council called upon the Commission to organise, in consultation with the government of the Republic of (Greek) Cyprus, the requisite contacts to be made with the Turkish Cypriot community.

In an effort to strengthen the country's infrastructure the EU has provided financial assistance through four protocols covering technical and economic support for the period 1979–99, providing for total financial aid of €210 mn (Table 10.2).

In response to the need for a more liberal economic regime, a limited privatisation programme has been pursued, embracing desalination plants and two airports. Some initial moves have also been made on the deregulation and liberalisation of telecommunications. However, the government of the Republic of Cyprus has shown a reluctance to speed up the privatisation of such enterprises as the Cyprus Tourist Development Agency, the Cyprus Forest Industries and the Pancyprian Company of Bakers (European Commission, 1999a).

Prior to the important December 1999 Helsinki Summit, The European Commission's report (1999b) on (the Republic of) Cyprus's progress toward EU accession concluded that it:

- had fulfilled the Copenhagen political criteria;

- was a functioning market economy and should be able to cope with the competitive pressures and market forces within the EU;

- should renew efforts in the areas of structural reform and deregulation: progress toward privatisation had been slow, and the process needed to be accelerated;

- had made very little progress in further alignment with the internal market *acquis* over the past year: there had been no new legislation in the area of standardisation, and the adoption of a new law regulating this area was urgently needed as only 15 per cent of existing European standards had been adopted;

- had made some progress in preparing for participation in the Common Agricultural Policy (CAP), but alignment in the veterinary and phytosanitary areas was only partial;

- needed to adopt several pieces of sectoral legislation to permit alignment with the environment *acquis*;

- had made little progress in the areas of immigration and asylum legislation;

- needed to reinforce administrative capacity in the maritime transport and environment sectors (European Commission, 1999b).

The EU and the Cyprus problem

The EU position is that the *status quo* imposed by the Turkish invasion of 1974 and the continued occupation by Turkish troops of 37 per cent of the island's territory is unacceptable. The EU supported the efforts of the United Nations to reach a negotiated and comprehensive settlement of the Cyprus question that would respect the sovereignty, independence, territorial integrity and unity of the country within a bi-communal and bi-zonal federation. These principles – the Ghali 'set of ideas' – established by the UN Secretary General Boutros Boutros-Ghali in 1992 and endorsed by the UN Security Council, stipulated that the question of EU membership should be decided upon only *after* a settlement of the Cyprus problem and through separate referendums of the two peoples (Bolukbasi, 1995, 1998). In February 1994 the EU's increasing interest in the Cyprus problem saw the appointment of its own observer to the UN-sponsored intercommunal talks.

However, at the UN-led direct talks between the leaders of the two communities in Montreux, Switzerland, the Turkish Cypriot leadership set pre-conditions for progress. These implied the freezing of the EU's commitment to start accession negotiations with Cyprus in 1998. As such, they were unacceptable to the Commission, which reconfirmed that the launch of those negotiations would proceed in March 1995. EU Commissioner Hans van den Broek subsequently regretted the lack of Turkish Cypriot participation in the island's EU negotiations, despite invitations for them to do so. But he also welcomed the progress achieved by 'Cyprus' toward accession and recognised that the Turkish government was making a serious attempt to improve the human rights situation (Anon, 1995).

In July 1997 the Commission, in *Agenda 2000* – its communication to the European Parliament on the future development of the Union – re-assessed the situation since the publication of its *Opinion* on Cyprus in 1993 and confirmed that accession negotiations would begin as planned. *Agenda 2000* reiterated the EU's determination to play a positive role in bringing about a just and lasting settlement in accordance with the relevant UN resolutions.

The timetable agreed for accession negotiations to start with Cyprus meant that they could start before a political settlement was reached. The EU argued that the decision to open negotiations should be seen as a positive development that could promote the search for a political settlement. If sufficient progress was made between the parties to allow representatives of the Turkish Cypriot community to be involved in the accession process, this would permit a faster conclusion to the accession negotiations. Nevertheless, *Agenda 2000* indicated that if progress toward a settlement had not been reached before the negotiations were due to begin, they should be opened with the government of the Republic of Cyprus, as the only authority recognised by international law.

Conflicting perceptions

The Cyprus problem has had the potential to confound negotiations for enlargement. Greece has repeatedly indicated that Athens would block expansion if Cyprus was kept out, arguing that the admission of other countries into the EU could not proceed if the reason for not admitting Cyprus was the island's political problem. The Greek position was that Cyprus could not be allowed to become a 'hostage' of Turkey, and that the EU must not accept a Turkish veto on the admission of Cyprus. Further, until the Helsinki Summit of December 1999, Greece had vetoed any move toward inaugurating enlargement discussions with Turkey (Anon, 1998).

As noted in Chapter 17, since the end of the Cold War, Turkey's relationship with Europe has changed: Turkey's strategic importance to the West has declined, just as the EU has forged ahead in economic and political integration. Turkey has also been experiencing domestic instability concerning the role of Islam in its society and the rights of its Kurdish minority population. Until the Helsinki Summit there had been growing friction and recrimination between the EU and Turkey as the latter had watched countries from CEE leapfrog its own application for membership.

The Turkish Cypriot view of the July 1990 application for EC membership was that it was a unilateral action on the part of the Greek Cypriot administration and not properly by or on behalf of Cyprus (as a whole). The 'north's' position was that the bi-communal Republic of Cyprus established in 1960 in accordance with the February 1959 Zurich and London agreements signed by the five parties – although destroyed by force of arms, in 1963, by the Greek Cypriot partner – was still in force. The Turkish Cypriots viewed the Greek Cypriots as aiming to destroy these fundamental rights and status by the accession application, and by so doing to destroy the balance between Turkey and Greece over Cyprus in favour of Greece. Once 'Cyprus' was accepted as a member of the EU, the Treaty of Guarantee would be inapplicable against a member state of the EU and, by virtue of EU laws, all the basic principles enshrined in the Ghali 'set of ideas' regarding a bi-zonal, bi-communal settlement would be of no effect (Richmond, 1999).

Since 1963 the Turkish Cypriot and Greek Cypriot communities have lived under their own separate administrations. Turkish Cypriots argue that there is no joint administration enjoying the mandate of both peoples and capable of speaking for both, or of applying for EU membership and conducting accession negotiations with the EU on behalf of the whole of the island. Indeed, the suggestion from the November 1998 EU Luxembourg Summit – that the 'Turkish Cypriot community' should become part of the EU membership process initiated by the Greek Cypriot application – was treated as an affront. Further, for Turkish Cypriots, agreeing to become a member of the EU, of which Turkey was not a full member while Greece was, would mean the destruction of the balance between the two motherlands over Cyprus. This would be tantamount to an indirect unification of the island with Greece. Rauf Denktash, the Turkish Cypriot leader, argued that Cyprus should be two confederated states, one guaranteed by Greece, the other by Turkey, but both available for simultaneous EU membership (Preston, 1998).

In December 1997, at talks with his NATO counterparts, Turkish Foreign Minister Ismail Cem said Ankara would proceed with the 'partial integration' of the Turkish-controlled north of the island if the EU started membership negotiations with the Greek Cypriot government in the spring of 1998. Cem said the move on Cyprus would provide for much closer economic, political and military ties between Turkey and the Turkish Cypriots, but would fall short of full annexation. Cem, however, distanced himself from threats by some Turkish politicians that they could block the entry of the Czech Republic, Hungary and Poland to NATO by refusing to ratify that organisation's expansion. The Greek Cypriot government's ordering of an S-300 missile system from Russia further heightened tension (Mather and Krushelnycky, 1998).

However, at the December 1999 EU leaders' summit in Helsinki, Greece lifted the veto it had wielded for the past decade on accession talks with Turkey. It was indicated to the Ankara government that Turkey was now assigned the status of a candidate country, although a timetable for accession discussions was not established. Indeed, Greece had not accepted the principle of eventual Turkish EU membership without imposing conditions. In addition to the normal EU requirements for improving human rights, democratic structures and economic reform, Turkey would have to agree to take any territorial disputes with Greece in the Aegean to the International Court of Justice in the Hague. And, of course, Turkey still faced the prospect of 'Cyprus' becoming an EU member before any internal political settlement (Watson, 1999).

Conclusion

Meanwhile, integration between northern Cyprus and Turkey has grown stronger. In 1998 a water supply project by sea from the Turkish coast was inaugurated. Turkey also plans to provide electricity through an underwater cable. The TRNC is now being treated as a Turkish province in economic matters. Since 1974, 120,000 Turkish Cypriots have left while 110,000 settlers from the mainland have moved in. There are also some 30,000 Turkish troops. In 1998 the president of Turkey promised that Turkish Cypriot industrialists and farmers would qualify for credits and soft loans on the same basis as Turkish citizens and that Turkish Cypriot companies would no longer be treated as foreign companies in Turkey. Turkish Cypriots working in Turkey would no longer have to register as aliens and renew their permits to stay every three months (Mather, 1998b).

The hopes for co-operation are not, however, abandoned. Planned to be more permanent than the water supply system noted above, a 78 km floating maritime 'peace pipeline' is to carry additional fresh water from Turkey's Dogon river to Cyprus, but, with US commercial involvement, is designed for a capacity that can provide for the south as well as the north of the island (Munir, 2000). The Nicosia sewerage system remains a single network run jointly by Greek and Turkish Cypriots: the pipes cross under the 'Green line' (or 'Attila' line) separating the two communities. Parts of the system on the Turkish side include the treatment plant, which is operated by Turkish Cypriots (Mather, 1998a). The system is run by a bi-communal team and presents a prime example of continuing, mutually beneficial co-operation, which the EU has hoped to reinforce and promote as a precedent for wider (re-)collaboration on the island.

The EC *Opinion* is that as a potential EU member (Greek) Cyprus is a democratic, European country with a competitive market economy and a high level of economic development, thus meeting the convergence criteria for economic and monetary union. The 'Cypriot government' has made accession one of its primary goals, and 'Cyprus' is in a position to harmonise its legislation and its policies with those of the Union. 'Cyprus' has much to benefit from accession to the EU. Its potential for the EU includes:

- acting as a geographical, cultural, economic and political bridge with its southern and Middle Eastern neighbours;

- the availability of highly educated professionals;

- a good communications network and well-functioning infrastructure; and

- a legal system based on internationally accepted principles of jurisprudence (Republic of Cyprus, 1998).

As the EU pursued accession negotiations with Greek Cypriots, and UN negotiations for a political settlement were resumed, the USA was becoming more actively involved in the situation of Cyprus. Clearly the futures of Cyprus are likely to be largely determined by the strategic interests of the major international actors involved (Müftüler-Bac, 1999). And as the Gordian knot of Cyprus's role within Europe begins to be loosened, five sets of political and economic relationships appear crucially intertwined:

- the political status and internal relationships of Cyprus;

- the EU's attitude and relations with Cyprus, separate or whole;

- the Greek government's position, to a large extent determined by the contemporary state of relations with Turkey;

- Turkey's EU role; and

- Turkey's relationship with the USA.

From a range of possibilities, two scenarios appear most likely. On the one hand, continued obstacles to Turkey's accession talks could lead to frustration in Ankara and a 'permanent', albeit not internationally recognised, division of Cyprus. (Greek) Cyprus would probably prosper within the EU without any wider settlement of the island's political condition being instituted. On the other hand, if relatively rapid progress of domestic reforms within Turkey took place, and fast-track EU membership resulted, agreement on the (re-)establishment of a confederated Cyprus could come about, but now within the auspices of the EU and overseen by the three guarantors as EU member states.

Ironically, even in the globalised 21st century, an island as small as Cyprus potentially holds one of the major keys to EU enlargement, eastern Mediterranean stability and CEE incorporation into mainstream Europe.

References

Anon, 1995, Cyprus and Malta are 'no problem' says Minister. *European Parliament* – EP News, 10 July, p. 3.

Anon, 1998, Cyprus problem could threaten EU expansion. *Cyprus Mail*, 11 November.

Bolukbasi, S., 1995, Boutros-Ghali Cyprus initiative in 1992 – why did it fail? *Middle Eastern Studies*, 31 (3), 460–482.

Bolukbasi, S., 1998, The Cyprus dispute and the United Nations: peaceful non-settlement between 1954 and 1996. *International Journal of Middle East Studies*, 30 (3), 411–434.

Boulton, L., 1999, Stubborn obstacle or stout defender? *Financial Times*, 30 October.

Clements, M. A., Georgiou, A., 1998, The impact of political instability on a fragile tourism product. *Tourism Management*, 19 (3), 283–288.

European Commission, 1997, *EU–Cyprus relations.* Washington DC: European Commission. http://www.eurunion.org/legislat/extrel/cec/cyprus.htm.

European Commission, 1999a, *European economy. Supplement C. Country notes: Cyprus.* Brussels: European Commission. http://europa.eu.int/comm/economy_finance/document/eesuppc/1999_3/cyp.htm.

European Commission, 1999b, *Regular report from the Commission on progress towards accession: Cyprus – October 13, 1999.* Brussels: European Commission. http://europa.eu.int/comm/enlargement/cyprus/rep_10_99/.

Fisk, R., 1998, Divided they stand, separated by eternal hatred and suspicion. *The Independent*, 10 December, p. 10.

Gilmor, D. A., 1989, Recent tourism development in Cyprus. *Geography*, 74 (3), 262–265.

Hughes, K., 1999, Bridge over troubled water. *Times Higher Education Supplement*, 19 March, p. 10.

Kammas, M., Salehiesfahani, H., 1992, Tourism and export-led growth – the case of Cyprus, 1976–1988. *Journal of Developing Areas*, 26 (4), 489–506.

Kliot, N., Mansfeld, Y., 1997, The political landscape of partition: the case of Cyprus. *Political*

Geography, 16 (6), 495–521.

Lockhart, D., 1994, Tourism in northern Cyprus – patterns, policies and prospects. *Tourism Management,* 15 (5), 370–379.

Mather, I., 1998a, Nicosia. *The European,* 29 June, p. 33.

Mather, I., 1998b, Union's big mistake hardens the divide. *The European,* 17 August, pp. 12–13.

Mather, I., Krushelnycky, A., 1998, Moscow's missile meddling raises spectre of war. *The European,* 6 April, pp. 14–16.

Mavratsas, C. V., 1997, The ideological contest between Greek-Cypriot politics, social memory and identity. *Ethnic and Racial Studies,* 20 (4), 717–737.

Müftüler-Bac, M., 1999, The Cyprus debacle: what the future holds. *Futures,* 31 (6), 559–575.

Munir, M., 2000, Turkey: 'Peace pipe' to carry water to Cyprus. *The Financial Times,* 18 January. http://www.ft.com/hippocampus/q3258c2.htm.

Panayiotopoulos, P., 1999, The emergent post-colonial state in Cyprus. *Journal of Commonwealth and Comparative Politics,* 37 (1), 31–55.

Papadakis, Y., 1998, Greek Cypriot narratives of history and collective identity: nationalism as a contested process. *American Ethnologist,* 25 (2), 149–165.

Preston, P., 1998, A tragedy of two races. *The Guardian,* 26 October.

Republic of Cyprus, 1998, *Cyprus–EU relations.* Nicosia: Republic of Cyprus Press and Information Office. http://www.pio.gov.cy/ir/cyprus_eu/recent_developments.htm.

Richmond, O. P., 1999, Ethno-nationalism, sovereignty and negotiating positions in the Cyprus conflict: obstacles to a settlement. *Middle Eastern Studies,* 35 (3), 42–63.

Scott, J., 1995, Social and national boundaries in tourism. *Annals of Tourism Research,* 22 (2), 385–403.

Warner, J., 1999, North Cyprus: tourism and the challenge of non-recognition. *Journal of Sustainable Tourism,* 7 (2), 128–145.

Watson, R., 1999, Turkey a step closer to EU as Greece lifts veto. *The Herald* (Glasgow), 13 December. http://www.theherald.co.uk/news/archive/13-12-99-23-59-19.html.

Zetter, R., 1994, The Greek-Cypriot refugees: perceptions of return under conditions of protracted exile. *International Migration Review,* 28 (2), 307–322.

11

SLOVAKIA

Frank Carter

Slovakia, or the Slovak Republic, covers an area of 49,035 sq km and became an independent state on 1 January 1993 with the dissolution of the Czech and Slovak Federal Republic (former Czechoslovakia) (Figure 11.1). In 1997 its borders constituted a total length of 1,672 km, shared between the Czech Republic in the west (252 km; 15 per cent of total length), Poland in the north (547 km; 33 per cent), Ukraine in the east (99 km; 6 per cent), Hungary in the south (669 km; 40 per cent) and Austria in the south-west (106 km; 6 per cent). The country's terrain is predominantly mountainous. In the north the highest peak, Gerlach (Gerlachovský štít), reaches an altitude of 2,655 m, forms part of the High Tatras (Visoké Tatry) in its border with Poland, and constitutes the country's major mountain ranges along with the Low Tatras (Nízké Tatry) in the east and centre; all form part of the Carpathian Mountains' most westerly chain. Several rivers drain the mountains, including the Váh (367 km), Hron (278 km), Ipel' (198 km) and Hornád (179 km). The river Danube forms a section (172 km) of Slovakia's southern border. The main lowland areas, an extension of the Pannonian Plain, are located in the south-west and south-east of the country and contain the major zones of agriculture and settlement. The lowest altitude (94 m) is located in the south-east, where the river Bodrog flows into Hungary. In 1997 more than two-fifths (40.6 per cent) of Slovakia was forested; half (49.8 per cent) was utilised as agricultural land, but less than a third of this total was used for arable purposes (30.0 per cent) (ŠúSR, 1997).

Slovakia experiences a continental climate, with warm summers and cold winters. Average temperatures in the capital, Bratislava, vary from -0.7 °C in January to 19.1 °C in July. Temperatures in the more mountainous areas can on average be ten degrees lower than the rest of the country. Precipitation (Bratislava: annual average 649 mm) is usually heavier in summer, with thunderstorms; autumn normally has dry clear weather, while spring is damp, both seasons having a short duration. Temperature inversions in the winter months frequently cause pollution problems in urban and more industrialised areas.

Figure 11.1: Slovakia

The March 1991 census recorded a total population of 5,283,404, of whom 51.2 per cent were female. Since the early 1920s the population has increased by nearly three-quarters (73.6 per cent) as seen in Table 11.1.

Table 11.1 Slovakia: population growth, 1923–1996

Year	Total population	Year	Total population
1923	3 094 700	1965	4 373 595
1930	3 315 459	1980	4 984 331
1940	3 553 461	1990	5 297 774
1950	3 463 446	1996	5 373 810

Source: *ŠúSR, 1997: 156–157*

Vital statistics for 1996 reveal there were 60,123 live births (11.2 per 1,000 inhabitants), 51,236 deaths (9.5), 27,484 marriages (5.1), 9,402 divorces (1.7) and 615 deaths in infancy (10.2 per 1,000 live births). Population data on nationality in 1996 showed 4,608,245 were ethnic Slovaks (85.7

per cent), 568,444 (10.6 per cent) were Hungarians, mostly concentrated along the southern border, and 86,383 (1.61 per cent) Roma (Gypsies). Some scepticism has been attached to this latter figure, due to the belief that there was considerable under-enumeration of the Roma community, many of whom claimed other nationalities, particularly Hungarian. There were also 58,652 (1.1 per cent) Czechs, including Moravians and Silesians, as well as small communities of Ruthenians and Ukrainians (32,165; 0.6 per cent), Germans (5,373; 0.1 per cent) and Poles (3,147; 0.06 per cent).

Formerly known as Pressburg, Bratislava, the Slovakian capital, is located in the extreme south-west of the country on the river Danube, a mere 50 km from Vienna. The capital forms one of the country's eight administrative regions (kraj) as seen in Table 11.2.

Table 11.2 Slovakia: administrative regions by area and population, 1997

Region	Chief city	Area		Population	
		sq km	%	No.	%
Bratislavský	Bratislava	2 053	4.2	618 904	11.5
Trnavský	Trnava	4 148	8.5	548 898	10.2
Trenčiansky	Trenčín	4 501	9.2	610 135	11.4
Nitriansky	Nitra	6 343	12.9	717 585	13.3
Žilinský	Žilina	6 788	13.8	687 771	12.8
Banskobystrický	Banská Bystrica	9 455	19.3	664 024	12.3
Prešovský	Prešov	8 993	18.3	773 121	14.4
Košický	Košice	6 753	13.8	758 494	14.1

Source: *ŠúSR, 1997: 577*

Table 11.3 Slovakia: population of cities with more than 70,000 inhabitants, 1997

City	No. of inhabitants
Bratislava	452 288
Košice	241 606
Nitra	87 569
Žilina	86 811
Banská Bystrica	85 052
Trnava	70 202

Source: *ŠúSR, 1997: 592–594*

From this table it is apparent that nearly half the population (46.4 per cent) live in the western regions (Bratislavský; Trnavský; Trenčiansky and Nitriansky), a quarter (25.1 per cent) in the central regions (Žilinský and Banskobystrický) and the rest (28.5 per cent) in the eastern regions of Prešovský and Košický.

Of the 136 urban centres in Slovakia, 117 (86 per cent) have populations of over 5,000; major settlements with over 70,000 inhabitants are seen in Table 11.3. Clearly, Bratislava dominates the urban hierarchy, with nearly double the number of inhabitants of Košice, the second largest city. In turn, Košice is more than twice as big as the next three cities, and more than three times larger than Trnava.

A brief history

Within the present-day territory of Slovakia evidence exists of early prehistoric settlements dating from 6000 BC to 4500 BC; they were mainly located in the valleys of the middle Váh, the lower stretches of the Hron and Ipel', the Torysa valley and the eastern lowlands. Between 500 BC and 400 BC Celtic proto-urban defensive settlements (*oppidiae*) were constructed on hill sites, for example at Bratislava, at nearby Devín, and at Zemplín, south of Košice. The Romans established most of their military camps (*castrae*) along the Danube (e.g. Rusovce) to guard the *limes* of the Empire between AD 100 and AD 400, but there were also small military outposts along the Váh valley (e.g. at Mlanovce and Trenčín). During the 6th and 7th centuries the Slovaks, along with other members of the western Slavic tribal branch, migrated to central Europe from the eastern steppe. In AD 830 the Great Moravian Empire was established, later extending into western and central Slovakia. This coincided with the second proto-urban phase, with settlements again favouring the river valleys, especially from Nitra southward to the Danube at Bina (Hruská, 1971). Moravian forces were defeated by the Hungarians at the Battle of Pressburg in AD 907; by the 11th century the Slovak lands were consolidated into the Kingdom of Hungary. They became known as Upper Hungary and were to remain under Hungarian rule until 1918.

During the Middle Ages the nucleus of the first urbanisation phase took place between the 10th and 13th centuries. This consisted mainly of constructing castles on hills and locating fortified monasteries along strategically significant trade routes. The addition of numerous new towns (so-called planted towns) took place in the 13th and 14th centuries during the period in the Later Middle Ages prior to the Black Death. These settlements were to form the basis for later urbanisation. For 15th-century Slovakia (Upper Hungary) the Peace of Pressburg (1491) was an important event for it confirmed Habsburg inheritance claims to the Hungarian throne. This period was noted for the rulers, conflicts with the nobility and the emergence of peasant uprisings; more importantly, however, it signalled the Ottoman Turkish advance through the

Balkan peninsula. The death of the Hungarian king, Louis II, at the Battle of Mohács (1526) signified the Austrian Habsburgs' inherited claim to Hungary. The Kingdom of Hungary was divided up between the victorious Ottomans and the defeated Habsburgs, who managed to retain control of Upper Hungary (Slovakia). Pressburg became the new capital of Hungary and the place where their monarchs were crowned over the next three centuries.

Economically, Upper Hungary (Slovakia) was to experience a growth in raw material exports to western Europe, especially metal ores, in the 16th and 17th centuries. In particular, the mines of Upper Hungary were exploited for copper by enterprises like that of Jacob Fugger. Ores from Banská Bistrica, Gelnica and Smolnik and other mines were dispatched to western Europe along trade routes via Kraków–Gdańsk and Wrocław–Frankfurt or along the Oder/Elbe rivers to Hamburg and beyond (Carter, 1994). In the 18th century a period of early industrialisation came to Upper Hungary. This stimulated the emergence of a new urbanisation pattern, based on natural resources and steam power, for the manufacture of glass, iron and textile goods in particular. Between 1781 and 1785 this process was accompanied by the abolition of serfdom.

Several significant events took place in Slovakia during the 19th century. In retaliation to the potential Hungarian threat (1844) of expulsion abroad for anyone writing in the Slovak language, the Slovak leaders Ludevit Štúr and Jozef Hurban officially proclaimed the existence of the Slovak language. In 1844 the first Slovak grammar book was published and the Slovak literary language was authenticated (Polišenský, 1991). Four years later, in 1848, there was an unsuccessful Slovak rebellion against Hungarian rule; even this did not deter further dissent. In 1861 the Memorandum of the Slovak Nation issued by the National Congress of Slovaks demanded autonomy for their country. Unfortunately, such hopes were thwarted by the compromise (*Ausgleich*), which created the Habsburg dual monarchy of Austria–Hungary in 1867; this decree subjected Slovakia to full Hungarian control. It was rapidly followed by a policy of 'magyarisation', resulting in a swift increase of Slovak emigration abroad. Nevertheless, at the end of the 19th century Slovakia's industrial revolution began, based on mineral ore extraction and iron working in the central region and oil exploration in the lower Krupinica valley. In turn, this stimulated rural-to-urban migration, leading to an intensive concentration of population in settlements established in the new industrial regions around Košice and the south-western lowlands.

In May 1918 Czech and Slovak exiles signed the Pittsburg Agreement, which provided the basis for a new Czech–Slovak state; in October of that year the Republic of Czechoslovakia was established as one of the new post-war succession states. Even so, the Hungarian government ordered an attack on southern Slovakia in the summer of 1919, which was repulsed only with great difficulty. Finally, in 1920 the Treaty of Trianon led to the demarcation of Hungary's frontiers. More trouble for Slovakia came with the economic crisis of the late 1920s. Unemployment at home encouraged increasing emigration abroad, particularly to west

Europe's industrial regions and overseas. The Munich Agreement of September 1938 led to the collapse of the First Czechoslovakian Republic; in November of that year, Hungary annexed parts of southern Slovakia. Slovakia was to achieve its own autonomy in 1939 under the pro-fascist leadership of Monsignor Jozef Tiso, and on 14 March Hitler agreed to Tiso proclaiming the 'free state of Slovakia'. A policy of Jewish extermination was adopted by Tiso's government in 1941. An August 1944 uprising against Tiso's Slovak National People's Party was suppressed by German troops in late October. An agreement that Slovakia should have limited autonomy was made on the return of Czechoslovakia's government-in-exile in April 1945.

In Slovakia's May 1946 elections the Democratic Party won 62 per cent of the seats against the Communist Party's 30 per cent. In retaliation, the following year a communist coup in Slovakia was organised by Gustav Husák, on the pretext that the Democratic Party was supportive of Tiso's National People's Party; Tiso received a sentence of death by hanging.

The communists had seized practically all power in Slovakia by 1948. The Policy Plan of 1948 promoted an equal distribution of industry throughout the country; being the poorest part, Slovakia experienced an intensive industrialisation drive. Politically, several significant events occurred. In 1960 a new constitution limited Slovak autonomy. In January 1968 Alexander Dubček, leader of the Slovakian Communist Party, became the country's first secretary and demanded 'socialism with a human face' in his 'Prague Spring' reforms. Warsaw Pact military intervention ended his aspirations in August 1968. A federal system of government was introduced in January 1969, creating the Czech and Slovak Federal Republics, and in April 1969 Husák replaced Dubček as first secretary. In January 1977 the dissident 'Charter 77' manifesto called for an end to the persecution of civil and political rights. Anti-government demonstrations grew in number during the late 1980s and by November 1989 the Communist Party had lost its monopoly on political power.

Trade and economic development

In the early 1990s the Slovak economy was far more dependent on exports to the Czech Republic than the reverse. Slovak exports to former socialist bloc countries were also very important. Prior to the split, over a quarter (27 per cent) of all Slovak goods went to Czech Lands, whilst in the opposite direction it was only 11.5 per cent. Unlike the Czech economy, Slovakia was more reliant on imports, which mainly came from the former USSR and other socialist bloc states. In 1992 the Czech Lands provided a destination for nearly half (48.5 per cent) of all Slovak exports. Of Slovakia's other trading partners, the EC countries took a fifth (21.4 per cent) of exports, and other western nations a further 6.5 per cent. By then a mere 8.5 per cent of Slovakia's exports went to the former USSR and, with the exception of the Czech Republic, only 8.6 per cent went to other central and east European states. By 1996 less than a third (31 per cent) of Slovak exports went to the Czech Republic and only 16 per cent to the former Soviet bloc; of the EU countries, Germany led with 21 per cent, followed by Austria, with 6 per cent and Italy with 5 per cent (Done, 1997a).

During the period 1990–97 the Slovak economy experienced early growth, but this has since declined (Okáli *et al.*, 1995). Early devaluation in 1991 and 1993 improved the country's foreign trade balance, but the influence has now waned. Since 1995 the earlier impact of currency devaluation has become dissipated and there has been a net decrease in exports. GDP growth by 1996 came only from the domestic market (Němec and Prachár, 1997). Part of the answer lies in low competitiveness and restricted imports. It was hoped to reverse the GDP decline through better investment plans and a higher share of fixed capital in domestic production, in spite of limited internal resources. Unfortunately, these hopes have yet to materialise, in spite of efforts to trade with developing countries (Michník and Bal'áková, 1997).

By June 1998 Slovakia's trade deficit with EU countries reached 8.73 bn Slovak crowns ($250 mn). Slovakia's largest trade exchange was still with Germany – for over a quarter (27.4 per cent) of Slovak exports and more than a fifth (23.6 per cent) of imports (Anon, 1998g). By the end of 1998 Slovakia's overall trade deficit was expected to reach 70 bn Slovak crowns ($2,005 mn), or about 9.4 per cent of GDP. The country's foreign trade commodities reveal that imports in 1997 were dominated by machinery/transport equipment (35.2 per cent), followed by fuels and related products (16.7 per cent) and chemicals and related products (11.5 per cent); but only 6 per cent on food and live animals. Over a fifth of exports (23.2 per cent) were in machinery/transport equipment and more than a tenth (12.4 per cent) in chemicals, but only 4.9 per cent in fuels and 3.8 per cent in food/live animals (ŠúSR, 1997).

Foreign investment in Slovakia before 1993 was governed by the former Czechoslovakian law of May 1990. Under its provisions foreign investors could form wholly owned subsidiaries, established and governed by Czechoslovakian law; through these companies, foreign investors could buy land or existing Czechoslovakian companies (Dobosiewicz, 1992). After the split the early years proved fruitful; in 1994 Germany was the highest foreign investor in Slovakia, followed by Austria, the Czech Republic, the USA and France. These countries represented about four-fifths of Slovakia's total foreign trade volume. In that year Mečiar announced the delay of a $1 bn privatisation programme. The suspension reawakened doubts in the West about Slovakia's commitment to a free market and discouraged foreign investment, which already lagged behind it neighbours, the Czech Republic and Hungary (LeBor, 1994). By 1997 foreign investors still remained cautious about moving into Slovakia, which proved one of the reasons for the country's growing foreign debt. The situation had improved somewhat after the official declaration (1996) that the full integration of Slovakia into the EU and other international organisations remained an unaltered priority for Slovak foreign policy (Šesták, 1997; Anon, 1997a; Kárász, 1996).

Table 11. 4 Slovakia: six most attractive districts for foreign capital, 1 January 1997

District	Total number of firms	Of which foreign	% of total foreign capital
Bratislava	4 704	2 491	65.0
Prievidza	147	40	3.7
Žiar nad Hronom	59	16	3.6
Humenné	43	13	3.1
Nitra	279	87	3.1
Trnava	403	165	3.0

Source: *ŠúSR, 1997: 568*

As of January 1997, over four-fifths (81.5 per cent) of the country's foreign capital was invested in the six districts listed in Table 11.4, with two-thirds going to the capital, Bratislava; the remaining 32 districts had less than a fifth (18.5 per cent) between them. There was little overall difference compared with August 1994, when the top six districts totalled 82.4 per cent. At that time Bratislava was still dominant (60.36 per cent), followed by Poprad (6.57 per cent), Humenné (5.94 per cent), Nitra (3.86 per cent), Banská Bystrica (3.23 per cent) and Rožňava (2.44 per cent). The other 32 districts shared just 17.6 per cent (Mikelka, 1995). Clearly, the leading district's local industries and services have received the most benefit (Zemplinerová, 1997). The strong investment preference has not only been toward metropolitan areas but has also endorsed the main urbanised regions in the north-west. The limited foreign investment interest demonstrated in the south proved particularly discouraging for the main Hungarian minority located in this area.

After the demise of communism, economic development in Slovakia began in 1990 with the transformation process. This was based on 'shock therapy', namely brisk privatisation, anticipation of foreign capital inflow, more liberal attitudes to prices and foreign trade; it also included restrictive monetary, budgetary and wage policies to forestall inflationary pressures and the liquidation of inefficient enterprises (Paulov, 1996). Prior to the 'velvet divorce', 1991 was the worst year in terms of economic performance; although shock-therapy policies continued to be executed, some slight improvement occurred in 1992. For example, by November 1992 four-fifths (81 per cent) of all assets selected for 'small-scale privatisation' were sold; sales revenue totalled 213.7 Czechoslovak crowns ($500 mn) (Takla, 1994). Unfortunately, the economic basis for Slovakian independence was delicately balanced; the loss of Comecon trade (in 1988 Slovakia accounted for two-thirds of the Czechoslovak military output) and then much of the Czech market occurred in quick succession. The effects of economic reform were being more sharply experienced in Slovakia than in the Czech Republic. This was the result of

Slovakia containing some of the least effective state-run industries established under communist rule (Shen, 1993).

By 1994 the adverse consequences of the 'velvet divorce' had not yet been completely assimilated and short-term economic prospects were rather depressing (Bilsen, 1994; Schwartz *et al.*, 1994; Okáli *et al.*, 1995). The slowdown in economic growth during the second half of the 1990s has been blamed on the restrictive monetary policy adopted by the National Bank of Slovakia, which in turn has blamed the finance ministry for a too expansive budget that resulted in a deficit (Anon, 1998c). Signs of improvement in the GDP are, however, encouraging: percentage comparison with 1989 (100 per cent), showed it dropped to 75 per cent in 1993, but had risen to 95 per cent by 1997 (Sáková, 1998).

Unemployment remains a serious problem both in the EU and in post-communist countries of central and eastern Europe. Transition to the market economy in Slovakia has led to increasing unemployment and the associated social problems. As a result of the 'shock' scenario in 1990–91 there was growth in long-term mass unemployment (Brhlovič, 1994). Unemployment was experienced in almost all regions, but the south-eastern regions suffered more markedly than those in the north-west. Least affected were the districts of Bratislava, Trnava, Trenčín, Nitra and Banská Bystrica (Bezák, 1996). The major drop was in the manufacturing industry, with over a fifth (23 per cent) of total unemployment (Olexa, 1994). Romany inhabitants experienced over 60 per cent unemployment rates in the districts of Rožňava, Rimavská Sobota, Veľký Krtíš and Spišská Nová Ves and over a third in other eastern Slovakia districts (Rajčáková, 1994). By 1995 continued unemployment increased mainly among the under-25s, many of whom were without any, or had low, qualifications (Rievajová, 1996; Boeri *et al.*, 1998). In June 1998 the unemployment rate reached 13.5 per cent; 352,271 of these people were available for immediate work (Anon, 1998f).

Much of Slovakia's industrial capacity during the communist period was concentrated in large clumsy enterprises utilising many thousands of workers; nearly two-thirds (62 per cent) of the labour force were employed in companies with over 500 personnel (Kopačka, 1992–93). Come independence, the collapse of the Comecon markets steered Slovakia's smoke stack industries into depression. One of the hardest hit was the armaments industry, particularly in places like Martin in the Žilina region (Moran, 1997). Rising world demand for steel, chemicals and other basic industrial products in 1994 led to a rapid and profitable revival (Boland, 1994). However, a policy of 'swords to ploughshares' restructuring led to large enterprises being divided into smaller units manufacturing anything from tractors to diesel engines (Smith, 1994). The post-1995 period has experienced the filling of structural gaps, particularly toward the growing tertiary sector, and a greater emphasis on research and development through better industrial technology (Outrata, 1997; Smith, 1996, 1997). In this the East Slovak Steelworks (VSŽ), the country's largest company, has been a driving force for growth (Anon, 1997e; Riečan, 1998).

Slovakia's poor energy resources have also led to changes, centred on the Horná Nitra coalmining region and the Jaslovské Bohunice nuclear power station (Szőllős, 1994; Anon, 1997c). The increasing use of imported oil has led to an investment boom in oil companies (Anon, 1998d).

Agricultural output declined in the early 1990s. In 1992 the 1.78 million ha of arable land suffered a 11.7 per cent drop in crop production; animal farming fell by 12.1 per cent and cereal production by 13 per cent. Livestock in the state and co-operative sectors included 1.24 million cattle (of which a third were milk cows), 2.05 million pigs, 0.36 million sheep, and 11.51 million poultry in 1992. A federal law in May 1991 returned land seized under the communists to their original owners, with a ceiling of 150 ha of arable per owner. There had been some 3.5 million claimants when ownership claims terminated on 31 December 1992. The real problem for Slovak agriculture was a dearth in investment and essential equipment, accompanied by a reduction of over two-fifths in state subsidies and a sharp drop in agricultural incomes. Long-term plans demanded agricultural privatisation; on independence, land was almost entirely collectivised or organised in co-operatives. During the second half of the 1990s the growth of private farming has been slow. Would-be private farmers have lacked vital capital stocks as well as the knowledge to run a small farm system (Drgoňa, *et al.*, 1998).

Changes in land use are shown in Table 11.5. Since privatisation 34,000 ha of grasslands in hilly and mountain areas have been converted into meadows/pastures, changing a pre-1990 trend. In contrast, arable land has decreased by 34,000 ha. Overall however, by 1998 Slovak agriculture had made considerable progress in the privatisation and restructuring process, as well as in the related agro-food industries (Spišiak, 1996; OECD, 1997; Hutník *et al.*, 1997).

Table 11.5 Slovakia: land use, 1990–1997 ('000 ha)

Land use	1990	1993	1997
Agricultural land	2 448	2 446	2 444
arable	1 509	1 483	1 475
hop-gardens and vineyards	33	31	30
meadows and pastures	808	835	842
Forests	1 989	1 911	1 993
Water surfaces and urban	466	466	466

Source: *ŠúSR, 1997*

The Slovak tourist industry is also showing signs of potential growth. Prior to 1989 it was of minor importance for the country, impeded by a poor infrastructure, by passport and visa barriers, by a poorly developed market economy and by communist ideology; all these factors meant international tourist receipts were low (Baláž, 1997a). Since independence in 1993 the situation has gradually improved (Elliott, 1993; Baláž, 1994; Kačírková, 1994), with international tourist receipts rising from $70.0 mn in 1990 to $672.8 mn in 1996 (Baláž, 1997b), and arrivals at borders increasing from 15.7 million in 1992 to 33.1 million in 1996 (ŠúSR, 1997: 436).

The role of borders, transport, migration and refugees

Government policy after 1989 led to changes in border procedures: passport barriers were removed and no-visa-required agreements were signed with 30 states. One major difference to Slovakia's international borders after 1993 was the creation of a 'new' frontier with the Czech Republic. Its appearance was not new: in medieval times it was the frontier between the former Bohemian and Hungarian kingdoms, and this was further confirmed in 1648 in the Treaty of Westphalia. Regarded as one of the most important events in modern history, it divided the Czech Lands (of the Holy Roman Empire) from Slovakia, which remained under Hungarian control. After 1993 a customs union existed between the Czechs and Slovaks, but the smuggling of cheaper, state-subsidised Slovak goods remained a problem (Boyes, 1992; Daněk and Svět, 1993). To the north, Poland's border with Slovakia was discussed in recent EU entry discussions in Warsaw. On gaining EU membership it will probably be necessary for Poland to introduce entry visas for citizens from non-EU countries such as Slovakia. Three other Slovakian frontiers (with the Czech Republic, Hungary and Austria) would also have to implement entry visas and these arrangements could lead to Slovak friction with these states. The introduction of visas would prove detrimental for the lucrative trade in informal exports by discouraging small traders who come to shop at Slovak bazaars (Anon, 1998e).

In its drive for energy independence Slovakia has had a long and painful dispute with Hungary over the construction of the Gabčikovo–Nagymáros 'water steps' dams along the Danube border (Ostry, 1988; Fitzmaurice, 1994) (see also Chapter 6). A positive sign toward solving this problem came in March 1998 when Hungary and Slovakia agreed in principle to build a new dam (at Nagymáros or Pilismarot) within the next eight years (Anon, 1998b). Failure to do so could lead to further conflict and would affect Slovakia's Hungarian minority, who could find themselves at the centre of this dispute.

Slovakia has a modernised but overall relatively low-density transport system (Table 11.6). Motorway construction began in 1969 but the Bratislava–Brno–Prague link was completed only in 1980 (Podhorský, 1995). After independence Slovakia had a dearth of motorways. These covered only 198 km and were mainly concentrated in the west, leaving an estimated 400 km deficit in the northern and eastern regions. A government plan for road improvement, accepted in 1997, aimed at providing 450 km of motorways (including 28 tunnels) by 2005 (Anon, 1997d). Such improvements are much needed for Slovakia's 1.5 million vehicles, 70 per cent of which are passenger cars.

Table 11.6 Slovakia: transport infrastructure, 1992–1996 (km)

Type	1992	1993	1994	1995	1996
Railways	3 661.00	3 661.00	3 661.00	3 665.00	3 673.00
Of which electrified	1 373.00	1 415.00	1 430.00	1 472.00	1 516.00
Roads	17 880.00	17 865.00	17 889.00	17 869.00	17 867.00
Of which motorway	198.00	198.00	198.00	198.00	215.00
Navigable water	172.00	172.00	172.00	172.00	172.00
Of which canals	38.45	38.45	38.45	38.45	38.45

Source: *ŠúSR, 1997: 390*

Under communism, rail links eastward profited from an extensive reconstruction/ electrification programme. Many lines followed river valleys through difficult mountain terrain. This legacy has helped the present rail network to play an increasing role in the transformation process, although high-speed rail facilities need to be improved (Podhorský, 1996). Help is at hand through a $150 mn five-year term loan to Slovakia provided by a western bank syndicate. Most probably, the loan will be used to improve main European rail corridors lines through the country (Anon, 1997a).

Most of Slovakia's interior rivers are unnavigable, leaving the river Danube as the mainstay for the country's water transport system. It forms the western third of southern Slovakia's border with Hungary, Bratislava and Komárno being the main ports. The latter contains the main shipbuilding activity, now struggling to find sources for long-term foreign investment (Done, 1997b). Air transport is widely distributed throughout the regions, with airports at Lučenec, Žilina, Zvolen, Poprad and Košice. Bratislava is Slovakia's main airport for international passenger and freight traffic; between 1993 and 1996 international passenger numbers rose from 34,000 to 125,000. Over the same period natural gas pipelines in Slovakia increased transport capacity from 64,000 to 81,500 million cu m.

Since the first days of independence Slovakia has made considerable strides in revamping its telecommunications network. It inherited from the communist regime a rather poorly installed infrastructure, but this has been changed under privatisation. A new telecom law in 1998 should improve the telecommunications network by harmonising it with EU legislation. By 1998 the telephone density had reached 23 lines per 100 inhabitants. Of the 1.25 million lines in service, about two-fifths (38 per cent) are digitalised; the target is to increase this to four-fifths by 2003.

The general trend of internal migration in Slovakia over recent years is seen in Table 11.7. Overall internal migrant movement decreased by over a fifth (22.7 per cent) between 1992 and 1996. This is partly due to increased unemployment, but there was also a migration outflow from the poorer eastern districts (Carter, 1997, 1998; Catten *et al.*, 1998). There was a sharper decrease in the internal migration of males than of females, the ratio being a quarter (25 per cent) to just over a fifth (20.5 per cent). Most movement was from municipality to municipality within the same district; this dropped by over a third (34.3 per cent), with, again, a greater decline in the migration of males (37.3 per cent; against 31.5 per cent for females). Movement between districts was more buoyant, with a decline of only 6.2 per cent (males 7.4 per cent; females 5 per cent.)

Table 11.7 Slovakia: internal migration, 1992–1996

Migrants	1992	1993	1994	1995	1996
Total	103 705	97 072	94 419	78 466	80 188
Within district	60 743	55 169	52 875	42 129	39 888
District to district	42 962	41 903	41 544	36 337	40 300

Source: *ŠúSR, 1997: 172*

Table 11.8 Slovakia: international migration, 1996

Continent	Total immigrants		Total emigrants		Total net migration	
	No.	%	No.	%	No.	%
Europe	2 115	85.4	192	87.0	1 923	85.3
Asia	112	4.5	3	1.3	109	4.8
America	173	7.0	13	5.9	160	7.0
Africa	31	1.3	3	1.3	28	1.3
Australia/Oceania	45	1.8	10	4.5	35	1.6
Total	2 476	100.0	221	100.0	2 255	100.0

Source: *ŠúSR, 1997: 173–174*

International migration on a continental basis is shown in Table 11.8. Clearly, Europe is the dominant migrant source, accounting for well over four-fifths of the movement in 1996. Nearly two-thirds came from neighbouring countries, namely the Czech Republic (47 per cent) and Ukraine (12.6 per cent), followed by Romania (7.6 per cent), Germany (5.1 per cent) and Bulgaria (4.1 per cent). Together the former Yugoslavia provided 5 per cent of the immigrants, with two-thirds coming from Serbia. Of the other continents, only America was of note with three-fifths (59 per cent) from Canada and nearly a third (30.6 per cent) from the USA. Emigration from Slovakia was negligible, nearly half (46.3 per cent) went to the Czech Republic, 16.1 per cent to Germany and 8.8 per cent to Austria.

Perhaps the most irritating question facing Europe today is what to do about refugees and asylum seekers, some of whom are escaping from countries where poverty and persecution are problems of everyday life (Brochmann and Hammar, 1999). In Slovakia the refugee problem is mainly centred around the Roma (Gypsies), who number at least 85,000. Roma are often the poorest members of Slovak society, and with the changing economic conditions after 1990 many have lost opportunities for temporary or seasonal work. Numerous communities, particularly in eastern Slovakia, have excessive unemployment rates. The number of Roma living in unbearable conditions in rural communities and devastated central city zones is growing and represents an extremely serious social and economic problem (Carter, 1998). Clearly, there is a need in Slovakia for better support structures toward ethnic minorities like the Roma. This would stem the tide of their migration to the industrial Czech Lands, where they either seek work or, possibly, larger welfare benefits.

Curfews on Roma in Slovak villages were imposed in 1997, and the government reduced their child benefit allowances to curb the 'reproduction of socially unacceptable people' (Boyes and Gledhill, 1997). These restrictions – plus personal attacks on Roma by groups of skinheads – encouraged many to leave. An attractive portrayal on television of the policy of some western countries toward Roma acted as a 'push' factor during the second half of 1997. Canada, the early destination of some Slovak Roma, declined after the imposition of stricter entry rules; many then came to Britain. Over 1,000 Slovak Roma arrived in 1997–98, prior to stricter immigration controls being imposed, and now await decisions on their refugee status by the British immigration service (Ford, 1998).

Politics and culture

Free elections in Slovakia (June 1990) saw the Public Against Violence Party (VPN) win an overall majority and its leader, Vladimir Mečiar, elected Slovak premier (Bútora, 1991; Mihaliková, 1995). With the political decline of the VPN in 1991, Mečiar became chairman of the newly formed Movement for Democratic Slovakia (HZDS) and, following the June 1992 elections, was chosen to lead an HZDS-dominated Slovak government. This situation continued after independence in January 1993 until a successful no-confidence vote on the government in March 1994. Subsequent elections in September saw Mečiar's HZDS retain power in a coalition with the Agrarians' Party of Slovakia (RSS). Together, they polled 35 per cent of the vote and 61 of the 150-member parliamentary seats. They capitalised on public dissatisfaction with the transition, and their strongest regional support came from five districts in central Slovakia (Baráth et al., 1995).

The new government faced several basic demands: to construct a democratic regime based on the rule of law; to develop a market economy; to clarify a new cultural identity while resolving minority issues; to solicit new external security arrangements; and to devise an infrastructure for bonding civil society. Not least of these difficult internal problems was the rise in crime, which was evident in all districts of Slovakia, particularly in the south and west (Michálek, 1995).

Even more serious was co-existence with the Hungarian minority, who formed over a tenth of Slovakia's total population (Wolchik, 1994; Williams, 1996). Problems between the two states have arisen from Hungary's centuries-long domination of Slovakia, which ended only in 1918. Most of the half-a-million-strong minority live along the country's southern border with Hungary (Koscis and Koscis-Hodosi, 1995). Many living there feel that since independence Slovak–Hungarian relations have deteriorated. The reason relates to Mečiar's populist government's attitude toward treatment of the Hungarian minority. This, along with problems associated with the Gabčikovo–Nagymáros Danube dam, have aroused emotions in both countries. The Hungarian minority objects to the rekindling of Slovak nationalism. This was exemplified by the language law of July 1994, which abolished dual-language signs for roads and urban centres and forced Hungarian women to add the Slovakian grammatical suffix 'ova' to their names. In July 1996 Mečiar's government passed a law that redrew Slovakia's administrative regional and district boundaries; these now led to an under-representation of the Hungarian minority influence in regional governments responsible for the infrastructure, education and other services (Anon, 1996b).

By 1997 Mečiar's government was being subjected to increasing national criticism for overheating the economy, for creating a poor image of Slovakia abroad and for the country's failure to be among the first new members of the EU and NATO. His response was to levy a 400 per cent VAT increase on newspapers and magazines critical of the government and suspend independent radio stations. Unfortunately, such acts reflected the immaturity of the Slovak political scene, creating concern among the international community and unintentionally isolating the country unnecessarily from its central European neighbours (Done and Anderson, 1997).

The political situation came to a head in 1998. In January criticism of the government's failure to live up to western democratic standards after five years of independence was made by the Slovak president (Michal Kováč). On his retirement from office in March, the position remained vacant; Mečiar took over some presidential powers and appeared reluctant to accept any changes that jeopardised his position. Unless voters could divest Mečiar of his control, little would change (Samson, 1998). However, in the September 1998 parliamentary elections Mečiar lost power to an opposition coalition, which meant the eclipse of his authoritarian rule. A four-party opposition group – including reformed communists and free-market conservatives – won 93 seats and aimed to use this majority to promote sweeping political reform. This would include constitutional safeguards against usurping power. Democracy appears to be making a comeback, but it is in need of urgent support.

The post-1989 period in Slovakia has been accompanied by vigorous cultural activity, in spite of rapid change and frequent anxious times during political and social development. A large variety of cultural attitudes (liberal, populist, postmodernist, mimetic and experimental) have been expressed, some of them depicted in stylistic ways, others with an emphasis on purity of the language. Further, the country's topographical diversity has reflected the population's regional and cultural heterogeneity, based on the many ethnic minorities living in Slovakia. There are Polish, German, Ukrainian, Ruthenian, Croatian and Bulgarian citizens in addition to the Hungarians, Roma and, since 1993, Czechs. Their influence, for example, has been demonstrated in the creation of Slovak–Roma literature, Slovak–Hungarian culture, and in the contributions of the Jewish community toward Slovak cultural life. National minorities partly use state finances to run their own schools, newspapers and journals, books, theatres and societies.

Besides the ethnic quilt, Slovakia also experiences another cultural division. One side of this partition is located in urban life, with its cosmopolitan, mainly heterogeneous, character closely linked to the multi-cultural central European scene. In contrast, the other side of Slovakia's culture is steeped in tradition, characterised by a greater ethnic and cultural homogeneity with an emphasis on folklore and history. Folklore straddles both urban and rural centres, many of which have their own folk ensembles, bands and theatres, whilst creative artistic potential is most notable in song-writing and dance routines. Art, especially popular art, is held in high esteem by many Slovaks, whilst other outlets for cultural life are represented in Franco–Slovak poetry links, Slovak contemporary cinema and the appearance of new Slovak 'pulp fiction'.

To this varied mixture of cultures and nationalities one can add further differences based on a miscellany of dialects, values and behaviour patterns. These are evident not only in the urban–rural divide, but also in regional location patterns. One consolidating feature over time, however, has been the strong Christian influence on Slovakia's cultural life. Christian beliefs have been bolstered by the population's long-term low mobility, which resulted in a powerful feeling for tradition that is still evident in contemporary Slovak life. Over three million Slovaks are practising Roman Catholics, and more than a quarter of a million are Protestant Evangelists and Reformed Christians. Other notable denominations include Greek Catholics, members of the Eastern Orthodox Church and Jehovah's Witnesses. There is also a small Jewish community. It is commonplace in some urban centres, such as Bardejov, to find as many as five different church denominations in existence. In contrast, about half a million Slovaks profess no religious affinity.

Slovakia and the EU

Early aspirations for closer co-operation with the rest of Europe (Filip, 1994; Mikelka, 1995; Kosír, 1995; Backé and Linder, 1996) were fortified in June 1997 when the Slovak government officially stated that full integration of its country into the EU and other international groupings remained a foreign policy priority. Unfortunately, in July 1997, the statement failed to convince either the heads of the EU or NATO to admit a country that had failed to make the grade either in politics or human rights. The EU refused Slovakia's application for admission to accession talks for the first wave of new entrants from central and eastern Europe. In the same month the referendum for Slovakia joining the NATO alliance was also rejected in spite of its commendable performance in the Partnership for Peace programme. Yet Slovakia's bargaining position to join the North Atlantic Treaty Organization remains strong, particularly since the Kosovo war, and failure to include it would make any future effort to admit Ukraine and Romania geographically anomalous (Hamberger, 1996). Slovakia is also trying to obtain membership of the Organization for Ecomonic Co-operation and Development but has problems in meeting the necessary free-market criteria.

Following the demise of Mečiar's populist government in 1998 – a regime characterised by an increasingly nationalist political atmosphere with a concomitant tendency to authoritarianism – the current coalition government under Prime Minister Mikulas Dzurinda and President Rudolf Schuster has to persuade the country that it can handle problems and issues on the domestic front. It also has to improve the country's image abroad, especially in relation to the EU. There have been encouraging signs: a new non-governmental organisation, the Foundation for a Civil Society (*Nadácia pre občiansku spoločnost*), organised a survey of 380,000 potential first-time voters in the September 1998 elections. The results revealed that, compared to their elders, many younger people had a much less cynical attitude toward the EU (Anon, 1998i).

In order for Slovakia to obtain future EU membership – i.e. by fulfilling the criteria set by the Copenhagen European Council in June 1993 – certain improvements have to be made. If one assumes that political and human rights are ameliorated, then the major hurdle concerns economic performance (Baláž and Trenčianská, 1997; Kramplová, 1998). Since independence the early stimulating effect of devaluation has gradually deteriorated, placing greater pressure on export development (Goldman, 1999). An austerity programme launched by the government in spring 1999 led to a slowdown in domestic demand, which was compensated by increased exports. The timing proved beneficial because Slovakia has been carrying out economic reforms in an expansive external environment, whereby exports and export-oriented industries are stimulating internal growth. Most exports are destined for neighbouring Poland, Hungary and the Czech Republic, as well as for EU countries (Anon, 1999). Slovakia's best hopes for 2000 lie in continuing this export trend, especially to the EU, and in an influx of foreign direct investment (FDI).

The country has to reverse the earlier slow pace of FDI (Carter, 1999a, b), a pace that arose from the previous government's enthusiasm for encouraging foreign investors without having the support of a safe financial regulatory system. Also the government had only a limited influence on decision-making within enterprises, resulting in the investment process being uncoordinated vis-à-vis the national strategy. This explains why, by September 1999, foreign investment stock in Slovakia had reached only $1.8 bn, a much lower level than its CEE neighbours. Future competitive policies need to be structured to maximise benefits from enterprise competition/co-operation, but price collusion has to be strictly prevented (Šesták, 1997; Outrata, 1998). In addition, improved policy decisions have to be made about infant industries, especially about locating them in the country's developing regions (Smith, 1999; Buček, 1999).

Finally, Slovakia must adapt to the EU's environment policy. According to measurements by the Environment Monitoring and Evaluation Programme (EMEP), Slovakia is located on the south-eastern boundary of Europe's highest level of regional air pollution and precipitation acidity. The country fulfilled its commitment to the first sulphur emission reduction protocol of 1979 (30 per cent reduction of European SO_2 emissions by 1993, over against the 1980 level). In compliance with the second sulphur protocol, there has been a decrease of precipitation acidity over its territory (SO_2 reduction of 60 per cent by 2000 compared with 1980) and there are future hopes of diminishing this further (65 per cent by 2005 and 72 per cent by 2010) (Mitošinková, 1997). Water pollution continues to be a problem. Regional government officials in charge of monitoring water quality – after years of refusing to pay attention to results from the Košice-based SOSNA Foundation's testing programme – agreed in 1997 to co-operate more closely with this non-governmental organisation (NGO) and share test results (Anon, 1998h). Specific study projects on environmental conditions have also been established; for example, diagnosis of water pollution problems in the industrialised Hron river basin (Anon, 1996a). PHARE projects have helped with studies on forest pollution (Anon, 1998a). Local NGOs have concentrated on specific regional problems: for example, the Ipel' Union NGO aims to conserve and revitalise the natural and cultural heritage of the Ipel' river watershed in south-central Slovakia (Wollant, 1998).

Less progress has been made by local NGOs against prestigious government nuclear power projects such as at Mochovce, where the first reactor was activated in June 1999. Critical in this context is the need to ease Austria's concerns about the safety of Slovakia's nuclear power stations. This is necessary because it impairs Slovakia's position with regard to EU accession negotiations: states wishing to join have to ensure that their plants meet EU safety standards. Austria has taken a tough line, threatening to boycott Slovakia's chances within the fast-track enlargement process unless it closes its Soviet-built Jaslovské Bohunice plant by 2003. Constructed in the 1970s, this is situated just 60 km from the Austrian border.

Conclusion

Slovakia's legacy of difficult terrain and turbulent history, along with its contemporary political and economic problems, was never the best preparation for a modern state. The new Slovak government has vowed to pursue closer links with the West, improve its relations with neighbouring states and try to create a more democratic society. This aim is hindered by the regional disparities suffered by the country, no better illustrated than in the difference in GDP between the capital, Bratislava, at 5 per cent above the EU average, and eastern Slovakia at 64 per cent below. Clearly problems have to be faced in the smoke stack industries of the eastern regions (Košice and Prešov), the rural backwaters of Rimavska Sobota in the south-east and the mountainous Orava region in the north (Moran, 1999).

This is but one of the many difficulties facing the coalition government. Many observers believed in 1998 that it would not survive a year in office; but if the economy shows sufficient improvement, the coalition's longevity could be maintained beyond 2000 – a possibility that was given a considerable boost at the EU leaders' Helsinki Summit in December 1999. This gave Slovakia encouragement and provided the opportunity for the country to join the fast-track countries for accession negotiations. In this process, the economy, not Austria's nuclear power fears, may prove to be the critical factor. The establishment of a proper market economy will create better conditions for investment. The role of FDI is vital: it has the ability to increase the inflow of more advanced technology and management techniques and also bears a large part of the risks involved. Such new influences can help to negate many of the problems of recalcitrance that the country has inherited from its past, and they can help Slovakia adjust more easily to the demands of the 21st century.

References

Anon, 1996a, Hron decision support system. *Hydro Delft*, 85, 13–14.

Anon, 1996b, Mečiar, Magyars and maps. *The Economist*, 10 August, pp. 34–35.

Anon, 1997a, Banks launch syndication of $150 mln railways loan. *New Europe*, 7 December, p. 16.

Anon, 1997b, Integration is still the target. *The Times, Slovakia Supplement*, 29 July, p. 1.

Anon, 1997c, Nuclear plants to grow by 1999. *The Times, Slovakia Supplement*, 29 July, p. 11.

Anon, 1997d, Road networks keep cars on the move: new projects will meet Slovakia's increasing transport needs. *The Times, Slovakia Supplement*, 29 July, p. 17.

Anon, 1997e, Steel giant is looking to broaden its horizons. *The Times, Slovakia Supplement*, 29 July, p. 6.

Anon, 1998a, Die nationalstrategie des Schutzes der Biodiversität lehnt sich um Rechtsnormen. *Informations-Bulletin SIA, Slowakische Informations-Agentur* (Bratislava), 20, 11–16.

Anon, 1998b, Hungary and Slovakia agree to build Danube dam. *New Europe*, 8 March, p. 16.

Anon, 1998c, New FinMin Maxon wants balanced budget in 1999. *New Europe*, 25 January, p. 16.

Anon, 1998d, Oil sector shares good investment. *New Europe*, 15 January, p. 16.

Anon, 1998e, Poland must tighten border with Slovakia, minister says. *New Europe*, 22 February, p. 16.

Anon, 1998f, Slovakia: unemployment rate rises to 13.5% in June. *New Europe*, 2 August, p. 16.

Anon, 1998g, Slovak trade deficit slows again in June. *New Europe*, 9 August, p. 2.

Anon, 1998h, Sowing seeds of environmentalism in Slovakia. *The Conservation Foundation*, 9, 20.

Anon, 1998i, The voters' veto. *Business Central Europe*, 6 (54), 63.

Anon, 1999, Economic indicators shimmy up. *New Europe*, 19 December, p. 29.

Backé, P., Linder, I., 1996, European Monetary Union: prospects for EU member states and selected candidate countries from central and eastern Europe. *Focus on Transition* (Vienna), 2, 20–45.

Baláž, V., 1994, Tourism and regional development in the Slovak Republic. *European Urban and Regional Studies*, 1 (2), 171–177.

Baláž, V., 1997a, Regional tourism management in the Slovak Republic. *Ekonomický Časopis*, 45 (1), 38–62.

Baláž, V., 1997b, Transition countries in central Europe and international tourism. *Ekonomický Časopis*, 45 (5), 350–370.

Baláž, P., Trenčianská, E., 1997, Joining the European Union – economic inevitability or political ambition for the Slovak Republic? *Ekonomický Časopis*, 45 (8–9), 685–703.

Baráth, J., Szőllős, J., Černák, P., 1995, Analýza stability územia volebnej podpory vybraných politických strán na základe výsledkov volieb 1990, 1992 a 1994. *Geografický Časopis*, 47 (4), 247–259.

Bezák, A., 1996, The relationship between regional and national unemployment trends in Slovakia, 1991–1994. *Acta Facultatis Rerum Naturalium Universitatis Comenianæ: Geographica*, 37, 104–110.

Bilsen, V., 1994, Privatization, company management and performance: a comparative study of privatization methods in the Czech Republic, Hungary, Poland and Slovakia. *In* Jackson, M., Bilsen, V., eds, *Company management and capital market development in the transition*. Guildford: Avebury, pp. 35–96.

Boeri, T., Burda, M. C., Köllö, J., 1998, *Mediating the transition: labour markets in central and eastern Europe*. New York/Prague/Budapest/Košice/Kyiv/Brussels: Institute for East–West Studies, Economic Policy Initiative No. 4.

Boland, V., 1994, Austerity begins to pay dividends. *Financial Times, Survey on Slovakia*, 16 December, p. IV.

Boyes, R., 1992, Lack of consent sours break-up. *The Times*, 31 December, p. 6.

Boyes, R., Gledhill, R., 1997, Romany refugees head for Britain after Canada closes the door. *The Times*, 20 October, p. 5.

Brhlovič, G., 1994, Analýza vývoja zamestnanosti a nezamestnanosti v rokoch 1990–1993 v Slovenskej republike. *Ekonomický Časopis*, 42 (11), 842–857.

Brochmann, G., Hammar, T., 1999, *Mechanisms of immigration control: a comparative analysis of European regulation policies*. New York: Berg.

Buček, M., 1999, Regional disparities in transition in the Slovak Republic. *European Urban and Regional Studies*, 6 (4), 360–364.

Bútora, M., 1991, The hard birth of democracy in Slovakia. *Journal of Communist Studies*, 7 (4), 15–25.

Carter, F. W., 1994, *Trade and urban development in Poland: an economic geography of Cracow, from its origins to 1795*. Cambridge: Cambridge University Press.

Carter, F. W., 1997, Czechoslovakia in transition: migration before and after the 'velvet divorce'. *In* Institut für Migrationsforschung und Interkulturelle Studien, *IMIS-Beiträge, Heft 6*. Osnabrück: Universität Osnabrück, pp. 35–63.

Carter, F. W., 1998, Geographical problems in east Slovakia. *Region and Regionalism* (Łódź/Opole), 3, 187–203.

Carter, F. W., 1999a, The role of foreign direct investment in the regional development of central and south-east Europe. *In* Vaishar, A., ed., *Regional prosperity and sustainability: proceedings of the 3rd Moravian Geographical Conference*. Slavkov u Brna: Institute of Geonics, Academy of Sciences of the Czech Republic, pp. 16–23.

Carter, F. W., 1999b, The geography of foreign direct investment in central-east Europe during the 1990s. *Wirtschafts-Geographische Studien*, 24–25, 40–70.

Catten, N., Grasland, C., Řehák, S., 1998, Migration flows between the Czech and Slovak Republics – which forms of transition? *In* Carter, F. W., Jordan, P., Rey, V., eds, *Central Europe after the fall of the Iron Curtain: geopolitical perspectives, spatial patterns and trends*. Frankfurt: P. Lang, 2nd edn, pp. 319–336.

Daněk, P., Svět, R., 1993, Tschechoslowakei oder Tschechische Republik und Slowakische Republik? *Geographische Rundschau*, 45 (3), 160–165.

Dobosiewicz, Z., 1992, *Foreign investment in eastern Europe*. London/New York: Routledge, pp. 46–48.

Done, K., 1997a, Serious tensions are developing. *Financial Times, Slovakia Survey*, 28 October, p. 21.

Done, K., 1997b, Awash with orders – but struggling. *Financial Times, Slovakia Survey*, 28 October, p. 20.

Done, K., Anderson, R., 1997, Facing isolation in the heart of Europe. *Financial Times, Slovakia Survey*, 28 October, p. 19.

Drgoňa, V., Dubčová, A., Kramáreková, H., 1998, Slovakia. *In* Turnock, D., ed., *Privatization in rural eastern Europe: the process of restitution and restructuring.* Cheltenham/ Northampton MA: Edward Elgar, pp. 251–273.

Elliott, H., 1993, Start now, before the rush. *The Times,* 7 November, p. 5.

Filip, J., 1994, Otázky rozvojovej stratégie ekonomiky Slovenskej republiky v podmienkach európskeho integračného procesu. *Ekonomický Časopis,* 42 (7–8), 489–504.

Fitzmaurice, J., 1994, *Damming the Danube: Gabčikovo and post-communist politics in Europe.* Boulder CO/Oxford: Westview.

Ford, R., 1998, Straw acts to stem tide of Slovakia Gypsies. *The Times,* 8 October, p. 5.

Goldman, M. F., 1999, *Slovakia since independence: a struggle for democracy.* New York: Praeger.

Hamberger, J., 1996, Slovakia's geopolitical situation. *International Studies,* 2, 5–18.

Hruská, E., 1971, Reflections on the origin and development of settlement structure in Czechoslovakia. *Ekistics,* 182, 105–107.

Hutník, F., Tomovčík, J., Štanga, R., 1997, Námety na urýchlenie štruktúrnych zmien v agropotravinárstve Slovenska. *Ekonomický Časopis,* 45 (12), 1010–1028.

Kačírková, M., 1994, Cestovný ruch a jeho úloha v procese transformácie ekonomiky regiónov. *Ekonomický Časopis,* 42 (10), 765–776.

Kárász, P., 1996, Macroeconomic features of foreign capital invested in the Slovak Republic. *Ekonomický Časopis,* 44 (11), 829–836.

Kopačka, L., 1992–3, Československo zaniklo, at' žijí Česká republika a Slovenská republika. *Geografické Rozhledy* (Prague), 2 (2), 35–41.

Koscis, K., Koscis-Hodosi, E., 1995, *Hungarian minorities in the Carpathian Basin: a study in ethnic geography.* Toronto/Buffalo: Matthias Corvinus.

Kosír, I., 1995, Slovakia. *In* Mizsei, K., Rudka, A., eds, *From association to accession: the impact of the Association Agreements on central Europe trade and integration with the European Union.* Warsaw/Prague/Budapest/Košice/New York: Institute for East–West Studies, pp. 85–104.

Kramplová, Z., 1998, *Die Slowakei auf dem Weg in die EU.* Vienna: IDM-Info Sonderheft, Institut für den Donauraum und Mitteleuropa.

LeBor, A., 1994, Investors scared off by block on privatisation in Slovakia. *The Times,* 20 December, p. 4.

Michálek, A., 1995, Priestorová diferenciácia kriminality a vybraných trestných činov v SR na úrovni okresov. *Geografický Časopis,* 47 (4), 93–108.

Michník, L., Bal'áková, G., 1997, Súčasný stav a d'alšie močnosti zahraničnoobchodnej spolupráce Slovenskej republiky s vybranými rozvojovými krajinami. *Ekonomický Časopis,* 45 (11), 899–918.

Mihaliková, S., 1995, *Democratic political culture - dream or reality? Slovakia after 1989.* Colchester: University of Essex, Centre of European Studies, Occasional Papers in European Studies No. 8.

Mikelka, E., 1995, Integrácia Slovenska do európskej a svetovej ekonomiky. *Ekonomický Časopis,* 43 (7–8), 635–667.

Mitošinková, M., 1997, Regional air pollution and quality of precipitation. *In* Pukančiková, K., ed.,

Air pollution in the Slovak Republik, 1996. Bratislava: Air Protection Department, Ministry of the Environment of the Slovak Republic, pp. 1–5.

Moran, T., 1997, Regional focus: Žilina. *Business Central Europe*, 5 (44), 70.

Moran, T., 1999, Eastern promises: Slovakia needs to tackle its regional disparities. *Business Central Europe*, 6 (67), 40.

Němec, J., Prachár, I., 1997, Slovenska ekonomika signalizuje zmenu tempa rastu. *Ekonomický Časopis*, 45 (12), 1029–1050.

OECD, 1997, *Slovakia: review of agricultural policies in non-member countries.* Paris: OECD.

Okáli, I., Gabrielová, H., Hlavatý, E., Outrata, R., 1995, Economic development of Slovakia in 1994. *Ekonomický Časopis*, 43 (3), 175–204.

Olexa, M., 1994, Labour force survey in the Slovak Republic. *Statistics in Transition* (Warsaw), 1 (4), 509–513.

Ostry, D., 1988, The Gabčikovo–Nagymáros dam system as a case study in conflict of interest in Czechoslovakia and Hungary. *Slovo*, 1 (1), 11–24.

Outrata, R., 1997, Structural changes and competitiveness in Slovak industry. *Ekonomický Časopis*, 45 (6–7), 480–499.

Outrata, R., 1998, Medzinárodná konkurencieschopnost' slovenského priemyslu a process probližovania k Európeskej únii. *Ekonomický Časopis*, 46 (2), 186–201.

Paulov, J., 1996, The transformation process in Slovakia: some thoughts on spatio-temporal regularities, regional pattern and possible regional shift. *Acta Facultatis Rerum Naturalium Universitatis Comenianæ: Geographica*, 37, 112–120.

Podhorský, F., 1995, Dial'nice na Slovensku. *Geografický Časopis*, 43 (2), 150–161.

Podhorský, F., 1996, The position of transport in the transformation of the regional systems in Slovakia. *Acta Facultatis Rerum Naturalium Universitatis Comenianæ: Geographica*, 37, 242–248.

Polišenský, J. V., 1991, *History of Czechoslovakia in outline.* Prague: Bohemia International.

Rajčáková, E., 1994, The main characters of process and state of unemployment in Slovakia. *Acta Facultatis Rerum Naturalium Universitatis Comenianæ: Geographica*, 34, 173–188.

Riečan, M., 1998, Slovenské železárny VSŽ míří vzhuru. *Hospodářské Noviny*, 5 August, p. 7.

Rievajová, E., 1996, Nezamestnanost' v Slovenskej republike – jej vývoj a špecifiká. *Ekonomický Časopis*, 44 (11), 879–895.

Sáková, B., 1998, Slovensko: hospodářství funguje, míní vláda. *Hospodářské Noviny*, 13 July, p. 9.

Samson, I., 1998, *Die Nationalratswahlen in der Slowakischen Republik von 25–26 September 1998.* Vienna: IDM-Aktuell Donauraum und Mitteleuropa, Zeitschrift des Institutes für den Donauraum und Mitteleuropa No. 2.

Schwartz, G., Stone., M., van der Willigen, T., 1994, Beyond stabilisation: the economic transformation of Czechoslovakia, Hungary and Poland. *Communist Economies and Economic Transformation*, 6 (3), 291–313.

Šesták, J., 1997, Niektoré aspekty prílevu priamych zahraničných investícií na Slovensko vo vnútornych a v medzinárodných súvislostiach. *Ekonomický Časopis*, 45 (2), 121–139.

Shen, R., 1993, *Economic reform in Poland and Czechoslovakia: lessons in systematic transformation*. New York: Praeger.

Smith, A., 1994, Uneven development and the restructuring of the armaments industry in Slovakia. *Transactions of the Institute of British Geographers*, 19 (4), 404–424.

Smith, A., 1996, From convergence to fragmentation: uneven development, industrial structuring and the 'transition to capitalism' in Slovakia. *Environment and Planning A*, 28, 135–156.

Smith, A., 1997, Constructing capitalism? Small and medium enterprises, industrial districts and regional policy in Slovakia. *European Urban and Regional Studies*, 4 (1), 45–70.

Smith, A., 1999, *Reconstructing the regional economy: industrial transformation and regional development in Slovakia*. Cheltenham/Northampton MA: Edward Elgar.

Spišiak, P., 1996, The current rural landscape and agriculture in Slovakia. *Acta Facultatis Rerum Naturalium Universitatis Comemeianœ: Geographica*, 37, 214–221.

ŠúSR (Štatistiký úrad Slovenskej Republiky), 1997, *Štatistická Ročenka Slovenskej Republiky 1997*. Bratislava: VEDA.

Szőllős, J., 1994, Energy industry of Horná Nitra and its position in Slovak energetics. *Geografický Časopis*, 46 (2), 160–171.

Takla, L., 1994, The relationship between privatization and the reform of the banking sector: the case of the Czech Republic and Slovakia. *In* Estrin, S., ed., *Privatization in central and eastern Europe*. London/New York: Longman, pp. 154–175.

Williams, K., 1996, The Magyar minority in Slovakia. *Regional and Federal Studies*, 6 (1), 1–20.

Wolchik, S., 1994, Politics of ethnicity in post-communist Czechoslovakia. *East European Politics and Societies*, 8 (1), 10–21.

Wollant, I., 1998, Ipel'ská únia (Ipel' Union, Slovak Republic). *Newsletter Central and Eastern Europe* (European Programme IUCN, Prague), 15 (28), 9.

Zemplinerová, A., 1997, Small enterprises and foreign investors – key players in enterprise restructuring and structural change. *Ekonomický Časopis*, 45 (10), 810–850.

12

LATVIA

Darrick Danta

Although a relatively small country (Figure 12.1) not accustomed to centre stage of world events, Latvia is significant for its ability to persevere and even prosper with a limited resource base. The country is a land of contrasts: comprised of an ancient people, it is among Europe's youngest; topographically rather bland, its culture is rich and vibrant; long oppressed by outside forces, its government must today grapple with extending rights to its large Russian minority. The nation has also remained a cohesive entity at the centre of the Baltic region, sharing common traits and aspirations with its neighbours to the north and south, while being stretched between the Slavic world to the east and the Germanic one to the west.

This chapter seeks to provide an overview of Latvia, particularly in terms of its basic geography, history, economy and politics, with an eye to evaluating its potential for entry into the European Union. Latvia applied for admission to the EU in 1995, but, as discussed earlier (Chapter 2), the country was placed in the so-called second-wave group and entered accession negotiations only in 2000. The country is desirous of admission to the EU as a 'return to Europe' and for the security benefits that membership offers. As will be shown, Latvia is a good candidate for EU membership, although problems for entry include a sluggish economy, issues surrounding the country's Russian minority and a low level of popular support for membership. Given these impediments, Latvia most likely will not gain entry until sometime after 2005 at the earliest.

Resources

Latvia is relatively small in area – some 64,589 sq km – about the size of the Republic of Ireland or 42 per cent of the European average (Dreifelds, 1995: 104–110). The country is located on the Baltic Sea and surrounded by Estonia to the north, Lithuania to the south, Russia to the east and Belarus to the south-east. Extensive continental glaciation during the last ice age has left the country with little topographic relief: the land is generally flat to undulating, with a long (531 km), sandy coastline along the Baltic. However, what the country lacks in hills, it makes up for in hydrographic features, boasting some 3,000 small lakes, numerous rivers (the principal one being the Daugava or Western Dvina) and assorted marshes and bogs.

Figure 12.1: Latvia

The main geographical feature of Latvia is the Gulf of Riga, which exists as a large indentation in the north-west corner of what would otherwise be a roughly rectangular-shaped country. This gulf extends north into Estonia and is nearly enclosed by large islands, which belong to Estonia. Climatically, Latvia is in a transition zone between the maritime climate of western Europe and the continental climate of Russia. Winters are, therefore, fairly severe and summers warm, though temperatures in both seasons are moderated by the proximity of the Baltic Sea.

Approximately 46 per cent of Latvia is covered by oak and pine forests and woodlands, some 27 per cent is cultivated and 13 per cent used for pasture. Natural resources are scarce, consisting only of timber, peat and some minerals, mainly industrial-grade dolomite and limestone. The main environmental issue facing the country is pollution of air and water, especially in the Gulf of Riga, the Daugava river and around military bases (CIA, 1999: 1). Likewise, soil and groundwater contamination by chemical and petroleum products is a problem around industrial and military sites.

Latvia's population currently stands at 2.47 million and is comprised of 54 per cent Latvian, 30 per cent Russian, 4 per cent Belarusian and 3 per cent Ukrainian, along with some Poles and Lithuanians (Table 1.1 in this volume; Fernandez-Armesto, 1994; Dreifelds, 1995: 85–87,

110–130; Department of State, 1997; CIA, 1999). The country's main religions are Lutheran, Orthodox and Roman Catholic; main languages are Latvian and Russian. The population is ageing: some 15 per cent of Latvians are 65 years or older; the average age is in the mid-30s. Not surprisingly given this top-heavy age structure, the country's birth-rate is only eight per thousand, whilst the death-rate is sixteen per thousand. Adding to this demographic decline is a net out-migration of six per thousand, yielding an overall annual population decline of 1.4 per cent.

About 73 per cent of Latvians live in cities. Sitting atop the urban hierarchy is Riga (875,000), the country's capital, largest city and main seaport, located at the mouth of the Daugava river on the Gulf of Riga. Other major cities include Daugavpils (125,000), Liepāja (108,000) and Jelgava, which are industrial and trading centres located, respectively, in the south-east, western, and central coastal portions of the country.

The government of Latvia is a parliamentary democracy consisting of an executive branch, made up of a president, prime minister and council of ministers; a legislative branch made up of a 100-seat parliament; and a judicial branch headed by the supreme court. The country is divided into 26 counties.

The economy of Latvia, like other transition countries, is in flux, though the outlook is optimistic (Table 12.1). The latest (1998) estimates for GDP place Latvia's total economy at $6.4 bn, which yields $4,136 per capita purchasing power parity (PPP). The economy's growth rate reached its lowest point in 1992, rebounded to about 6 per cent during the second half of the 1990s, but dipped back to negative values at the end of the decade. Likewise, inflation reached extreme levels in the early 1990s, but has fallen to low levels more recently; unemployment generally has remained below 10 per cent over the last decade. The labour force, which stands at 1.4 million, is distributed between 9 per cent agriculture, 34 per cent industry and 57 per cent service sector.

The country's main industries produce vehicles (buses, vans and rolling stock), machinery, consumer goods, petrochemicals, pharmaceuticals, textiles and food products. Agricultural products include grains, vegetables, meat, dairy products and fish. Exports, valued at $0.5 bn in 1999, down from $1.4 bn in 1995, consist mainly of wood and wood products, textiles and foodstuffs; imports, valued at $0.8 bn, were mainly fuels, machinery and chemicals. Latvia's main trading partners are Russia, CIS countries, Sweden, the UK, and Finland.

A brief history

Contemporary Latvians are descendants of an ancient group of peoples collectively known as the Balts (Fernandez-Armesto, 1994; Dreifelds, 1995: 83–102; Latvia, 1999). Their language,

Table 12.1 Latvia: economic structure, 1990–1995

	1990	1991	1992	1993	1994	1995	1996	1997	1998
Nominal GDP ($ bn)	na	1.0	1.5	2.2	3.6	4.5	5.1	5.6	6.4
GDP per capita (PPP; $)	5 472.0	5 118.0	3 463.0	3 070.0	3 213.0	3 312.0	3 515.0	3 920.0	4 136.0
GDP (% change)	−3.5	−10.4	−34.9	−14.9	0.6	−0.8	3.3	8.6	3.6
Industrial production (% change)	na	−2.1	−46.2	−38.1	−9.5	−6.3	1.4	6.1	−0.7
Budget balance (% of GDP)	na	na	−0.8	0.6	−4.1	−3.9	−1.7	0.1	−0.8
Unemployment (%)	na	na	2.3	5.8	6.5	6.6	7.2	7.0	9.2
Average monthly wage ($)	na	na	na	na	119.0	161.0	183.5	211.8	225.9
Inflation (%)	10.5	172.0	951.0	108.0	36.6	25.1	17.6	8.4	4.7
Exports ($ bn)	na	na	0.8	1.1	1.0	1.4	1.5	1.8	1.9
Imports ($ bn)	na	na	1.0	1.1	1.3	1.9	2.3	2.7	3.0
Trade balance ($ bn)	na	na	−0.2	0.0	−0.3	−0.5	−0.8	−0.9	−1.8
Current-account balance ($ bn)	na	na	0.0	0.3	0.0	−0.2	−0.2	−0.3	−0.7
Foreign direct investment flow ($ m)	na	na	43.0	51.0	155.0	244.0	376.0	515.0	200.0
Foreign exchange reserves ($ bn)	na	na	na	0.4	0.5	0.5	0.7	0.7	1.0
Foreign debt ($ bn)	na	na	0.0	0.2	0.4	1.4	2.0	0.4	0.4
Discount rate (%)	na	na	na	27.0	37.8	21.1	9.7	4.0	4.0
Exchange rate (/$)	na	na	0.7	0.7	0.6	0.5	0.6	0.6	0.6
Population (mn)	2.7	2.7	2.6	2.6	2.6	2.5	2.5	2.5	2.5

Source: *UNECE, 1999*

Lettish, although Indo-European, is related only to Lithuanian; it is unrelated to the several Slavic and Germanic languages used in surrounding areas. Many of the cultural and folklore elements developed by these early people remain prominent today, especially their reverence for natural elements – oak trees and lime hold symbolic significance in Latvian mythology – and the importance placed on song and music festivals.

Although mention of the area was made at least as early as the 1st century AD in connection with the amber trade with the Roman Empire, Latvian settlement of their present-day territory occurred during the 6th century when East Baltic tribes were driven westwards by the Slavonic

Kryvycy. Loose tribal associations generally held sway during the 10th and 11th centuries in spite of pressure from Slavic tribes from the east and Swedes from the west. This situation changed from the 12th century as the Latvians entered a period of subjugation that would last for 800 years.

During the mid-1100s Saxon merchants began pushing into the Gulf of Riga, where they encountered the Finnish speaking Livs, which explains the German name for the region *Livland* or its Latin equivalent *Livonia*. Missionaries, though, soon replaced merchants, as those with the crusader spirit were drawn to the area bent on converting the pagan tribes. The first monk arrived in 1180 and was made bishop in 1186. His successor, Albert, bishop of Livonia, founded Riga in 1201 and formed the Order of the Brothers of the Sword the following year. By the time the Brothers merged with the Knights of the Teutonic Order in 1237, they had conquered all the Latvian tribal kingdoms. Thus began German rule in the guise of the Livonian confederation, which pitted the Teutonic Order, archbishopric of Riga and free city of Riga in a three-way tug-of-war for control of the territory. Apart from some prosperity enjoyed after Riga joined the Hanseatic League in 1282, Latvians generally languished under their subject status.

The next 400 years saw much of the same treatment, although from different masters. During this period Latvia was divided first between Lithuania and Poland (1561 and 1581) and later with Sweden (1621 and 1629). Latvians also found themselves pulled between the Catholic and Lutheran worlds as successive leaders exercised their predilections – although pagan practices apparently survived, as evidenced by laws against black practices and the imposition of compulsory church attendance. Finally, over the period 1710–95 the Russians, under Peter I, were able to wrest from the Swedes and Poles first Riga and then the several additional pieces of territory that today make up Latvia. Russian rule continued until 1918, during which time Latvian serfs gained little by way of increased freedoms or ability to own land.

Taking advantage of the vacuum created by the 1917 Bolshevik Revolution, Latvians proclaimed their independence on 18 November 1918. Almost immediately, though, the Soviets, after setting up a communist government, took Riga and forced the elected government to flee. The ebb and flow of first German and then Russian military incursions into the country continued until 1920. By 1922 Latvia had a constitution and was well on its way toward establishing an independent and prosperous state in spite of the considerable damage that had been wrought during the years of domination and war. The government was able to implement land reform and facilitate industrialisation, although only 17 per cent of the workforce was engaged in industry in the late-1930s.

The beginning of the end of Latvia's brief period in the sun began in August 1939 with the Molotov–Ribbentrop Pact (Kirby, 1994). Considering it 'theirs', the Red Army invaded Latvia in 1940, and soon a puppet government was formed that quickly voted to incorporate the nation into the USSR. After a second German occupation of the country from 1941–44, which saw the massacre of 95 per cent of the Jewish population and widespread destruction of the industrial capacity, Latvia was fully incorporated in the Soviet system. The early period of Soviet-style administration produced typical results: mass deportations (35,000 in 1940, followed by at least another 100,000, mainly in 1949); expropriation of most private property; forced industrialisation; collectivisation of agriculture; participation of Latvia in the division of labour; and bombardment by the Soviet propaganda machine (Latvia, 1999: 3). Particularly troubling for the Latvians was the extreme Russification of the nation's culture along with the relocation of ethnic Russians into the country, which eventually changed the proportions of natives from over three-quarters to just over one-half. Nearly all government and other key posts were reserved for ethnic Russians, whose language largely replaced Latvian.

The history of Latvia – or more accurately the Latvian SSR – during the period from the 1950s until the mid-1980s is essentially that of the Soviet Union (Bradshaw *et al.*, 1994: 158–168). On the one hand, Latvia remained a small republic with limited resources, located on the periphery of the rest of the Union. On the other hand, Soviet planning strategy sought to integrate Latvia's economy tightly into the rest of the Union, thereby making the country dependent on Soviet resources and products and thus less likely to seek independence. For example, in 1987 over half of Latvia's imports and exports were with Russia alone, and nearly 75 per cent of this was with the Slavic republics of the USSR (Bradshaw *et al.*, 1994: 173). By 1989 general levels of economic development and quality of life were higher in the Baltic republics than in the USSR; overall, Latvia's values were better than or intermediate with its neighbours (Table 12.2).

Table 12.2 Quality of life indicators for the USSR and the Baltic republics, 1988–1989

Indicator	USSR	Estonia	Latvia	Lithuania
Per capita income index	100.0	109.8	119.0	117.2
Retail trade turnover: roubles per capita	1 282.0	1 609.0	1 831.0	1 965.0
Life expectancy (years)	69.5	71.8	70.4	70.6
Infant mortality (per 1000 live births)	22.7	10.7	11.1	14.7
No. of doctors per 1000 residents	116.9	126.7	126.5	115.7
Living space per resident (sq m)	15.1	18.7	19.2	21.1
Average salary (roubles)	235.8	242.7	260.9	300.9
Rural telephones per 1000 persons	32.0	78.0	119.0	97.0

Source: *Bradshaw et al., 1994: 167*

Post-Soviet developments

The general thaw brought on by Gorbachev's dual policies of *glasnost* and *perestroika*, beginning in the mid-1980s, created the opportunity for people throughout the Soviet Union to press for reform (Shoemaker, 1999). In 1987 Latvians began mass demonstrations based on ecological and political concerns. In 1988 they formed an independent political party, the Latvian Popular Front, which easily won the lion's share of posts in the 1990 elections (aided, of course, by voting requirements that favoured ethnic Latvians). Later that year the legislature passed a declaration of independence, and by late 1991 – in spite of a final effort by the Soviets to keep the former republic under its yoke – Latvia's independence was recognised internationally.

Problems, though, soon developed. As was the case for the other transition economies, Latvia was faced with the need to create a market economy, privatise industry, agriculture, housing, etc. and reorient trade – all the while keeping inflation, unemployment and social unrest to a minimum. The initial period, 1990–93, was difficult: inflation hit 951 per cent in 1992; industrial production fell by 46 per cent and 38 per cent in the years 1992 and 1993; per capita GDP fell 44 per cent between 1990 and 1993; trade volume dropped (Table 12.1; Bradshaw *et al.*, 1994; Barnard, 1999); and banking scandals rocked both economy and government (Anon, 1996a).

However, the country has made a very rapid turnaround. Latvia's new currency, the lat, was introduced in 1993 and has proven stable on world markets; Latvia's budget has enjoyed relative stability since 1997. A bottom-up growth of a free-market economy has proceeded hand-in-glove with governmental efforts at privatisation, which has occurred fastest in agriculture and small firms; however, the housing sector and large industries remain largely state owned. Most employment is in the private sector, which also contributes by far the most to the country's GDP. Latvia is still struggling, though, to secure new trading partners to replace Russia, Ukraine and Belarus. So far, the Netherlands, Germany and Sweden are Latvia's main western trade partners. Foreign investment in Latvia has been limited, totalling only $1.2 bn for the period 1990–99. Major investing countries are Germany, the USA, Sweden, Switzerland and Austria. Latvia's lack of resources is proving detrimental to attracting investment, though its coastline may prove to be a valuable asset in promoting a tourism industry (Hofheinz, 1991: 70).

Latvia has made considerable progress on the diplomatic front. After declaring independence in 1991, the country quickly joined the UN and most other international organisations. Latvia has established embassies in many countries and is eager to expand its international role. Even relations with Russia are improving, largely as a result of Russian troop withdrawals. However, language and naturalisation laws remain a thorny issue among non-ethnic Latvians (Anon, 1996b).

Fitness to join the European Union

This section provides an overview of Latvian–EU relations, outlines some of the main obstacles to admission and discusses efforts made to address these problems. Overall, Latvia has made good progress at addressing the concerns raised by the EU and should be in good position to be admitted during the period 2005–10.

Latvia–EU relations

Latvia applied for EU membership in June 1995 but was not chosen as one of the first-wave countries included in the accession negotiations that began in 1998. Latvians understandably were irritated by this exclusion, especially given the apparent preferential treatment of their Baltic neighbour Estonia. They argued that outdated statistics were used in the evaluation and that they should be considered with the first group. The EU countered with the argument that Latvia had not progressed as quickly as Estonia in pursuing reform. A second blow came in 1997 when Latvia, along with the other Baltic nations, was denied admission to the North Atlantic Treaty Organization (NATO).

Latvian politicians have made EU entry a major goal for two main reasons (Herd, 1999). First, given their long history of subjugation under various powers, and especially their most recent experience with the Soviet Union, they see membership in the EU as a tangible path of return to the European family (and as a device for distancing themselves from Russia). The symbolic significance of this should not be understated. Second, Latvians are justifiably gravely concerned over security issues, in particular the threat of Russian aggression. They see EU membership as providing medium-term protection, with an eye to eventual NATO membership affording a long-term solution.

However, despite some evidence suggesting strong sentiment for joining the EU (Anon, 1998), popular support in Latvia for entering the Union is weak, perhaps a response to the perception that the EU has not been as welcoming as it should have been. Polls conducted by the European Commission in 1997 showed that only 34 per cent of Latvians would vote in a referendum in favour of EU membership, the second lowest level of all the candidate countries (Table 1.3 in this volume; Grabbe and Hughes, 1999). By the end of 1999 the level of support had increased to just 49.7 per cent (EIB, 1999). Interestingly, the concern over EU entry causing loss of sovereignty, common among most CEE nations, is largely absent in Latvia – no doubt the result of long association with other countries.

Latvia continues to align itself more closely with the EU. Trade with EU countries, mainly Germany, the UK and Sweden, continues to increase and reached 56.6 per cent of total exports in 1998. Furthermore, Latvia continues to receive EU financial assistance through the PHARE programme. Between 1992 and 1999 Latvia was allocated EURO 248 mn, and a further EURO 16.1

mn in 1999, to support language training for non-Latvian speakers, reinforce institutional and administrative capacity and improve infrastructure (Lusis, 1998; European Commission, 1999).

Political considerations

In 1998 the EU Commission found that Latvia's institutions function smoothly and that it fulfils the Copenhagen political criteria for entry in the EU. Latvia has achieved stability of its various branches of government, guarantees democracy and rule of law, has made progress on combating corruption and has acceded to the major international human rights instruments (European Commission, 1999).

A remaining issue, though, concerns Latvia's integration of non-citizens, especially with regard to language laws (Smith *et al.*, 1994). Approximately 600,000 (25 per cent) of those living in Latvia are non-citizen residents, mostly Russians. Previously, gaining Latvian citizenship was rather difficult (Anon, 1998), but since new legislation came into force in 1998 there has been a dramatic rise in the number of persons naturalised. Furthermore, the government has made increasing efforts to expand Latvian language training.

Although not addressed in formal documents, another concern has been Latvia's lack of regional co-operation. In 1989 Estonia, Latvia and Lithuania formed the Baltic Assembly, whose aim was to create a free trade zone and generally participate in regional decision-making. However, intra-Baltic co-operative efforts as a means of furthering EU entry potential never materialised.

Economic considerations

In its 1997 *Opinion* the European Commission (1999) concluded that Latvia has made considerable progress in the creation of a market economy but that it would face serious difficulties in coping with competitive pressures and market forces within the Union in the medium term. One problem facing Latvia is the continued economic crisis in Russia and the consequent loss of stability and markets. A further problem concerns Latvia's low level of per capita GDP: compared to the average EU15 countries, it is only 8 per cent; when expressed as purchasing power parity (PPP), the value rises to 18 per cent, but this is still the lowest value of any of the applicant countries (Ardy, 1999: 108). In 1998 Latvia's GDP was only 58 per cent of that in 1989 (Jones and Fallesen, 1999: 32). Considerable room for improvement still exists in the performance of Latvia's economy.

Environmental considerations

As mentioned earlier, environmental problems, particularly pollution of air, water and soil, were an early topic of protest by Latvians during the Soviet regime. The state of the environment in Latvia also has been recognised as problematic by the EU, but the problem is viewed more in terms of a limited set of 'hot spots' than a general condition. The European Commission (1999) has further pointed to the potential for trans-boundary pollution (e.g. various types of contaminants entering Latvia from Russia and Belarus) and the inadequacy of investment levels to combat existing problems. The EC's *Opinion* is that Latvia can meet the requirements of the environmental *acquis* in the medium term and ensure full compliance in the long term.

Conclusion

Latvia is a country with a troubled past, but the future is promising. After centuries of outside domination, punctuated by the period 1940–1991 when it was fully incorporated within the USSR, Latvia is emerging as a prosperous, democratic society.

In terms of entering the EU, Latvia has fulfilled or is making good progress toward fulfilling all of the stipulations of the Europe Agreement. It fulfils the political criteria, particularly concerning the integration of non-citizens, but further efforts must be made to strengthen the judiciary, fight corruption and increase Latvian language training. Latvia has achieved a functioning market economy and has privatised nearly all of the former state-owned enterprises. Regulators need only ensure that macroeconomic stability is maintained, especially in the face of crises in Russia, and continue improvements to the infrastructure so that long-term growth of the economy can continue. Latvia has also made progress on environmental protection and in aligning all the various aspects of legislation as a precursor to EU entry. The country should be ready for admission sometime after 2005; however, given the low level of support, the referendum for joining the EU may not receive sufficient popular vote.

References

Anon, 1996a, How to go bust in the Baltics. *The Economist*, 20 January, p. 79.

Anon, 1996b, Them and us. *The Economist*, 17 August, pp. 67–69.

Anon, 1998, Latvia votes for Europe. *The Economist*, 10 October, p. 57.

Ardy, B., 1999, Agricultural, structural policy, the budget and eastern enlargement of the European Union. *In* Henderson, K., ed., *Back to Europe: central and eastern Europe and the European Union*. London and Philadelphia: UCL Press, pp. 107–128.

Barnard, B., 1999, The Baltics. *Europe*, 390, 23–25.

Bradshaw, M., Hanson, P., Shaw, D., 1994, Economic restructuring. *In* Smith, G., ed., *The Baltic States: the national self-determination of Estonia, Latvia and Lithuania*. New York: St Martin's Press, pp. 158–180.

CIA, 1999, Latvia. *In* CIA, *The world factbook*. Washington DC: CIA. http://www.odci.gov/cia/publications/factbook/lg.html.

Department of State (USA), 1997, *Background notes: Latvia*. Washington DC: Department of State.

http://www.state.gov/www/background_notes/latvia_0997_bgn.html.

Dreifelds, J., 1995, Latvia. *In* Iwaskiw, W. R., ed., *Estonia, Latvia, and Lithuania: country studies*. Washington DC: Library of Congress, pp. 85–165.

EIB (European Integration Bureau), *Latvia, 1999: EIB information*. Riga: EIB. http://www.eib.lv/www/owa/NOTIK_INFO_ENG?IN_ID=1660&in_gads=1356.

European Commission, 1999, *Regular report from the Commission on progress towards accession: Latvia*. Washington DC: European Commission. http://www.europa.eu.int/ comm/enlargement/latvia/rep_10_99/index.htm.

Fernandez-Armesto, F., ed, 1994, *The Times guide to the peoples of Europe*. London: Times Books.

Grabbe, H., Hughes, K., 1999, Central and east European views on EU enlargement: political debates and public opinion. *In* Henderson, K., ed., *Back to Europe: central and eastern Europe and the European Union*. London/Philadelphia: UCL Press, pp. 185–202.

Herd, G. P., 1999, The Baltic states and EU enlargement. *In* Henderson, K., ed., *Back to Europe: central and eastern Europe and the European Union*. London/Philadelphia: UCL Press, pp. 259–273.

Hofheinz, P., 1991, Opportunity in the Baltics. *Fortune*, 124 (9), 68–74.

Jones, B., Fallesen, L., 1999, The newly independent states. *Europe*, 383, 30–36.

Kirby, D., 1994, Incorporation: the Molotov–Ribbentrop Pact. *In* Smith, G., ed., *The Baltic States: the national self-determination of Estonia, Latvia and Lithuania*. New York: St Martin's Press, pp. 69–85.

Latvia, Embassy of, 1999, *History of Latvia: a brief synopsis*. Washington DC: Embassy of Latvia. http://www.latvia-usa.org/hisoflatbrie.html.

Lusis, J., 1998, Latvia: potential and opportunity at the centre of the Baltic. *In* Nicholl, W., Schoenberg, R., eds, *Europe beyond 2000: the enlargement of the European Union towards the east*. London: Whurr Publishers, pp. 169–178.

Shoemaker, M. W., 1999, *Russia, Eurasian states, and eastern Europe 1999*. Harpers Ferry WV: Stryker-Post Publications, 30th ed.

Smith, G., Aasland, A., Mole, R., 1994, Statehood, ethnic relations and citizenship. *In* Smith, G., ed., *The Baltic States: the national self-determination of Estonia, Latvia and Lithuania*. New York: St Martin's Press, pp. 181–205.

UNECE, 1999, *Trends in Europe and North America: Latvia*. New York: UNECE. http://www.unece.org/stats/trend/lat.htm.

13

LITHUANIA

Darrick Danta

Lithuania is a small Baltic country with a proud past struggling to regain a foothold in its European home (Figure 13.1). This chapter examines the resource and historical contexts of the country and evaluates Lithuania's evolving relations with the European Union. Since applying for membership in 1995, Lithuania has made good progress at continuing to reform its economy, improving relations with Russia, and strengthening its administrative capacity for the internal market. Lithuania, therefore, is a worthy candidate for EU membership and should be eligible for entry with the other countries comprising the second wave sometime in the period 2005–10. However, public support for entry remains low.

Resources

Lithuania's land area covers 65,300 sq km, making it almost identical in size to Latvia (Vardys and Slaven, 1996; Department of State, 1998; CIA, 1999; Lithuanian Home Page, 2000). It is located on the Baltic Sea and surrounded by Latvia to the north, Belarus to the east and south-east and Poland to the south. The outstanding geographical feature of this otherwise circular country is the presence of the Russian *oblast* Kaliningrad, located on the Baltic and wedged between Lithuania and Poland. Of course, this exclave, still politically part of the Russian Federation although separated from it by Lithuanian (and Belarusian) territory, has the potential to significantly affect relations between the two countries.

Lithuania occupies the rim of the North European Plain, and as such is largely flat with moraine hills grouped mainly in the west and east of the country. Nearly 3,000 lakes, several rivers (the principal one being the Nemunas or Niemen river), plus many bogs and marshes in the central part of the county account for Lithuania's main hydrographic features. Because of the moderating effects of the Baltic Sea, Lithuania's climate is transitional between the maritime climate of western Europe and the continental climate of Russia (Vardys and Slaven, 1996: 186–189).

Figure 13.1: Lithuania

Approximately 49 per cent of Lithuania is arable land, 22 per cent pasture and meadows and 16 per cent forests and woodlands (Department of State, 1998: 1). Apart from peat, limestone and gravel, natural resources are limited, although potentially economically viable reserves of oil, iron ore and granite also exist. The main environmental issue facing the country is soil and groundwater contamination from chemicals and petroleum products, mainly around industrial and military sites. Another potential problem concerns the continued operation of Lithuania's nuclear power plant. Currently, two 1,500 MW RBMK graphite-moderated nuclear reactors – the same design that caused the Chernobyl disaster in 1986 – are located about 60 km from Vilnius at Ignalina and produce 80 per cent of Lithuania's electricity supply (Synovitz, 1999). All 15 such reactors located in Europe are potential safety risks due to their lack of any containment structure (Recknagel and Holland, 1996).

Lithuania is the most populous of the Baltic countries, with 3.7 million inhabitants, 81 per cent of whom are Lithuanian, 9 per cent Russian, 7 per cent Polish and 2 per cent Belarusian (CIA, 1999). Lithuanians are primarily Roman Catholic, although the Lutheran, Orthodox and Jewish religions are also represented. The official language is Lithuanian, but Polish and Russian are also widely spoken. The demographic situation in Lithuania is similar to other CEE countries: the average age is in the mid-30s, the birth-rate is 10 per thousand, the death-rate 13 per thousand and net emigration 2 per thousand, yielding an overall annual population decline of 0.4 per cent. Adding to this decline is the highest suicide-rate in Europe: in 1996 nearly 50 Lithuanians per 100,000 ended their own lives, a rise of 70 per cent from 1989 (Anon, 1998). Apparently the stress of economic, social and political transition is taking its toll.

The population of Lithuania is 69 per cent urban. The capital, largest city and centre of industry is Vilnius (population 590,000), located in the south-east part of the country. If Europe is defined as extending to the Ural Mountains, its geographic centre is located 25 km north of the Lithuanian capital (Lithuania, 1999: 1). Other cities include Kaunas (430,000) and the ice-free port city Klaipėda (210,000). The government of Lithuania is a parliamentary democracy, consisting of an executive branch made up of a president and prime minister; a legislative branch comprised of a 141-seat parliament; and a judicial branch headed by the supreme court. The country is divided into 11 city and 44 rural districts.

Lithuania is currently facing the problems of adjusting to a market economy, just like the other transition countries. Total GDP for 1998 was $10.7 bn, which yields $4,425 per capita purchasing power parity (Table 13.1). The labour force, which stands at 1.8 million, is distributed between 20 per cent agriculture and forestry, 42 per cent industry and construction and 38 per cent services (Department of State, 1998). The unemployment level in 1999 was 8.1 per cent.

Lithuania's main industries include machine tools, motors, electronic components, computers, consumer goods, petrochemicals, ships, furniture, textiles and food products. The main agricultural products are grains, potatoes, sugar beets, vegetables, meat, dairy products and fish. Exports, valued at $4.3 bn in 1998, consisted mainly of machinery and equipment, mineral products, textiles, chemicals and foodstuffs; imports, valued at $5.9 bn, were mainly minerals, energy, machinery, electronics and chemicals. Lithuania's main trading partners are Russia, Germany, Poland and UK.

A brief history

Lithuanians are descendants of the Balts, who moved to the western shores of the Baltic Sea from central Russia perhaps as early as 3000 BC (Fernandez-Armesto, 1994: 283–288; Vardys and Slaven, 1996: 177–186; Lithuanian Home Page, 2000). Beginning around AD 900, Baltic

Table 13.1 Lithuania: key economic indicators, 1990–1998

	1990	1991	1992	1993	1994	1995	1996	1997	1998
Nominal GDP ($ bn)	na	na	na	2.7	4.2	5.9	7.9	9.6	10.7
GDP per capita (PPP; $)	na	na	na	3681.0	3409.0	3612.0	3853.0	4164.0	4425.0
GDP (% change)	−6.9	−5.7	−21.3	−16.2	−9.8	3.3	4.7	6.1	4.5
Industrial production (% change)	na	−26.4	−28.5	−34.4	−26.5	5.2	1.3	5.6	4.7
Budget balance (% of GDP)	−5.4	2.7	0.5	−3.3	−5.5	−1.8	−2.5	−1.0	−1.3
Unemployment (%)	na	0.3	1.3	4.4	3.8	6.1	7.1	5.9	6.4
Average monthly wage ($)	na	na	na	na	91.0	163.3	193.5	202.3	288.1
Inflation (%)	8.4	225.0	1021.0	410.0	72.2	39.6	24.6	8.9	5.1
Exports ($ bn)	na	na	1.1	2.0	2.0	2.7	3.4	4.2	4.3
Imports ($ bn)	na	na	1.0	2.2	2.2	3.4	4.3	5.3	5.9
Trade balance ($ bn)	na	na	0.1	−0.2	−0.2	−0.7	−0.9	−1.1	−1.6
Current-account balance ($ bn)	na	na	0.2	−0.1	−0.1	−0.6	−0.7	−1.0	−1.5
Foreign direct investment flow ($ m)	na	na	25.0	30.0	31.0	72.0	152.0	328.0	950.0
Foreign exchange reserves ($ bn)	na	na	0.1	0.4	0.6	0.8	0.8	1.1	1.5
Foreign debt ($ bn)	na	na	0.1	0.3	0.5	0.8	2.3	1.4	1.7
Discount rate (%)	na	na	na	98.3	24.9	22.4	10.7	7.6	6.1
Exchange rate (/$)	na	na	1.8	4.3	4.0	4.0	4.0	4.0	4.0
Population (mn)	3.7	3.7	3.7	3.7	3.7	3.7	3.7	3.7	3.7

Source: *UNECE, 1999*

languages began to divide into Lithuanian, Latvian and the now extinct Prussian, whose speakers inhabited the region of today's Kaliningrad (formerly East Prussia) but who were destroyed in the mid-1200s by the Teutonic Knights who, ironically, kept the name.

Unlike Latvia to the north, for Lithuania the medieval period of history was marked by territorial expansion. Responding to the threat of Germanic monastic military orders, notably the Teutonic Knights, Duke Mindaugas created the Grand Duchy of Lithuania in the 1230s to 1240s; after adopting Catholicism, he was crowned king of Lithuania in 1253. A point of clarification, though, is needed here. Although 'Lithuania' appears in its title, the history of this duchy belongs as much to the Poles, Belarusians and Ukrainians as it does to the Lithuanians.

Many ethnic Lithuanian élites actually preferred to speak Polish, seeing their mother tongue as inferior and useful only as a means of peasant communication. Writing in the language was thereby postponed: the first book written in Lithuanian was not published until 1547, and the first Bible in the language did not appear until 1735 (Fernandez-Armesto, 1994: 283–284).

From the early 1300s rulers of the Gediminas dynasty (who held power until 1572) expanded Lithuanian territory eastwards, eventually (by 1430) reaching the shores of the Black Sea, and thereby creating one of the largest states of Europe at the time. These rulers grappled with the dilemma of whether to look east or west for political and cultural influences. Jogaila chose a westward orientation, accepted the Polish crown with the blessing of the pope in 1386, and with his cousin Vytautas began converting Lithuania, the last pagan corner of Europe, to Christianity in 1387. Conflict with the Teutonic Knights continued until they were defeated in 1410, thereby halting Germanic eastward expansion.

Growing pressure from Russia brought Lithuania into closer partnership with Poland, culminating in the 1569 Union of Lublin, which joined the two countries in a commonwealth. Afterwards, Lithuania experienced a period of stability that saw the development of agriculture, the founding of towns, the rise of culture and learning and the codification of law. However, by the end of the 18th century the commonwealth was weakened by wars with Russia, Sweden, Ukraine and Belarus. In 1795 most of Lithuania became part of Russia, which began a process of cultural assimilation and even banned (from 1864 to 1904) the printing of Lithuanian using Latin characters (Fernandez-Armesto, 1994: 283–284).

Following German occupation during the First World War, Lithuania declared independence, which was recognised by Russia in 1920. Two years later, the country had a constitution and was busily working out boundary disputes, proceeding with land reform, developing light industry and agriculture and improving systems of education and cultural facilities. However, the 1939 Molotov–Ribbentrop Pact opened the door for Soviet domination: by 1940, 100,000 troops were stationed on Lithuanian soil and within two months the country was proclaimed a Soviet Socialist Republic (Kirby, 1994). The Soviets immediately began the all too familiar process of establishing totalitarian rule and exiling Lithuanians to Siberia. Further developments, though, were postponed by German occupation of the country from 1941 to 1944, a time that saw the repression of Lithuanians, the massacre of 200,000 Jews, and the destruction of property and infrastructure. Following the Second World War, the Soviets tightened their grip further by restricting personal freedoms, restocking the political apparatus with ethnic Russians and stepping up deportations (Shtromas, 1994; Department of State, 1998). Armed resistance by Lithuanian guerrillas to foreign rule continued into the Soviet period (Lithuanian Home Page, 2000).

As was typical of experiences in other countries of central and eastern Europe, Soviet planning brought large-scale intensive industrialisation to Lithuania as well as economic integration with the Soviet Union (Bradshaw *et al.*, 1994: 158–168). Between 1949 and 1952 private ownership of agriculture was abolished as collective and state farms were established. Levels of urbanisation rose from below 40 per cent in the 1950s to nearly 70 per cent by the 1990s. However, Soviet planning paid little regard for labour, health or environmental issues, and levels of air, water and soil pollution rose, especially in the face of out-dated industrial technology and the extensive use of chemical fertilisers. By the end of the Soviet period, Lithuania enjoyed better overall quality of life than the average for the Soviet Union, and was slightly ahead of its Baltic neighbours in some economic indicators, slightly behind in health and medical services (Table 12.3).

Post-Soviet developments

The opportunity for change created by Mikhail Gorbachev's policies of *glasnost* and *perestroika* of the mid-1980s was quickly seized upon by Lithuanians, who began organising demonstrations and, by 1989, had adopted multi-party politics. Independence was declared on 11 March 1990. Following a brief, armed intervention by the Red Army, which saw the death of 15 civilians, Lithuania won international recognition and joined the United Nations in September 1991. By the close of 1993 Lithuania had joined the Council of Europe, introduced its new currency, the litas, and bade farewell to the last Russian troop (Shoemaker, 1999: 236–245; Lithuanian Home Page, 2000).

Economic reform has been proceeding since 1993, albeit at a pace that has been somewhat impeded by the government's early reliance on voucher-based privatisation. Currently, most small firms are owned privately and over 50 per cent of the labour force is privately employed, although large plants, which account for a majority of Lithuania's capital stock, remain in the state sector. Farm production has declined recently, partly because of difficulties with agricultural privatisation (Davis, 1997). Other aspects of the economy, specifically transport infrastructure and financial institutions, are still in a rather underdeveloped state, although the situation is generally improving. Poverty, though, has been a very real problem. Indeed, scenes of ordinary Lithuanians scavenging through rubbish tips for anything of value remain some of the most poignant images of post-communist CEE. Furthermore, crises in Russia and banking scandals have had a significant impact on Lithuania's economy (Anon, 1996; Barnard, 1999).

After an uncertain start to economic reforms (WPR, 1993), Lithuania's economic performance has been improving in recent years under the guidance of governments who have taken a more disciplined approach to market reforms and the stricter monetary policies imposed by the IMF. GDP per capita increased 30 per cent from 1994 to 1998; after registering losses of 26 per cent to 34 per cent for much of the 1990s, industrial production has stabilised; inflation, which hit 1021 per cent in 1992, has been brought under control; and unemployment has been kept to single digits. However, much progress remains to be achieved: although GDP is rising, its value in 1998 was less than two-thirds of the 1989 level (Jones and Fallesen, 1999: 31). Trade with western countries has risen dramatically since 1992, although Russia remains Lithuania's main trading partner (accounting for 24 per cent of both exports and imports), followed by Germany, Belarus and Poland (Paleckis, 1998: 191). Lithuania has attracted $2.2 bn in foreign direct investment (FDI), mainly from Sweden, Germany and the USA (Paleckis, 1998: 193; EID, 1999).

Lithuania's future looks bright, at least if the government is to be believed. The chairman of the parliament, Vytautas Landsbergis, sees Lithuania becoming 'the Hong Kong of the west', linking Russia with Europe (Hofheinz, 1991: 70). The country is quickly becoming a Baltic trade hub, attracting overseas investment and experiencing increasing GDP growth since 1995 (Phillips, 1999). This is due to:

- ongoing economic reforms, including establishment of a central bank, price liberalisation and mass privatisation;

- a well-educated labour force;

- a strategic location and an enviable infrastructure; and

- the establishment of Free Economic Zones.

Fitness to join the European Union

This section presents a review of Lithuania's experience thus far with the European Union, and discusses the main obstacles to admission identified by the European Commission in its *Opinion* on Lithuania's readiness to become an EU member as well as the efforts made to address these problems. Lithuania has established a good track record at pursuing economic reforms and for making other administrative and fiscal adjustments as prelude to entry into the European Union. The country should therefore be ready for full admission in the period 2005–10, although more cautious observers see 2007–15 as a more realistic window (Anon, 2000b).

Lithuania–EU relations

Lithuania's formal involvement with the European Union began in 1994 with the signing of a free-trade agreement (EID, 1999). Then, in June 1995, Lithuania signed the Europe (Association) Agreement (which entered into force in 1998), and submitted an application to join the EU in December of that year. However, despite considerable efforts on the part of both parties and a Commission *Opinion* that found Lithuania to be mostly in compliance with conditions for membership, the Council decided in late 1997 that Lithuania would have to wait with the second wave of entrants. Lithuanians of course were disappointed by this exclusion, particularly since their Baltic neighbour Estonia was placed in the first wave (Herd, 1999). A second cause for disappointment came in 1997 when the North Atlantic Treaty Organization (NATO) turned down the country's application for membership. The Lithuanian response to this decision was particularly vocal.

Over the past three years Lithuania and the Union have continued to hold bilateral talks and generally gear-up for the accession process. In particular, the procedures and institutional frameworks of implementing the Association Agreement were adopted in early 1998, and a progress report on Lithuania's steps toward accession was produced later that year, as was an approved Plan of Priority Measures for 1998–99 (EID, 1999; EU–LAC, 1999). During 1999 the analytical examination of the *acquis*, or screening, for entry into the EU was completed for Lithuania; in October of that year the Commission recommended starting accession negotiations (Anon, 2000b). The PHARE programme had allocated $328 mn to Lithuania during the period 1992–99 for improvement of administrative capacity, to help make the economy better equipped to withstand internal market competition, to support agriculture and to improve environmental monitoring.

However, Lithuanian public opinion of the European Union apparently remains quite low. Asked (in 1996) how they would vote in a referendum on the question of joining the EU, only 35 per cent of Lithuanians polled said they would vote 'yes'; this value is near the bottom of the range of responses for candidate countries, whose average positive response was 61 per cent (Grabbe and Hughes, 1999: 187; see also Table 1.3). On the one hand, Lithuanians are attracted to the EU because of the security benefits membership would bring, especially in relation to the continuing potential for Russian aggression (Matloff, 1998). On the other hand, they feel that such western institutions as the EU and NATO should have been more accommodating to the CEE countries.

Political considerations

The 1998 regular report of the EU Commission concluded that Lithuania fulfils the political criteria as stipulated during the Copenhagen Council meetings, but that it needs to intensify the fight against corruption and pursue reforms in the judiciary (European Commission, 1999). The government is stable and supports entry into the EU although there have been difficulties in the Lithuanian political scene in the recent past. For the first two years following independence, government activities were constrained by a lack of clear delineation of power between the different branches, by political infighting and by mismanagement. Turmoil struck again in 1995, when a financial crisis forced the resignation of the prime minister. Since then, Lithuania has made great progress in fine-tuning legislation and installing a bureaucracy that is more conducive to political and economic restructuring.

One issue not addressed specifically in EU documents concerns Lithuanian–Russian relations in general, and the Kaliningrad situation in particular. As mentioned previously, this exclave – which remains a Russian *oblast* – is separated from Russia by a significant swath of Lithuanian (and Belarusian) territory. The importance of Kaliningrad is that it contains an ice-free port and is the home of Russia's Baltic fleet (Vesilind, 1997: 115). Clearly, Kaliningrad is important to Russia; at least one observer fears that conflict over it may trigger war (Coleman, 1997). However, a recent agreement to set up an EU–Russian working group to examine the Kaliningrad issue, coupled with a relatively low level (compared to Latvia) of conflict over ethnic Russians in Lithuania, augur well for the future (Anon, 2000a).

Economic considerations

The 1998 regular report of the EU Commission found that Lithuania's sustained implementation of its reform agenda will bring about a functioning market economy that will enable the country to progress in the medium term and to withstand the competitive pressure of market forces within the Union (European Commission, 1999). The Commission noted that Lithuania has maintained macroeconomic stability, even in the face of the Russian crisis. However, priority must be given to cutting the fiscal deficit, to completing structural adjustments and to implementing ongoing reforms. Further, the country needs to continue re-orienting its trade towards the EU and other developed market economies, to invest more in infrastructure development, to improve the quality of the labour force and to attract more foreign direct investment.

Lithuania has made progress on fulfilling these objectives. Trade with EU countries has risen from only 2 per cent of Lithuania's total foreign trade in 1991 to 48 per cent in the first half of 1999. Further, 63 per cent of Lithuania's FDI came from EU countries in 1999. The country appears poised to continue with economic reforms, to increase privatisation, to achieve a balanced budget and to maintain productivity growth with little inflation (EID, 1999).

Particularly troubling, though, is Lithuania's relatively low standard of living. According to the most recent statistics, per capita GDP has fallen to only $930, just 5 per cent of the EU15 average and the lowest of all the candidate countries. When expressed as purchasing power parity, its relative percentage rises to 24, equal to that for Bulgaria (Ardy, 1999: 108). Although not necessarily an impediment to EU admission, overcoming the country's low level of economic development needs to be a top priority of Lithuanian strategists.

Environmental considerations

The European Commission (1999) *Opinion* is that Lithuania is able to transpose the environmental *acquis* in the medium term and to achieve full compliance in the long term. As is the case with Latvia, Lithuania suffers more from environmental 'hot spots' than from widespread problems. Although not an official consideration, the fact that newly elected Lithuanian president Valdas Adamkus worked for 27 years at the US Environmental Protection Agency certainly looks good on the country's environmental score sheet.

A major impediment to Lithuania's accession to the EU, though, concerns the continued use of the Ignalina nuclear power plant (Jones and Fallesen, 1999). As early as 1993 EU officials identified the reactors as problematic and awarded $50 mn to improve safety conditions. Lithuania has agreed to shut down Ignalina Unit 1 in 2005, but has yet to set a date for decommissioning Unit 2. Since the facility currently produces 80 per cent of Lithuania's electricity and has been a source of export revenue, its closure will have significant economic repercussions by raising energy prices and making the country dependent on foreign sources for energy (Anon, 2000b).

Conclusion

Today Lithuania finds itself clinging to the glory of its medieval past, on the one hand, and reeling from 50 years of Soviet legacy, on the other. Lithuanians are seeking their place in Europe, and look to institutions such as the EU to facilitate a smooth passage.

Lithuania has made good headway toward fulfilling all of the requirements of its Europe Agreement with the European Union. The country fulfils the Copenhagen political criteria but must continue to fight corruption and pursue reforms in the judiciary. Lithuania is also on target to fulfil the economic criteria in the medium term, provided sustained efforts are made at continuing the reform agenda that will complete the establishment of a functioning market economy. The country is also in compliance with the environmental *acquis*, though it must take steps to close its nuclear power plant. However, Lithuania must step up efforts to complete legislative frameworks and strengthen institutions for entry into the internal market.

In short, despite a gloomy economic picture at present, Lithuania has already established a solid basis for continued prosperity and stability. The country should be ready for accession into the European Union when invited, which should be in the period 2005–10.

References

Anon, 1996, How to go bust in the Baltics. *The Economist*, 20 January, p. 79.

Anon, 1998, The pain of being set free. The Economist, 29 August, p. 50.

Anon, 2000a, Cosy up. *The Economist*, 14 February, pp. 45–46.

Anon, 2000b, Lithuania: Westward ho! *The Economist*, 8 January, p. 50.

Ardy, B., 1999, Agricultural, structural policy, the budget and eastern enlargement of the European Union. *In* Henderson, K., ed., *Back to Europe: central and eastern Europe and the European Union*. London/Philadelphia: UCL Press, pp. 107–128.

Barnard, B., 1999, The Baltics. *Europe*, 390, 23–25.

Bradshaw, M., Hanson, P., Shaw, D., 1994, Economic restructuring. *In* Smith, G., ed., *The Baltic States: the national self-determination of Estonia, Latvia and Lithuania*. New York: St Martin's Press, pp.158–180.

CIA, 1999, Lithuania. *In* CIA *The world factbook*. Washington DC: CIA. http://www.odci.gov/cia/publications/factbook/lh.html.

Coleman, F., 1997, The Kaliningrad scenario: expanding NATO into the Baltics. *World Policy Journal*, 14 (3), 71–75.

Davis, J. R., 1997, Understanding the process of decollectivisation and agricultural privatisation in transition economies: the distribution of collective and state farm assets in Latvia and Lithuania. *Europe–Asia Studies*, 49 (8), 1409–1432.

Department of State (USA), 1998, *Background notes: Lithuania*. Washington DC: Department of State. http://www.state.gov/www/background_notes/ Lithuania_9801_bgn.html.

EID (European Integration Department), 1999, *Integration of Lithuania into the European Union*. Vilnius: EID. http://www.urm/lt/eu/.

EU–LAC (Lithuanian Association Committee), 1999, *Position paper of the Lithuanian delegation*. Vilnius: Association Committee. http://www.urm.lt/comm2.htm.

European Commission, 1999, *Regular report from the Commission on progress towards accession: Lithuania*. Brussels: European Commission. http://www.europe.eu.int/comm/ enlargement/Lithuania/rep_10_99/index.htm.

Fernandez-Armesto, F., ed, 1994, *The Times guide to the peoples of Europe*. London: Times Books.

Grabbe, H., Hughes, K., 1999, Central and east European views on EU enlargement: political debates and public opinion. *In* Henderson, K., ed., *Back to Europe: central and eastern Europe and the European Union*. London/Philadelphia: UCL Press, pp. 185–202.

Herd, G. P., 1999, The Baltic states and EU enlargement. *In* Henderson, K., ed., *Back to Europe: central and eastern Europe and the European Union*. London/Philadelphia: UCL Press, pp. 259–273.

Hofheinz, P., 1991, Opportunity in the Baltics. *Fortune*, 124 (9), 68–74.

Jones, B., Fallesen, L. B., 1999, The newly independent states. *Europe*, 383, 30–36.

Kirby, D., 1994, Incorporation: the Molotov–Ribbentrop Pact. *In* Smith, G., ed., *The Baltic States: the national self-determination of Estonia, Latvia and Lithuania*. New York: St Martin's Press, pp. 69–85.

Lithuania, 1999, *About Lithuania*. Vilnius: Ministry of Foreign Affairs. http://www.urm.lt/ about/.

Lithuanian Home Page, 2000, *Land and People*. Vilnius: MII KTL. http://neris.mii.lt/homepage/lietuva.html.

Matloff, J., 1998, Heart of Europe waits to join Europe's alliance. *Christian Science Monitor*, 6 March, p. 7.

Paleckis, J. V., 1998, Lithuania is at the centre and crossroads of Europe. *In* Nicholl, W., Schoenberg, R., eds, *Europe beyond 2000: the enlargement of the European Union towards the east*. London: Whurr Publishers, pp. 179–196.

Phillips, S., 1999, Lithuania: trade hub of the Baltics. *AgExporter*, 11 (4), 7–9.

Recknagel, C., Holland, L., 1996, Chernobyl part IV: despite the disaster, nuclear power grows in former Soviet Union. *Radio Free Europe/Radio Liberty*, 19 April. http://www.rferl.org/nca/special/chernobyl/f.ukr.96041919490612.html.

Shoemaker, M. W., 1999, *Russia, Eurasian states, and eastern Europe 1999*. Harpers Ferry WV: Stryker-Post Publications, 30th ed.

Shtromas, A., 1994, The Baltic states as Soviet Republics: tensions and contradictions. *In* Smith, G., ed., *The Baltic States: the national self-determination of Estonia, Latvia and Lithuania*. New York: St Martin's Press, pp. 86–117.

Synovitz, R., 1999, Broken nuclear promises could jeopardize EU membership chances. *RFE/RL Newsline*, 22 February. http://wwwrferl.org/newsline/1999/02/5-not/not-220299.html.

UNECE, 1999, *Trends in Europe and North America: Lithuania*. New York: UNECE. http://www.unece.org/stats/trend/lit.htm.

Vardys, V. S., Slaven, W. A., 1996, Lithuania. *In* Iwaskiw, W. R., ed., *Estonia, Latvia, and Lithuania: country studies*. Washington DC: Government Printing Office, pp. 169–242.

Vesilind, P. J., 1997, Kaliningrad: coping with a German past and a Russian future. *National Geographic*, 191 (3), 110–123.

WPR *(World Press Review)*, 1993, Troubled Lithuania. July, p. 37.

14

BULGARIA

Derek Hall

A brief history

A small country (110,994 sq km; 8.2 million people) in a troubled region (Figure 14.1), Bulgaria has tended to depend either on the patronage of great powers or on playing them off against each other. Although predominantly Slavic, Bulgarians take their name from central Asian nomads who founded the first Bulgarian state in AD 681 and became Christianised in the 9th century. In 1396 this powerful regional state fell to the Ottoman Turks, who proceeded to dominate for almost five centuries until the Russo–Turkish war of 1876–78. However, the extensive territory that was granted to the new state in 1878 by the Treaty of San Stefano was almost immediately cut back by the Treaty of Berlin later that year, as the great powers sought to restrict Russian influence in Europe. A German prince was installed as monarch. Bulgaria allied itself with Germany in both world wars, although in the Second World War, Tsar Boris III refused to declare war on the Soviet Union or to allow Bulgaria's Jews to be deported (Roussinov, 1969; Crampton, 1997).

An anti-German coup took place in September 1944, just as Soviet forces entered the country. The monarchy was abolished by a referendum in 1946, and within the following year the Bulgarian Communist Party (BCP) had consolidated its position. A severe imposition of agricultural collectivisation and nationalisation of industry followed.

In 1954 Todor Zhivkov reached the top of the party and used tactics similar to those of Nikita Khrushchev in Moscow – anti-Stalinism and moderate reforms. Surviving Khrushchev's overthrow in 1964, Zhivkov held power for a further 25 years and maintained Bulgaria's unfailing loyalty to Moscow. Indeed, it was the only full Warsaw Pact member believed loyal enough not to need Soviet troops on its soil. Zhivkov reportedly argued for a time that Bulgaria actually be absorbed into the Soviet Union.

A relatively flexible, albeit cautious, approach to economic reform produced one of the Soviet bloc's more successful agrarian economies and a relatively dynamic industrial sector. In the 1980s, however, foreign debt rose sharply, owing to increased oil prices, reduced Soviet subsidies

Figure 14.1: Bulgaria

and delays in structural reform. An incomprehensible campaign of forced assimilation of Bulgaria's ethnic Turks in the mid-1980s attracted international disapproval and eventually led to an exodus of ethnic Turks, which significantly depleted Bulgaria's agricultural workforce.

In November 1989 politburo colleagues forced Zhivkov's resignation 'on health grounds', and the process of political change began in earnest. The first seven years after communism were, however, marked by political instability. A parliamentary election in June 1990 gave the Bulgarian Socialist Party (BSP – the renamed communists) 48 per cent of the vote and 52 per cent of the seats – an outcome some dismissed as fraudulent. Political and economic upheaval resulted in a 'government of experts' emerging in late December 1990. The following year saw a package of price- and foreign-exchange liberalisation, a foreign investment law, a commercial code, competition law and a new constitution, providing for a multi-party system, free elections on the basis of universal adult franchise and human civil rights (Zloch-Christy, 1996).

Privatisation proceeded slowly and industrial restructuring made little progress. The economy deteriorated particularly rapidly in 1996. The BSP's defeat in the November presidential election prompted Zhan Videnov to resign as prime minister and party leader. A round of violence, peaceful demonstrations, strikes and road blockages eventually dissuaded the new BSP leadership from forming a government, thereby averting a potential civil war.

A caretaker government dealt with fuel shortages, stabilised the currency, brought down inflation, reached an accommodation with the International Monetary Fund (IMF), launched a drive against crime and corruption and purged the bureaucracy. With its allies in the United Democratic Forces (UtdDF), the Union of Democratic Forces (UDF) won a comfortable majority in parliamentary elections in April 1997, and more than two years of stability followed. At the turn of the decade, however, privatisation and restructuring remained a slow process, and economic growth was sluggish. Further, the government's support for NATO action in Kosovo in 1999 proved controversial.

Social and demographic issues

Officially, Bulgaria's population was 8.23 million at the end of 1998, but in reality it was probably slightly less than 8 million because official figures exclude emigration and take into account only births and deaths since the last census in 1992. Between 1989 and 1996 around 650,000 people emigrated, 238,000 of them between 1993 and 1996. Some 19,000 people returned in 1996 after being away for more than a year, but there is still a net outflow and, in the absence of detailed statistics, unofficial estimates suggest that this was around 40,000 in both 1997 and 1998. Emigration has been caused by discontent with post-communist conditions and the desire of ethnic Turks to move to Turkey. Emigrant numbers swelled, especially among the highly skilled, during the rapid deterioration of economic conditions in 1996 and 1997.

Turks (9.4 per cent) and Roma (3.7 per cent) represent the major ethnic minorities in an otherwise relatively homogeneous country (85.7 per cent Bulgarian). Ethnic relations are less of a problem than elsewhere in the Balkans. No significant ethnic conflict has occurred since the communist regime's maltreatment and attempted assimilation of the Turkish minority in the 1980s when, between 1985 and 1990, more than 300,000 emigrated from Bulgaria to Turkey (Bocharov, 1997). However, in the European Commission's 1998 report on Bulgaria's progress toward EU accession, concern was expressed about the treatment of the Roma (European Commission, 1998). A framework programme for their integration into Bulgarian society was adopted in April 1999 following consultations between the government, most of the country's Roma organisations and human rights non-government organisations. Whilst the Turkish minority is reasonably well integrated and represented in political life, some of the regions where this minority is concentrated are beset by economic problems and suffer from low investment and high unemployment, and Turks are heavily over-represented in the rural population. Although it is the dominant faith, Orthodox Christianity, claimed by 83 per cent of the population, does not play a major role in Bulgarian life. Other faiths include Islam, Roman Catholicism and Protestant Christianity.

The Refugees Law, which came into force during 1999, addresses the organisation of the system of granting asylum and provides a framework to allow asylum seekers to exercise their rights and duties in a way that is compatible with European standards. Continued problems of human trafficking, especially of women, need to be addressed in relation to a strengthening of border control (European Commission, 1999b).

Sixty-eight per cent of the population live in towns, although the administrative definition of 'town' includes 12 settlements with fewer than 2,000 inhabitants. Only the capital, Sofia, has more than a million inhabitants (1.114 million), and it accounts for 13.5 per cent of the population. In total, only 31.3 per cent of the population lived in towns of 100,000 or more at the end of 1997: Plovdiv (340,000), Varna (299,000), Burgas (194,000), Ruse (166,000), Stara Zagora (148,000) and Pleven (123,000).

New decentralised institutions (dependent on the central authorities) have been created in the 28 administrative regions (*oblasti*). These should co-ordinate the action of the government in each region under the authority of a regional governor appointed by the council of ministers. In June 1999 these regions were combined into six macro-regions in accordance with EU regionalisation methodology.

Health and health service provision has deteriorated since 1989, having been subjected to some privatisation of provision and to severe funding constraints. Male life expectancy declined from 68.2 years in 1984–86 to 67.2 in 1995–97, compared to an EU average in 1997 of 73.1. Infant mortality rose from 12.4 per 1,000 live births in 1988 to 16.9 per 1,000 in 1991. In the crisis year of 1997 the rate averaged 17.5 per 1,000, although it fell sharply to 14.4 in 1998 (the EU average in 1995 was 5.9) (EIU, 1999).

The education system, although traditional, is of relatively high quality and attracts students from neighbouring and developing countries. However, vocational training has suffered since 1989, and the shortage of western-style business education, particularly in financial and marketing skills, is greater than in the Višegrád countries, although engineering and information technology skills are strong.

Corruption remains a serious problem, the sectors most affected being customs, municipalities, medical services, universities, the police, taxation authorities and the courts. Bulgaria has ratified the major anti-corruption conventions, although Bulgarian legislation does not yet provide a concrete definition of 'corruption', and a stronger legal framework is required in areas of public financing and the judiciary. There remain concerns about the abuse of power by law enforcement bodies, especially the police.

Economic development and restructuring

Bulgaria's total area is 110,994 sq km, of which 38 per cent is arable land and 35 per cent forest: in all there are 6.2 million ha of agricultural land. The agricultural sector accounted for 21 per cent of GDP and 24.7 per cent of the working population in 1998. The long and often acrimonious process of agricultural land restitution (e.g. see Mileva, 1994; Yarnal, 1994; Carter, 1998) was to have been completed by the end of 1999, but the provision of appropriate land rights documentation had reached only about 20 per cent of coverage, severely crippling the development of a rural land market. Even so, completion of the restitution process is unlikely to turn the agriculture sector into an engine of economic growth (Meurs and Begg, 1998: 259).

Viticulture has a long tradition (e.g. Batakliev, 1939) and wine is by far the largest agriculture-related export, for which the UK is the biggest market. Russia is the principal market for fresh fruit and vegetables, as well as cigarettes, whilst the USA is the largest market for raw tobacco. Progress was made in the liberalisation of the price and marketing system by removing government controls on domestic farm-gate prices in August 1998.

Regional development legislation aims at establishing prerequisites for a sustainable and balanced development of the different regions, for reducing disparities in employment and income and for carrying out regional and cross-border co-operation and integration. But up to 80 per cent of the rural population live in poverty, and there are regional contrasts between the relatively poor northern part of the country, which mainly borders Romania, and the more affluent southern and coastal regions, which border the Black Sea, Turkey and Greece (Buckwalter, 1995).

Communist location policies tended to spatially disperse industry. Structurally, Bulgarian industry suffered considerably from the disintegration of the Council for Mutual Economic Assistance (CMEA), as many of the country's subsidised specialist products were uncompetitive on world markets. Post-communist industrial decline has been most severe in the machine building, defence and electronics sectors, although the latter has shown some signs of rejuvenation (Rosenberg and Whitford, 2000).

The share of the private sector in GDP has increased dramatically since 1989. By 1998 the private sector accounted for 63.7 per cent of GDP, including 60.5 per cent of the services component and 98.2 per cent of the agricultural component. However, its share of industry and construction was still quite low, at 44.2 per cent. On a simple GDP per capita basis, Bulgaria is poorer than the nine other CEE applicant countries to the EU, although the country is ahead of

Table 14.1 Bulgaria: key economic indicators, 1991–1999

	1991	1992	1993	1994	1995	1996	1997	1998	1999
Current account ($ mn)	−406	−801	−1 386	−203	−59	117	433	−252	−650
Exports ($ mn)	2 734	3 956	3 727	3 935	5 345	4 890	4 925	4 293	3 200
Imports ($ mn)	2 330	4 169	4 612	3 952	5 224	4 703	4 544	4 609	4 200
Trade balance ($ mn)	404	−213	−885	−17	121	187	381	−316	−1 000
Net FDI ($ mn)	56	42	40	105	82	100	497	401	700
GDP per capita ($)	872	1 016	1 280	1 157	1 559	1 170	1 228	1 315	na
Share of industry in GDP (%)[a]	37.4	40.5	35.0	32.1	32.7	28.5	25.3	25.5	na
Share of agriculture in GDP (%)[a]	14.3	11.7	10.3	12.0	13.1	14.5	23.8	18.7	na
Unemployment (%)	11.1	15.3	16.4	12.8	11.1	12.5	13.7	12.2	na

[a] After 1995 the industrial classification was changed; using the old classification, industry as a share of GDP was 32.4% in 1996 and the share of agriculture was 12.8%.

Source: *EBRD, 1999: 205*

Romania on the basis of purchasing power parity. Economic activity recovered in 1998, with real GDP growth of 3.5 per cent, although the official forecast for 1999 was down to 1.5 per cent (European Commission, 1999a) (see also Table 14.1).

Since 1989 internal obstacles to reform and a variety of external shocks have constrained economic development. These have included:

- the relatively prosperous times experienced in the late-communist period;

- covert privatisation and monopolistic forms of private enterprise pursued by certain sections of the communist élite, before and after 1989;

- an economy initially geared to the needs of the former CMEA;

- a UN trade embargo on Yugoslavia in 1992–95, which denied Bulgaria access to an important market and debtor, as well as an important transit route to new west European markets; and

- embargoes on Iraq, which also cut off an important energy supplier (EIU, 1999).

Lax regulatory control in the early 1990s encouraged a private sector that comprised both small trade, retailing and service enterprises, and larger 'red capital' firms, whose strength originated in old regime capital and *nomenklatura* connections. By the end of 1996 only around 5 per cent in value of medium and large state industrial assets had been sold, and just 30 sales had involved foreign companies, none of which was very large.

Sales of smaller companies have proceeded swiftly since the UtdDF came to power. Small- and medium-sized enterprises (SMEs) account for well over 90 per cent of all registered economic entities. The vast majority have fewer than five employees, and their main activities are in retail business. However, the share of SMEs in total employment, at about 41 per cent, is low compared with the EU average. There are inadequacies in both the general business environment and in the availability of long-term financing to support it. To help ameliorate this situation, a state bank lending only to SMEs was established, and this participates in the EU's multi-annual programme for SMEs. The Agency for SMEs (ASME), founded in July 1997 at the industry ministry, has been strengthened through an SME law adopted in September 1999, and is now the central governmental unit for the promotion and co-ordination of SME policy in Bulgaria. There is a need, however, for the strengthening of a national network of SME intermediaries, particularly in terms of the quality of services and advice, such as on business plans, management, partnerships, and the possibilities of participating in international business events (European Commission, 1999b). The government's Bulgaria 2001 programme aims to sustain economic growth and the acceleration of privatisation and restructuring as the framework conditions for industrial development and the competitiveness of enterprises, and in particular to establish an environment conducive to SME growth. In 1999 the government adopted a strategy for the development of high-technology industry, aiming to create a dynamic sector for manufacturing of high-tech products and services.

Some estimates suggest that the unofficial economy accounts for around 50 per cent of GDP (EIU, 1999). Private-sector firms tend to declare salaries at or near the minimum wage for their employees to minimise tax and social security payments. The percentage of the workforce registered as unemployed has been in double figures since 1992 and reached 13.3 per cent in April 1999. Enterprises have tended to lay off workers, or to not replace those leaving, rather than embark on radical restructuring. Unemployment figures are subject to distortion, however: some registered unemployed work in the grey economy, and some unemployed do not register, since only around one-third of those registered receive benefits, which are usually low.

Of the service industries, investment (especially foreign) in the tourism sector holds much promise, but this has been held up by delays in privatisation. Powerful local economic groups and hotel and resort managements have often made advantageous leasing arrangements rather than buying outright. Poor service and administration and lack of adequate promotion continue to constrain development (Koulov, 1996; Bachvarov, 1997).

Trade

With the EU predominating, the Organization for Economic Co-operation and Development (OECD) is Bulgaria's most important trading bloc. Of the EU countries, Germany, Italy and Greece are the most important for both imports and exports. Russia remains the major source of Bulgaria's imports (Table 14.2), providing mostly fuels and raw materials.

Table 14.2 Bulgaria: major trading partners, 1998

Exports to		Value ($ mn)	%	Imports from		Value ($ mn)	%
EU		2 135.1	49.7	EU		2 248.4	45.0
Of which:	Italy	544.3	12.7	Of which:	Germany	686.1	13.7
	Germany	448.7	10.5		Italy	385.1	7.7
	Greece	377.1	8.8		Greece	295.1	5.9
	France	146.9	3.4		France	227.1	4.6
Turkey		341.3	8.0	Russia		1 003.2	20.1
Russia		234.1	5.5	United States		197.8	4.0
Total exports		4 292.9	100.0	Total imports		4 995.2	100.0

Sources: *EIU, 1999: 43, author's additional calculations*

An EU association agreement, in force since February 1995, has facilitated trade, especially on the export side, but unfulfilled agricultural quotas emphasise problems of supply-side constraints, as well as those of trade restrictions. Of non-EU OECD states, the potential of the USA is limited by distance, and trade with Turkey is being encouraged by a free-trade agreement inaugurated in 1999. Although the Višegrád countries have relinquished their former trade significance, Bulgaria's entry into the Central European Free Trade Agreement (CEFTA) in 1998 brought a reinvigoration to trade relations: CEFTA's share of imports rose from 5.0 per cent in 1997 to 5.6 per cent in 1998, and its export share increased from 3.4 per cent to 4.9 per cent.

Cumulative foreign direct investment (FDI) since 1989 exceeded $1 bn only in 1997, although totals of more than $600 mn in both 1997 and 1998 reflected an upturn, albeit tempered by slow privatisation and the impact of the conflict in Kosovo. Increased greenfield investment, re-equipment of privatised firms and infrastructural work should, however, ensure some growth of FDI in coming years (EIU, 1999).

A transit country

Bulgaria is situated on the traditional overland route from the Middle East to central and western Europe, and the role of transit is significant. A riparian of the Danube, the country has no other rivers that are navigable by sizeable ships. Sofia is recognised as having potential as an air transport hub, and there are plans to build a new airport there.

In terms of surface transport, four of the proposed and long-anticipated European rail and road transport corridors pass through Bulgaria:

- Corridor IV from Calafat in Romania, through Sofia to Promachin in Greece and on to Svilengrad on the Bulgarian–Turkish border;

- Corridor VIII from Gushevo on the Bulgarian–Macedonian border, via Sofia to the ports of Burgas and Varna;

- Corridor IX from Giurgiu in Romania, via Ruse to Alexandroupolis in Greece; and

- Corridor X from the Serbian border to Edirne in Turkey.

An infrastructure investment plan for 1998–2000 has been linked to participation in the Trans-European Infrastructure Needs Assessment (TINA), which has identified priority projects for ISPA pre-accession EU financing. The issue of a second bridge across the Danube between Bulgaria and Romania has been under discussion for some time. Despite PHARE-funded feasibility studies, the two countries have disagreed on the usefulness and location of the bridge. Although Bulgaria's transport infrastructure is relatively well developed, it has suffered from low spending and poor maintenance in recent years.

Energy and the nuclear question

Bulgaria's 'Strategy for the development of the energy sector until 2010' was approved in March 1999, in line with a short-term priority of the accession partnership. It has a stated objective of meeting the requirements of accession, but is based on a continuous growth in energy production, which does not appear realistic.

Nuclear capacity generated from the Kozloduy complex has provided an increasing proportion of national electricity supply, now representing more than 40 per cent. Environmental and safety concerns about the station's Soviet technology and its operation led the EU to press for the early closure of the four oldest reactors in accordance with an agreement reached in the early 1990s. However, alternative energy sources have been less certain, notably oil from Iraq and Libya, and Russian gas. Post-communist decline in industrial production has lowered domestic energy demand, although the industry response has been to export surplus energy rather than to cut back on production. Bulgaria's geographical position makes the country potentially important for transit pipelines, and the construction of lines to supply Russian gas to Turkey, Greece and the western Balkan states is planned. A pipeline for Caspian oil from Burgas on the Black Sea to Alexandroupolis in northern Greece has also been under discussion.

Kozloduy is a major factor in accession negotiations. The Cologne European Council emphasised the importance of high standards of nuclear safety in CEE, not least in the context of EU enlargement. Four VVER 440 MW (K1–4) and two VVER 1,000 MW (K5–6) reactors, of Soviet design, are located at Kozloduy. The Nuclear Safety Account Agreement (NSAA) signed by Bulgaria in 1993, foresaw the closure of reactors K1–4 by 1997/98 because they represented a high safety risk. In *Agenda 2000* the European Commission called upon candidate countries operating non up-gradable reactors to close them at the earliest practicable date. For Bulgaria, as the original deadline passed, the EC took the view that K1–2 should close in 2001 and K3–4 in 2001/02. In November 1997 the Bulgarian government requested a revision of the NSAA, suggesting operation of K1–4 until the end of their economically justified life. The long-term energy strategy adopted by the Bulgarian government in 1998 foresees the closure of K1–2 in 2005 and of K3–4 after 2010. These dates are clearly not in line with the country's international commitments in the NSAA nor with *Agenda 2000*, and in March 1999 the European Parliament called on Bulgaria to comply with its nuclear commitments.

The European Commission is willing to assist Bulgaria in the early closure of K1–4, both technically and financially. It has considered the granting of a Euratom (European Atomic Energy Community) loan for the modernisation, including safety upgrading, of K5–6, which is a key element in the NSAA conditionality. It would also consider substantial multi-annual PHARE grant assistance to Bulgaria's energy sector, over and above the national allocation. However, further assistance, including the Euratom loan, is conditional upon agreement for the closure of the older units. This takes into account Bulgaria's future electricity requirements and the country's need, as a future member of the EU, to develop its energy sector on the basis of security of supply, competitiveness, environmental considerations and energy efficiency. In March 1999 the European Commission and the Bulgarian government agreed to work toward setting a realistic timetable for the closure and decommissioning of K1–4, but progress made during 1999 was considered inadequate.

The Bulgarian Nuclear Safety Authority still lacks the required number of staff to pursue its duties properly, although its strengthening is being envisaged. Low levels of remuneration pose obstacles to retaining or engaging competent staff.

International collaboration

In its post-communist phase of integrating with the 'international community', Bulgaria became a member of the World Bank in 1990, joined the Council of Europe in 1992, and acceded to the European Bank for Reconstruction and Development (EBRD), the IMF and the World Trade Organization in 1996 (European Commission, 1997b). Under the UtdDF government, Bulgaria's economic orientation toward western Europe was given an impetus – aspirations to EU membership and to defence integration with the North Atlantic Treaty Organization (NATO) – although resentment has sometimes been expressed over issues such as visa restrictions and EU demands for the decommissioning of Kozloduy's reactors.

Bulgaria has been included in NATO's Partnership for Peace programme since 1994 and has both participated in and hosted various military exercises. It also has military co-operation agreements, concluded since 1989, with a variety of NATO member states. Russia has been more sensitive to the prospect of Bulgaria's membership in NATO than to that of most other former allies. The consensus before NATO's war with Yugoslavia, in which Bulgaria granted the use of airspace to NATO, was that Bulgaria would not be ready for membership in economic or military terms for some time. The need for NATO to improve its relations with Russia after the war with Yugoslavia underlined this assumption.

Ethnic and linguistic affinities with FYR Macedonia are keenly felt in Bulgaria, which was early to recognise the new state and to be supportive during the 1994–95 Greek embargo. But the fact that Bulgarians view Macedonian as a Bulgarian dialect rather than as a separate language tended to obstruct inter-state relations until a compromise was reached in 1999 (Bocharov, 1997; EIU, 1999).

Relations with Yugoslavia (Serbia–Montenegro) were relatively good in the years after 1989, despite Bulgarian support for UN sanctions during the Bosnian war – partly due to pro-Serb, pan-Slav and anti-Islamic opinion within the BSP. The UtdDF government, less well-disposed to the Serbs, led regional initiatives to bring about a negotiated settlement in Kosovo in 1998/99, but went along with financial sanctions in 1998 against Belgrade and supported NATO military action from March 1999, making Bulgarian airspace available when requested despite some public opposition. Open hostility to the Milošević regime has been tempered by assurances that no ill-will is held for the Serbian people.

The position of Bulgaria's ethnic Turkish minority has improved since the 1980s, thus removing one important source of friction between the two countries (Vasileva, 1991). A free-trade agreement was signed early in 1999, enhancing Bulgarian access to an important export market, and Turkish investment in major road-building and hydro-electric projects is an important ingredient for Bulgarian infrastructure improvements.

A long-standing dispute with Greece over the use of the waters of the Mesta river was settled in 1977, and the question of what the Bulgarians see as a Bulgarian-speaking minority in northern Greece is a low priority issue. No territorial or ethnic disputes exist with Romania. The most serious disagreement concerns the location of a proposed second bridge over the Danube.

EU–Bulgaria relations

Diplomatic relations with the EU were first established in 1988, and a trade and co-operation agreement was signed in 1990. The present contractual relationship is regulated by the Europe Agreement of 1995. This is a preferential agreement, of which the trade element aims to establish a free-trade area over a maximum period of ten years. Bulgaria was included in the Community general system of preferences from 1991 (European Commission, 1997b).

The EU share of Bulgaria's foreign trade rose from 44.7 per cent of exports in 1997 to 49.7 per cent in 1998 (see Table 14.2) and 60.3 per cent in the first quarter of 1999. The share of imports rose from 38.7 per cent in 1997 to 45 per cent in 1998 and to 49.3 per cent for the first quarter of 1999. The two main product categories that are both exported and imported by Bulgaria are textiles and chemical products. Bulgaria exports base metals to the EU and imports machinery equipment from the EU.

Bulgaria participates in a number of European Community programmes: Youth for Europe, Socrates, Leonardo da Vinci, Save II, Third Programme for SMEs, Kaleidoscope, Ariane, Raphael, AIDS Prevention and Combat against Cancer. Bulgaria is also included in the Fifth Framework Programme for research and development.

The PHARE programme has been the main source of financial assistance for Bulgaria's pre-accession strategy, concentrating support on the accession partnership priorities that help to fulfil the Copenhagen criteria. Around 30 per cent of the PHARE allocation is used for institution capacity building. The other 70 per cent is shared between financing investments to strengthen the regulatory infrastructure needed to ensure compliance with the *acquis* and to reinforce economic and social cohesion. The PHARE programme allocated €865.5 mn to Bulgaria during 1989–99. The 1999 PHARE programme allocation of €50.5 mn was focused on the following priorities:

- further integration of the Roma community (€0.5 mn);

- economic reform through management training and SME promotion (€4.8 mn);

- reinforcement of the institutional and administrative capacity in public administration, competition and state aid (€6.5 mn);

- strengthening of co-operation in border management, police and judicial reform (€9.5 mn);

- support for the environment (€4.9 mn);

- development of agriculture (€10.3 mn);

- labour market initiatives (€4.5 mn); and

- participation in Community programmes and TEMPUS (€9.6mn).

An additional €30 mn have been allocated for cross-border co-operation (CBC) programmes to provide support for transport infrastructure, telecommunications and environmental rehabilitation. In addition, funding is being provided under the catch-up facility – special assistance given to Latvia, Lithuania, Slovakia, Bulgaria and Romania for projects aimed at accelerating EU accession preparations in certain areas – for projects relating to job creation and the promotion of foreign direct investment (€14 mn).

During the period 2000–06 pre-accession aid to the candidate countries will be more than doubled. Alongside the PHARE programme, SAPARD (agricultural and rural development) and ISPA (a structural instrument) will give priority to measures in their fields in the same way as the cohesion fund assists with regard to environment and transport. For 2000–02 indicative figures for total financial assistance available amount to around €300 mn for PHARE (including CBC), €156.3 mn for SAPARD and €249–375 mn for ISPA (European Commission, 1999b).

The EC *Opinion* of October 1999 (European Commission, 1999b) confirmed that Bulgaria fulfilled the Copenhagen political criteria. However, further efforts need to be undertaken to:

- strengthen the rule of law and protect human and minority rights, particularly those of the Roma population;

- fight against corruption; and

- improve the functioning of the judicial system.

Until publication of *Agenda 2000* a high degree of consensus among Bulgarians in support of EU membership masked a lack of realistic debate or understanding of EU issues. A *Eurobarometer* survey undertaken in late 1996 indicated that Bulgarians were third only to Romanians and Poles in their strength of support for their country's EU entry, although the reported level was only 42 per cent (Grabbe and Hughes, 1998: 83). A 1997 survey of Bulgarian attitudes indicated clearer support: more than 91 per cent of respondents answered positively when asked whether they personally supported Bulgaria's decision to join the EU (UNDP, 1998). This did, however, beg the question of the level of knowledge and motivation (e.g. see Bransten, 1997) behind such support: for example, 12.6 per cent believed that the Czech

Republic, Poland and Hungary were already EU members, and the majority of Bulgarians surveyed expressed little knowledge of EU institutions or of the practical aspects of integration. Indeed, although over 78 per cent felt that Bulgarian accession would bring gains both for the country and for the EU, 70 per cent could not explain how the EU would benefit.

Conclusions

Promoted during 1999 from one of the 'second six' to being part of the leading 12 candidate countries, Bulgaria was none the less not yet considered to be in a position to cope with competitive pressures and market forces within the EU in the medium term. Despite moving forward with its reform programme, more was required to improve the competitiveness of the Bulgarian economy. Sustained levels of domestic and foreign investment were required to upgrade Bulgaria's infrastructure and accelerate enterprise restructuring (Nicholls, 1999).

Priority needed to be given to completing privatisation and to accelerating restructuring of the enterprise and banking sectors. Further steps were needed to ensure a stable and transparent legal framework for business. Bulgaria had made determined efforts during 1998–99 to put in place the key elements of internal market legislation, and this needed to be maintained in the first years of the new century. Bulgaria had also made progress in meeting all of the short-term priorities of the accession partnership – except in the critical nuclear sector (European Commission, 1999b). This could yet pose a major stumbling block to EU accession for both political and economic reasons.

References

Bachvarov, M., 1997, End of the model? Tourism in post-communist Bulgaria. *Tourism Management*, 18, 43–50.

Batakliev, I., 1939, Viticulture in Bulgaria. *Geography*, 24, 85–94.

Bocharov, P., 1997, Bulgaria: Turkey opens new chapter in relations with neighbor. *Radio Free Europe/Radio Liberty*, 10 December. http://search.rferl.org/nca/features/1997/12/F.RU.971210145649.html.

Bransten, J., 1997, Bulgaria: EU's rebuff could signal new toughness. *Radio Free Europe/Radio Liberty*, 31 January. http://search.rferl.org/nca/features/1997/12/F.RU.970131164243.html.

Buckwalter, D. W., 1995, Spatial inequality, foreign investment, and economic transition in Bulgaria. *Professional Geographer*, 47 (3), 288–298.

Carter, F. W., 1998, Bulgaria. *In* Turnock, D., ed., *Privatization in rural eastern Europe*. Cheltenham: Edward Elgar, pp. 69–92.

Crampton, R. J. 1997, *A concise history of Bulgaria*. Cambridge: Cambridge University Press.

EBRD, 1999, *Transition report 1999*. London: EBRD.

EIU, 1999, *Bulgaria: country profile 1999–2000*. London: EIU.

European Commission, 1997a, *Agenda 2000: Commission opinion on Bulgaria's application for membership of the European Union*. Brussels: European Commission. http://europa.eu.int/comm/dg1a/enlarge/agenda2000_en/op-Bulgaria/.

European Commission, 1997b, *EU–Bulgarian relations*. Washington DC: European Commission. http://www.eurunion.org/legislat/extrel/cec/bulgaria.htm.

European Commission, 1998, *Regular report from the Commission on progress towards accession: Bulgaria* (November 4, 1998). Brussels: European Commission.

European Commission, 1999a, *Economic reform monitor no. 3 – October 1999. Country notes: Bulgaria*. Brussels: European Commission. http://europa.eu.int/comm/ economy_finance/document/eesuppc/1999-3/bul.htm.

European Commission, 1999b, *Enlargement: regular report from the Commission on progress towards enlargement: Bulgaria – October 13, 1999*. Brussels: European Commission. http://europa.eu.int/comm/enlargement/bulgaria/rep_10_99/.

Grabbe, H., Hughes, K., 1998, *Enlarging the EU eastwards*. London: Pinter.

Koulov, B., 1996, Market reforms and environmental protection in the Bulgarian tourism industry. *In* Hall, D., Danta, D., eds, *Reconstructing the Balkans: a geography of the new Southeastern Europe*. Chichester/New York: John Wiley and Sons, pp. 187–196.

Meurs, M., Begg, R., 1998, Path dependence in Bulgarian agriculture. *In* Pickles, J., Smith A., eds, *Theorising transition*. London/New York: Routledge, pp. 243–261.

Mileva, N., 1994, Bulgarian agriculture in the period of transition. *In* Avramov, R., Antonov, V., eds, *Economic transition in Bulgaria*. Sofia: Sofia Press, pp. 169–194.

Nicholls, A., 1999, A survey of Bulgaria: the limits of stability. *Business Central Europe*, 6 (63), 39–50.

Rosenberg, S., Whitford, R., 2000, Rebooted. *Business Central Europe*, 7 (68), 23–24.

Roussinov, S., 1969, *Bulgaria: a survey*. Sofia: Sofia Press.

UNDP, 1998, *National human development report: Bulgaria 1998. The state of transition and transition of the state*. Sofia: UNDP. http://abs.bg/undp-hdr98/.

Vasileva, D., 1991, Bulgarian Turkish immigration and return. *International Migration Review*, 26 (2), 342–352.

Yarnal, B., 1994, Decollectivization of Bulgarian agriculture. *Land Use Policy*, 11 (1), 67–70.

Zloch-Christy, I., ed., 1996, *Bulgaria in a time of change: economic and political dimensions*. Aldershot: Avebury.

15

ROMANIA

David Turnock

The chapter begins with an introduction on the origins of the Romanian nation, showing how the Romanised Dacian population in the Carpathian–Danubian zone provided the ethnic basis for an independent state by the end of the 19th century. After a particularly brutalising experience under communism, the politics of transition have been dominated by caution on the part of both governments and investors. Reform is proceeding slowly because it is poorly resourced and heavily resisted by a largely sceptical and dispirited population. However, the present government has gone all out for integration with Europe and has recently introduced a new regional policy in harmony with the EU's structural funding arrangements. There are also some new arrangements to meet the needs of rural areas where social problems have been accentuated by a spate of mine closures. However, Romania has arguably been the most stable of the south-eastern European post-socialist states, and the growing business community is trying to make the best of a home market plagued by pathetically low incomes for the great majority of the population (Figure 15.1).

A brief history

Romania is unusual in being an east European country whose mainstream community claims descent from the indigenous population of pre-history; most nations in the region derive from the Dark Age migrations that introduced a largely Slavonic population. Further distinction arises from the claim that a not inconsiderable Slavonic influence has been far less significant than a decisive Roman impact, which leads directly to the name of the state, the nation and the language. The result is an 'island' of Roman/Latin culture anchored deep in south-eastern Europe and isolated from other territories where Romance languages are spoken. There is, of course, a community of interest with west European peoples, and the point is not infrequently made that the Romanians and the British enjoy a sort of antipodean relationship at opposite 'poles' of the Roman Empire, poles at which conquest was protracted and there was preoccupation about defining the imperial limits. Links with France are particularly close through language and culture: the modern Romanian administration followed the French model

Figure 15.1: Romania

and Bucharest has been referred to as 'Little Paris'. There is a natural sympathy in the West for Romania's aspiration to play a full part in the institutions of the continent.

And yet Romania is different because its geopolitical position in a Carpathian–Danubian–Pontic territory meant exposure to the post-Roman migrations (and produced the 'miracle' of survival). This was followed by the imposition of constraints on political formations through the pressures of strong neighbouring kingdoms (Bulgaria, Hungary and Poland) before the Ottoman–Russian struggle began to dominate the affairs of the Balkans. However, the principalities of Moldavia, Transylvania and Wallachia did crystallise, and in view of the strategic significance of the Danube estuary there seems to have been a consensus that these territories should retain their integrity through shifting compromises between independence, on the one hand, and occupation and annexation, on the other. There was strong Hungarian and Habsburg influence in Transylvania, whilst Ottoman suzerainty was imposed on Moldavia and Wallachia. Russian influence became stronger during the 18th century and parts of Moldavia (Bessarabia and Bucovina) were annexed, while the Habsburgs imposed a brief occupation of western Wallachia. Unification of the principalities was, however, unacceptable and was a tenet of the Great Powers' balkanising mentality of the 19th century. But the rise of Romanian nationalism forced a change of heart at a time when crucial assistance was given to the Russian campaign in Bulgaria, and the subsequent Congress of Berlin (1878) confirmed the independence declaration of the unified principalities of Moldo–Wallachia, henceforth to be known as Romania.

The greatest threat to the country's security was always seen in the east, and consequently defence was normally secured through alliances with states most able to contain Russian ambitions to control the Straits. A secret treaty with the Habsburg Empire was in force at the beginning of the 20th century, but it was renounced in favour of support for the allies during the First World War, which ended with major territorial gains and the realisation of 'Greater Romania'. But in the Second World War, defending these gains from the Soviet threat took Romania into the Axis camp. The result this time was disastrous because of the eventual occupation of the country by the Red Army and the imposition of the communist system in a particularly oppressive manner. Attempts by the Romanian Communist Party to regain the initiative merely perpetuated a neo-Stalinist dictatorship, which was consolidated by Nicolae Ceauşescu and eventually overthrown in December 1989 by a combination of spontaneous resistance and longer-term contingency planning by communists in tune with Gorbachev's *glasnost* culture.

The politics of transition

Major dislocation of Romania's commerce arose through the 'trade shock' of German unification, which meant that East Germany started trading in Deutschmarks. There followed the collapse of the USSR, which brought many long-standing exchanges to an abrupt conclusion; meanwhile civil war in Yugoslavia led to a UN trade embargo against Serbia, another important Romanian trading partner. The result was a transition marked economically and socially by extreme 'gradualism' (Hunya, 1998; Shen, 1997). After the execution of President Ceauşescu and his wife – which conveniently left the rest of the old party hierarchy blameless for the years of oppression – the National Salvation Front (NSF) was able to offer a home to former communists and to gather an effective constituency among the managers and workers of the state sector, who had most to fear from the introduction of market reforms. The need for stability after the trauma of the later Ceauşescu years – which were marked by the most severe austerity combined with extravagant and socially disruptive public works (Teodorescu, 1991) – meant that the end to central planning, and the toleration of private enterprise, went hand in hand with state subventions for state-owned enterprises and a very gradual dismantling of price controls, which prevented a 'level playing field' for all forms of business (Heller, 1998).

The NSF was flanked on the centre right by the Democratic Convention of Romania (DCR), which drew strong support from the towns (especially from Bucharest and the Transylvanian cities of Braşov and Timişoara (Banat)) through its programme of market reform (Fischer, 1992; Pop-Eleches, 1999). The DCR was ideologically close to the ethnically based Democratic Alliance of Hungarians in Romania (DAHR), although a formal alliance was constrained by the sensitive nature of politics involving ethnic groups until the treaty of friendship was signed with Hungary in 1996 (Bakk, 1998). On the other side of the political spectrum were the nationalist parties – the Greater Romania Party (GRP) and the Romanian National Unity Party (RNUP) – which opposed both foreign penetration of the economy and concessions to the ethnic minorities. When the NSF failed to deliver its promises, it had to play the nationalist card and work with parties that had emerged through regional movements like Vatra Românească in Transylvania (reflecting a sense of conflict against the indigenous Hungarian population by Romanian migrants from Moldavia who could not qualify for land restitution; Eyal, 1993). But such alliances ruled out the possibility of co-operation with the DCR, which regarded the nationalists as extremist (Calinescu and Tismaneanu, 1991) and deplored the tendencies towards 'protochronism' (projecting the originality of Romanian culture as a justification for isolationism) and an alternative to synchronism and the 'spirit of Europe' (Marga, 1993: 21). Such an outlook was a hangover from communism, when dictatorship and economic failure was excused on the grounds that Romania's destiny ran counter to socialist integration (Kligman, 1990).

An important part of the NSF strategy concerned the peasantry and the near universal desire to reclaim family landholdings from the communist co-operatives. Many peasants took matters into their own hands, and the local authorities were unable to prevent the *de facto* collapse of the system in many areas. Although the government wanted to retain large farms, it was astute enough to recognise the inevitability of land reform. The NSF legislated for the private restitution of holdings with a maximum size (10 ha arable equivalent), which would, on the one hand, leave the vast majority of *de facto* restitutions on the right side of the law and, on the other, allow a large section of the peasantry to own land, at the very least through the symbolic 1.0 ha plots (0.5 ha in the case of families who were not members of co-operative farms). When the centre-right opposition, which gradually consolidated as the DCR, advocated restitution on a more generous scale (that would also benefit the former owners of small estates), the NSF was able to hold out the spectre of further expropriation of smallholders (or alternatively of bankruptcy in the face of radical market reforms). So, the NSF and its successors were able to control the rural areas, almost solidly in Moldavia and Wallachia, and this was the key to its electoral successes until 1996 (Verdery and Kligman, 1992).

Early experience with reform

Price liberalisation attracted protest, and in 1991 misgivings over the pace of reform forced President Iliescu to replace the dynamic Petre Roman with the cautious Teodor Stolojan as prime minister. But the NSF subsequently split, with the reformist Roman wing retaining the original name and the president's party becoming the Democratic National Salvation Front (DNSF) A further metamorphosis converted the latter into the present-day Party of Social Democracy of Romania (PSDR), which went into opposition in 1996. The Stolojan cabinet prevented escalation of social tension during the winter months of 1992, and the 1992 elections were successfully fought on a government platform of very gradual reform. Iliescu was returned as president with a reduced majority, and the DNSF became the largest party in parliament. A new government headed by Nicolae Vacaroiu consisted of DNSF ministers and was supported by the nationalist parties (Tismaneanu, 1993). The government bureaucracy and the large workforces maintained by the nationalised industries and utilities were bastions of conservatism. There seemed a distinct danger that a Latin American model would prevail, with a small, rich and corrupt oligarchy ruling a poor nation. While people accepted market competition, they expected government to be protective: 'most people do not want to replace government control with more seriously binding contracts that are inflicted by market-related institutions' (Nicolaescu, 1993: 103–104). Although happy with the idea of free competition, they did not want government control replaced by the vagaries of a society governed by market forces, and political parties seeking major economic reforms found the going hard. The government argued that the country needed a period of calm after the traumas of the Ceauşescu years, and it believed that restructuring would incur heavy social costs and increase instability (van Frasum *et al.*, 1994). However, the opposition thought these fears were exaggerated and argued that failure to introduce market reforms would make for difficulties later.

Heavy industry was in great need of restructuring due to low productivity and because it was inefficient in using the large steel capacities built under communism (dependent on imported ore and energy) to turn out ships and railway rolling stock for export at competitive prices (Ben-Ner and Montias, 1994). Pollution problems often centre around such industries: there are heavy concentrations of dust, sulphur dioxide and other gases in the vicinity of the main industrial centres, and damage over wider areas was evident through deterioration in the quality of river water and the health of the forests. Massive lay-offs were avoided, compulsory 'holidays' were taken in rotation and wage rises in line with inflation were invariably delayed.

Strong worker resistance to job cuts at the Semanatoarea agricultural machinery plant in Bucharest forced New Holland to abandon its ownership bid and, with the company on the verge of bankruptcy, a new buyer would agree only to a very modest investment programme. In the case of smaller enterprises, mass privatisation eventually got under way in 1994–95, after the failure of an earlier attempt in 1992 (Earle and Telegdy, 1998). Meanwhile, foreign investment remained modest but it did grow from small and medium ventures in 1990–91 to larger-scale projects by transnational corporations like ABB, Alcatel, Amoco, Coca-Cola, Colgate-Palmolive, Shell and Siemens over the following three years. From 1995 some large strategic investments were made in the context of an improved international environment, with pride of place going to the Daewoo (South Korea) $150 mn stake in the former Oltcit car factory in Craiova. Hydrocarbon exploration was opened up to foreign companies in 1990 through production-sharing agreements. UK Enterprise Oil has found gas in the Black Sea, while Shell has drilled for gas beneath a salt layer in Transylvania at depths of 1,500 m, which is beyond the capacity of Romgaz who operate in shallower fields. Amoco have also prospected onshore.

Although it seemed that the PSDR had a good chance of re-election in 1996 – in view of its astute reading of the public mood of extreme caution over the DCR's more radical approach to reform – the campaign found the government undermined by bad economic news (Neve, 1998). This was largely a result of the economic boom engineered in 1995 when heavy borrowing (capitalising on the low debt levels of the early 1990s) led to inflation, devaluation and industrial slowdown. At the same time, the value of the minimum wage continued to fall and agriculture suffered a poor harvest after a difficult planting season that was beset by delayed provision of credit. Also, the PSDR was hit by scandal through party links with the state-owned foreign trade bank BANCOREX and misuse of bank funds with respect to unsecured loans. Meanwhile, the DCR offered a vigorous reform programme that paved the way for a new governing coalition, and the DCR's presidential candidate (Emil Constantinescu, running for the second time against Iliescu) was also effective in promoting his own programmes for educational reform, cultural transformation and moral leadership, as well as for resolving the ethnic tensions that followed the treaty with Hungary, entered into during the last months of the outgoing government. Led by Victor Ciorbea, and subsequently by Radu Vasile, the new government has persevered with privatisation: Daewoo took a majority stake in the Mangalia '1 Mai' shipyard; and the Bucharest heavy engineering industries IMGB and FECNE (linked with the country's nuclear programme) were taken over by the Norwegian transnational Kvaerner (though a further sale is now pending in view of a revised company strategy). But the investment surge evident in 1996 and 1997 has not been maintained, and turbulence arising from Russia's economic crisis also impacted negatively on the country's prospects. With little money for rapid restructuring or for generous programmes to modernise farming and infrastructure, the reform process became highly contested within the governing coalition and this led to Vasile's resignation in 1998. Despite substantial external assistance, including support for Romania's desire to join the EU and the North Atlantic Treaty Organization (NATO), a delicate balancing act is needed to satisfy the Internation Monetary Fund (IMF) and other international economic institutions as well as the electorate.

However, the country has a record of stability and now supports a large, efficient and well-equipped private sector. Romania still suffers from the poor image acquired in the last communist years: the forced industrialisation is now evident in the concentrations of declining industries and the underdeveloped infrastructure in such counties as Bistriţa-Năsăud, Botoşani, Buzău, Dolj, Neamţ, Tulcea and Vaslui, where 45 per cent of the people living in 'high poverty' are to be found (Puwack, 1992: 39-40). The high birth-rate under Ceauşescu is another unfortunate legacy (Kligman, 1992), evident in the 100,000 abandoned children in specialised institutions. The rise in the maternal death-rate due to self-inflicted abortion has now ceased – 3 abortions for each live birth in 1990 dropped to 2.1 in 1995 – and the birth-rate has fallen sharply: the current fertility level of 1.3 children per couple is among the lowest in Europe. But while the 1995 infant death-rate of 21.2 per 1,000 is the lowest in Romania's history, it is still high by European standards. There are serious nutrition problems induced by poverty (Anon, 1998). Low incomes lead to the purchase of cheaper food products, which means that more bread and low-quality cereals are consumed rather than the meat, fish and fruit that are necessary for an adequate intake of vitamins and mineral elements. There has been an explosion of diseases generated by poverty (TB and infectious diseases), an increase in underweight new-born babies and a rising number of abandoned children (Ion-Tudor, 1997).

Regional policy

In the early 1990s there was little explicit regional policy, which was unfortunate because foreign direct investment (FDI) was not only modest in absolute terms but also highly polarised spatially, with the bulk of the capital going to Bucharest and a handful of other urban centres (Guran, 1998) (Table 15.1). Transylvanian cities are among the most dynamic in the country, notably Cluj–Napoca, which has recovered from its association with the Caritas pyramid investment scandal. Cluj has a local development association and seeks to build on its successful industries, such as the privatised Ursus brewery (with a majority stake by the German brewery Bräu und Brunnen) and Porcelaine Manufacturers, a Romanian–German joint venture, which began production in 1990. However, much of the north and east is neglected, and the natural population growth is highest in these areas where there is poverty and out-migration (Ianoş, 1998; Lazaroiu, 1998). The government was sensitive to poverty problems and provided assistance in such lowland counties as Botoşani, Giurgiu and Vaslui, where large rural populations were heavily dependent on small farms. Some help was also forthcoming in Tulcea in connection with the changes associated with the Danube Delta Biosphere Reserve; and flooding in the mountains of Alba lay at the root of a special programme approved in 1997 to repair the infrastructure in an area of dispersed settlement. Such a measure must be seen in the context of limited aid for the mountain regions provided through a commission for mountainous regions set up within the ministry of agriculture immediately after the revolution

Table 15.1 Romania: regional variations in population, budget revenues and investment, 1994–1997

Region	Total population 1995	Natural change 1995	Migration (annual average) 1994–96	Budget revenues (lei mn per 1 000 population 1994–95)		Foreign investment ($ per capita, March 1990–February 1997)	
				A	B	A	B
Bucharest	2 332 620	–9 489	+6 831	472.1	+247.1	554.9	+456.1
Centre	2 678 153	–3 560	+747	208.2	–16.8	50.8	–48.0
North-east	3 784 564	+8 191	–5 376	183.3	–41.7	17.9	–80.9
North-west	2 883 233	–4 758	–2 114	207.6	–17.4	57.0	–41.8
South	3 524 974	–9 577	–1 881	166.7	–58.3	25.8	–73.0
South-east	2 954 688	–2 428	+89	252.4	+27.4	39.9	–58.9
South-west	2 437 179	–5 971	–781	178.6	–46.4	78.9	–19.9
West	2 085 540	–7 440	+5 477	244.0	+19.0	98.8	na
Romania	22 680 951	–35 032					

A = Absolute figures.   B = Deviation from the national average.

Source: *CNS (various)*

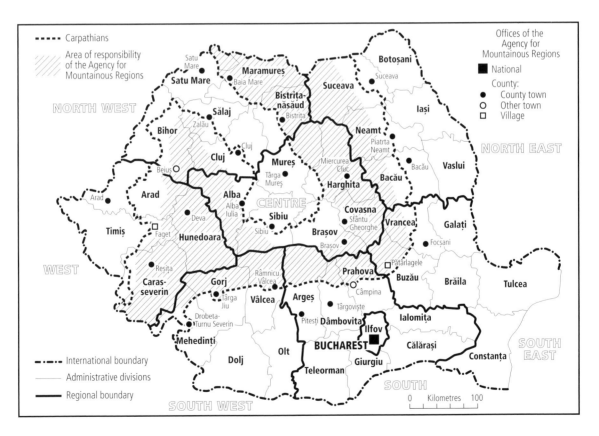

(Figure 15.2). This owed much to the advocacy of western-style 'mountainology' within the NSF government, which extended a platform that was constructed in the 1980s as a modest critique of official Communist Party policy on the consolidation of rural settlement.

As Romania is an EU candidate country, structural funding will play an important role in its future regional policy (Phinnemore, 1997). For example, the EU is helping to disseminate information and know-how through Euro-Info Bucharest and a network of regional offices, such as Euro-Info Baia Mare (which covers the counties of Bihor, Maramureş, Sălaj and Satu Mare), and 250 sub-centres. There is also an important European dimension in the reform of the planning system through the INTERREG IIc programme on 'Prospects and Strategies of Space Development Policies in the Central European Danubian and Adriatic Areas', which covers urban areas and transport systems and aims to safeguard the natural and cultural heritage. Another initiative deals with spatial planning in the Danube Basin, aiming at reduced regional differences and co-ordinated sector development policies. In the case of border areas there is now a good prospect of co-operation in places that previously felt the full rigour of the central planning system's logic of self-sufficiency within virtually closed frontiers (Dobraca, 1998). Since the new government came to power in 1996, Euroregions have been created in the east with Moldova and Ukraine (Lower Danube and Upper Prut) and in the west with Hungary and Yugoslavia (Danube–Criş–Mureş–Tisa), and a group of northern counties are now members of the Carpathian Euroregion, which works for co-operation between Hungary, Poland, Romania, Slovakia and Ukraine.

Most important, however, is EU structural funding with emphasis on direct links between Brussels and the regions in order to stimulate local democracy and satisfy the need for additionality and transparency. Development councils and agencies were set up in 1998 to co-ordinate regional development in eight large regions created by the grouping of existing counties, and these remain the top-tier units of local government (Guvernul României, 1997). Romanian experts drawn from planning and the social sciences have identified areas that are functionally coherent, polarising around major provincial cities, and roughly similar in population (in excess of two million). The aims are to reduce disparities (and permit the recovery of disadvantaged areas) through balanced development; to provide an institutional framework for the EU and for access to structural funds; to correlate government policies and sectoral activities at the regional level and use the available resources to secure durable economic and social development; and to stimulate interregional and international (cross-border) co-operation. Each council will include representatives of every town and village council, and an agency will formulate and implement the plans. The agency will also identify disadvantaged areas, in collaboration with the local or county councils, and submit proposals to World Bank specialists. A national council (chaired by the prime minister) and a national agency will approve EU structural funding and allocate resources from the national regional development fund while providing specialised assistance for individual councils. There was to be 1.5 bn lei from the 1998 budget for regional development and €35 mn from the EU for disadvantaged areas.

The new agencies are now getting organised and selecting the towns where they will locate (probably Alba Iulia, Alexandria, Bucharest, Cluj, Craiova, Galați, Iași and Timișoara). Although the richer counties may have reservations about being paired with poorer ones, the allocations from the central fund will reflect these variations. There has been little controversy over the extent of the regions themselves. The priorities will have to be worked out, but the government sees high unemployment as a major consideration (Miron, 1995). Much of the assistance will be earmarked for disadvantaged areas where poverty arises through concentrations of declining manufacturing and mining industries (with unemployment more than 25 per cent above the national average rate) and an underdeveloped infrastructure. Thus in Caraș-Severin county (part of the West Region) a series of mine closures have taken place affecting Anina (coal), Bocșa (iron ore), Moldova Nouă (non-ferrous ores), Ruschița (lead-zinc) and Sasca Montană (copper). Accordingly most of the relevant zones (Anina-Moldova Noua, Bocșa and Rusca Montană) will be designated disadvantaged areas so that efforts can be made to rebuild the economy with 3–10 year fiscal concessions to generate employment.

The most serious problem arises in the Jiu valley (in the southernmost part of Hunedoara county), which is Romania's leading pit-coal producer. Mining here is relatively high cost (exceeding the cost of imported coal) and demand is falling. The government is making heavy cutbacks, combined with relatively generous redundancy terms and attempts to introduce alternative employment. Under communism female employment was neglected, but now that there are fewer relatively well-paid jobs for men more attention must be given to food processing and textiles. A professional training and re-conversion centre is now operating, and a business consulting service is being provided in Petrosani by a local foundation that was established in 1997 for the promotion of SMEs and is supported by the UN Development Programme and the local business community. A new cigarette factory was opened in the area (in Lupeni) in 1998 by Romned International: a DM 7.0 mn project using Romanian capital and Dutch/Italian technology. Two hundred locals will be employed (plus 70 key employees from the Tg. Jiu cigarette factory) and the firm intends to invest in a tobacco plantation in Gorj, which lies immediately to the south. Meanwhile local water and power supplies are being improved, and many jobs will be created by the planned road link with Baile Herculane, a project that has great significance for the tourist industry. However, the miners' attempted march on Bucharest in January 1999 has demonstrated the scale of this reorganisation and the need for a slower programme of mine closures. But after five weeks of general strike the mines are in an extremely bad condition and a viable industry is a long way off.

Rural areas

Some progress has been made in the modernisation of agriculture through the opening, in 1997, of the Bucharest Central Wholesale Market, which is linked with a network of collecting centres and production co-operatives (Mazura, 1998). But the rural situation is difficult: although land restitution was politically unavoidable, millions of small farms in the hands of a predominantly elderly workforce do not provide a sound basis for investment in modern agriculture; and, despite promises, governments have been unable to find money for generous support of farming throughout the country (von Hirchhausen, 1998). World Bank statistics show that 30 per cent of Romanian homesteads are 'poor' and that the poverty rate is twice that of the towns. Some money is available to farmers through coupons (issued in proportion to farm size) which can be exchanged to pay for necessities such as seeds and fertilisers. But there is a need for a land market so that ambitious farmers can make profits and reinvest them (Gavrilescu, 1997). However, foreign investment is now possible through the amendment to the foreign investment law that permits land ownership by foreign companies registered in Romania. And to encourage agriculture the agriculture sales tax has been suspended until 2000. It is expected that cereal production will reach 20 million tonnes by 2000, giving an exportable surplus of 5 million tonnes. This will be a boost to impoverished areas in south Moldavia and in the Danube Valley. Meanwhile efforts are being made to improve essential rural services: water, electricity, lighting and telecommunications. Rural tourism is making progress thanks to foreign support, fiscal incentives and national promotion by a non-governmental organisation (ANTREC) dedicated to ecological and cultural tourism (Ureche and Ureche, 1997). ANTREC highlights a 'quality' network of 100 addresses (out of a total number of 2,000 actually in business) (Ion-Tudor, 1996, 1998). Returning migrants decrease the ancestral conservatism of rural populations and spread initiative, and small towns and key villages are witnessing a significant growth of tertiary activities (Turnock, 1998).

Assistance is to be given to disadvantaged rural areas. There is World Bank support for a $45 mn social development fund to help with rural housing, infrastructure and community centres, and $20 mn has been set aside specifically for the disadvantaged rural areas of eastern Moldavia (Botoşani, Iaşi and Vaslui counties), the Danube valley (including Călăraşi, Giurgiu and Teleorman) and Dobrogea (Constanţa). But there is a desire to assist all rural areas through the EU Special Accession Programme for Agriculture and Rural Development (SAPARD): ECU 500 mn per year from 2000 for Romania and the other nine candidate countries (Neagu and Stanciu, 1996). An agricultural consulting agency (ANCA) will now operate within the Ministry of Agriculture, and there will be free consultancy services for farmers covering all aspects of farming and food production. There will also be PHARE-funded training for agricultural extension in 100 villages in 16 counties. Meanwhile, there is assistance from the United Nations Food and Agriculture Organization (FAO) with regard to soil pollution and rural conservation through pilot studies at Sageata (Buzău) and Negreşti (Vaslui). The government produced a

Green Paper for reform of the agri-food sector (1998–2000), which provides for the integrated development of rural communities through World Bank support for 'unfavoured zones' and environmental conservation (Government of Romania, 1998). It is hoped that depopulation can be reduced by settling young farmers and offering compensation to older people to induce them to release their land.

Priority should be given to the further development of institutions as an essential component of community life. There is a lead from Europe through the 1998 programme to encourage citizens to participate in decision-making through contact between local authorities and both NGOs and individual people. Five projects are now being supported by the European Fund for Community Development. A National Forum of Small- and Medium-Sized Private Companies was founded in 1992 to represent the 40,000 SMEs in 41 branches and work for a national strategy to develop SMEs (Barboi, 1996a). Romania's chambers of commerce and industry have launched a programme to facilitate closer communication between the political leadership and private companies and create an improved business climate to meet international political objectives (Barboi, 1996b). Mioara Stoian from Bran (near Braşov) has started the National Association of Women from Rural Regions to enhance appreciation of the work of peasant women, protect women's rights and promote rural culture and folklore art. But a far higher level of activity is needed to mobilise local talent and initiative in a way that harmonises with the macroeconomic constraints under which the country is labouring.

Conclusion

Romania's transition has been painful and controversial. In the early years the country seemed to be a refuge for the conservatives and reform was restricted to a trickle of relatively insignificant measures taken by a neo-communist governing élite. According to this analysis, western help was misappropriated in order to support the regime of subsidies to non-viable state-owned enterprises. On the other hand, it is undeniable that Romania faced massive problems in restructuring large firms that had for so long been managed without prime concern for economic efficiency. Given the experience of the Ceauşescu years, the country understandably wavered in the face of a problematic market economy model, and even the reformist coalition – returned in 1996 when the Romanian electorate made a clean break with the past – has found it difficult to find the resources to maintain a radical programme. Romanian society has been charged with political apathy, yet a clear preference has been expressed for western democracy and EU membership. Because Romania is now firmly on the escalator leading to European integration, conservative factions have little credibility, ethnic violence has subsided and the terror tactics of the past (notably the interventions by 'miners' in Bucharest) appear to have been consigned to history. The early start to EU accession negotiations promised in late 1999 is something of a boost, and one that may help to keep the country on a reformist path if there is a change of government after the elections due in 2000.

The economic situation is difficult, for there is a limit to what indigenous business can do when there is only modest home-market demand and limited funding to support new enterprises. Yet local actions can only succeed in the context of a strong market economy, and until greater resources are available local actors will only be able to take small steps in line with prevailing opportunities and potentials. Arguably there is a 'cultural' gulf between the local and the national. On the other hand, despite beneficial changes since 1989 people are worried about negative trends in Romanian life, but there is little sense of personal involvement in and responsibility for the development of civil society. On the other hand, the national government (especially the present one, seeking EU membership) is aware of the limits of intervention in a democratic European system and of the primary importance of economic success to generate resources for welfare programmes at all levels. Also, awareness that economic growth depends on external assistance accentuates the tendency to think in broad terms of macroeconomic policy. Ways must be found to bridge the gap, most obviously through further evolution of local democracy so that the responsibility for taking 'small steps' is more readily accepted at both the regional and local levels.

References

Anon, 1998, Infant nutrition: the essence of health of a generation. *Romanian Business Journal*, 5 (42), 6.

Bakk, M., 1998, *The Democratic Alliance of Hungarians in Romania*. Budapest: Institute for Central European Studies, Teleki Laszlo Foundation Paper 9.

Barboi, D. C., 1996a, National Forum of Small and Medium-Sized Private Companies. *Romanian Business Journal*, 3 (24), 7.

Barboi, D. C., 1996b, CCIR: a factor of development. *Romanian Business Journal*, 3 (37), 8.

Ben-Ner, A., Montias, J. M., 1994, Economic systems reforms and privatization in Romania. *In* Estrin, S., ed., *Privatization in Central and Eastern Europe*. London: Longman, pp. 279–310.

Calinescu, M., Tismaneanu, V., 1991, The 1989 revolution and Romania's future. *Problems of Communism*, 40 (1–2), 42–59.

CNS (Comisia Naţionala de Statistica), Annual, *Anuarul statistic al România*. Bucharest: CNS.

Dobraca, L., 1998, Potenţialul de interacţiune spatială în ariile transfrontaliere: studiu de caz euroregiunea Dunărea-Mureş-Tisa. *In* Deica, P., Alexandrescu, M., Dobraca, L., Guran, L. eds, *Euroregiunile din Europa Centrală şi de Est: zonele transfrontaliere de România*. Bucharest: Academia Română, Institutul de Geografie, pp. 51–59.

Earle, J. S., Telegdy, A., 1998, The results of mass privatization in Romania: a first empirical study. *Economics of Transition*, 6, 313–332.

Eyal, J., 1993, Romania. *In* Whitefield, S., ed., *The new institutional architecture of eastern Europe*.

London: Macmillan, pp. 121–142.

Fischer, M. E., 1992, The new leaders and the opposition. *In* Nelson, D. N., ed., *Romania after tyranny*. Boulder CO: Westview, pp. 45–65.

Gavrilescu, D., ed., 1997, *Agricultural restructuring and rural transition in Romania*. Bucharest: Agro International.

Government of Romania, Ministry of Agriculture and Food, 1998, *Rural development in Romania: Green Paper*. Bucharest: EU PHARE Programme.

Guran, L., 1998, Rolul investiţiilor străine în cadrul teritoriului românesc cuprins în euroregiunile Dunărea-Tisa-Mureş şi Carpatică. *In* Deică, P., Alexandrescu, M., Dobraca, L., Guran, L. eds, *Euroregiunile din Europa Centrală şi de Est: zonele transfrontaliere de România*. Bucharest: Academia Română, Institutul de Geografie, pp. 39–50.

Guvernul României şi Comisia Europeană, 1997, *Politica de dezvoltare regională în România*. Bucharest: Programul PHARE.

Heller, W., ed., 1998, *Romania: migration, socio-economic transformation and perspectives of regional development*. Munich: Südosteuropa-Gesellschaft, Südosteuropa Studien 62.

Hunya, G., 1998, Romania 1990–2002: stop-go transformation. *Communist Economies and Economic Transformation*, 10, 241–259.

Ianoş, I., 1998, The influence of economic and regional policies on migration in Romania. *In* Heller, W., ed., *Romania: migration, socio-economic transformation and perspectives of regional development*. Munich: Südosteuropa-Gesellschaft, Südosteuropa Studien 62, pp. 55–76.

Ion-Tudor, C., 1996, Durable development in Romania's Carpathians. *Romanian Business Journal*, 3 (29), 16.

Ion-Tudor, C., 1997, The child: a victim of transition. *Romanian Business Journal*, 4 (31), 8.

Ion-Tudor, C., 1998, Romanian rural tourism joins international circuit. *Romanian Business Journal*, 5 (16), 16.

Kligman, G., 1990, Reclaiming the public: a reflection on creating civil society in Romania. *East European Politics and Societies*, 4, 393–438.

Kligman, G., 1992, The politics of reproduction in Ceauşescu's Romania: a case study in political culture. *East European Politics and Societies*, 6, 364–418.

Lazaroiu, S., 1998, Post-communist transformations in Romania and their effects on migration behaviour and ideology. *In* Heller, W., ed., *Romania: migration, socio-economic transformation and perspectives of regional development*. Munich: Südosteuropa-Gesellschaft, Südosteuropa Studien 62, pp. 36–54.

Marga, A., 1993, Cultural and political trends in Romania before and after 1989. *East European Politics and Societies*, 7, 14–32.

Mazura, O., 1998, The first collecting centre for the wholesale market opened in Mihaieşti-Argeş. *Romanian Business Journal*, 5 (14), 6.

Miron, M., 1995, Romania: the challenge of unemployment. *In* Jackson, M., ed., *Unemployment and evolving labor markets in central and eastern Europe*. Aldershot: Avebury, pp. 31–47.

Neagu, V., Stanciu, G., 1996, *Romania: charta europeana a spatiului rural*. Bucharest: Editura Ceres.

Neve, G. de, 1998, Political dimensions of transformation in Romania. *In* Heller, W., ed., *Romania: migration, socio-economic transformation and perspectives of regional development*. Munich: Südosteuropa-Gesellschaft, Südosteuropa Studien 62, pp. 23–35.

Nicolaescu, T., 1993, Privatization in Romania: the case for financial institutions. *In* Fair, D. E., Raymond, R. J., eds, *The new Europe: evolving economic and financial systems in eastern Europe*. Dordrecht: Kluwer.

Phinnemore, D., 1997, Romania and the EU: prospects for entry. *In* Light, D., Dumbraveanu-Andone, D., eds, *Anglo-Romanian geographies: proceedings of the second Liverpool–Bucharest Geography Colloquium*. Liverpool: Liverpool Hope Press, pp. 119–130.

Pop-Eleches, G, 1999, Separated at birth or separated by birth? the communist successor parties in Romania and Hungary. *East European Politics and Societies*, 13, 117–147.

Puwak, H., 1992, *Poverty in Romania: territorial distribution and the intensity of poverty level*. Bucharest: Institute for Quality of Life, Romanian Academy.

Shen, R., 1997, *The restructuring of Romania's economy: a paradigm of flexibility and adaptability*. Westport CT: Praeger.

Teodorescu, A., 1991, The future of a failure: the Romanian economy. *In* Sjöberg, Ö., Wyzan, M. L., eds, *Economic change in the Balkan states*. London: Pinter, pp. 69–82.

Tismaneanu, V., 1993, The quasi revolution and discontents: emerging political pluralism in post-Ceauşescu Romania. *East European Politics and Societies*, 7, 309–348.

Turnock, D., 1998, Human resources for regional development in the Romanian Carpathians. *In* Heller, W., ed., *Romania: migration, socio-economic transformation and perspectives of regional development*. Munich: Südosteuropa-Gesellschaft, Südosteuropa Studien 62, pp. 90–115.

Ureche, C., Ureche, I., 1997, Le tourisme comme moyen de développement de l'espace rural roumain. *In* Cristea, V., ed., *L'espace rural: approche pluridisciplinaire*. Cluj-Napoca: Editura Risoprint, pp. 154–158.

van Frasum, Y. G., Gehmann, U., Gross, J., 1994, Market economy and economic reform in Romania: macroeconomic and microeconomic perspectives. *Europe–Asia Studies*, 46 (4), 735–756.

Verdery, K., Kligman, G., 1992, Romania after Ceauşescu: post-communist communism. *In* Banac, I., ed., *Eastern Europe in revolution*. Ithaca NY: Cornell University Press, pp. 117–147.

von Hirschhausen, B., 1998, *Nouvelles campagnes roumains: paradox d'un retour paysan*. Paris: Edition Belin.

16

MALTA

Derek Hall

A brief history

The Maltese archipelago consists of three islands: Malta, Gozo and Comino (Kemmuna). Malta, the largest, is 237 sq km in area, Gozo 68 sq km and Comino 2 sq km (Figure 16.1). The total population is 378,000, of whom 28,000 live on Gozo; Comino is inhabited only by a few farmers. The islands have a high natural demographic growth rate (3.8 per 1,000 in 1998, 5.2 in 1997), coupled to relatively high net migration rates (1.6 per 1,000 in 1997). Infant mortality was down to 5.3 per 1,000 live births in 1998 (from 10.7 in 1996), and life expectancy in 1998 was 80.1 years for women and 74.4 for men (European Commission, 1999b). English is the second official language of the islands, and the official religion is Roman Catholic. There are no other denominations of substantial size among the Maltese, although churches of other faiths are present.

Because of their strategic position in the Mediterranean, Malta and Gozo have been inhabited for at least 7,000 years, and exhibit some of the earliest known stone buildings in existence. Neolithic, Copper and Bronze Age civilisations lasted more than 4,000 years. The first known people to settle from outside were the Phoenicians, who arrived as traders in the 9th century BC. They were succeeded by the Carthaginians, who were eventually conquered by the Romans in the 3rd century BC. Romans governed until the division of the Empire in the 4th century AD.

Arabs from North Africa occupied the islands from the 9th to the 13th century and left behind notable imprints of their culture, particularly on the language of the Maltese people, which is the only Semitic language written in Latin characters. Norman, Swabian and Angevin dynasties subsequently ruled the islands, which, at the beginning of the 14th century, fell to the throne of Aragon. In 1530 Charles V of Spain granted the islands on fief to the international Order of the Knights of St John of Jerusalem. The knights administered the islands for the next 268 years until Napoleon Bonaparte occupied the country in 1798 in the name of the French Republic. But after just two years the French were forced to surrender following a land-and-sea blockade by combined British and Maltese forces, and in 1800 Malta became part of the British Empire.

Figure 16.1: Malta

In 1964 Malta gained its independence and was declared a republic within the British Commonwealth in 1974. Until the 1960s the Maltese economy depended mostly on the British armed services and the naval dockyard. After independence, light industry (e.g. see METCO, 1999) and tourism were developed (see Tables 16.1, 16.2) (MTA, 1999b).

Since 1993 Malta's GDP per capita has increased by about one-quarter in real terms, but it remains low relative to the EU average (and Maltese statistics do not permit a direct comparison on a PPP basis) (European Commission, 1999a). Weakening domestic demand in the economy

Table 16.1 Malta: main economic indicators, 1994–1998

	1994	1995	1996	1997	1998
GDP ($ bn)	2.7**	3.1**	3.1**	3.2**	4.3*
Real GDP change	na	6.2*	4.0*	4.9*	4.1*
(%)	2.1**	7.3**	4.2**	2.8**	2.8§
Exports ($ bn)	1.4**	1.8**	1.6**	2.1*	2.3*
Imports ($ bn)	2.4**	2.9**	2.8**	2.9*	3.0*
Unemployment	na	3.7*	4.4*	5.0*	5.1*
(%)	4.0**	3.6**	3.7**	4.4**	4.9§
Agriculture (% of gross value-added)	2.8*	2.9*	2.9*	2.9*	2.8*
Industry excluding construction (% of gross value-added)	26.1*	25.5*	24.7*	24.3*	24.7*
Construction (% of gross value-added)	3.4*	3.3*	3.1*	3.0*	2.8*
Services (% of gross value-added)	67.7*	68.3*	69.3*	69.7*	69.7*
Inflation rate (%)	4.1*	4.0*	2.5*	3.1*	2.4*
FDI (% of GDP)	na	5.6*	9.7*	3.8*	na
Current account balance (% of GDP)	na	−11.0§	−10.7§	−6.2§	−4.8§

Sources: *European Commission, 1999a* (§), *1999b* (*); *UNECE, 1999* (**)

has led to a reduction in the trade and current account deficits from the high levels of the mid-1990s.

International tourism showed a resurgence in the later 1990s, with a 6.4 per cent increase in arrivals in 1998 (Table 16.2). This was likely to be strengthened with the decision of one of the world's leading cruise operators to use Malta as a hub port from 1999. In launching a new brand image for Maltese tourism in that year (MTA, 1999a), the Malta Tourism Authority laid emphasis on high-income generating niche, leisure and tourism products such as culture and conference tourism, language studies and underwater diving.

VAT was reintroduced in January 1999, and although it induced a temporary increase in the inflation rate, overall the inflation trend has been downwards, reaching just 1.4 per cent by May 1999 (European Commission, 1999a). Notably, the Maltese economy was not significantly affected by the turbulence on international financial markets during 1998–99. However, Malta's high dependence on tourism and a limited number of export products makes its trade performance vulnerable to shifts in international demand (European Commission, 1999b).

The Maltese government initiated a privatisation process and a restructuring of the public sector only in the second half of the 1990s. Although a task force has been set up for this purpose, there

Table 16.2 Malta: tourism statistical trends, 1994–1998

	1994		1995		1996		1997		1998	
	No.	%	No.	%	No.	%	No.	%	No.	%
International tourist arrivals	1 176 223	100	1 115 971	100	1 053 788	100	1 111 161	100	1 182 240	100
Source of which:										
UK	530 385	45.1	461 159	41.3	398 899	37.9	436 899	39.3	448 763	38.0
Germany	200 281	17.0	187 761	16.8	184 110	17.5	193 020	17.4	203 199	17.2
Italy	98 746	8.4	97 384	8.7	89 439	8.5	90 190	8.1	90 558	7.7
France	68 711	5.8	72 876	6.5	64 453	6.1	62 457	5.6	72 512	6.1
Netherlands	45 328	3.9	45 526	4.1	48 928	4.6	52 238	4.7	56 534	4.8
Libya	40 668	3.5	37 186	3.3	50 950	4.8	39 289	3.5	37 509	3.2
Belgium	17 880	1.5	22 008	2.0	21 879	2.1	25 567	2.3	25 146	2.1
Switzerland	19 988	1.7	18 502	1.7	19 900	1.9	17 924	1.6	24 776	2.1
Austria	19 000	1.6	20 095	1.8	15 909	1.5	17 913	1.6	23 741	2.0
Russia	7 277	0.6	10 593	1.0	13 596	1.3	21 339	1.9	23 717	2.0
Other	127 959	10.9	142 881	12.8	145 725	13.8	154 325	14.0	175 785	14.8
International excursionist (day-tripper) arrivals	62 820	-	77 216	–	69 240	–	126 645	–	144 064	–
Direct employment in hotels and catering establishments	8 154	–	8 561	–	8 457	–	9 078	–	9 713	–

Sources: *MTA, 1999a; author's additional calculations*

is strong opposition within the country. Utilities remain in state hands, and other corporations, such as shipbuilding and dry-dock companies (METCO, 2000), continue to be supported by large subsidies. State-guaranteed debts accumulated by loss-making public enterprises amount to more than 40 per cent of GDP (European Commission, 1999a, 1999b).

The European Commission's 1999 regular report (1999b) concluded that Malta was a functioning market economy and should be able to cope with competitive pressure and market forces within the EU provided it continues with industrial restructuring. The report saw the main challenge for Malta's economic policy to be the need to reduce the government deficit.

Malta–EU relations

In 1967, three years after its independence, Malta informed the European Economic Community (EEC) that it wished to establish formal contractual relations. Negotiations were soon initiated, leading to the signing of the EC–Malta Association Agreement in December 1970. This agreement, only the third of its kind signed by the EC with a third country, came into force in April 1971. It formalised close links between the EU and Malta and has remained the cornerstone of relations. Under the agreement the EU–Malta Association Council was established and a joint parliamentary committee was set up. The main focus of the agreement was the gradual removal of trade barriers to allow unhindered access to each other's markets. The result has been close trade relations, with the EU accounting for 52.8 per cent of Malta's exports and 69.3 per cent of its imports in 1998 (albeit down from, respectively, 74.0 and 75.7 per cent in the peak year 1994) (European Commission, 1999b).

Although remaining in its first stage, the Association Agreement has been extended: in 1976 after the accession of Denmark, Ireland and the UK, and again in 1988 after the accession of Spain and Portugal. The amendments allowed for a significant deepening of relations, the most notable change being the introduction of a package of technical and financial assistance in the form of a financial protocol, which entered into force in November 1978 (Table 16.3). To date the EU and Malta have signed four successive protocols allocating ECU 138.5 mn in assistance to cover specific projects in the fields of infrastructure, professional training and the environment (Table 16.4). In July 1990 Malta formally applied for European Community membership. The publication of a favourable *Opinion (avis)* by the European Commission in June 1993 added momentum and, subsequently, EU–Malta relations were oriented toward the goal of membership.

Following a change of government in October 1996 Malta's application for EU membership was placed in abeyance. Malta was subsequently excluded from the pre-accession strategy and the structured dialogue was suspended. The policy of the new Maltese government was that of 'closest ties', falling short of full membership. This position was noted by the Council of Ministers, who then requested the Commission to prepare a communication on the nature and scope of relations in light of the new objective of the government of Malta.

At the beginning of 1998 the future relations between the EU and Malta were defined in a communication to the Council. The key element of the communication was the completion of a free-trade area as a first step toward a customs union. The communication paved the way for the first council of association. As such a joint declaration was made which set out the parameters of future EU–Malta relations. It was envisaged that barriers to trade would be removed over a three-year period, starting from the entry into force of a legal protocol (to be negotiated). It was

Table 16.3 Malta: chronology of EU relations, 1970–1999

1970

December Signing of the EEC–Malta Association Agreement.

1978–83

1st financial protocol: ECU 26 mn

1983–88

2nd financial protocol: ECU 29.5 mn

1988–93

3rd financial protocol: ECU 38 mn

1990

Malta applies to join the European Community.

1992

September EU–Malta joint parliamentary committee set up.

1993

June European Commission's *Opinion (avis)* on Malta's application for membership.

1994

March Agreement on a programme and a timetable for implementing economic reforms.

June European Council of Corfu states that the next enlargement will involve Malta and Cyprus.

December The Essen Council confirms this.

1995

January Malta's economic reform programme comes into force.

July European Parliament adopts a resolution in favour of accession by Malta.

1995–98

4th financial protocol: ECU 45 mn

1996

October General election: new administration puts EU membership application on hold, while expressing the desire for close relations.

1997

April Second Euro-Mediterranean ministerial conference in Valletta. The Maltese government expresses its full commitment to the Euro – Mediterranean Partnership and calls for urgent action to strengthen it.

May European Commissioner van den Broek pays an official visit to Malta to discuss the definition of the new EU–Malta relationship.

1998

February The Council of Ministers adopts the Commission's communication on future relations with Malta.

September General election: new government reactivates Malta's application for EU membership.

October The European Council asks the Commission to prepare a report assessing Malta's present progress of reforms. The European Parliament approves a resolution for a positive stance to reactivate, as soon as possible, Malta's application for EU membership.

1999

February The European Commission adopts an *Opinion* on Malta's application for EU membership.

December Helsinki EU leaders' summit invites Malta to join enlargement negotiations. Commission President Romano Prodi tells press he considers Malta one of the most prepared candidates.

Sources: *EUDEL, 1999; MFA, 1999*

also agreed that the restructuring of Maltese manufacturing, a process already under way, would be given financial support under the terms of a fourth financial protocol.

The outcome of a snap general election held in September 1998 saw EU accession negotiations recommencing. The European General Affairs Council of October considered positively the Maltese request for membership reactivation and invited the European Commission to present

Table 16.4 Malta: outline of EU protocols, 1978–1999

Protocol	Aims	Main measures
1st (1978–1983) ECU 26 mn	Help finance technical assistance and training, development of industrial and agricultural production, tourism and scientific co-operation	• Rehabilitation and expansion of telecoms • Redevelopment of commercial port • Power station upgrading • Civil aviation staff training • Upgrading hospital x-ray department • Training and equipping university mechanical engineering
2nd (1983–1988) ECU 29.5 mn	Help finance economic and social development	• New air terminal • Recycling plan • Tourism promotion programme • Institute for hotel and tourism studies • New physical planning law and structure plan • Water resource management projects • Sewerage master plan • Upgrading educational and technical standards
3rd (1988–1993) ECU 38 mn	Help finance infrastructure improvement	• Desalination plant • Sewerage facility upgrading • Upgrading air traffic control • Coastline protection measures • Upgrading hospital radiotherapy • Rehabilitation of Valletta telephone network • Strengthening EC scholarships, fellowships and educational support programmes • Marketing assistance for manufacturers • Upgrading of standards, metrology testing and quality assurance sectors
4th (1995–1998; extended to December 1999) ECU 45 mn	Promote development of the economy and fulfil the objectives of the Association Agreement, to offer technical assistance and training to facilitate Malta's economic transition with a view to accession	• Contribution towards risk capital formation • Support for SME investment • Financing equity participation in joint ventures between EU partners and Maltese entrepreneurs in the industrial and tourism sectors • Water supply and waste-water treatment • Further upgrading of tourism, telecoms and transport infrastructures

Source: *EUDEL, 1999*

an evaluation of the position since the 1993 *Opinion*. The European Parliament then voted a resolution asking the European Council and the Commission to support Malta's accession 'as soon as possible in full respect and procedures of the Treaty'. The European Parliament also asked the Council to include Malta as a member of the European Conference. In February 1999 the European Commission adopted a report updating the 1993 *avis*. It recommended that the Council give the go-ahead for the screening of Malta's legislation with a view to enabling the start of negotiations by the end of 1999. However, it was reported in the Maltese press that Brussels was concerned that the anti-EU membership lobby – led by the opposition Labour Party – appeared to be more organised and vocal than its counterpart on the pro-membership side. It was claimed that Brussels was arguing that the Maltese government needed to organise a distinctive and clear policy in favour of EU membership, as had been done by other applicant countries (Manduca, 1999).

The EU and Malta have established a number of additional co-operation ties within multilateral frameworks. Malta has participated in the fourth framework programme for research and development, as well as in a wide range of Community programmes in the context of the EU's Mediterranean policy. It actively participates in the networks in support of small- and medium-sized enterprises (SMEs), such as Europartenariat, MedPartenariat and Med-Interprise, as well as in the programme of decentralised regional co-operation (Med-Campus, Med-Urbs and Med-Media). The latter falls within the framework of the Euro-Mediterranean Partnership, of which Malta is a full member.

Conclusion

As a cultural bridge between southern Europe and North Africa, and as a popular tourism destination for north Europeans, Malta sees itself as having an important international role in Europe. However, those involved in heavily subsidised state and para-statal sectors of the economy and in the myriad of offshore businesses and services are likely to be less enthusiastic about the requirements for EU membership. Indeed, despite optimistic noises from Brussels on Malta's suitability, the relatively slow process of privatisation and subsidy removal might suggest that the path toward Malta's EU accession may not be wholly smooth.

References

EUDEL (Delegation of the European Commission – Malta), 1999, *An introduction to EU–Maltese relations*. Ta'xbiex: EUDEL. http://mlt.eudel.com/eudel/introduc.htm.

European Commission, 1999a, *Economic developments and structural reform in the candidate countries. Country notes: Malta*. Brussels: EC Economic Reform Monitor No. 3 (ECFIN/D.1). http://europa.eu.int/comm/economy_finance/document/docum_en.htm.

European Commission, 1999b, *Regular report from the Commission on progress towards accession: Malta – October 13, 1999*. Brussels: European Commission. http://europa.eu.int/comm/enlargement/malta/rep_10_99/x.htm.

Manduca, A., 1999, Brussels wants pro-EU lobby to be better organised. *The Malta Business Weekly*, 26

August. http://www.business-line.com/business-weekly/archives/253/15.html.

METCO (Malta External Trade Corporation), 1999, *Company profiles*. Valletta: METCO. http://metcowww.com/bd_01.htm.

METCO, 2000, *Malta Drydocks*. Valletta: METCO. http://metco.com.mt/co/drydocks/home.html.

MFA (Ministry of Foreign Affairs, Malta) 1999, The EU leaders meeting in Helsinki formally invited Malta and five other applicants to start accession talks in February 2000. *Foreign Affairs Diary* (Valletta), 6 December, pp. 1–3. http://www.foreign.gov.mt/news/hron1.htm.

MTA (Malta Tourism Authority), 1999a, *A new brand image for Malta*. Valletta: MTA. http://visitmalta.com/history.htm.

MTA, 1999b, *History of Malta*. Valletta: MTA. http://visitmalta.com/history.htm.

UNECE, 1999, *Trends in Europe and North America: Malta*. New York: UNECE. http://www.unece.org/stats/trend/mlt.htm.

17

TURKEY

Jesus del Río Luelmo and Allan M. Williams

Turkey occupies a strategic position in the interface of Europe, Asia and the Middle East (Figures 17.1, 17.2) and has borders with both existing and applicant EU members. The questions of whether its destiny is as an eastern or western, European or Asian, developed or peripheral country are just some of the dilemmas conditioning Turkey's role in the international community, its relationship with the EU and the applicant member states and the evolution of its domestic policy.

Turkey's long-term goal of full integration into the EU has been a centrepiece of both domestic and foreign politics since the signing of the Treaty of Rome (Buzan and Diez, 1999). This was mainly due to two sets of circumstances: first, Kemalist obsession with the West has been

Figure 17.1: Turkey

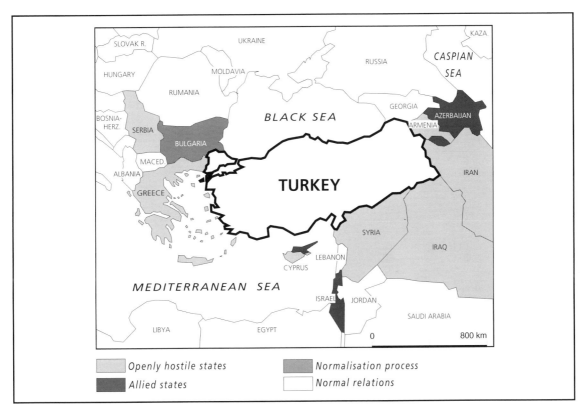

Figure 17.2: Turkey: living in a tough neighbourhood

virtually unquestioned since the creation of the republic (Heper *et al.*, 1993); second, Greece has played a significant dual role as Turkey's major external enemy and part of the western bloc (Eralp, 1993). While a progressive approach to Europe has been a dominant feature of Turkey's approach to the West, this relationship has been subject to sharp fluctuations in recent decades. Although EU integration has been the dominant option for Turkish decision-makers, it has encountered a number of obstacles. These were being overcome, in one way or another, until the watershed of the 1990s. Turkey's present relationships with the EU are extremely delicate, perhaps to a greater degree than ever before. For some commentators, the obstacles to the normal development of this relationship seem to be unsurmountable at present. This chapter explores whether the 1990s were a turning point in this relationship, or simply a new chapter in its long and difficult history (Müftüler-Bac, 1998). A brief history of the institutional relations between Turkey and the EU is followed by an account of the main difficulties – including the issue of mutual misperceptions. The chapter concludes with an assessment of future prospects. This provides the framework for considering relationships not only with the EU but also with the other applicants for EU membership.

Turkey and the EU: always a difficult relationship?

From the Ankara Agreement to the customs union

Institutional relations between Turkey and the European Community were officially initiated on 31 July 1959, when Turkey formally applied for membership. The driving forces behind this were twofold: concerns over Greek influence in Europe, and reinforcement of the westernisation project initiated by Atatürk (Kinross, 1964). The onset of the Cold War presented Turkey with an unprecedented opportunity for approaching the West. Its pivotal position was optimised by Turkish decision-makers, and application for EU membership was a logical consequence of the process of integration into a series of organisations representing the western alliance: OECD, NATO, the Marshall Plan and the Council of Europe. An openly pro-European option was not considered to be contradictory to foreign policy toward the USA, given the strength of US–European relations at this time. Moreover, in the 1950s, economic difficulties and tensions with the USA (Eralp, 1993) contributed to Turkey's vision of Europe as the guarantor of its westernisation project.

Turkey's early application was perceived by the Community as a possible threat to its own integration process. The main concerns were Turkey's low level of socio-economic development and the perceived cultural differences. The initial approach had been to offer Ankara a package of general co-operation measures, including economic and financial co-operation and trade and customs privileges, but without provision for integration. However, the signing of the EC's association agreement with Greece posed a serious dilemma, in the context of the need for parity of treatment for the two rival states at a time of Cold War sensitivity. Therefore, the Ankara Agreement (12 September 1963) offered association membership to Turkey. The decision reveals a lack of foresight by the EC. There was little appreciation of either the potential regional impact of the integration process on Turkey and south-east Europe, or of the symbolic – almost obsessive – value that full membership would acquire in Turkey's foreign policy (Öymen, 1997). This continues to be a source of friction, which the eastern enlargement project has exacerbated.

The Ankara Agreement included a timetable for the staged convergence of Turkey with EC standards. It provides for a consultative joint parliamentary committee, and for an association council to manage the association. But the landmark decision was provision for eventual full integration after a lengthy transition period. After Turkey had fulfilled all the conditions of the transitional stages, the agreement set out a schedule for the free movement of workers (provisionally from 1 December 1986), together with a customs union, and these were to be the final steps before full integration. The agreement has cast a long shadow over Turkey's European policy ever since. A supposedly smooth process of integration became progressively more complex for the beleaguered Turkish state in late 1960s and early 1970s. However, despite certain delays and difficulties in the early stages, Ankara could envisage the possibility of medium-term success: adaptation was slow but in the required direction.

Turkey's domestic situation posed a serious challenge for the agreement in this period. During the 1970s the approach to the Community was no longer seen by Turkish economic leaders as a matter of foreign policy, but rather as a purely economic issue. Fears of the negative consequences of a customs union for an already weakened Turkish economy reduced enthusiasm for integration. For the first time, the coupling of westernisation and development, hitherto considered indivisible, began to split. The Cyprus issue in the international arena, together with internal conflicts, lay at the root of this. Economic pressures led to negotiation of a number of extensions to the original timetable, so as to adapt the process to Turkey's domestic circumstances. It was precisely at this moment of Turkey's uncertainty and weakness that Greece (in the mid-1970s) applied for full membership, and thereby changed the political balance in south-east Europe. It was an extremely delicate period for Ankara: internal violence and economic and political instability led to the 1980 military *coup d'état*. EU membership was not the priority for the Turkish state in such circumstances, and the opportunity to counter the Greek application was missed. This was to change Turkey's relationships not only with existing members of the EU, but also with potential future members.

After Greek accession to the EU in 1981, Ankara progressively realised the magnitude of its strategic, and now historical, error, and desperately sought to reverse the situation and restore confidence at both the domestic and international levels. Economic and political reforms, and progressive liberalisation, created a more optimistic environment in Turkey. EU membership was again seen to be feasible, and Türgüt Özal (President 1989–93) made full membership the central goal of foreign policy, lodging Turkey's application with the EU in 1987. However, this policy and popular aspirations were to be thwarted by Greek hostility, and the threat of a veto on any membership application, although this provided a convenient cloak of hesitation for other member states and for the EU itself. In 1989 Turkey's membership application was deferred, and this heralded a more uneasy relationship with the EU during the 1990s.

Uncertainty related to the collapse of the Soviet Union also affected Turkey's role as a strategic ally for the West. The 1990s witnessed a continuous struggle by Turkey to define a new role in the region, one which would appeal to EU interests. Moreover, the growing gap between the US and Europe in the post-Cold War era, made it more difficult for Turkey to navigate its relationship among the western powers. At the same time, the end of the Cold War had a significant double implication for Turkey: it opened up a new wave of potential membership applicants in central and eastern Europe and also led to the series of political and humanitarian crises that have surrounded the fragmentation of the former Yugoslavia.

The customs union

With or without full membership, the effective economic integration of Turkey into the EU is already under way. Approximately one half of Turkey's trade was with the EU by the 1990s. The customs union – signed in 1995 and implemented from 1996 – was the final step in the economic integration, in this sense. It can be considered as a significant Turkish success in the aftermath of the 1987 membership decision, although there are limits to the union. First, 'sensitive' Turkish products, such as textiles, have been subject to quotas, but these are perhaps its most competitive exports. In addition, the transition to a full customs union was supposed to have been accompanied by financial support for Turkey's integration into the EU market. In practice, Greece has vetoed these promises, and Turkey receives less financial support from the EU than most other Mediterranean countries (Williams, 1993).

The logic behind the customs union is open to interpretation. While Ankara sees it as the step prior to full integration, the EU and most of the member states have understood it to be the highest stage of integration available to Turkey in the foreseeable future. Assessment of the success of the union depends fundamentally on which perspective is adopted. But if the question of full membership is set aside for the moment, then the union can be seen as an economic success, although it has been more favourable to the EU than to Turkey. The share of Turkey's exports destined for the EU have stagnated, while imports have increased consistently (see Table 17.1). Nevertheless, a provisional balance offers a moderately optimistic panorama on market integration. However, the lack of financial support is creating strong tensions as Turkish industry faces growing European competition. Additionally, the union severely constrains Turkey's trade ambitions in the surrounding regions: while part of this customs union, the country cannot be part of other free-trade areas.

Key issues in the Turkey–EU relationship

Turkey's international position was relatively strong in the Cold War period: it was a respected ally for the West, an opponent for the East and an instrument of US influence in the Middle East. This strategic role contributed to its close relationship with the EU and the West, but this has been weakened by a number of problematic issues. These have a twofold dimension – domestic and international – but they are interlinked and difficult to isolate.

Domestic issues

The treatment of human rights has been one of the most persistent obstacles to Turkey's integration into wider western associations. A lack of legal guarantees for detainees, human rights abuses by the police and army, legal restrictions on the freedom of the press and of speech, party political restrictions, the role of paramilitary forces and the excessive powers of the

Table 17.1 Turkey: trade with the EU, 1987–1998

	Imports from the EU (% of Turkish imports)	Exports to the EU (% of Turkish exports)	
1987	39.9	48.7	
1988	41.1	43.6	
1989	38.6	46.5	
1990	42.6	53.1	
1991	46.1	51.8	
1992	44.6	51.6	
1993	43.5	48.5	
1994	44.2	48.5	
1995	47.2	51.2	
1996	52.0	49.5	
1997	49.4	46.2	
1998 (January–June)	51.6	48.8	

Source: *SIS, 1999*

military in the east of the country have all contributed to creating a negative image of Turkey in many western circles. Although there have been improvements in recent decades, these have arisen largely from international pressures rather than from reform movements within Turkish society.

The Kurdish issue

This is closely linked to the above problem (MacDowall, 1996). Despite the hope created in the Özal years that a way could be found to integrate Kurds into Turkish society relatively harmoniously, there has been heightened tension, and it is difficult to foresee an early end to the unofficial civil war in the east of the country (Beriker-Atiyas, 1997). This conflict, led on the Kurdish side by the PKK (Kurdish Workers' Party), has left more than 30,000 dead. The related issue of contested sovereignty is extremely sensitive in Turkish politics and society, and European concerns – there were 13 condemnations by the Council of Europe for human rights abuses in 1999 alone – do not facilitate a closer relationship. The position is further exacerbated by the distribution of Kurds among Turkey, Iraq and Syria, so that domestic issues are intertwined with international territorial issues.

The omnipresence of the military

In recent decades such an omnipresence qualifies any western assessment of Turkish democracy. The army is attributed a far greater role in Turkey than is acceptable in western societies. It is considered to be a guarantor of the republican order created by Atatürk, and its intervention is considered as normal – and often welcomed – by the vast majority of the population. *Coups d'état* in 1960, 1971 and 1980 have been the most dramatic chapters in this history of protagonism. Although Turkey's claims that an enhanced democratic system was instituted after the 1980 *coup* are formally justified, the practices of democracy remain flawed. The arrival in power of Erbakan, leader of the Islamist Welfare Party, was seen to challenge the secularisation of the Turkish state, one of the cornerstones of Atatürk's vision of a modern Turkey. This provoked a rapid response by the army, even if this was more discreet than in the past. Increasing military pressure culminated in an ultimatum to the government and eventually led to Erbakan's resignation. This 'soft' *coup* reinforced the negative image of Turkish politics and society in the West, and it is difficult to see how the obstacle can be overcome given the present configuration of the country's civil society.

Economic and political stability

Weaknesses in civil society are also an obstacle to the development of relations with the EU and with its future members. For example, the unhealthy links between political power, organised crime and the security forces were exposed several times during the life of the Çiller government (June 1993–March 1996), which was eventually partly undermined by revelations of corruption, especially in respect of privatisation. In addition, Turkey lacks a strong civil society able to impose a more acceptable (to the West) political model on internal politics. The system of élites and the weight of clientelism – particularly, although not exclusively, in the east of the country – contribute to this negative perspective. A further complication has been the arrival in power of political Islam, due particularly to the liberalisation of Turkey's political system, to recurrent socio-economic difficulties and to the so-called Bosnian effect (related to the perceived persecution of Muslims). Although it is neither a violent nor a radical form of political Islam, fears in the West have increased (Lapidot, 1996) and have been fuelled by a western failure to appreciate that Islam is a heterogenous set of religious, social and political movements (Acar, 1993).

There are parallels in the economy. Whilst Turkey's economic system is relatively strong, and has produced impressive GDP growth rates in individual years in the 1990s, there are also structural weaknesses (Cioclea, 1998). Among the major challenges are (Balkir and Williams, 1993):

- Unbalanced foreign trade with the EU: the weight of agriculture in Turkish exports is a weakness, given inelastic demand conditions, and contributes to a sustained growth of foreign debt.

- Budget deficit: despite efforts to liberalise the economic system and to reduce the role of the state since the 1980s, public expenditure habitually exceeds state income, particularly because of the lack of an efficient tax system.

- Inflation has become an accepted part of daily life, with annualised rates in excess of 50 per cent and even of 100 per cent in much of the period since the 1970s. High levels of foreign debt, budget deficits, currency devaluations and increases in oil prices are contributory factors.

- High unemployement rates, together with uneven regional development, are a barrier to EU integration, given concerns about the potential for emigration. The regional inequalities would also cause enormous potential demands on the EU's structural funds, especially given the challenges that have already been posed by the proposed eastern expansion.

Foreign policy issues

Immigration

One of the most delicate issues in the relationships with the EU, this has been heightened by the end of chronic northern European labour shortages after the 1960s. The issue of Turkish migration is strongest in Germany. Anti-Turkish violence, the rejection of foreigners, a reluctance to adapt to the host society or import outside problems – such as Kurdish violence – represent only a few examples of an issue that questions the very basis of European society (Elmas, 1998b). In this context, there is little possibility that the free movement of Turkish workers into or within the EU will be accepted by the member states. In practice, this is likely to have been one of the most powerful reasons for the rejection of the Turkish application, even though it is not formally admitted by representatives of either the member states or of the European Commission.

Geopolitics: uneasy relations with neighbouring countries

While Turkey's geo-strategic position has been advantageous for its insertion in the international community, relationships with neighbouring countries in this tense geopolitical zone have been difficult, and this has added to barriers to further integration with the EU.

The historical animosity between Greece and Turkey, with the Cyprus issue to the forefront, is no doubt the main problem posed by relations with neighbouring countries to EU integration. Recent incidents have reinforced this mutual hostility. But this is not the only source of tension.

For a variety of reasons, relations with other bordering states are not much better: with Syria and Iraq due to conflicts over access to water and to the Kurdish issue; with Iran because of the clash between Turkey's secular regime and political Islam (Calabrese, 1998); with Armenia (Vaner, 1998) as a result of historical events. Turkish membership of the EU would, therefore, pose very serious challenges for the fledgling common foreign and security policy.

Turkey as a strategic ally

Despite the emphasis placed so far on barriers, Turkey is an interesting partner for the West in general and for the EU in particular. Turkey occupied a strategic geographical position both before and after the end of the Cold War (Mango, 1994), and this is complemented by its pivotal role in cultural, religious, political and economic terms (Bazin, 1998). Relationships with Turkey's neighbours in the Middle East and with the central Asian republics of the former Soviet Union are important for the West, and Turkey has the potential to influence these (Bishku, 1992). The Gulf War and interventions against Iraq provide one example of this (Bali Aykan, 1996), the use of the Incirlik air base (Adana) having been especially useful to the western allies (Sayari, 1992).

Turkey is, of course, a member of the North Atlantic Treaty Organization (NATO), which it joined in 1952, an event that gave a significant impulse to the westernisation project. It provided Turkey with a voice in western military decision-making and the possibility of counterbalancing Greek influence in the international community (Krebe, 1999). Not least, it provided a significant bargaining card, given that NATO decision-making is based on consensus. However, there are limitations to this, as became clear at the time of the EU's negative response to Turkey's application. The Turkish authorities insinuated, if half-heartedly, that they would veto NATO's eastern enlargement if the country's EU membership application was unsuccessful. This provoked a sharp reaction in western Europe, which led Turkey to deny this possibility. After the eastern enlargement was agreed in 1997, Turkey lost its main bargaining ploy with the Union.

Despite minor frictions, Turkey remains an important strategic ally for the western powers. The USA has emphasised its interest in sustaining an alliance with Turkey even in difficult circumstances, such as those after the Luxembourg Summit (1997). The end of the Cold War has not diminished Turkey's weight as a strategic ally, but its European partners have been slower to understand this than the USA. A more flexible framework of relations has been created by the end of the Cold War and other related developments, and this has provided opportunities for Turkey to develop a higher degree of autonomy in its foreign policy. With hindsight, the Cold War framework constricted Ankara's goals in many respects (Calogeropoulos-Stratis, 1997). A number of examples illustrate the nature of the new environment for Turkish international relations:

- being able to exert more pressure on water resources which it shares with its neighbours, and an associated military build-up on the Syrian border;

- the arrest of the PKK leaders Öcalan and Soysal in circumstances that suggest the end of Turkey's relative timidity in world affairs;

- serious threats against (southern) Cyprus regarding the intention to deploy S–300 Russian missiles (see Chapter 10);

- increasing pressure on Greece, which has been facilitated by some of the confessions made by Öcalan during his trial;

- a more aggressive and negative attitude toward negotiations with the EU;

- the signing of a new Turkish military co-operation agreement with Israel, in the face of opposition from its Arab neighbours (Encel, 1998).

Bayart (1998: 16) has expressed concerns that if Turkey was to become a 'free rider' in international relations, this would be destabilising for the EU and for the West. An independent and aggressive foreign and security policy could put at risk both internal stability and the regional balance. The future of Cyprus provides evidence of this more autonomous role. It offers Turkey a strong bargaining ploy in the international arena, perhaps its last major card, and Ankara has considerably hardened its position on this issue, despite EU concerns and condemnations. American support has reinforced this new tendency, presenting Turkey, without qualification, as 'a good ally', and criticising the EU's decision to exclude it from the list of applicants. In the longer term, Turkey could also be seen as an alternative to Israel in the Middle East as a vehicle for American policy in the region.

The December 1999 EU Helsinki Summit redrafted the map of Turkish international relations, by virtue of its acceptance of Turkey as a candidate country. This does not put the country on an equal footing with the other 12 applicants, as membership application will not be opened until Turkey has fully met a number of political and human rights criteria. However, Turkey's chilly relations with the EU have been thawed, and there is now considerable optimism that this marks an historic watershed in relations. In practice, the negotiations are likely to be long and tortuous and may bring new tensions to the relationships between Turkey and the Union, especially if popular enthusiasm turns to disenchantment in the former.

The failure of the European option: the search for alternatives

In the 1990s growing uncertainty regarding the possibility of full integration into the EU contributed to the rise to power of Erbakan and the Islamist Welfare Party. As prime minister, he sought closer ties with Turkey's eastern neighbours, emphasising a shared Islamic identity.

Symbolically, his first official trips were to Islamic countries such as Libya, Iran and Indonesia. These moves were initially highly criticised by both the élites and the Turkish army, but they were soon cautiously but widely celebrated. Journalists, bureaucrats, military leaders and politicians admitted that Turkey's obsession with Europe had been less positive than expected, and that alternatives should be explored in order to unlock the eastern flank. This shift has also been boosted by the rise of nationalist parties, focusing on the central Asian Turkic republics and following pan-Turkic ideology (Landau, 1995; Balci, 1999).

Despite these initiatives, Europe remained the focus of Turkey's goals and activities (del Río Luelmo, 1998). The new options have opened up political and economic opportunities in relations with Turkey's neighbours, although these remain constrained. Turkey is not strong enough to provide regional leadership (Rubinstein and Smolansky, 1995), and historically poor relations form a difficult backcloth for relationships. Initiatives like the Black Sea Economic Co-operation Council (BSECC) have provided only limited results in the economic field and are more symbolic than operational. There may also be opportunities for new alliances in the Balkans in the aftermath of the Bosnian and the Kosovo crises. Perhaps the most important implication of these new initiatives is that – if successful – they will strengthen Turkey's relations with the West, especially as eastern enlargement approaches. Most commentators consider that, at best, they will be complementary, and never an alternative, to Turkey's European vocation.

Recent developments: growing pains in context of eastward expansion

Toward the end of the 1980s the dominant hypothesis in Turkish politics was that political and economic consolidation could be achieved through integration – in one way or another – into the EU. This extended to the progressive reconciliation of traditional opponents (Balkir and Williams, 1993): Kemalism and Islam, Kurds and the Turkish state. The construction of this reconciliatory programme had barely commenced during the Özal presidency, and it has collapsed in recent years. The reasons behind this failure are varied and include the realities of both domestic and international politics (Yesilada, 1999). The long-expected customs union with the European Union did not provide the expected benefits: the initial conditions were disappointing given Turkish expectations; and Brussels has not been able to fulfil its financial promises, mainy due to the Greek veto.

The conclusions of the Luxembourg Summit, which effectively sidestepped the Turkish application, inevitably made international relations with the EU more tense. Subsequently, a more aggressive approach to the EU by Turkish decision-makers has created additional friction. The rise of political Islamism, and its implications for domestic politics, has also increased the gap with Europe. The 'soft' *coup* by the army in 1998, concerned with the challenge to the secularist destiny of the country, had a similar distancing effect. This *coup* involved overt pressure and implicit threats rather than armed intervention. Economic reforms to liberalise and privatise the economy, reduce the public sector deficit and bring rampant inflation under control have also been laggardly. Nevertheless, the Helsinki Summit placed Turkey's eventual integration into the EU back on the agenda.

Meanwhile, a number of other issues have contributed to make Turkey's relationship with the EU more problematic:

- On 19 May 1998, the French National Assembly took the first steps toward recognising the Armenian genocide of 1915, creating tensions with France, which was traditionally viewed as being favourable to Turkey's approach to Europe.

- Increasing tension in Cyprus during the late 1990s intensified friction with a number of member states, particularly after the island's acceptance as a candidate for full integration in the EU.

- The signing of a military co-operation agreement with Israel has increased tension with the Arab world, particularly with Syria.

- The contested sovereignty of the Imia islands (Athanassoupoulou, 1997; Hickok, 1998) has posed a further obstacle to improved relationships with the EU: again rivalries with Greece have been under the spotlight (Angrand, 1997).

In 1999 the arrest of the Kurdish leader, Öcalan, made Turkey's international situation even more delicate. The use of (Turkish-controlled) water resources as a bargaining card, paired with a display of military force, brought about his expulsion from Syria. Following a long chase – via Italy, Greece and Russia – the PKK leader was arrested by Turkish secret services in the Greek embassy in Kenya, reputedly with the co-operation of the CIA. Öcalan's trial and death sentence were carefully monitored by the West. Although the trial was accepted to have been fair and according to Turkish law, after the removal of military judges, it raises important issues.

First, it attracted international attention to the Kurdish issue at the same time as the NATO intervention in Kosovo, thus invoking unwelcome comparisons. But the major issue was whether or not the death penalty would be commuted. The weight of nationalism, after the 1999 elections won by Ecevit, is under scrutiny: the government's weak electoral base does not allow it to take risky decisions, in the face of popular and military calls for the death penalty to be implemented. Moreover, parliament, which has to ratify the verdict, is unlikely to vote for clemency. For some political leaders this offers an opportunity for Turkey to reassert its independence, its position as a free rider, and to snub the EU, which had earlier snubbed its membership application. However, the Helsinki Agreement, has since made this more a potential barrier to further improvements to Turkey's international rather than a vehicle for a more independent foreign policy.

There are powerful reasons for Turkish decision-makers not to implement the death sentence. Turkish politics is dominated by the weight of its bureaucracy, and the bureaucrats – as followers of Kemalism – are likely to seek to avoid the further distancing of Turkey from Europe. The opportunities offered to Turkey by the trial and its aftermath are unique. Öcalan has already proved useful to the Turkish state. He has already accused Greece, the Greek Orthodox church, the Syrian government, Cyprus and some Armenian groups of supporting him, and this has considerably reinforced Turkey's regional position. Furthermore, he has made an official offer to the Turkish state to mediate with Kurdish activists in a search for peace. His death would deprive Turkey of this valuable asset, besides creating a hostile international atmosphere, particularly in Europe. Execution would make Öcalan a martyr and would weaken the Turkish position on the Kurdish issue, both in the domestic and international spheres. In short, it would deepen the gap between Turkey and the EU at the very time when relationships were again warming.

Conclusions: a future for Turkey in Europe?

Turkey, without doubt, has a future in Europe, although its future alignment to the EU remains problematic. Turkey's stormy relations with the EU have not fundamentally modified either the powerful Turkish bureaucrats' will to follow Atatürk's dictates or Europe's interest in close relations with its large and strategically important neighbour. The Helsinki Agreement, while putting these relations on a more stable and co-operative basis, has also opened a number of other potential conflicts. The pathway to opening negotiations, let alone the negotiations themselves, will test the strength of the relationship, and the skills of the politicians and bureaucrats, to the limit.

Close relations do not necessarily imply full membership; despite recent reverses and the Helsinki 'olive branch' offered to Turkey, the search continues for a new institutional relationship. The rebirth of the 'democratic European' scenario still enjoys very strong support among the country's élites, but both sides will be required to redefine their approach to the relationship (del Río Luelmo, 1997). Realistically, a new form of integration that falls short of full membership may be required in the short- to medium-term. Historically, Turkey–EU relations have been conditioned by the different approaches of the two parties (Elmas, 1998a). While Turkey has been – and remains – historically committed to full integration, the EU – notwithstanding Helsinki – has sought a balance between a closer alliance without full integration. This difference in goals and aspirations has obviously created tensions and distortions in what otherwise could be viewed as a model of EU relationships with a third country (Pesmazoglou, 1997).

Many western and Turkish commentators have argued that the time has arrived for Turkish decision-makers to realise that the obsession with full and relatively early integration is damaging the possibility of a more stable and fruitful relationship. The difficulty is that accepting anything less than full membership poses questions about Turkey's Kemalist principles and identity, so that there are strong pressures to reject any such compromise. The EU, in turn, has also reached an extremely delicate point (Wood, 1999). Avoidance of sensitive issues and lack of sincerity toward Turkey, paired with a critical lack of sensibility in some bilateral issues, led to damaging friction (Akagül, 1998). The risks were and are far from negligible. On the one hand, Turkey's survival as a powerful secular and pro-European state is in question; on the other hand, the security of the EU's eastern flank is at risk. Moreover, the stability of the surrounding regions – including the Balkans (Turan and Barlas, 1999), the Middle East (Aras, 1998) and central Asia – depends to a great extent on Turkey's pivotal role in relation to Europe. The proposed eastern enlargement enhances rather than diminishes the importance of this role, if only because of Turkey's geographical position in respect of the former communist bloc.

The eastern enlargement has posed Turkey a series of questions. Whilst it is true that it offers Turkey some opportunities in strategic terms, the 1997 EU move angered Ankara, which perceived this initiative to be a threat to its own membership bid. The possible creation of a stronger Greek front within the EU, in the form of a Greece–Greek Cyprus axis, is also unacceptable to Turkey. Confrontations with Greece over a series of issues, continuous Greek vetoes on EU aid to Turkey and the long-standing division about the future of Cyprus have been significant obstacles to 'normal' international relations between Turkey and the EU. The accession of Greek Cyprus is set to exacerbate these tensions, notwithstanding some easing of relations following the assistance provide by Greece after the 1999 earthquake in north-west Turkey.

The integration of the central and eastern European countries is also seen as an economic threat by the Turkish authorities. The CEE states have already started to attract foreign investment and financial aid, which arguably has been partially diverted from Turkey. The enlargement will also add to the potential migration into the existing members of the EU, thereby increasing west European concerns about Turkish migration. The second wave of CEE countries, including Bulgaria and Romania, is seen to be even more problematic for Turkey's membership bid and its attempt to reshape relations with the EU.

Acknowledgement

This chapter was prepared with the support of a research grant from the Nuffield Foundation.

References

Acar, F., 1993, Islam in Turkey. *In* Balkir, C., Williams, A. M., eds, *Turkey and Europe*. London: Frances Pinter, pp. 219–240.

Akagül, D., 1998, Le cinquième enlargissement de l'Union européenne et la question de la candidature turque: la fin d'un cycle, mais quelles perspectives? *Revue du Marché commun et de l'Union européenne*, 419, 359–369.

Angrand, J., 1997, Le conflit entre la Grèce et la Turquie au sujet du plateau continental de la mer Egée: problèmes politiques et juridiques. *Revue de droit international, de sciences diplomatiques et politiques*, 75 (20), 101–130.

Aras, B., 1998, *Palestinian Israeli peace process and Turkey*. Commack NY: Nova Science.

Athanassoupoulou, E., 1997, Blessing in disguise? The Imia crisis and Turkish–Greek relations. *Mediterranean Politics*, 2 (3): 76–101.

Balci, B., 1999, Turcs et Turkmènes: les retrouvailles: carnet d'une mission au Turkménistan. *Revue Française de Géoéconomie*, 10, 165–175.

Bali Aykan, M., 1996, Turkey's policy in Northern Iraq, 1991–95, *Middle Eastern Studies*, 32 (4), 343–366.

Balkir, C, Williams, A. M., 1993, Introduction: Turkey and Europe. *In* Balkir, C., Williams, A. M., eds, *Turkey and Europe*. London: Frances Pinter, pp. 2–22.

Bayart, J.-F. 1998, L'Europe et la laïcité contre la démocratie en Turquie. *Critique Internationale*, 1 (1), 15–22.

Bazin, M., ed., 1998, *La Turquie entre trois mondes: actes du colloque international de Montpellier, 5, 6 et 7 octobre 1995*. Paris: Harmattan.

Beriker-Atiyas, N., 1997, The Kurdish conflict in Turkey: issues, parties and prospects. *Security Dialogue*, 28 (4), 439–452.

Bishku, M. B., 1992, Turkey and its Middle Eastern neighbors since 1945. *Journal of South Asian and Middle Eastern Studies*, 25 (3), 51–71.

Buzan, B., Diez, T., 1999, The European Union and Turkey. *Survival*, 41 (1), 41–57.

Calabrese, J., 1998, Turkey and Iran: limits of a stable relationship. *British Journal of Middle Eastern Studies*, 25 (1), 75–94.

Calogeropoulos-Stratis, A., 1997, Les ambitiones géopolitiques de la Turquie: risques et réalités. *Etudes helléniques*, 5 (1), 97–106.

Carter, F. W., Hall, D. R., Turnock, D., Williams, A. M., 1995, *Interpreting the Balkans*. London: Royal Geographical Society, Geographical Intelligence Paper No. 2.

Cioclea, S., 1998, Turquie: à la recherche de la stabilité. *Conjoncture*, 28 (11), 8–14.

del Río Luelmo, J., 1997, Hacia nuevas formas de integración con los espacios periféricos del continente? Las relaciones de la UE con Turquía. *Revista de Estudios Europeos*, 17, 27–50.

del Río Luelmo, J., 1998, Turkey and the EU. *In* Unwin, T., ed., *A European geography*. London: Longman, pp.141–146.

Elmas, H. B., 1998a, *Turquie–Europe: une relation ambigué*. Paris: Syllepse.

Elmas, H. B., 1998b, L'intervention du facteur 'immigration' dans les relations turco-européennes. *Revue Européenne des Migrations Internationales*, 14 (3), 77–101 .

Encel, F., 1998, Israël–Turquie, un nouvel axe stratégique. *Hérodote*, 90, 148–162.

Eralp, A., 1993, Turkey and the EC in the changing post-war international system. *In* Balkir, C., Williams, A. M., eds, *Turkey and Europe*. London: Frances Pinter, pp. 23–44.

Heper, M., Öncü, A., Kramer, H., eds, 1993, *Turkey and the West: changing political and cultural identities*. London: I. B. Tauris.

Hickok, M. R., 1998, The Imia/Kardak affair, 1995/96: a case of inadvertent conflict. *European Security*, 7 (4), 118–136.

Kinross, P., 1964, *Atatürk: the rebirth of a nation*. London: Weidenfeld and Nicolson.

Krebe, R. R., 1999, Perverse institutionalism: NATO and the Greco–Turkish conflict. *International Organization*, 53 (2), 343–377.

Landau, J. M., 1995, *Pan-Turkism: from irredentism to cooperation*. London: Hurst.

Lapidot, A., 1996, Islamic activism in Turkey since the 1980 military take over. *Terrorism and Political Violence*, 8 (2), 62–74.

MacDowall, D., 1996, *A modern history of the Kurds*. London: I. B. Tauris.

Mango, A., 1994, *Turkey: the challenge of a new role*. Washington: Praeger/Center for Strategic and International Studies.

Müftüler-Bac, M., 1998, The never-ending story: Turkey and the European Union. *Middle Eastern Studies*, 34 (4), 240–258.

Öymen, O., 1997, Turkey's European foreign policy. *Perceptions*, 2 (1), 7–14.

Pesmazoglou, S., 1997, Turkey and Europe, reflections and refractions: towards a contrapuntal approach. *South European Society and Politics*, 2 (1), 138–159.

Rubinstein, A. Z., Smolansky, O. M., eds, 1995, *Regional power rivalries in the new Eurasia: Russia, Turkey and Iran*. Armonk NY: Sharpe.

Sayari, S., 1992, Turkey: the changing European security environment and the Gulf Crisis. *Middle East Journal*, 45 (1), 9–21.

SIS (Republic of Turkey, Prime Ministry State Institute of Statistics), 1999, *SIS world wide web service*. Ankara: SIS. http://www.die.gov.tr/.

Turan, I., Barlas, D., 1999, Turkish–Greek balance: a key to peace and cooperation in the Balkans. *East European Quarterly*, 32 (4), 469–488.

Vaner, S., 1998, La Turquie face à la Transcaucasie: retrouvailles, ouvertures et frictions. *Noveaux Mondes*, 8, 43–65.

Williams, A. M., 1993, Turkey: the Mediterranean context. *In* Balkir, C., Williams, A. M., eds, *Turkey and Europe*. London: Frances Pinter, pp. 45–67.

Wood, C., 1999, Europe and Turkey: a relationship under fire. *Mediterranean Quarterly*, 10 (1), 95–115.

Yesilada, B. A., 1999, The worsening of EU–Turkey relations. *SAIS Review*, 19 (1), 144–161.

Part III

The Balkans and the European Newly Independent States

INTRODUCTION

Derek Hall and Darrick Danta

This section of the book addresses those components of the former Yugoslavia, Albania and the European newly independent states (NIS) of the former Soviet Union, which are not current candidates for EU entry and for whom any such consideration is likely to be far distant. Although during 1999 a Stability Pact for South-eastern Europe was formulated, and a new EU attitude toward the former Yugoslavia and Albania was declared in the wake of the Kosovo conflict, these have only acted to confirm the vulnerability and inappropriateness of the candidature of the countries involved. The one possible exception is Croatia (Chapter 18): following President Tudjman's death toward the end of 1999, both parliamentary and presidential elections were held in the early months of 2000 and their outcome heralded a new political direction for the country and a government dedicated to internal reforms to set Croatia on a course for EU accession. This process is being strongly encouraged by western Europe.

The former Soviet republics of Moldova, Belarus and Ukraine each have their own mix of economic and political problems. Constituting the eastern borderlands for much of the currently projected enlarged EU, these countries represent an important east–central European 'buffer zone' with Russia. However, their potential instability and relationships with Moscow raise questions concerning the perception of and response to the needs of those eastern borderlands within future EU regional and trans-boundary policies.

After some debate, a decision was taken not to include a separate chapter on Russia in this volume. Russia's attitude to the EU is at best ambivalent, and while closer relations between the two are to be encouraged, realistically no discussion of the former being embraced by the latter is likely to take place within the next generation. Clearly what is of some importance is Russia's attitude toward former Soviet satellites and indeed toward members of the former Soviet Union seeking to join and gaining admittance to western multinational institutions such as the EU and the North Alantic Treaty Organization (NATO). Such an attitude is alluded to in some of the individual country chapters in this section. For Russia, however, such considerations are overlain by a continuing domestic economic and political instability which renders any evaluation of future trends in the Russia–EU relationship at best speculative (e.g. see Lane, 1995; Bradshaw *et al.*, 1998; EBRD, 1999: 261).

Further, the conflict that continues within Russia's borders and overspills beyond them, and the human rights issues which accompany it, would seem critical in the EU's attitude toward Russia. The December 1999 European Council meeting in Helsinki, for example, adopted an emergency statement on the situation in Chechnya. The Council condemned the bombardment of Chechen cities and the threat levelled at the residents of Grozny. As a sign of its disapproval of Russian policy, the implementation of the EU's Common Strategy on Russia would be reviewed and the TACIS budget for 2000 would be limited to priority areas such as human rights, the rule of law, support for civil society and nuclear safety.

References

Bradshaw, M., Stenning, A., Sutherland, D., 1998, Economic restructuring and regional change in Russia. *In* Pickles, J., Smith, A., eds, *Theorising transition*. London: Routledge, pp. 147–171.

EBRD, 1999, *Transition report 1999*. London: EBRD.

Lane, D., ed., 1995, *Russia in transition: politics, privatisation and inequality*. Harlow: Longman.

18

CROATIA

Derek Hall

Croatia is borderland: straddling or acting as an historical dividing line between central Europe and the Balkans, between the Mediterranean world and continental Europe and between eastern Byzantine Christendom and the Latin west (DGSP, 1993/94, Klemencić, 1996; Tanner, 1997). The very shape of the country reinforces a frontier impression: arcing round Bosnia like a horseshoe, squarely facing central and western Europe, yet with tails trailing back into the Balkans (Figure 18.1). In the far south, the country is only a few kilometres wide, hemmed in between the Adriatic Sea and the mountains of Bosnia. The people of this periphery tend not to be relaxed about their heritage or culture. They fear not only being forgotten by the rest of Europe, but, much worse, that they be confused with the peoples to the east and south, and be thought of as 'Balkan'.

A brief history

Croats came to south-eastern Europe in the 6th and 7th centuries, migrating south across the Carpathians and settling along the shores of the Adriatic. By the 10th century they had established a Croatian kingdom, uniting most of what is now Croatia and parts of present-day Bosnia and Hercegovina. In 1102 Croatia entered a dynastic union with Hungary, although this provided no defence against the Tatars who swept in from the east in the 13th century and razed Zagreb to the ground, nor against the Ottomans who reached Croatia in the 15th century and annihilated the country's nobility in 1493. In the 1520s, as the Ottoman armies overwhelmed more territory, the pope sent a message to the Croatian parliament, urging it to continue to resist the tide of Islam and referring to the Croats as the 'ramparts of Christendom'. The Turks swept on, almost to the gates of Zagreb, destroying most of the seven-century-old civilisation that they encountered (Tanner, 1997).

Following Hungary's defeat at Ottoman hands in 1562, the Hungarian crown, including Croatia, was claimed by the Habsburgs. In the 17th century the Habsburg emperor created a military frontier (*krajina*) along the border with the Ottoman Empire (which included Bosnia and Hercegovina until 1878), detaching it from Zagreb's rule. The population of this region

Figure 18.1: Croatia

received privileges in return for defending the frontier, and settlers from the Ottoman Empire were encouraged to live there, including large numbers of Serbs. The maritime regions of Dalmatia and Istria, which had been under Venetian control and exhibited strong Italianate influences going back to Roman times (Katušić, 1971; Beritić and Suljak, 1972; Letcher, 1989), passed to Austria after the Napoleonic wars. In 1867 the Habsburg empire was reorganised as the Austro–Hungarian empire, and Croatia was divided between the Hungarian and Austrian halves, the latter retaining Dalmatia and Istria (Gazi, 1973).

Nineteenth-century national movements included expressions of both Croatian nationalism and pan-'Yugoslavism', seeking collaboration and unification with other south Slav peoples. Following Austria–Hungary's collapse in the First World War, Croatia became part of the Kingdom of Serbs, Croats and Slovenes, under the Serbian Karadjordjević dynasty. This state was characterised by regional and ethnic tensions, particularly between dominant Serbs and dissatisfied Croats (Banac, 1984). The 1928 assassination of Croat political leader Stjepan Radić in Belgrade was followed by the imposition of a royal dictatorship as King Aleksandar sought to impose unity on his country, the name of which was changed to Yugoslavia. Aleksandar in turn was assassinated in 1934 by the Ustaša, extreme Croat nationalists. In an effort to unite the country prior to the Second World War, Croatia was granted autonomy within Yugoslavia in 1939 (Boban, 1993).

Germany invaded Yugoslavia in April 1941 and, with Italian support, established a puppet independent state of Croatia (NDH – Nezavisna Država Hrvatska), on territory comprising most of present-day Croatia, all of Bosnia-Hercegovina and part of present-day Serbia. Exiled Ustaša leader Ante Pavelić was installed as leader (*poglavnik*) and modelled himself closely on the Führer. The regime pursued the systematic genocide of Serbs, Jews and Roma, often with Muslim support (Jelavich, 1983: 264), and estimates suggest that 350,000 Serbs were killed (Tomasevich, 1969: 78). This galvanised resistance by Serbs and many Croats, in which the communist-led Partisan movement of Josip Broz Tito (who was half Croat, half Slovene) took the main initiative (Doder, 1979). From 1943 the Partisans consolidated power and established Yugoslavia as a communist federation of six republics, one of which was Croatia. None the less, inter-ethnic distrust, particularly between Serbs and Croats, had been heightened by wartime experiences, and often only the combination of Tito's charisma and the strong arm of the internal security machine was able to suppress internal conflict.

Following Yugoslavia's break with the Soviet bloc in 1948, centralised communist rule was gradually relaxed and Yugoslavia became more western-oriented. By the mid-1960s the country had been decentralised to a considerable degree, and Croatia's communist leadership was in the forefront of those seeking further liberalisation. Decentralisation also emphasised the considerable socio-economic inequalities between the country's developed north-west (Slovenia, Croatia) and the relatively poor and undeveloped south-east (Macedonia, Montenegro, Kosovo). By 1971 political and cultural liberalisation was such that, fearing Croatia's communists were losing control, Tito tried to impose tighter party discipline. None the less, high levels of labour migration to western Europe and especially to west Germany, the hosting of most tourists coming to Yugoslavia, and links to a widespread diaspora, saw Croatians maintaining a strong relationship with the outside world and feeling themselves firmly to be part of central and western Europe – their Catholicism reinforcing their cultural self-perceptions.

The 1974 Yugoslav constitution introduced further decentralisation, but after Tito's death in 1980, republican leaders found it difficult to take a united approach to the country's economic problems, each jealously guarding their autonomy and interests. Stoked up by an ascendant Slobodan Milošević, nationalist ferment in Serbia in the late 1980s (and notably on the 600th anniversary of the seminal defeat of the Serbs at the hands of the Ottomans at Kosovo Polje in 1389), provoked a strong counter-reaction in other parts of the federation.

Free parliamentary elections in the spring of 1990 allowed an outpouring of resentment and nationalism in Croatia, as the Croatian Democratic Union (UDZ) led by Franjo Tudjman, a former communist general turned nationalist dissident, won convincingly. Parliament elected him as Croatian president and approved amendments to the constitution downgrading the Serb minority from its status as a constituent nation of the republic. The new regime also restored Croat national symbols, including the Sahovnica. This chequerboard crest had been suppressed by the communists as it had been adopted previously by the Ustaša and was thus tainted with fascist associations. In response, Serbs in the Krajina proclaimed autonomy from Zagreb; after the Croatian declaration of independence in June 1991, this led to confrontation with the Croatian authorities and armed insurrection.

Serbia failed in its attempts to manipulate the collective federal Yugoslav presidency to bring about a state of emergency that, with the help of the Yugoslav National Army (JNA), could be used to thwart independence moves by Slovenia and Croatia. Following a brief war in Slovenia, which saw a JNA withdrawal in July 1991, Serb paramilitaries in Croatia began to expand the area of land under their control and, in support, the JNA became involved in the fighting. In October 1991 it laid siege to the town of Vukovar. By the end of the year a third of Croatian territory was beyond Zagreb's control. A ceasefire was negotiated at the beginning of 1992, and a UN force was deployed in the Serb-controlled areas, from which the JNA withdrew. The EU recognised Croatia's independence in January 1992; the conflict became frozen, and the war moved on to Bosnia.

The loss of so much territory, the disruption it caused and the large number of refugees from Serb-controlled regions dominated the Croatian political agenda. Frustration deepened at the UN's failure to make progress toward a settlement that would return these areas to Zagreb's control. Although Croatia reluctantly agreed in March 1995 to a renewal of the UN mandate, two months later Tudjman seized control of western Slavonia by force (Anon, 1995) and in August launched an assault on the Krajina. This prompted the flight of an estimated 180,000 Serbs living there (UNHCR, 1998). Previously Croats had been expelled *en masse* by Serbs controlling the Krajina.

Under the Erdut Agreement of November 1995, which complemented the Dayton Peace Agreement for Bosnia–Hercegovina, a transitional UN administration was established in the last Serb-controlled region of eastern Slavonia. The region was gradually reintegrated into Croatia in 1997 and reverted to Zagreb's full control the following year. Despite international insistence that Croatia provide assurances to the local Serb population and guarantee their rights, the number of Serbs in eastern Slavonia dwindled. Likewise, international pressure for the return of Serb refugees, culminating in the adoption of a return programme in June 1998, resulted in a mere trickle. This confirmed to the international community that the Croatian authorities had no desire to protect the rights of Serbs in Croatia. Croatia itself was host to 160,000 displaced persons, including 77,000 Croatians expelled during fighting in eastern Slavonia and 45,000 Muslim and Croat refugees from Bosnia's Serbian enclave (UNHCR, 1998).

From 1996 Croatia's relations with the USA and the EU soured, largely as a result of Croatian policy in Bosnia–Hercegovina, whereby Bosnian Croats blocked measures to strengthen the federation. Croatia's treatment of Serb refugees and of minorities, and its stance on media and other domestic freedoms, also constrained western support.

As a result Croatia was denied access to many assistance programmes that became available to other CEECs, such as the EU PHARE programme. The preclusion of an EU Association Agreement placed Croatian companies at a relative disadvantage in exporting to the EU. In April 1999, however, the US softened its position in response to Croatia's co-operation with NATO in its air strikes in Yugoslavia, and membership of NATO's Partnership for Peace appeared possible for the first time. However, Croatia's apparent lack of enthusiasm for attempts to foster regional co-operation, such as the EU's regional approach and the USA's South-east European Co-operation Initiative (SECI), did not endear the country's UDZ leadership, as reflected later in the poor international representation at Tudjman's funeral.

Although formally a parliamentary democracy, from independence in 1991/92 until the death of Franjo Tudjman in December 1999 and the elections of January and February 2000, Croatia functioned as a presidential-style republic, dominated by Tudjman and his ruling Croatian Democratic Union party (HDZ). Nowhere else in the region, apart from Serbia, had the ruling party fused together the interests of state, party and president so comprehensively. With Tudjman gone, such a fusion made the HDZ's collapse more comprehensive (LeBor, 2000).

A centre-left coalition won Croatia's January 2000 parliamentary elections, promising democratic change. The leading coalition partner, the Social Democrats (formerly communists) were viewed as the inheritors of the old Yugoslav tradition of ethnic tolerance. The new government was eager to establish good relations with the European Union (Anon, 2000; Poolos, 2000) and soon declared three aims: (a) to end Croatia's international isolation; (b) to initiate concern for human rights and freedom of the press; and (c) to increase Croatian co-operation with the UN war crimes tribunal at The Hague.

Human and natural resources

Croatia's population was 4.78 million in the 1991 census, of whom 3.74 million (78 per cent) were Croats. Although only Slovenia had a more homogenous population within the Yugoslavia of that time, over 12 per cent of Croatia's population – almost 582,000 people – were Serbs (Klemencić, 1996). By 1997 the official estimate saw the total population of Croatia reduced to 4.57 million. The country has a land area of 56,500 sq km, of which 26.2 per cent is arable, 20.4 per cent pasture and 36.7 per cent forest. The country has 1,777 km of continental coastline and some 1,185 islands – 66 inhabited – adding a further 4,000 km of coast. Croatia's main urban centres are the capital Zagreb (population 868,000 in 1991), Split (200,000), Rijeka (168,000), Osijek (130,000) and Zadar (80,000). Although migration has been a major factor in demographic change, the birth-rate fell below 11 per 1,000 inhabitants during the first half of the 1990s. Because of an ageing population, the death-rate rose slightly, and remained above 11 per 1,000. Although the birth-rate picked up after the end of the war with Yugoslavia, there is estimated to have been a natural decline of 8,400 during 1996–98 (EIU, 1999).

Although relatively small, Croatia is diverse and can be divided into three major geographical regions: the coast, with a Mediterranean climate; inland mountains; and the lowlands of Slavonia, with a continental climate. Landscapes vary between the flat, agriculturally rich plains in Slavonia, gently rolling hills in the Zagorje region around Zagreb and the bare mountains of the Dinaric Alps, inland from the coast. Widely different regional patterns of livelihood and culture reflect these environmental variations, particularly between the largely pastoral economy of the Dinaric and the Slavonian plains, where cultivation predominates.

Transport and communications

Some of the main trunk-routes linking central and western Europe with south-eastern Europe pass through Croatia. The war disrupted the main rail-lines east and south from Zagreb, and also the *autoput* (motorway) of 'brotherhood and unity', which runs across the flat plains of Slavonia from Zagreb to Belgrade. The road and rail networks are particularly in need of substantial upgrading. The 1997 Pan-European Transport Conference proposed that two out of ten east–west European road and rail corridors should pass through Croatia and that a third route should link Slavonia with the port of Ploče via Bosnia–Hercegovina.

Rail traffic declined with the break up of Yugoslavia and the 1991–95 war. The network carried 17 million passengers in 1997, compared with 40 million in 1990. Yet the country's 2,726 km of track (36 per cent electrified) is insufficient in both extent and quality. Of the 27,800 km road system, only 330 km is motorway – the Croatian section of the Zagreb–Belgrade *autoput* and a short link between Zagreb and Karlovac. Extending the network has been a priority for some time. In 1995 contracts were awarded for the construction of a new road in Istria to cater for tourism traffic. There are plans for a motorway from Zagreb to the Hungarian border and for extending the Zagreb–Karlovac highway to the major port of Rijeka. In April 1998 a $600 million contract was signed with the US Bechtel Corporation to build a motorway linking the Slovene border with Zagreb, which will be extended to southern Dalmatia.

Maritime communications are important for Croatia, with its long coastline and large shipping fleet (Potter, 1999). Goods carried rose to 36 million tonnes in 1997, compared with 23 million in 1986. Although passenger numbers fell from over 8 million before 1991 to 5.4 million in 1994, post-war figures recovered to almost 7 million by 1997.

Telecommunications have developed steadily in recent years. The number of fixed telephone lines rose from 20.9 per 100 people in 1993 to 35 per 100 in 1998, a level similar to Hungary. The proportion of digitalised local exchanges more than doubled to 81 per cent, and a mobile-telecoms systems was established. This expansion was undertaken largely by the state, partly with loans from multilateral financial institutions, whereas in Hungary and the Czech Republic the private sector led such developments.

Economic structure

In 1997 industry and mining represented around 27 per cent of GDP, while agriculture accounted for 10 per cent and services for more than 56 per cent. Important export industries include chemical products, textiles, shipbuilding, food processing and pharmaceuticals. Disruption caused by the Yugoslav wars and by the loss of much of the former Yugoslav market has exacerbated restructuring problems. Manufacturing sectors, such as shipbuilding, furniture, machinery and equipment, have strengthened, whilst textiles, food products, beverages and tobacco, have declined in importance.

The gradual recovery of tourism in Dalmatia and Istria – initially given impetus from such central European markets as the Czech Republic – has been an important factor in economic growth and the recovery of export earnings (Table 18.1), but the Kosovo conflict acted to depress growth in 1999. Although direct damage to Croatia's tourism infrastructure was limited during the 1992–95 conflict with Serbia and Montenegro, images of the shelling of Dubrovnik (e.g. see Oberreit, 1996; Vierda, 1998) and continuing Balkan instability acted as a lingering deterrent to the return of high-spending international tourists and investors. Further, the use of hotels to house refugees left many facilities in urgent need of refurbishment. Between 1985 and 1990 tourism accounted for 6 per cent of Croatia's GNP and provided employment for up to 200,000. Since 1996, when a DM 50 mn credit line was extended, the European Bank for

Table 18.1 Croatia: economic structure, 1994–1998

Economic indicators	1994	1995	1996	1997	1998
GDP at current prices ($ bn)	14.6	18.8	19.9	20.3	21.8
GDP per capita ($)	3 139.0	4 029.0	4 422.0	4 362.0	4 663.0
% retail GDP growth	5.9	6.8	6.0	6.5	2.3
% share of industry in GDP	27.9	28.4	26.5	26.9	25.4
% share of agriculture in GDP	11.5	10.7	10.3	9.6	8.9
Registered unemployment (%)	14.5	14.5	16.4	17.5	17.6
Retail price inflation (av. %)	98.0	2.0	3.5	3.6	5.7
Population (mn; mid-year)	4.65	4.67	4.49	4.57	4.57
Exports ($ mn)	4 260.0	4 633.0	4 546.0	4 210.0	4 613.0
Imports ($ mn)	5 229.0	7 510.0	7 788.0	9 104.0	8 383.0
Current-account balance ($ mn)	826.0	−1 452.0	−1 148.0	−2 343.0	−1 543.0
Total external debt ($ mn; December)	2 054.0[a]	3 729.0[a]	4 933.0	6 842.0	7 998.0[b]
Nights spent in tourist facilities ('000)	19 977.0	12 885.0	21 456.0	30 314.0	31 287.0
Of which, foreigners	15 556.0	8 515.0	16 546.0	24 697.0	26 002.0
Earnings from foreign tourists ($ mn)	1 801.0	1 351.0	2 014.0	2 259.0	2 276.0

[a] These figures do not include the $1.45 bn Croatian share of unallocated debt inherited from the former Yugoslavia.
[b] EIU estimate.

Sources: *EBRD, 1999b: 209; EIU, 1999: 5, 38, 40*

Reconstruction and Development (EBRD) has taken a close interest in assisting the recovery of Croatia's tourism industry (EBRD, 1996, 1999a).

Post-war reconstruction, including housing and infrastructure, has had an important role in reinvigorating the economy. Economic restructuring picked up after 1995, and most manufacturing industry was at least partly privatised by 1996, although often based on the hybrid Yugoslav model of enterprise management. This brought virtually no new capital for industry as existing management largely remained in control. However, FDI (foreign direct investment) inflows more than doubled between 1997 and 1998, reaching a level of 4 per cent of GDP. Yet, over half of all FDI has gone into the banking sector and to the internationally expanding pharmaceutical company *Pliva*. FDI has been minimal in other sectors (EBRD, 1999b): investors have been deterred by complicated capital structures and entrenched vested interests.

Two tranches of an IMF three-year $486 mn extended fund facility (EFF) were delayed in 1997, as a result of Croatia's undermining the Dayton Peace Agreement. When they were later released, the government argued that the strength of foreign currency inflows was now such that the EFF was not needed. However, in April 1999 negotiations with the International Monetary Fund were pursued for a $200 mn standby agreement to cover a financing gap for the year, following recession during 1998 (Kapoor, 1999). A depreciated currency and weak domestic demand helped to reduce a large trade deficit in 1999, offsetting the loss of tourism receipts resulting from the Kosovo conflict (Bucan, 1999; EBRD, 1999b).

Regional trends

Croatia is divided administratively into counties (*zupanije*), but their areas of authority are limited and the country is relatively centralised. The geographical diversity of the country was compounded by the varying experience of the war in different parts of the country, as a result of which very different patterns of economic development have emerged in recent years. The tourism sector is still far from regaining its pre-war high level of activity. Dalmatia, for example, was badly affected by the war, as the tourism industry came to a standstill – and has also been adversely affected by close proximity to the Croat-controlled areas of western Hercegovina, where widespread avoidance of taxes and customs duties is evident.

In the northern peninsula of Istria, away from the wars, tourism suffered much less, and Istria has remained relatively prosperous, although resentment at the high taxes needed to prosecute the war fuelled ill-feeling toward the central authority in Zagreb. Istria was incorporated into Croatia and Yugoslavia only in 1945 (previously being part of Italy) and has an Italian-speaking minority. Unique in Croatia, regional expression is articulated by a political party, the Istrian Democratic Assembly.

The regions of Slavonia and Krajina, which were under Serb control during the war, are particularly depressed and depopulated; most Serbs have left, and many Croats are reluctant to move to areas where economic prospects appear bleak.

Trade in goods

Foreign trade fell sharply when war broke out at the beginning of the 1990s; a statistical upturn in 1992 mainly reflected a redefinition of transactions with other former Yugoslav republics that had previously been classified as domestic trade. The level of export receipts peaked in 1995 at just over $4.6 bn. Although Croatia's military campaigns in 1995 and the subsequent peace agreements allowed the country to restore trade routes, exports of goods had fallen to around $4.2 bn by 1997. The strength of the dollar was one reason for the decline in 1997; in *kuna* terms, by contrast, receipts rose by 4.1 per cent. In 1998 exports recovered to 1992 levels at around $4.6

bn. By contrast, Hungary's export receipts more than doubled in dollar terms between 1992 and 1998, and Slovenia's exports rose by around 40 per cent during that period (EIU, 1999). Croatia's higher level of wages and taxes, combined with the EU's refusal to sign an Association Agreement, has placed exporters at a regional disadvantage.

The declining competitiveness of Croatian exports is reflected in a fall in the proportion of exports going to the EU, although it remains the country's most important market. In 1998 the EU took 47.6 per cent of exports (Table 18.2) compared to 59.4 per cent in 1994. Italy (17.7 per cent) and Germany (16.9 per cent) were the largest single markets in 1998. The proportion of exports to former Yugoslav states was up just a little at 25.6 per cent in 1998, compared to 24.7 per cent in 1993. There has been a steady decline in exports to neighbouring Slovenia, and Bosnia–Hercegovina has become the third largest market for Croatian goods, exports there totalling $653 mn in 1998.

Just under 60 per cent of imports come from the EU (Table 18.2). Germany (19.3 per cent) and Italy (17.9 per cent) were the most important sources of imports in 1998. Other former Yugoslav republics have declined in significance, accounting for 10.4 per cent of imports in 1998 compared to 16.6 per cent in 1993. However, imports from Slovenia, which declined to $772 mn in 1998, fell considerably less than Croatian exports to Slovenia, which dropped from $712 mn in 1993 (18.2 per cent of the total) to $432 mn (9.5 per cent) in 1998. The most striking change has been the increase in imports from other CEECs, such as the Czech Republic (up 332 per cent between 1993 and 1998 to $181 mn) and Hungary (up 171 per cent to $212 mn).

In June 1999 a number of laws were passed covering customs and barriers to trade, intellectual property rights and differential excise tax – all aimed at improving the country's position for accession to the World Trade Organization (EBRD, 1999b).

Croatian–EU relations

At an extraordinary ministerial meeting in December 1991, the EC declared that it intended to recognise the independence of all the Yugoslav republics, and that the implementation of this decision would take place on 15 January 1992. It invited all the Yugoslav republics to state by 23 December 1991 whether they wished to be recognised (Trifunovska, 1994: 431). However, on that date the Bonn government announced its intention to recognise Croatia and Slovenia, although the decision would not take effect until the 15 January EC foreign ministers' meeting.

This 'Christmas recognition', as it was called in Croatia, pre-empted EC discussion (Anon, 1999). The European Community went through the motion of passing requests for recognition from Croatia, Slovenia, Macedonia and Bosnia (Serbia and Montenegro insisted that the rump Yugoslavia did not need recognition) to a commission of arbitration under Robert Badinter of

Table 18.2 Croatia: main trading partners, 1994–1998

| | *Percentage of total value* | | | | |
	1994	*1995*	*1996*	*1997*	*1998*
Exports to					
Italy	21.3	23.7	21.0	20.8	17.7
Germany	22.1	21.5	18.6	17.8	16.9
Bosnia and Hercegovina	7.9	8.3	12.2	14.9	14.4
Slovenia	13.1	13.1	13.5	12.2	9.5
Austria	3.5	4.3	4.4	5.1	5.4
EU total	59.4	57.7	51.0	51.2	47.6
Imports from					
Germany	21.2	20.1	20.6	20.2	19.3
Italy	19.0	18.2	18.2	18.9	17.9
Slovenia	10.3	10.7	9.9	8.3	8.6
Austria	6.8	7.7	7.7	7.8	7.3
Russia	3.4	6.1	2.9	5.0	4.3
EU total	59.2	62.1	59.7	59.5	59.4

Source: *EIU, 1999: 41*

France. On 11 January the Badinter commission turned down Bosnia's request; Macedonia and Slovenia were approved unconditionally. It ruled that the Republic of Croatia met the conditions for recognition, subject to constitutional changes on minority rights. Only Germany opened an embassy in Zagreb immediately. The pretence of European unity had been maintained, but Croats knew that they owed recognition of their independence almost exclusively to German efforts (Tanner, 1997).

Following recognition of Croatia's independence, the establishment of contractual relations with the EU was made conditional on Zagreb's observance of a 'code of good democratic conduct' (European Commission, 1996). In March 1995 it was agreed to extend PHARE assistance and to open negotiations on a trade and co-operation agreement, but following Croatia's military offensives in August 1995 both developments were suspended. None the less, trade preferences have been granted, and from 1996 the EU has contributed to the rehabilitation and reconstruction of eastern Slavonia.

In March 1998 the EU released a statement on Croatia's international commitments and called for improvements in four areas: (a) compliance with the Dayton and Erdut peace agreements for the former Yugoslavia; (b) the safe return of refugees to Croatia; (c) internal democracy; and (d) measures to prevent the exodus of Serbs from eastern Slavonia, which had been returned to Croatian control by the UN just two months previously (Clarke, 1998).

In 1999, prompted by the Kosovo conflict, the European Commission (1999) recommended a strategy for neighbouring countries for adoption by the Helsinki European Council (summit meeting) of December 1999. Notably, it proposed 'to confirm the vocation for membership' of countries of former Yugoslavia and Albania but under strict conditions. In addition to the Copenhagen criteria, these countries would be required to recognise each other's borders, settle all issues relating to the treatment of national minorities and pursue economic integration in a regional framework as a precondition for their integration in the EU.

After the elections of January/February 2000 – which brought declarations from the new government and new president of an eagerness to 'rejoin' Europe and aspirations for EU membership – the European Council decided to set up a Joint EU–Croatia consultative task force, in order to start preparing the ground for future contractual relations, within the framework of the stabilisation and association process. The European Commission would send a fact-finding mission to Croatia, mandated to assess the needs and establish the priorities with a view to enhancing Community assistance. As soon as conditions allowed, a feasibility study on the Stabilisation and Association Agreement would be envisaged.

With a view to future Croatian integration in European structures, the EU declared an 'expectation' for the new government to meet the conditions necessary for a closer relationship between Croatia and the EU. This would entail progress on constitutional, electoral, media and judicial reform, full respect of human rights and fundamental freedoms, economic reform, active progress on Croatia's obligations under the Dayton Agreement (including refugee return) and a full commitment to regional co-operation.

Conclusions

With the first post-Tudjman government's declaration of wanting to reintegrate Croatia into Europe, to address human rights and media freedoms and to co-operate with international organisations in addressing the mass abuses of the Yugoslav wars, both an important platform was laid out and a significant message sent to the international community that Croatia wished to put the first decade of compromised and bloodstained independence behind it and seek its rightful place in Europe. The ability to pursue this aspiration rests in no little way on the ability of the Croatian political system to mature into a democratically functioning system based neither on cronyism nor on the suppression of opposition voices. The territorial dimensions of Croatian democracy are of particular importance in this spatially irregular and ethnically sensitive country (Pusich, 1996).

The absence of an Association Agreement with the EU has suggested to commentators that any realistic date for Croatia's EU entry will not be before 2010. Certainly, the EU will not commit itself to Croatian membership until there is strong evidence over a significant period that the country has abandoned nationalism and has a stable government. Economic reform, ability to attract significant FDI and a reduction in the defence budget (currently 7 per cent of GDP – double central European levels) are part of that process (Kapoor, 2000).

Croatia is a significant country with notable natural resources and occupying – geographically, culturally and historically – an important position in Europe. That position should be secured by a combination of domestic maturity and international support and encouragement. That the EU, driven by Bonn, so quickly recognised the independence of Croatia and Slovenia in January 1992 – in stark contrast to its lack of urgency in subsequent actions in the former Yugoslavia – continues to place a moral responsibility on that international body for the reintegration of Croatia at the appropriate moment. That moment should be sooner rather than later.

References

Anon, 1995, Croatia takes on the Serbs. *The Economist*, 6 May, pp. 43–44.

Anon, 1999, German politicians in doubt: was Croatia recognised too soon or not soon enough? *Vjesnik*, 15 January, p. 3. http://www.dalmatia.net/croatia/politics/croatia_recognised_too_soon. htm.

Anon, 2000, Thankfully, the Communists have won this election. *The Independent*, 5 January, p. 3.

Banac, I., 1984, *The national question in Yugoslavia*. Ithaca NY: Cornell University Press.

Beritić, D., Suljak, T., 1972, *Dubrovnik and its surroundings*. Zagreb: Turistcomerc.

Boban, L. J., 1993, Croatian borders 1918–1993. Zagreb: Skolska knjiga.

Bucan, C., 1999, Room vacant: is Croatia ready to sell its coast? *Business Central Europe*, 6 (65), 31.

Clarke, J., 1998, *Persecution of Serbs in Croatia*. New York: The Serbian Unity Congress. http://suc.suc.org/news/who_articles/suc49.html.

DGSP (Department for Geography and Spatial Planning, University of Zagreb), 1993/94, *Croatia – a new European state*. Zagreb: DGSP.

Doder, D., 1979, *The Yugoslavs*. London: George Allen and Unwin.

EBRD, 1996, *Croatia's tourism sector gets DM 50 million from EBRD*. London: EBRD. http://www.ebrd.com/english/opera/PRESSREL/PR1996/39JUNE27.HTM.

EBRD, 1999a, *EBRD activities in Croatia*. London: EBRD. http://www.ebrd.com/english/opera/COUNTRY/CROAFACT.HTM.

EBRD, 1999b, *Transition report 1999*. London: EBRD.

EIU, 1999, *Croatia: country profile 1999–2000*. London: EIU.

European Commission,1996, *EU–Croatia relations*. Washington DC: European Commission. http://eurunion.org/legislat/extrel/formyugo/croatia.htm.

European Commission, 1999, *Commission sets out an ambitious accession strategy and proposes to open accession negotiations with six more candidate countries.* Brussels: European Commission. http://www.europa.eu.int/comm/enlargement/report_10-99/intro/index.htm.

Gazi, S., 1973, *A history of Croatia.* New York: Philosophical Library.

Jelavich, B., 1983, *History of the Balkans: twentieth century.* Cambridge: Cambridge University Press.

Kapoor, M., 1999, The price of exile. *Business Central Europe*, 6 (64), 16–21.

Kapoor, M., 2000, Out of the cold? *Business Central Europe*, 7 (68), 14–17.

Katušić, I., 1971, *The Croatian littoral.* Zagreb: Naprijed.

Klemencić, M., 1996, Croatia *rediviva. In* Carter, F. W., Norris, H. T., eds, *The changing shape of the Balkans.* London: UCL Press, pp. 97–117.

LeBor, A., 2000, Leftist allies take power as Croatia rejects nationalism. *The Independent*, 5 January, p. 11.

Letcher, P., 1989, *Yugoslavia: mountain walks and historic sites.* Chalfont St Peter, Buckinghamshire: Bradt Publications.

Oberreit, J., 1996, Destruction and reconstruction: the case of Dubrovnik. *In* Hall, D., Danta, D., eds, *Reconstructing the Balkans: a geography of the new southeast Europe.* Chichester/New York: John Wiley and Sons, pp. 67–77.

Poolos, A., 2000, Croatia: elections signal democratic change. *RFE/RL*, 5 January. http://www.rferl.org/nca/features/2000/01/F.RU000105130024.html.

Potter, B., 1999, Rijeka. *Business Central Europe*, 6 (65), 62.

Pusich, S. M., 1996, The case for regionalism in Croatia. *In* Hall, D., Danta, D., eds, *Reconstructing the Balkans: a geography of the new southeast Europe.* Chichester/New York: John Wiley and Sons, pp. 53–65.

Tanner, M., 1997, *Croatia: a nation forged in war.* New Haven/London: Yale University Press.

Tomasevich, J., 1969, Yugoslavia during the Second World War. *In* Vucinich, W. S., ed., *Contemporary Yugoslavia: twenty years of socialist experiment.* Berkeley: University of California Press.

Trifunovska, S., ed., 1994, *Yugoslavia through documents from its creation to its dissolution.* Dordrecht: Kluwer.

UNHCR, 1998, *Country profiles: Croatia.* Geneva: UNHCR. http://www.unhcr.ch/world/euro/croatia.htm.

Vierda, V., 1998, Dubrovnik – five years without tourism: the new meaning of leisure, culture and tourism for reconstruction (case study). *In* Nahrstedt, W., Pancic Kombol, T., eds, *Leisure, culture and tourism in Europe.* Bielefeld: Institut für Freizeitwissenschaft und Kulturarbeit e.V., pp. 35–52.

19

BOSNIA AND HERCEGOVINA

Darrick Danta

From the outset Bosnia and Hercegovina (B–H) has not had an easy time. A rugged territory largely bereft of natural resources and located along religious, linguistic and cultural fault lines, Bosnia and Hercegovina today is a country struggling to rise from the ashes of recent wars to find its place in a very uncertain world (Figure 19.1). Indeed, while other chapters in this volume can point to multiple successes within the countries of central and eastern Europe, the same cannot be said for B–H, whose war-ravaged, partitioned status and almost non-existent industrial capacity hold little prospect for rapid recovery.

This chapter evaluates the country's resources and offers a brief history before turning to a discussion of its recent experiences and potential for EU entry. Given its current disjointed political structure, wrecked economy and lack of infrastructure and industrial capacity, decades will be needed before B–H will be in a position to rejoin the European community in a mutually beneficial manner.

Before proceeding, though, a point concerning the country's name is in order. For much of its history, the region known as 'Bosnia–Hercegovina' has existed more or less as a single unit and was recognised as such, even though it is technically composed of two parts: Bosnia, constituting roughly the northern two-thirds of the territory; Hercegovina, the southern third. Today, former distinctions between the two entities have faded to obscurity, and have been replaced by more important internal divisions.

Resources

Although larger than other former Yugoslav Republics, B–H, which covers 51,233 sq km, is only one-third of the European average. The triangular-shaped country is located in the centre of what was Yugoslavia, surrounded by Croatia (932 km of border) to the north, west and south, Serbia (312 km of border) to the east and Montenegro (215 km of border) to the south-east (Hoffman, 1963; Danta and Hall, 1996; Berentsen, *et al.*, 1997; CIA, 1999; Department of State, 1999; Shoemaker, 1999: 384). Apart from a sliver of land that crosses Dalmatia (Croatia) to the

Figure 19.1: Bosnia and Hercegovina

Adriatic coast at Neum just north-west of Dubrovnik, B–H is landlocked and generally consists of mountainous topography. The predominantly limestone lithology of the Dinaric Alps has undergone solution weathering, which has produced the underground drainage, caverns and sinks or *poljes* characteristic of karst topography. The climate is largely determined by elevation and distance from the sea, the norm being hot summers and mild, rainy winters in the lowlands and cool summers and severe winters in the highlands. B–H has no significant lakes and, apart from the Sava, which flows along the northern border with Croatia, very few rivers. The Bosna and Drina, although unnavigable, are important in the region's history.

Approximately 39 per cent of B–H is forest (mainly pine, beech and oak) and woodland, 20 per cent pasture, 14 per cent arable land and 5 per cent in permanent crops; the remaining 22 per cent is unclassified (CIA, 1999). Natural resources include timber, coal, iron ore and bauxite, along with some manganese, copper, chromium, lead and zinc. Agriculture consists of animal grazing on pasturelands and mixed farming mainly along the Sava valley in the north of the country, with some cultivation of citrus, olives, grapes and tobacco in the warmer lowlands of the south. The environment of B–H prior to the civil strife of 1992–95 was fairly good, with air pollution being limited to the area surrounding metallurgical plants. However, the loss of sewerage and water treatment facilities, disruption of rubbish collection and the introduction of so much lead and other harmful products from ordinance discharged during three years of locally intense fighting have contributed significantly to a severe reduction in environmental quality in the country.

The population of Bosnia–Hercegovina stands at 3.48 million, although this figure is debatable due to the problems of accurate counting in the face of the recent conflicts. B–H has long been an ethnically diverse region, with no clear majority. Table 19.1 lists the population breakdown by ethnicity for the years 1981, 1991 and 1999 according to the most recent estimates. During the 1980s the most numerous group, although not an absolute majority, was Bosnian Muslim, followed by the Serbs and the Croats; percentages remained about the same for each group. However, the group who considered themselves to be 'Yugoslav' declined from nearly 8 per cent in 1981, to 5.5 in 1991 and to nil by the end of the 1990s. Over the period 1991–99 the proportion of Muslims declined due to migration and ethnic cleansing. In terms of religion, 40 per cent are (Sunni) Muslim (sometimes also called Bosniacs), 31 per cent Orthodox, 15 per cent Catholic, 4 per cent Protestant and 10 per cent other (Poulton, 1991: 39–46; CIA, 1999). Languages spoken are Serbian, written in the Cyrillic alphabet; Croatian, which is virtually identical to Serbian, though written using the Latin alphabet; and Bosnian, which is merely a dialect of Serbo-Croatian, although some claim it to be the purest form of the south Slavic tongue (Malcolm, 1994: 102). Currently, the crude birth-rate in B–H is estimated to be 9 per 1,000, the death-rate 11 per 1,000 and the net migration rate 33 per 1,000, yielding an overall population growth rate of 3.2 per cent (CIA, 1999). However, due to the fluid situation in the region, these rates are subject to considerable variation. Health conditions are currently well below European standards, as indicated by B–H's relatively high infant mortality rate of 25 deaths per 1,000 live births (CIA, 1999).

The population of Bosnia and Hercegovina is approximately 42 per cent urban. The main cities are the capital Sarajevo (390,000), Banja Luka, Mostar (the 'capital' of Hercegovina), Tuzla and Bihać. The government is technically classified as an 'emerging democracy' (Department of State, 1999), though in practice the country operates under two systems. According to the terms of the 1995 Dayton Peace Agreement, Bosnia–Hercegovina was partitioned into two areas of roughly equal size: the Muslim/Croat Federation and the Republika Srpska (RS). The agreement established a two-tiered executive branch: the office of president for the whole country rotates every eight months between the three groups (Muslim, Croat and Serb; the two non-presidents act as co-prime ministers), while the Federation and RS is each represented by a president. The legislative branch is comprised of the parliamentary assembly, which in turn is made up of the House of Peoples (15 members total: 5 Croat, 5 Muslim and 5 Serb) and a 42-member House of Representatives. The constitutional court heads the judiciary.

The economic situation in B–H at present is bleak (Table 19.2). The infrastructure and industrial capacity were all but destroyed by three years of intense fighting, so that now the country must survive on international aid. Due to the nature of the economy, based as it is on official and unofficial transfer payments, small-scale informal retailing operations and a large black market, reliable economic data are impossible to obtain. The latest CIA estimates, however, place B–H's economic production at $5.8 bn, which yields $1,720 per capita purchasing power parity, with a real growth rate of GDP placed at 30 per cent (CIA, 1999).

Table 19.1 Bosnia and Hercegovina: ethnic structure, 1981–1999

Ethnic group	1981		1991		1999	
	No.	%	No.	%	No.	%
Muslims	1 629 375	39.5	1 902 954	43.6	1 323 348	38.0
Serbs	1 320 000	32.0	1 370 476	31.4	1 392 998	40.0
Croats	759 000	18.4	755 071	17.3	766 149	22.0
Yugoslav	325 875	7.9	240 052	5.5	–	–
Others	90 750	2.2	96 021	2.2	–	–
Total	4 125 000	100.0	4 364 574	100.0	3 482 495	100.0

Sources: *Bugajski, 1994: 3–4; CIA, 1999; author's additional calculations*

Table 19.2 Bosnia and Hercegovina: major economic indicators, 1994–1998

	1994	1995	1996	1997	1998
GDP ($ mn)	1 254	1 867	2 741	3 423	4 082
GDP % change in real terms	na	21	69	30	18
GDP per capita ($)	299	455	669	815	972
Exports ($ mn)	91	152	336	575	817
Imports ($ mn)	894	1 082	1 882	2 333	2 573

Source: *EBRD, 1999b: 201*

A brief history

Throughout much of its history Bosnia–Hercegovina has been a land either lying at the edge of empires or between them. Although settlement of the territory extends back to neolithic times, the narrative of history begins in the early Middle Ages after the Slavic infiltration of the Balkan peninsula (Singleton, 1985; Bugajski, 1994: 5–10; Donia and Fine, 1994; Malcolm, 1994: 1–42; Danta and Hall, 1996; Shoemaker, 1999: 384–385). Since that time the people of B–H have been of the same ethnicity, Slavic, and have spoken essentially the same language, Serbo-Croatian; what distinguishes the three main groups today is religion. As early as AD 395 (formalised by the 1054 Greek Schism) European Christendom began to split between the western (Roman Catholic) and eastern (Roman-Orthodox-Byzantine) empires. The divide fell roughly through what is today B–H, which is why Catholic Croats using the Latin alphabet are found to the west, whilst Orthodox Serbs writing in Cyrillic are to the east.

Adding yet another ingredient to this Balkan stew was the introduction of the heretic religion Bogomil, which sprang from Macedonia during the 10th century and entered Bosnia under Ban Kulin (1180–1204). That Bogomilism, which became the state religion of Bosnia under Kulin, was rejected by both the Roman Catholic and Greek Orthodox churches placed the country in a difficult position and made it subject to attack in various forms. The territory of Bosnia thus fell into the hands of first one and then another neighbouring power (kingdoms of Serbia, Croatia and Hungary) and was divided into principalities. One ruler of the southernmost part of the territory became a Holy Roman vassal, for which he was made *Herzog* or duke of St Sava; hence the name Herzegovina or Hercegovina.

Bosnia became part of the Ottoman Empire in 1463, a condition that lasted for 415 years until 1878 (Sugar, 1977; Brown, 1996: xiii). Bosnia was one of the few areas of the Balkans that more or less welcomed the Turks, who were seen as less threatening than the Catholics. During this time many of the Bogomils converted to Islam and adopted the outward appearance of the Turks while maintaining their own language and much of their own culture. In doing so, they avoided the practice of giving up every tenth boy for Ottoman service (the *devesime*), were taxed less and were allowed greater political freedom than the Christians or Jews (Jelavich, 1983a: 88–90; Fernandez-Armesto, 1994: 240). Many Bosnian Muslims became important officials in the Ottoman military and administration throughout the empire. The religious/ethnic division that developed between Muslim Bosniacs and Orthodox Serbs, and to a lesser extent with Catholic Croats, also became manifest in a geographic divide between the predominantly Islamic city dwellers and the rural Christians. This urban–rural split, plus differing loyalties (Muslims to the empire, Christians to their church/nation), go a long way toward explaining the roots of the animosity that persist to the present (Brown, 1996: 41). The period of Ottoman control was also when numbers of Serbs moved into the *Krajina* (frontier) of eastern Croatia and the north-west shoulder of Bosnia.

Bosnia–Hercegovina passed into Austrian control by the 1878 treaty signed at the Congress of Berlin at the conclusion of the Turko–Russian War (Jelavich, 1983b: 59–63). Before this event, though, Serbs and Croats had sought in vain to ferment rebellion in the territory as a prelude to incorporating B–H into their lands. Austrian control of B–H and the adjacent Sanjak of Novi Pazar continued, and even strengthened, up to the outbreak of the First World War, which was ignited by the assassination of Archduke Ferdinand in Sarajevo in 1914.

From the time of the First World War, Bosnian Muslims were subjected to persecution, a practice that continued and intensified during the early days of the Kingdom of Serbs, Croats and Slovenes (1918–29) and during the pre-socialist phase of Yugoslavia, especially during the Second World War. Indeed, during this war B–H became a battleground not so much for the forces of Nazis against Partisans as for the Croatian Ustaša against the Serb Četniks. Death-tolls were high on all sides, but Muslims, whose ranks were reduced by some 100,000 during the war, were the hardest hit (Bugajski, 1994: 6).

Following the Second World War, Bosnia–Hercegovina was made a separate republic within Yugoslavia, with essentially its medieval borders (Department of State, 1999). B–H entered the post-war period as Yugoslavia's third poorest republic (after Macedonia and Montenegro), with a per capita income level that was only 86 per cent of the Yugoslav average (Table 19.3). This value rose slightly by 1952, but then dropped to only 71 per cent by 1964. B–H's relative position continued to slide, so that by 1989 it stood at 69 per cent, only slightly higher than Macedonia. Under Tito, industrial capacity was greatly increased in B–H, but much of it was based on the production of military hardware and metallurgy (see Dawson, 1987; Jancar-Webster, 1993). Of note is the large 'new industrial town' of Zenica located in eastern Bosnia. This industrial output accounts for the relatively strong position of B–H in terms of its export economy in 1990 (Gianaris, 1994: 141).

Post-communist experience and potential for joining the EU

B–H declared independence from Yugoslavia in early 1992 and within a month was recognised by the USA and by most European countries and admitted to the United Nations (Department of State, 1999). Soon thereafter, however, Bosnian Serbs, supported by their brethren to the east (who also controlled nearly all of the Yugoslav army and arsenal), began armed resistance with the apparent aim of establishing a 'Greater Serbia' that included much of eastern Bosnia (Bugajski, 1995: 115–123). Despite efforts by the UN and other western governments (Anon, 1993), this was the beginning of a three-year war that resulted in 200,000 casualties, the destruction of infrastructure and industrial capacity and the escalation of ethnic tension (Anon, 1996). Indeed, the horrors of the war rival the darkest pages of history. For example, in the so-called UN safe area of Srebrenica, some 7,000 Bosnian Muslims were massacred, most in truly

Table 19.3 Income per capita by Yugoslav region, 1947–1964

Region	1947	1952	1962	1964
Yugoslavia	100	100	100	100
Bosnia and Hercegovina	86	88	73	71
Montenegro	71	64	66	73
Croatia	107	117	121	120
Macedonia	62	59	57	69
Slovenia	175	188	198	195
Serbia proper	95	87	90	90
Vojvodina	110	89	103	105
Kosovo	52	50	34	37

Source: *Dyker, 1990: 55*

horrendous fashion (Anon, 1999d; Anon, 1999f). Despite efforts by western powers, notably those by the Vance–Owen team, an end to open warfare was not accomplished until 1995, when the Dayton Peace Agreement was signed by the presidents of the three factions to the conflict (Bosnian, Croatian and Serbian). Besides partitioning B–H into the Muslim/Croat Federation and Republika Srpska, the agreement put in place a 60,000-strong NATO-led peacekeeping force (IFOR), which was succeeded in 1996 by a smaller NATO-led stabilisation force (SFOR).

B–H currently faces huge problems, which it must address to achieve political and economic stability. First, it must struggle to rebuild infrastructure and productive capacity in order to generate economic growth (see Table 19.2). Progress has been made on this agenda: the EU pledged $1.2 bn in aid for 1996–99 (Ladika, 1998a), while Islamic nations, such as Turkey and Saudi Arabia, have also rendered financial aid (Sorabji, 1996). Even the stone bridge over the Neretva River in Mostar, blown up during the fighting, is being repaired (Young, 2000). However, international aid to the Bosnian Serbs in the RS has been withheld over non-compliance with provisions of the Dayton Agreement. The impact of aid on differential growth is clearly seen in GDP figures: according to World Bank estimates, growth in GDP was 62 per cent in the Federation and 25 per cent in the RS in 1996, 35 per cent and zero in 1997 (Anon, 1998a; CIA, 1999). Some degree of normality is returning to at least some parts of the country; for example, international flights have resumed at Sarajevo's airport, and café life has returned, at least to the capital (Ladika, 1998b; Anon, 1999a). Second, like all the countries of CEE, B–H needs to develop a market-based, private sector economy. Some progress along these lines has occurred in the form of incipient market vendors, but much more growth from both the bottom up and top down is needed for any kind of sustained growth. Third, the country needs to prepare for the loss of external financial support over the next few years and develop better internal financial mechanisms; in early 1999 B–H's central bank contained a mere $130 mn (Anon, 1999c). As a positive sign, the European Bank for Reconstruction and Development, after an initial focus on emergency projects, has shifted attention toward more long-term projects (EBRD, 1999a).

Perhaps a longer-term problem concerns repatriation of the 330,000 refugees currently living outside the country and of the 836,000 individuals who were forced from their homes during the conflict but remain in B–H (UNHCR, 1999). By early 2000 little progress had been made, due in large measure to hardline attitudes on the part of some Serbs (Anon, 1998b). As international support (especially Russian) for the Serbs continues to erode, though, they may have to soften the stance (Laird, 1994). Finally, the country needs to heal from the recent strife and find a way to defuse the time bomb of ethnic hatred that apparently can be ignited rather easily (Lyon, 1999). Indicted war criminals are only now being brought to trial for their part in the Bosnian conflict; others have been charged, including Serbian President Slobodan Milošević (Anon, 1999e).

Given the rudimentary state of the Bosnian economy, the primitive conditions of the (largely paper) government and administration (Anon, 1998a; Anon, 1999b), and the potential for continued turmoil (Anon, 1999g), talk of entry into the European Union is premature. Diplomatic relations between the EU and B–H were established in 1993, and since that time the European Commission has allocated ECU 1.2 bn in humanitarian aid, with more to follow (EU 1996; Walker, 1998). Clearly, though, at least two decades will be needed before B–H will be in any position to make a serious bid for EU membership.

Conclusion

A difficult road lies ahead for Bosnia and Hercegovina. Having suffered debilitating damage during three years of fighting, and with its infrastructure and industry in shambles, government and administration practically non-existent and civil order maintained through what amounts to an occupying army, the country's future at present does not look promising. The best outlook would be for the country to continue making progress on reconstruction, building its economy and civil society, welcoming back its refugees and generally healing from its recent trauma. A more pessimistic view would be for the country's internal political/ethnic divisions to become entrenched, thus paralysing the country in endless rounds of bickering that keep the nation on the international dole. If the issue of human rights legislation is any indication, this route, unfortunately, appears to be the most likely at present (see IHF, 1999). An even more pessimistic scenario would be for Serbia and/or Croatia to realise a long-held dream of annexing parts of Bosnia–Hercegovina, thereby plunging the region into yet another round of turmoil. In any event, the prospects for Bosnia's entry into the European Union in even the medium term are slight to non-existent.

References

Anon, 1993, EC leaders pledge unity, support in Bosnia. *Europe*, 328, 2.

Anon, 1996, In focus: Bosnia. *National Geographic*, 189 (6), 48–61.

Anon, 1998a, A precarious peace. *The Economist*, 24 January, pp. 6–8.

Anon, 1998b, Putting it right. *The Economist*, 21 November, p. 52.

Anon, 1999a, Balkan wars. *The Economist*, 24 April, pp. 14–15.

Anon, 1999b, Better luck next time. *The Economist*, 1 May, pp. 47–48.

Anon, 1999c, Building Bosnia on banknotes. *The Economist*, 1 May, p. 66.

Anon, 1999d, Lessons from Bosnia. *The Economist*, 20 November, p. 22.

Anon, 1999e, Seized. *The Economist*, 28 August, p. 38.

Anon, 1999f, The whole and awful truth. *New Republic*, 221 (24), 9.

Anon, 1999g, Two on the chin. *The Economist*, 13 May, p. 61.

Berentsen, W. H., Danta, D., Hoffman, G. W., 1997, East central and southeastern Europe. *In* Berentsen, W. H., ed., *Contemporary Europe: a geographic analysis*. New York/Chichester: John Wiley & Sons, pp. 494–553.

Brown, L. C., 1996, *Imperial legacy: the Ottoman imprint on the Balkans and the Middle East*. New York: Columbia University Press.

Bugajski, J., 1994, *Ethnic politics in eastern Europe: a guide to nationality policies, organizations, and parties*. Armonk, NY/London: M. E. Sharpe.

Bugajski, J., 1995, *Nations in turmoil: conflict and cooperation in eastern Europe*. Boulder CO: Westview Press.

CIA, 1999, Bosnia and Herzegovina. *In* CIA, *The world factbook*. Washington DC: CIA. http://www.odci.gov/cia/publications/factbook/bk.html.

Danta, D., Hall, D., 1996, Contemporary Balkan questions: the geographic and historic context. *In* Hall, D., Danta, D., eds, *Reconstructing the Balkans: a geography of the new southeast Europe*. Chichester/New York: John Wiley & Sons, pp. 15–32.

Dawson, A. H., 1987, Yugoslavia. *In* Dawson, A. H., ed., *Planning in eastern Europe*. New York: St Martin's Press, pp. 275–291.

Department of State (US), 1999, *Background notes: Bosnia*. Washington DC: Department of State. http://www.state.gov/www/background_notes/bosnia_9908_bgn.html.

Donia, R. J., Fine, J. V. A., Jr, 1994, *Bosnia and Herzegovina: a tradition betrayed*. New York: Columbia University Press.

Dyker, D., 1990, *Yugoslavia: socialism, development and debt*. London/New York: Routledge.

EBRD, 1999a, *EBRD activities in Bosnia and Hercegovina*. London: EBRD. http://www.ebrd.com/english/opera/COUNTRY/bosnfact.htm.

EBRD, 1999b, *Transition report 1999*. London: EBRD.

EU, 1996, *EU–Bosnia-Herzegovina Relations*. Washington DC: European Union. http://eurunion.org/legislat/extrel/formyugo/bos-herz.htm.

Fernandez-Armesto, F., ed., 1994, *The Times guide to the peoples of Europe*. London: Times Books.

Gianaris, N. V., 1994, *The European Community, eastern Europe, and Russia*. Westport CT/London: Praeger.

Hoffman, G., 1963, *The Balkans in transition*. Princeton NJ: Van Nostrand.

IHF (International Helsinki Federation for Human Rights), 1999, *Annual report 1999 on Bosnia–Hercegovina*. Vienna: IHF. http://www.ihf-hr.org/reports/ar99/ar99bos.htm.

Jancar-Webster, B., 1993, Former Yugoslavia. *In* Carter, F. W., Turnock, D., eds, *Environmental problems in eastern Europe*. London/New York: Routledge, pp. 164–187.

Jelavich, B., 1983a, *History of the Balkans: eighteenth and nineteenth centuries*. Cambridge: Cambridge University Press.

Jelavich, B., 1983b, *History of the Balkans: twentieth century*. Cambridge: Cambridge University Press.

Ladika, S., 1998a, Rebuilding Bosnia. *Europe*, 381, 28–29.

Ladika, S., 1998b, Sarajevo seeking tourists … again. *Europe*, 381, 30–31.

Laird, L., 1994, Shared history. *Europe*, 337, 19.

Lyon, J., 1999, Bosnia and Herzegovina: an impossible reconciliation? *The UNESCO Courier*, December, p. 35.

Malcolm, N., 1994, *Bosnia: a short history*. New York: New York University Press.

Poulton, H., 1991, *The Balkans: minorities in conflict*. London: Minority Rights Publications.

Shoemaker, M. W., 1999, *Russia, Eurasian states, and eastern Europe 1999*. Harpers Ferry WV: Stryker-Post Publications, 30th edn.

Singleton, F., 1985, *A short history of the Yugoslav peoples*. Cambridge: Cambridge University Press.

Sorabji, C., 1996, Islam and Bosnia's Muslim nation. *In* Carter, F. W., Norris, H. T., eds, *The changing shape of the Balkans*. Boulder CO: Westview Press, pp. 51–62.

Sugar, P. F., 1977, *Southeastern Europe under Ottoman rule, 1354–1804*. Seattle/London: University of Washington Press.

UNHCR, 1999, *Bosnia–Herzegovina*. Geneva: UNHCR. http://www.unhcr.ch/world/euro/bosnia.htm.

Walker, M., 1998, Is Bosnia ready for peace? *Europe*, 374, 18–19.

Young, P., 2000, Building bridges in Bosnia. *History Today*, 50 (2), 6–7.

20

SERBIA AND MONTENEGRO

Darrick Danta

Serbia and Montenegro, along with the formerly autonomous provinces of Kosovo and Vojvodina, constitute what is left over from the break-up of the former Yugoslavia (Figure 20.1). The current situation, though, is ambiguous: while Serbia and Montenegro have self-proclaimed the 'Federal Republic of Yugoslavia' (tacitly including Kosovo and Vojvodina), this entity has not been recognised by the international community.

Resources

The total land area of Serbia and Montenegro (S–M) is 102,200 sq km, which is 67 per cent of the European average. The roughly cone-shaped region is located near the centre of the Balkan Peninsula surrounded by Albania (287 km shared border) and (FYR) Macedonia (221 km) to the south, Bulgaria (318 km) and Romania (476 km) to the east, Hungary (151 km) to the north and Croatia (241 km border in north, 25 km in south) and Bosnia–Hercegovina (527 km) to the east (Danta and Hall, 1996; Berentsen *et al.*, 1997; CIA, 1999; Department of State, 1999; Shoemaker, 1999: 342–344). Within this territory, Serbia, at 88,412 sq km, was the largest of the former Yugoslav republics; Montenegro, with 13,928 sq km, the smallest. The two former autonomous regions Kosovo-Metohija (sometimes abbreviated as Kosmet) and Vojvodina cover, respectively, 10,886 sq km and 21,507 sq km. Montenegro has 199 km of coastline on the Adriatic Sea. Like most of this part of Europe, the topography of S–M is hilly to mountainous with extensive development of karst topography and associated sinks, or *poljes*, and caverns (Singleton, 1985: 7–9). Climate generally consists of cold winters with hot, humid summers in the northern portions of Serbia, becoming drier in the central portions and more Mediterranean in nature with proximity to the Adriatic coast in Montenegro. The major hydrographic feature of the region is the Danube river with its tributaries the Sava and Tisa, which flow from the north and west, join near Belgrade and thence flow eastward toward the Black Sea via the Romania/Bulgaria border. The only lake on the territory is Scutari (Shkodër), located along the border of Montenegro and Albania.

Figure 20.1: Serbia and Montenegro

Land use of Serbia–Montenegro is 26 per cent forest, 20 per cent pasture, 38 per cent agriculture-cultivated and 16 per cent other. Natural resources include petrochemicals (oil, gas and coal) along with mineral deposits of copper, lead, zinc, nickel, gold and chrome. Agricultural products consist mainly of cereals, fruits and vegetables, though livestock raising (chickens, pigs, goats, cattle and sheep) contributes significantly to primary sector output. The main natural hazard in the territory of S–M is earthquakes; until recently environmental degradation was confined to water pollution of rivers and air pollution, mainly around industrial plants (Jancar-Webster, 1993). Of course, the 1999 NATO air campaign brought considerable destruction to much of the infrastructure of Serbia, with a concomitant reduction in the country's ability to process effluent and other forms of waste. Continuing economic and political sanctions have also hampered the ability of the government to make repairs and attend to environmental concerns.

The population of Serbia and Montenegro is currently estimated to be 11.2 million (10.5 million in Serbia, 700,000 in Montenegro), though given the disruption of recent conflicts all population figures are subject to considerable variation (CIA, 1999). Of this, approximately 63 per cent are Serb, 14 per cent Albanian, 6 per cent Montenegrin, 4 per cent Hungarian and 13 per cent other. Religion is mainly represented by the Orthodox faith (65 per cent), but 19 per cent of S–M is Muslim and 4 per cent Roman Catholic, with Protestant and others comprising, respectively, 1 and 11 per cent. Languages spoken in the territory of S–M are Serbo-Croatian (95 per cent; although most such speakers would now refer to their language as Serbian) and Albanian (5 per cent). Of course, Serbs, who are overwhelmingly Orthodox, form the majority of the population of Serbia, and Montenegrins, also Orthodox, form the majority of Montenegro. The main area of (predominantly Catholic) Hungarian settlement is in the northern part of Vojvodina near the Hungarian border; until recently Kosovo has been some 85 per cent Albanian (Poulton, 1991: 57). Whilst it is safe to assume that most followers of Islam (almost exclusively found in Kosovo) are ethnic Albanians, not all Albanians there are Muslims; small numbers of Orthodox and Catholic Albanians also inhabit the province (Poulton, 1991: 71–73).

Serbia–Montenegro is approximately 57 per cent urban. The main cities are Belgrade (1.2 million), the capital of Serbia and former capital of Yugoslavia; Podgorica (formerly Titograd), the capital of Montenegro; Priština, capital of Kosovo; and Novi Sad, capital of Vojvodina. The current political situation of S–M is a self-proclaimed 'federal republic', but this entity has not been recognised by the international community. The economic status of the territory is likewise uncertain. As will be discussed in a later section, for much of the 1990s Serbia was subject to sanctions and experienced hyperinflation and outright attack; as such, economic data are suspect. However, the latest estimates place the GDP of S–M at $25.4 bn, which yields $2,300 per capita (CIA, 1999). Composition of the economy is 25 per cent agriculture, 50 per cent industry and 25 per cent service, although the unemployment rate is at least 35 per cent overall, and 100 per cent in much of Kosovo.

A brief history

The territory covered by present day Serbia–Montenegro has been occupied for thousands of years by various tribes, notably the Celts, Illyrians, Tracians and Avars among many others (Singleton, 1985: 10–13; Stoianovich, 1994: 7–46). These early peoples developed cultural, religious and economic practices that form an important basis for contemporary Balkan societies (Stoianovich, 1994: 47–185). They also introduced agriculture to the region, exploited the native metals and developed trade routes.

Roman expansion into the region began in the 2nd century BC and was complete by around AD 200. Besides founding important cities (e.g., Singidunum–Belgrade, Naissus–Niš), the Romans built roads and other protected routes along the Danube to the Black Sea and along the Morava and Vardar rivers to the Aegean Sea. The Romans also began the division of the empire between west and east in 285; a line established in 393, passing along the Neretva river (Schwartz, 1999: 42) in Hercegovina just to the west of today's Serbia-Montenegro, explains the use of the Cyrillic alphabet in the region and the adherence to Orthodoxy among the Serbs and Montenegrins. Slavic settlement of the Balkan Peninsula can be traced to the 4th century, and had become differentiated between Slovenes, Croats and Serbs by the 10th century (Singleton, 1985: 13–14).

The history of the Serbian people is one of periods of expansion under important dynasties, followed by subjugation from powerful neighbours (Bugajski, 1994: 131–137; Gwin, 1999; Jelavich, 1983a: 18–19; Singleton, 1985: 24–28). The first state dates from the mid-9th century, although Serbs soon fell under the influence of Bulgarians, Macedonians and Byzantines before emerging in 1282 under the Nemanjid dynasty. Based in Raška (southern Serbia, in what was later the Sandjak of Novi Pazar), the kingdom reached its zenith under Stefan Dušan (ruled 1331–55 from Skopje), who extended the territory of Serbia over much of the Balkan Peninsula (Danta and Hall, 1996: 20; Fernandez-Armesto, 1994: 231–232). However, the Serbian medieval kingdom was extinguished with Ottoman expansion into the Balkans in general, and more specifically through defeats at such battles as Maritsa River in 1371 and Kosovo Polje in 1389 (Jelavich, 1983a: 31; Sugar, 1977: 21). Thus began 440 years of Ottoman rule (Brown, 1996: xiv), during which time Serbs (after 1459) lost control of their lands, essentially becoming slaves. However, in 1346 the Serbian autocephalous church was founded and became the most important element of building and maintaining Serbian identity (Malcolm, 1998: 12). Throughout the centuries places of historic importance, mainly battlefields and church sites, have also been of great significance in defining Serb identity (White, 1996).

Serbs successfully began re-establishing their independence in the early 1800s, achieving autonomy in 1815 and independence in 1878 (with the Treaty of Berlin). Beginning with the Karadjordjević dynasty in 1903, Serbs have sought to regain, or create, the 'Greater Serbia' of their medieval glory days, an ambition that continues to the present. Serbia was the principal entity of the Kingdom of Serbs, Croats and Slovenes created following the First World War.

Montenegrins are religiously, culturally and linguistically indistinguishable from the Serbs; they differ only in terms of history (Bugajski, 1994: 171–174). The rugged territory of Montenegro has protected them from attack over the years, notably from Ottoman advances that swept over other Balkan regions (Singleton, 1985: 29–31). The Montenegrins thus remained independent during the long Turkish occupation in what was the medieval principality of Zeta. In the modern period western powers sought to keep Montenegro separated from Serbia. Austria was thus awarded protectorate status (by the 1878 Treaty of Berlin) of the Sandjak of Novi Pazar, which lies between the two territories (Jelavich, 1983b: 29).

Kosovo-Metohija, as it is technically known, occupies a small area to the south of Serbia. The area is of great importance to Serbs for two reasons: as the site of their 1389 defeat at the hands of the Ottomans; and for Peć, which is the site of the patriarchate of the Serbian Orthodox Church (Malcolm, 1998). During medieval times Kosovo was also an important source for gold and other valuable minerals, which have long ago been exhausted. Despite its importance and former wealth, Kosovo in the modern period has been the poorest region of the Balkans. However, what the region has lacked in wealth, it has more than made up for in potential for conflict: whilst the territory is of enormous emotional significance to the Serbs, who desire to retain control at all costs, Kosovo since at least medieval times has contained a majority of ethnic Albanians, who naturally claim it as theirs.

The Vojvodina is a province located to the north of the Danube river and bordering Hungary. Long a possession of Hungary, the territory received many Serb settlers fleeing Turkish domination. During much of the modern period the region has had a majority Serb population, though it contains several other groups as well.

The Socialist Federal Republic of Yugoslavia (SFRY) created following the Second World War was, like its predecessor, largely dominated by Serbia, politically and militarily. However, during the Yugoslav period the republic did not fare as well economically: income figures/indices indicate that Serbia remained just below or at the Yugoslav average (see Tables 19.3 and 8.1). Montenegro, on the other hand, remained among the poorer republics over the period. Vojvodina was actually above the Yugoslav average for the whole period, but Kosovo was consistently the poorest: in 1947 its per capita income index was only 52 per cent of the Yugoslav average, falling to 28 per cent by the end of the Yugoslav period.

Under the guidance of Tito the SFRY made some progress in creating a multi-ethnic society and an economy that was the envy of other centrally planned countries of CEE (see Dawson, 1987). However, soon after Tito's death in 1980 the country's economy began to deteriorate (Lazic and Sekelj, 1997: 1057). Despite reform efforts enacted in 1983 and again in 1989, the rate of economic growth dropped, foreign debt mounted, annual inflation soared to over 10,000 per cent, industrial production fell and unemployment rose. Years of economic mismanagement began to show as even premier industrial plants spiralled out of control (Palairet, 1997). The fabric of Yugoslav society seemed to start to crumble, and individual republics began to agitate for independence.

Post-1989 experience and potential for EU entry

Many of the events of the past decade in the SFRY and its successor are closely linked to the rise to power of Slobodan Milošević. Beginning in 1987 he began a campaign to encourage Serb nationalism; within two years the head of Serbia's Communist Party was able to use other events, significantly the occasion of the 600th anniversary of the Battle of Kosovo, *en route* to becoming president of Serbia and later to gain Yugoslavia's top political post (Gwin, 1999; Ladika, 1999c: 26). He quickly began creating – with the support or guidance of his wife – an empire based on communist ideology, personal ambition and unquestioning loyalty (Silber, 1999). His tenure thus far has seen the break-up of Yugoslavia, as Slovenia followed by Croatia, Bosnia–Hercegovina and then Macedonia seceded and formed independent nations. Carefully orchestrated wars in Croatia and Bosnia–Hercegovina – outwardly based on 'ancient ethnic hatreds', though in reality driven by a desire to build a 'Greater Serbia' and motivated by economic gain – have been equally disastrous (Schwartz, 1999).

In 1992 Milošević joined Serbia, Montenegro, Kosovo and Vojvodina in the still internationally unrecognised Federal Republic of Yugoslavia (FRY) (Sekelj, 2000). This entity contains the two provinces of Kosovo and Vojvodina, which according to the 1974 SFRY constitution (a document largely ignored by Milošević) existed within the federal framework (Malcolm, 1998: 327–328), not as part of Serbia as is now claimed (Anon, 1999m).

The past decade has been difficult for Serbia. The economic situation, which was bad in 1989, has worsened. Inflation, unemployment, falling industrial production and loss of trade partners remain problems. Furthermore, the loss of capital, imports and the markets of Slovenia (the wealthiest republic of the former Yugoslavia) and Croatia did not make matters any better. Wars in Croatia and especially Bosnia further drained the government's resources. More significant has been the imposition of economic sanctions on Serbia. In an effort to curb Serbia's ambitions vis-à-vis Bosnia, in 1992 the USA and the European powers imposed a comprehensive package of sanctions – mainly economic, but also political – against the FRY. Still in place, sanctions have had the unintended consequence of strangling legitimate commerce and thus hurting average Serbians, while promoting official corruption and the black market, as well as lining the pockets of the ruling élite (Walker, 2000). The West is now in the process of re-thinking this policy instrument (Gallagher, 1999).

Most significant, though, was the NATO air campaign of spring 1999. This action, brought on in retaliation for continued Serbian military actions in Kosovo, caused the death of some 6,000 Serb soldiers and a further 2,000 civilian casualties along with the destruction of much of Serbia's power-generating capacity, bridges and other transport lines and industrial infrastructure, as well as other general damage (Anon, 1999e).

The economy is on the verge of collapse (Anon, 2000b), with a greater likelihood of generating domestic conflict and lawlessness than sustained growth (Anon, 2000e). Although economic data are suspect, the EU (1996) reports that the GDP of Serbia–Montenegro nearly halved over the period 1991–95, from $24.6 bn to $13 bn; trade with EU15 countries in 1995 was just ECU 188.5 mn in exports and ECU 31.6 mn in imports. Politically, Serbia has tried to foster relations with other countries, but thus far only the traditional allies – Russia, Greece (Hope, 1999a) and China (Anon, 2000a) – have shown any support for the failing regime. On the other hand, political opposition within Serbia is growing (Anon, 1999a), and Milošević and four of his colleagues have been indicted for war crimes by the UN's International Criminal Tribunal in The Hague (Anon, 1999f). Serbia has also to deal either directly or indirectly with well over 800,000 refugees and internally displaced persons (UNHCR, 1999).

Currently, EU–FRY relations are non-existent. In 1991 the EU renounced its co-operation agreement with Yugoslavia, which dates from 1970 (Gianaris, 1994: 143), and has had no contact with the FRY during the period of sanctions (EU, 1996). However, the EU Commission has given ECU 224.9 mn to the FRY over the period 1991–96, although most of this went to Montenegro. Furthermore, the EU recognises that it will have to at least participate, if not lead, post-conflict rebuilding efforts in the region (Leonard, 1999). Currently, Serbia does not even come close to fulfilling the Copenhagen criteria for EU membership in economic, political, legal or administrative terms (IHF, 1999). The USA and other countries have stated that as long as Milošević remains in power, Serbia will receive neither recognition nor aid (Husarska, 1999: 17).

The situation in Montenegro is somewhat more hopeful. Montenegro is part of the FRY, but in name only. The Montenegrins are consistently moving away from Serbian control – though not without potential for conflict (Anon, 1999h; Anon, 1999l) – and trying to establish relations with western governments (Husarska, 1999; Ladika, 1999b; Anon, 2000d; Anon, 2000f). Montenegro has even adopted the Deutschmark as its currency (Anon, 1999c). The USA and other western powers have recognised the cleavage with Serbia and have 'rewarded' Montenegro with $20 mn in aid, with promises for more (Husarska, 1999: 17). Of course,

Montenegro has a long way to go before thoughts of EU entry can be seriously entertained, but its prospects at present are at least better than Serbia's.

Despite horrendous events over the past decade, even Kosovo's future holds some potential. One of the first acts performed by the Serbian president in 1989 was to pressure the Kosovo assembly into abolishing the province's autonomous status and to suppress Albanian cultural institutions (USIA, 1999). In 1990 Serbia dissolved the Kosovo assembly, prompting legislators to proclaim the Republic of Kosovo in 1991, although this political entity was recognised only by Albania. Tensions between Serbs and ethnic Albanians mounted over the next few years, flaring to open warfare in 1998. A tentative peace accord was reached in early 1999, but the worsening situation led to direct military action on the part of the North Atlantic Treaty Organization (NATO) to try and halt open Serb aggression in Kosovo. During the conflict the territory of Kosovo was devastated: whole villages and towns were burned and shelled and thousands of civilians, mainly Albanian but also Serb, lost their lives or became refugees (Ladika, 1999a; Ladika, 1999c). In 1998–99, the total population of Kosovo was reduced substantially, while the percentage of Albanians rose relatively to Serbs (Table 20.1). NATO peacekeeping forces have since occupied the territory to try and maintain order, allow refugees to return and oversee reconstruction efforts.

Table 20.1 Kosovo's ethnic population, 1998–1999

Ethnic group	1999 population	%	1998 population	%	1999 pop. as % of 1998
Albanian	1 394 200	93	1 829 119	84	76
Serb	70 000	5	190 669	9	37
Other	42 000	3	169 946	8	25

Source: *Anon, 1999d*

Currently, the situation in Kosovo is far from settled (Bugajski, 1995: 133–144). While rebuilding efforts, funded by the USA, the EU, and other western governments, are being undertaken (Anon, 1999g; Hope, 1999b; Leonard, 1999) and some measure of market activity is commencing (Anon, 1999k), the province remains under UN administration and NATO control (Anon, 1999j). Life for Albanians and Serbs alike is difficult in Kosovo (Anon, 1999b; Anon, 1999i). In towns like Mitrovica in northern Kosovo, tensions run high (Anon, 2000c), and officials admit that the goal of creating a multi-ethnic society is not achievable in the short term. Despite the problems, Kosovo is receiving considerable attention from the international community in general and the EU in particular. Indeed, recent talk has focused on the creation of 'autonomous states of the EU' for entities such as Croatia, Albania and FYROM, and 'autonomous regions of the EU' for those such as Bosnia and Kosovo who do not qualify for full membership, but who could benefit from closer EU association (Leonard, 1999: 5).

The situation in Vojvodina, while not drawing the same level of attention as its neighbours to the south, is also noteworthy (Bugajski, 1995: 144–150). Currently, efforts are under way to create a multi-ethnic, multi-religious community based on self-rule in the province (IHF, 1999: 8), though conditions remain uneasy (Anon, 1999n).

Conclusion

The current situation in Serbia and Montenegro, along with that in Kosovo and Vojvodina, reflects years of political mismanagement, criminal actions, economic sanctions, war and continued ethnic strife. Predicting the future with respect to the different entities currently comprising the Federal Republic of Yugoslavia is difficult. In due time Serbia, Montenegro, Kosovo and Vojvodina will be freer to negotiate directly with the European Union. Sometime much further into the future these entities may gain EU admission.

References

Anon, 1999a, Can the Serbs get rid of Milosevic? *The Economist*, 3 July, p. 39.

Anon, 1999b, Cooling down in Kosovo. *The Economist*, 26 June, p. 20.

Anon, 1999c, Independence? *The Economist*, 4 December, pp. 50–51.

Anon, 1999d, Kosovo resurgent. *The Economist*, 25 September, pp. 57–58.

Anon, 1999e, Messy war, messy peace. *The Economist*, 12 June, pp. 15–16.

Anon, 1999f, Nailing the war-criminals. *The Economist*, 26 June, p. 58.

Anon, 1999g, No killing to be made. *The Economist*, 31 July, pp. 53–54.

Anon, 1999h, Not so fast, Djukanovic. *The Economist*, 17 July, pp. 44–45.

Anon, 1999i, Sad Serbs. *The Economist*, 31 July, p. 41.

Anon, 1999j, State in embryo. *The Economist*, 27 November, pp. 52–53.

Anon, 1999k, The market-minded Kosovars. *The Economist*, 25 September, p. 58.

Anon, 1999l, The next Kosovo? *The Economist*, 14 August, p. 39.

Anon, 1999m, Unsatisfactory sanctions. *The Economist*, 6 November, p. 17.

Anon, 1999n, Worried. *The Economist*, 26 June, p. 59.

Anon, 2000a, A Serbian–Chinese liaison. *The Economist*, 5 February, p. 49.

Anon, 2000b, Down, but not out. *The Economist*, 8 January, p. 48.

Anon, 2000c, Kosovo untamed. *The Economist*, 26 February, pp. 57–58.

Anon, 2000d, Last bust-up in Yugoslavia? *The Economist*, 29 January, p. 24.

Anon, 2000e, Rebuilding the Balkans – theory and practice. *The Economist*, 19 February, pp. 49–50.

Anon, 2000f, The last divorce? *The Economist*, 22 January, pp. 52–53.

Berentsen, W. H., Danta, D., Hoffman, G. W., 1997, East central and southeastern Europe. *In* Berentsen, W. H., ed., *Contemporary Europe: a geographic analysis*. New York/Chichester: John Wiley & Sons, pp. 494–553.

Brown, L. C., 1996, *Imperial legacy: the Ottoman imprint on the Balkans and the Middle East*. New York: Columbia University Press.

Bugajski, J., 1994, *Ethnic politics in eastern Europe: a guide to nationality policies, organizations, and parties*. Armonk. New York/London: M. E. Sharpe.

Bugajski, J., 1995, *Nations in turmoil: conflict and cooperation in eastern Europe*. Boulder CO: Westview Press.

CIA, 1999, Serbia and Montenegro. *In* CIA *The world factbook*. Washington DC: CIA. http://www.odci.gov/cia/publications/factbook/sr.html.

Danta, D., Hall, D., 1996, Contemporary Balkan questions: the geographic and historic context. *In* Hall, D., Danta, D., eds, *Reconstructing the Balkans: a geography of the new southeast Europe*. Chichester/New York: John Wiley & Sons, pp. 15–32.

Dawson, A. H., 1987, Yugoslavia. *In* Dawson, A. H., ed., *Planning in eastern Europe*. New York: St Martin's Press, pp. 275–291.

Department of State (US), 1999, *Background notes: Serbia and Montenegro*. Washington DC: Department of State. http://state.gov/www/background_notes/serbia_9908_bgn.html.

EU, 1996, *EU–Former Yugoslavia relations*. Washington DC: European Union. http://eurunion.org/legislat/extrel/formyugo/fry.htm.

Fernandez-Armesto, F., ed., 1994, *The Times guide to the peoples of Europe*. London: Times Books.

Gallagher, D., 1999, The next step in the Balkans. *Christian Science Monitor*, 91 (139), 11.

Gianaris, N. V., 1994, *The European Community, eastern Europe, and Russia*. Westport CT/London: Praeger.

Gwin, P., 1999, Kosovo: overrun with ghosts of conflicts past. *Europe*, 386, 28–29.

Hope, K., 1999a, Greeks and Serbs: an overview of current affairs in Europe's capitals. *Europe*, 386, 38–39.

Hope, K, 1999b, Kosovo: rebuilding getting underway. *Europe*, 391, 30–31.

Husarska, A., 1999, Podgorica dispatch: FRYed. *The New Republic*, 221 (14), 17–18.

IHF (International Helsinki Federation for Human Rights), 1999, *Annual Report 1999 on Federal Republic of Yugoslavia (Serbia, Montenegro, Kosovo)*. Vienna: IHF. http://www.ihf-hr.org/reports/ar99/ar99yug.htm.

Jancar-Webster, B., 1993, Former Yugoslavia, *In* Carter, F. W., Turnock, D., eds, *Environmental problems in eastern Europe*. London/New York: Routledge, pp. 164–187.

Jelavich, B., 1983a, *History of the Balkans: eighteenth and nineteenth centuries*. Cambridge: Cambridge University Press.

Jelavich, B., 1983b, *History of the Balkans: twentieth century*. Cambridge: Cambridge University Press.

Ladika, S., 1999a, Balkan update. *Europe*, 390, 4.

Ladika, S., 1999b, Montenegro stuck between Serbia and NATO. *Europe*, 386, 24.

Ladika, S., 1999c, The Kosovo. *Europe*, 386, 25–26.

Lazic, M., and Sekelj, L., 1997, Privatisation in Yugoslavia (Serbia and Montenegro). *Europe–Asia Studies*, 49 (6), 1057–1070.

Leonard, D., 1999, Rebuilding the Balkans. *Europe*, 387, 4–5.

Malcolm, N., 1998, *Kosovo: a short history*. New York: HarperCollins.

Palairet, M., 1997, Metallurgical kombinat Smederevo 1960–1990: a case study in the economic decline of Yugoslavia. *Europe–Asia Studies*, 49 (6), 1071–1101.

Poulton, H., 1991, *The Balkans: minorities in conflict*. London: Minority Rights Publications.

Schwartz, S., 1999, Beyond 'ancient hatreds': what really happened to Yugoslavia. *Policy Review*, 97, 39–51.

Sekelj, L., 2000, Parties and elections: the Federal Republic of Yugoslavia – change without transformation. *Europe–Asia Studies*, 52 (1), 57–75.

Shoemaker, M. W., 1999, *Russia, Eurasian states, and eastern Europe 1999*. Harpers Ferry WV: Stryker-Post Publications, 30th edn.

Silber, L., 1999, Milosevic family values: the dysfunctional couple that destroyed the Balkans. *The New Republic*, 221 (9), 23–27.

Singleton, F., 1985, *A short history of the Yugoslav peoples*. Cambridge: Cambridge University Press.

Stoianovich, T., 1994, *Balkan worlds: the first and last Europe*. Armonk NY/London: M. E. Sharpe.

Sugar, P. F., 1977, *Southeastern Europe under Ottoman rule, 1354–1804*. Seattle/London: University of Washington Press.

UNHCR, 1999, *Federal Republic of Yugoslavia (Serbia and Montenegro)*. Geneva: UNHCR. http://www.unhcr.ch/world/euro/ fryugo.htm.

USIA (United States Information Agency), 1999, *Kosovo: timeline of important events 1989–1999*. Washington DC: USIA. http://www.usia.gov/regional/eur/balkans/kosovo/timeline.htm.

Walker, C., 2000, Tinkering rightly with Serb sanctions. *Christian Science Monitor*, 28 February, p. 9.

White, G., 1996, Place and its role in Serbian identity. *In* Hall, D., Danta, D., eds, *Reconstructing the Balkans: a geography of the new southeast Europe*. Chichester/New York: John Wiley & Sons, pp. 39–52.

21

FORMER YUGOSLAV REPUBLIC OF MACEDONIA

Darrick Danta

The Former Yugoslav Republic of Macedonia (FYROM), or more simply Macedonia, was once a wellspring of classical culture, but today finds itself at the vortex of Balkan turmoil. A small country with limited resources and surrounded by suspicious neighbours, FYROM none the less has made great strides in creating political stability, revamping its economy and accommodating different viewpoints, both internal and external (Figure 21.1). In many ways Macedonia serves as a model for other Balkan countries seeking to emerge from the maelstrom of the break-up of Yugoslavia. As such, although contact with the European Union and other organisations thus far has been limited, potential exists for future developments that would bring Macedonia into closer partnership with this institution. However, FYROM will not be entering the Union as a member in the near future; at least a decade will be needed before the country's economy will be on par even with the Union's poorest members.

Before proceeding, consideration must be given to the name of the country being discussed. 'Macedonia' refers to a geographic region of the southern Balkans that historically (336 BC) extended from the upper reaches of the Vardar river to the Aegean Sea. As will be discussed, this region has undergone considerable change since the time of Philip of Macedon, having been conquered by Romans, Byzantines and Ottomans; partitioned among Bulgarians and Serbs; and fought over by most parties to Balkan conflicts. Currently, the subject of this chapter occupies what was historically Vardar Macedonia; the rest of the geographic region today lies in south-west Bulgaria (so-called Pirin Macedonia) and northern Greece, whose province of Macedonia occupies the historic section of Aegean Macedonia (Poulton, 1995: xvi, 1–2). During the Yugoslav period Macedonia existed as a republic of that name, and so upon declaring independence in 1991 the government naturally called itself 'Republic of Macedonia'. However, Greece vigorously objected to this nomenclature on the grounds that the name refers to their current province and that it, along with the symbol originally used in the Macedonian flag, was Greek cultural property (Perry, 1996: 115). The interim compromise adopted in 1994 by most of the international community was to refer to the new country as the Former Yugoslav Republic of Macedonia, or by its acronym FYROM. Referring to the country by any of its names – Macedonia, Republic of Macedonia or FYROM – upsets someone. Therefore, in this chapter an

Figure 21.1: FYR Macedonia

attempt will be made to respect the desires of the government and inhabitants of the republic and to acknowledge Greek objections to this name.

Resources

The Republic of Macedonia covers an area of only 25,700 sq km, which is 16 per cent of the average of European countries (CIA, 1999). Its location is at the centre of the Balkan Peninsula, surrounded by Albania to the west (151 km border), Bulgaria to the east (148 km border), Greece to the south (228 km border) and Serbia to the north (221 km border). The topography generally is hilly to mountainous, with deep valleys, rolling plains and picturesque alpine settings (Pribichevich, 1982: 10–34; Hoffman, 1963: 9–24). A particular feature of this nearly circular shaped country is the extensive development of karst features, such as sinks, or *poljes*, artesian springs and caverns, which result from solution weathering of the predominantly limestone bedrock. Another is the tectonic instability of the region; indeed, as recently as 1963 a major earthquake destroyed much of the capital, Skopje (Vesilind, 1996: 120). Macedonia contains three major lakes (Ohrid, Prespa and Doiran), each shared with a neighbouring country (Albania or Greece). The major river of Macedonia is the Vardar (Axios in Greece), which nearly bisects the country flowing north to south through the capital and entering the Aegean Sea near the Greek port Thessaloníki. The climate of FYROM is mainly in the humid Mediterranean zone, although due to the many mountains it is continental in nature, with warm summers and cold winters accompanied by heavy snowfall.

Approximately 24 per cent of Macedonia is arable, 39 per cent forest and woodlands, 25 per cent pasture, only 2 per cent in permanent crops and 10 per cent is other (CIA, 1999). Like much of the Balkans, natural resources are in limited supply, having been exploited long ago. FYROM currently produces only small quantities of minerals, such as chromium, lead, zinc, manganese, tungsten and nickel, along with some low-grade iron ore, coal, asbestos and sulphur; timber, though, is exploited in significant quantities. Agriculture is limited due to the short supply of arable land, though grains, mainly wheat and rice, vegetables, cotton and tobacco are grown. Likewise, the abundant pasture land is used for grazing nearly two million sheep, cattle, pigs and goats, which are used for their meat, wool and milk, much of which is used for cheese manufacture. Macedonia has a relatively clean environment: air pollution is a problem only around metallurgical plants. On the other hand, several parks and wild areas have been established, notably Mavrovo National Park, to preserve Macedonia's rich natural heritage.

The population of FYROM currently stands at approximately two million, of which approximately 66 per cent is Macedonian and 23 per cent Albanian, along with Turks, Serbs and Roma. These are the official figures: the actual proportion of Albanians is perhaps 33–35 per cent (Anon, 1998a). The territory of Macedonia, though, has always been a complex mélange of ethnicities; it is little surprise that the French word for mixed salad is macédoine (Vesilind, 1996: 124). The major religions, corresponding to the ethnic groups, are Eastern Orthodox 67 per cent and Muslim 30 per cent (CIA, 1999); until the Second World War, a sizable Jewish population, which had formed strong communities in many south Balkan cities from the medieval period (Sugar, 1977: 223), lived in the southern part of the country. Macedonian is the official language, although Albanian is spoken widely in the north-western portion of the country adjacent to Albania and Kosovo. The population growth rate is a modest 0.64 per cent, comprised of a birth rate of 15 per 1,000, a death rate of 8 per 1,000 and a net migration rate of –0.8 per 1,000.

The FYROM population is 60 per cent urban. Major cities include the capital Skopje (0.5 million), Bitola, Tetovo and Prilep. The government is an emerging democracy composed of an executive branch headed by the president and a legislative branch with a 120-seat assembly; the constitutional court makes up the judicial branch. FYROM is divided into 34 counties.

The economy of Macedonia is underdeveloped by European standards. GDP currently stands at $2.1 bn, which yields only a little over $1,000 per capita, thus making it, along with Bosnia and Albania, among Europe's poorest countries (CIA, 1999). The sectoral employment breakdown is 20 per cent primary, 39 per cent secondary and 41 per cent tertiary, though unemployment has ranged between 30–40 per cent in recent years (Anon, 1999d). Major industries include metal works (chromium, lead, zinc and nickel), coal mining, textiles, wood and timber products and tobacco. Exports totaling $1.2 bn in 1997 were mainly in manufactured goods, machinery, tobacco and food products that were directed to Bulgaria, other former Yugoslav republics, Germany and Italy. Imports, valued at $1.6 bn, were mainly machinery and equipment, chemicals and fuels from other former Yugoslav republics, Germany, Bulgaria, Italy and Austria.

A brief history

The early period

Human habitation of the upper Vardar river valley extends back to neolithic times, when groups separate from the coastal peoples occupied the mountainous regions inland from the Mediterranean climate (Poulton, 1995: 11). Migrations during the Bronze Age brought Illyrians (the forerunners of the Albanians), Thracians (who are believed to be extinct) and others across the region. Macedonia has existed as a regional place name, though, since the time of King Karan (808–778 BC), and reached early prominence during the reign of Philip II and especially that of his son Alexander the Great (336–323 BC) (MOI, 2000). The ethnic identities of these individuals, of course, is hotly debated since it is upon such characteristics that issues of contemporary 'Macedonianness' revolve. Most evidence points to the Hellenic character of the royal house of early Macedonia, although these leaders remained distinct: Philip was King of Macedon, but *hegemon* of the Greek League, which he never entered (Poulton, 1995: 11–15; Pribichevich, 1982: 37–40). The common people of this region, though, were Greek in neither education, culture, nor civilisation. So, Greek claims of an entirely Hellenic origin of Macedonia are based on a weak historical footing; by the same token, though, contemporary Macedonian claims for Alexander the Great as theirs are completely spurious (Fernandez-Armesto, 1994: 223–224). In any event, the situation for much of the Balkans changed drastically with the arrival of the Romans, who by AD 146 had consolidated control over the area of Macedonia, which soon found itself dismembered and lying astride borders between Latin speakers to the north and Greek speakers to the south, and between western and eastern empires. Latin-speaking Vlachs still inhabit some remote towns and villages in Macedonia.

Slavic period

The real story of the FYROM, though, begins during the second half of the 6th century with the arrival of the Slavs (Pribichevich, 1982: 65–88: Singleton, 1985: 10–32; Danta and Hall, 1996). Responding to the vacuum left in the Balkans by the disintegration of the Roman Empire and a subsequent period of threat from various Asiatic (Hun, Avar) and Teutonic (Visigoth) tribes, Slavs infiltrated the territory of contemporary FYROM, mingling with those already present, transforming them and being themselves transformed. A unifying force came in the form of Christianity during the early 9th century, championed by the 'Slav Apostles' Cyril and Methodius, who founded a literary script (Glagolitic, which became Cyrillic) for use in translating holy texts into a language understood by the Macedonian masses. Toward the end of the 9th century, Saints Clement and Nahum established a Slavonic monastery at Ohrid in present-day FYROM, which became the centre of Orthodox scholarship and dissemination for the south Balkans, and which represents the birth of the Macedonian Orthodox Church. The influences of the Ohrid Literary School, the *en masse* conversion to Christianity in 864 of the Macedonians at the direction of the Bulgarian Boris, combined with the growth of the Bulgarian kingdoms established by Samuel (976–1018) and others, began the process of organising the loose tribal/clan associations that characterised medieval Macedonian society (Pribichevich, 1982: 70–72; Stoianovich, 1994: 132). The period from the early 11th century to the mid-14th generally saw the region of Macedonia pass from Bulgarian to Byzantine to Serb control as the various medieval kingdoms and empires ebbed and flowed across the Balkan Peninsula.

Ottoman period

The next development came with the Ottomans, who, apart for a short period in 1878, controlled the territory of FYROM (Skopje) for 542 years from 1371 (the Battle of Maritsa) to 1913 (the second Balkan war) (Sugar, 1977: 20; Pribichevich, 1982: 93–106; Jelavich, 1983a: 30–34; Singleton, 1985: 35–71; Poulton, 1995: 26–47; Brown, 1996: xiii–xv). The period of Turkish rule generally retarded economic, political and social development of the territory that is now FYROM: this area went from being the centre of Orthodox learning to becoming the most backward, underdeveloped portion of the Balkans, save for Albania. During this time 'nationalities' under the *millyet* system were organised by religion; thus, the Christian *rayah* were treated separately from Jews, who were second-class citizens to the followers of the Koran. Out of this arrangement grew the problem of multiple identities that so confounds attempts at neat classification (Papadopoulos, 1996; Prevelakis, 1996; Terkenli, 1996). One by-product of this classification, though, was the nascent growth of proto-nationalism, which became important during the 18th and 19th centuries. During this time Macedonia had no definite political boundaries but was divided between the three administrative districts (*vilayets*) of Selanik, Kosovo and Bitola (Jelavich, 1983b: 89). Later, it was split between the *vilayets* of Manastir, Kosovo and Salonika (Perry, 1996: 113).

With the crumbling of the Ottoman Empire during the 19th century, the problem arose as to how to divide Balkan territory into discrete national units. Macedonia soon drew the attention of ambitious Bulgarians, Serbs and Greeks bent on establishing control of the region in the guise of historical legitimacy. The Greeks could point to Philip and Alexander; the Serbs to the medieval kingdom of Dušan, which encompassed the territory of Macedonia for a brief time; while the Bulgarians based their claims on the close similarity of languages. Each contestant for the territory argued that Macedonians, and hence Macedonia, were not separate, and thus should not stand alone. The 1870s to 1890s were particularly eventful: Macedonia was awarded to Bulgaria by the Treaty of San Stefano (1878), which was annulled in the same year by the Treaty of Berlin, thus restoring control to the Ottomans; Serbs actively expanded in Macedonia, which they referred to as 'South Serbia'; Greeks also established schools and other organisations in the area to bolster their claim; while the Macedonian Revolutionary Organisation (VMRO) was established in 1893 to promote independence, although linked with the Slavic, as opposed to the Hellenic, world (Jelavich, 1983a: 333–334; Poulton, 1991: 46–55; Bugajski, 1994: 98–99; Fernandez-Armesto, 1994: 224; Shoemaker, 1999: 395).

The history of Macedonia during the early 20th century is one of national aspirations caught in a web of territorial expansions whose origins were both near and far. During this time Greek, Serb and Bulgarian interests remained strong; but now Russia, Austro–Hungary and other European powers entered the scene with ambitions of either expanding influence in the area and/or preventing such adventurism. Macedonia soon found itself overwhelmed by outside interests and at the centre of the first and second Balkan wars (1912–13), which finally ended Ottoman rule but led to partition of the territory between Serbia, Greece and Bulgaria into approximately the current boundaries (Jelavich, 1983b: 95–100; Fernandez-Armesto, 1994: 224; Bugajski, 1995: 150–152;). Only one year later the First World War broke out, the outcome of which not only was finally to put to rest the Ottoman and Austro–Hungarian empires, but also essentially to check Russian ambitions in the Balkans. In the aftermath, US President Wilson's notions of self-determination came to the fore, resulting in the creation in 1918 of the Kingdom of Serbs, Croats and Slovenes (with Vardar Macedonia subsumed within Serbia). However, when the name changed to Yugoslavia, Macedonia emerged as a separate republic.

Yugoslav period

The experience of the Republic of Macedonia within the Yugoslav Federation, especially after the institution of socialism in 1945, in many ways was a repeat of its experience under Ottoman rule. On the political front, Tito took steps to entrench Macedonia's claim to a history distinct from Greek or Bulgarian – often by freely usurping other's national heroes – and to a language distinct from Serbo-Croatian. The Greeks, fearing irredentist moves, relocated thousands of settlers into Aegean Macedonia to help solidify control of the region (Fernandez-Armesto, 1994: 224).

On the economic front, Macedonia slipped into the Yugoslav basement. Income data show that at the beginning of the socialist period the position of the republic was only 62 per cent of the Yugoslav average and 35 per cent of the wealthiest, Slovenia (Table 19.3). Macedonia's level dipped further by 1962, although recovered somewhat by 1964; only Kosovo showed consistently lower income levels. Other indicators of well-being also show Macedonia and Kosovo as having the lowest levels in Yugoslavia, if not in all of Europe (Berentsen *et al.*, 1997: 518–520). By 1989 Macedonia's employment consisted of 29 per cent agriculture and 24 per cent industry; 22 per cent were unemployed; 11 per cent of the population was illiterate; and the GNP index was only 67 per cent of the Yugoslav average, or 33 per cent of Slovenia's level (see Table 8.1). By 1990 Macedonia contributed only 4 per cent of Yugoslavia's export total (Gianaris, 1994: 141).

Macedonia was largely relegated to a back-stage position by government policies; most discussions of economic planning and development within Yugoslavia give Macedonia scant attention (cf. Dawson, 1987; Dyker, 1992). Within Yugoslavia, the republic of Macedonia remained tucked away in the extreme southern corner, so when the federal structure started to unravel in the early 1990s, most observers paid more attention to the richer and larger republics to the north. There was a general feeling that Macedonia would either stay within the Yugoslav structure, or else would be engulfed by Serbia. That neither occurred is a tribute to then president Kiro Gligorov (Anon, 1999b).

Post-communist experience and potential for joining the EU

Despite FYROM's less than lustrous experience during Yugoslav times, many of the developments experienced during the 1990s were promising.

First, the country avoided war, which is no small task given the Balkan cauldron. Indeed, the potential for conflict was recognised early (Anon, 1998b), and a NATO peacekeeping force of 12,500 was put in place in 1992 to monitor the situation (Hope, 1994; Hope, 1999a; Anon, 1999b). The situation was particularly perilous since the Macedonian army was left without arms when the Yugoslav army withdrew in the early 1990s (Harris, 1999).

Second, the country has established good relations both with its neighbours and with its large Albanian population. When the Republic of Macedonia declared its independence in 1991, it was recognised by Bulgaria and met the European Community's requirements for recognition (Perry, 1996: 114). However, Greece objected both to the use of the name 'Macedonia' and to the flag adopted by the new country and was able to rally support for its position in Europe, the UN and the USA, and thereby to delay recognition of the country. Once a compromise was reached to refer to the country as the 'Former Yugoslav Republic of Macedonia' the way became clear for recognition by the UN (in 1993), the US (1994) and the Organization for Security and Co-operation in Europe (OSCE), European Council and Partnership for Peace programme in 1995 (MOI, 2000). Recent elections in FYROM have helped to ease tensions with neighbouring countries (Anon, 1999c). The situation also seems relatively stable with respect to the Albanian minority, especially in regard to recent migrants from Kosovo who find life in FYROM better than elsewhere (Anon, 1998a, 1999a; Perry, 1998). Indeed, FYROM has done an excellent job in accepting some 260,000 refugees from Kosovo (UNHCR, 1999). The overall human rights situation in FYROM is viewed in optimistic terms (IHF, 1999).

The outlook for economic restructuring also looks less gloomy. During the early 1990s FYROM suffered greatly under embargoes against it from Greece and also from sanctions placed on Serbia. Greek embargoes hurt because landlocked FYROM's closest outlet is through Thessaloníki; some 90 per cent of its trade, valued at over $80 bn, normally travels this route (Hope, 1994: 337). In addition, loss of Serbia as a trade partner has meant the loss of $83 bn in trade revenue and has led to a 30 per cent decline in industrial output (Hope, 1994: 337). The situation at least with respect to Greece has improved, so that now FYROM can export to the south, Greeks are starting to invest there, and other types of economic partnerships are evolving (Hope, 1999b). Certain entrepreneurs are even finding ways to avoid the Serbian embargo and thus reap good profits (Anon, 1999e). GDP growth was, therefore, negative for much of the 1990s, although latterly it has shown signs of improvement (Table 21.1).

Table 21.1 FYR Macedonia: major economic indicators, 1994–1998

	1994	1995	1996	1997	1998
GDP % change in real terms	−1.8	−1.2	+0.8	+1.5	+2.9
GDP per capita ($)	1 500	1 917	1 971	1 663	1 548
Exports ($ mn)	1 086	1 204	1 147	1 237	1 322
Imports ($ mn)	1 272	1 439	1 464	1 623	1 722

Source: *EBRD, 1999b: 221*

Relations with the European Union are at the initial stages. A co-operation agreement was signed in 1997 (EUR-Lex, 1997) and came into effect on 1 January 1998 (EU, 1998). The European Bank for Reconstruction and Development has adopted a strategy for developing the private sector in FYROM (EBRD, 1999a). Furthermore, the privatisation process is moving ahead with great success (MPA, 2000). However, observers point to the need for reforming monetary policy in FYROM (Kraft, 1995) and for gaining needed entrepreneurial and managerial skills (Dana, 1998).

At present, FYROM is progressing toward eventual EU membership. The country has established the rule of law and is improving its overall level of administrative capacity. The government is taking measures to furthering a free-market economy, and new trade partners to replace Serbia are being found. Furthermore, the environmental situation is good (Jancar-Webster, 1993), and considerable potential exists for the development of a tourism industry in the near future (Allcock, 1991). Bulgaria is emerging as a new trade partner and political supporter and has pledged to back FYROM's entry into the EU.

Conclusion

Macedonia has led a long and complex existence. Currently, FYROM appears well on its way to distancing itself from the troubles in other parts of the Balkans. Its people desire entry into the EU and other international organisations, and, given the present course, should see this come to pass within a decade or so.

References

Allcock, J. B., 1991, Yugoslavia. *In* Hall, D. R., ed., *Tourism and economic development in eastern Europe and the Soviet Union*. London: Belhaven Press, pp. 236–258.

Anon, 1998a, Albanian calm. *The Economist*, 7 November, pp. 53–57.

Anon, 1998b, Next domino? *The Economist*, 7 March, pp. 55–56.

Anon, 1999a, In the balance. *The Economist*, 8 May, pp. 51–52.

Anon, 1999b, Macedonia's protection racket. *The Economist*, 6 March, p. 50.

Anon, 1999c, Methodical man. *The Economist*, 20 November, p. 59.

Anon, 1999d, Still nervous in Macedonia. *The Economist*, 12 June, p. 44.

Anon, 1999e, The Macedonian exit route. *The Economist*, 3 April, p. 18.

Berentsen, W. H., Danta, D., Hoffman, G. W., 1997, East central and southeastern Europe. *In* Berentsen, W. H., ed., *Contemporary Europe: a geographic analysis*. New York/Chichester: John Wiley & Sons, pp. 494–553.

Brown, L. C., 1996, *Imperial legacy: the Ottoman imprint on the Balkans and the Middle East*. New York: Columbia University Press.

Bugajski, J., 1994, *Ethnic politics in eastern Europe: a guide to nationality policies, organizations, and parties*. Armonk NY/London: M. E. Sharpe.

Bugajski, J., 1995, *Nations in turmoil: conflict and cooperation in eastern Europe*. Boulder CO/ San Francisco/Oxford: Westview Press.

CIA, 1999, Macedonia, the former Yugoslav Republic of. *In* CIA, *The world factbook*. Washington DC: CIA. http://www.odci.gov/cia/publications/factbook/mk.html.

Dana, L. P., 1998, Waiting for direction in the former Yugoslav Republic of Macedonia (FYROM). *Journal of Small Business Management*, 36 (2), 62–68.

Danta, D., Hall, D., 1996, Contemporary Balkan questions: the geographic and historic context. *In* Hall, D., Danta, D., eds, *Reconstructing the Balkans: a geography of the new southeast Europe*. Chichester/New York: John Wiley & Sons, pp. 15–32.

Dawson, A. H., 1987, Yugoslavia. *In* Dawson, A. H., ed., *Planning in eastern Europe*. New York: St Martin's Press, pp. 275–291.

Dyker, D., 1990, *Yugoslavia: socialism, development and debt*. London/New York: Routledge.

Dyker, D., 1992, Yugoslavia. *In* Dyker, D., ed., *The national economies of Europe*. London and New York: Longman, pp. 278–300.

EBRD, 1999a, *EBRD activities in FYR Macedonia*. London: EBRD. http://www.ebrd.com/english/opera/COUNTRY/ fyrmfact.htm.

EBRD, 1999b, *Transition report 1999*. London: EBRD.

EU, 1998, *EU–Former Yugoslav Republic of Macedonia (FYROM) relations*. Washington DC: European Union. http://eurunion.org/legislat/extrel/formyugo/fyrom.htm.

EUR-Lex (Community Legislation), 1997, *Community legislation in force*. Brussels: Official Journal L348. http://www.europa.eu.int/eur-lex/en/lif/dat/1997/en_297A1218_02.html.

Fernandez-Armesto, F., ed., 1994, *The Times guide to the peoples of Europe*. London: Times Books.

Gianaris, N. V., 1994, *The European Community, eastern Europe, and Russia*. Westport CT/London: Praeger.

Harris, M. F., 1999, Macedonia: the next domino? *The National Interest*, 55, 42–46.

Hoffman, G., 1963, *The Balkans in transition*. Princeton NJ: Van Nostrand.

Hope, K., 1994, The Macedonia question. *Europe*, 336, 8.

Hope, K., 1999a, Albania & Former Yugoslav Republic of Macedonia. *Europe*, 387, 28–29.

Hope, K., 1999b, Greeks invest in FYROM. *Europe*, 388, 43–44.

IHF (International Helsinki Federation for Human Rights), 1999, *Annual report 1999 on Macedonia*. Vienna: IHF. http://www.ihf-hr.org/reports/ar99/ar99mac.htm.

Jancar-Webster, B., 1993, Former Yugoslavia. *In* Carter, F. W., Turnock, D., eds, *Environmental problems in eastern Europe*. London/New York: Routledge, pp. 164–187.

Jelavich, B., 1983a, *History of the Balkans: eighteenth and nineteenth centuries*. Cambridge: Cambridge University Press.

Jelavich, B., 1983b, *History of the Balkans: twentieth century*. Cambridge: Cambridge University Press.

Kraft, E., 1995, Stabilizing inflation in Slovenia, Croatia and Macedonia: how independence has affected macroeconomic policy outcomes. *Europe–Asia Studies*, 47 (3), 469–492.

MOI (Ministry of Information), 2000, *Facts about Republic of Macedonia: history: chronology*. Skopje: MOI, Republic of Macedonia. http://www.sinf.gov.mk/Macedonia/EN/History/Chronology.htm.

MPA (Macedonian Privatization Agency), 2000, *Status report as of June 30, 1999*. Skopje: Ministry of Information. http://www.mpa.org.mk/front.htm.

Papadopoulos, A. G., 1996, Single human geography, multiple Macedonian histories. *In* Hall, D., Danta, D., eds, *Reconstructing the Balkans: a geography of the new southeast Europe*. Chichester/New York: John Wiley & Sons, pp. 79–88.

Perry, D. M., 1996, Macedonia: Balkan miracle or Balkan disaster? *Current History*, 95 (599), 113–117.

Perry, D., 1998, Destiny on hold: Macedonia and the dangers of ethnic discord. *Current History*, 97 (617), 119–126.

Poulton, H., 1991, *The Balkans: minorities in conflict*. London: Minority Rights Publications.

Poulton, H., 1995, *Who are the Macedonians?* Bloomington: Indiana University Press.

Prevelakis, G., 1996, The return of the Macedonian question. *In* Carter, F. W., Norris, H. T., eds, *The changing shape of the Balkans*. Boulder CO: Westview Press, pp. 131–155.

Pribichevich, S., 1982, *Macedonia: its people and history*. University Park: The Pennsylvania State University Press.

Shoemaker, M. W., 1999, *Russia, Eurasian states, and eastern Europe 1999*. Harpers Ferry WV: Stryker-Post Publications, 30th edn.

Singleton, F., 1985, *A short history of the Yugoslav peoples*. Cambridge: Cambridge University Press.

Stoianovich, S., 1994, *Balkan worlds: the first and last Europe*. Armonk NY/London: M. E. Sharpe.

Sugar, P. F., 1977, *Southeastern Europe under Ottoman rule, 1354–1804*. Seattle/London: University of Washington Press.

Terkenli, T. S., 1996, Macedonian cultural and national identity. *In* Hall, D., Danta, D., eds, *Reconstructing the Balkans: a geography of the new southeast Europe*. Chichester/New York: John Wiley & Sons, pp. 89–97.

UNHCR, 1999, *FYR of Macedonia*. Geneva: UNHCR. http://www.unhcr.ch/world/euro/macedon.htm.

Vesilind, P. J., 1996, Macedonia: caught in the middle. *National Geographic*, 189 (3), 118–139.

22

ALBANIA

Derek Hall

A brief history

The size of Wales or the state of Maryland, with a population of 3.3 million, Albania's average altitude of 708 m is twice the European mean (Figure 22.1). Two-thirds of the country is mountainous, yet it also contains the only fertile coastal plain on the eastern Adriatic. Varied relief and climatic conditions, significant water and mineral reserves, and a diversity of fauna and flora complement often stunning Ionian and Adriatic coasts. The Albanians see themselves as ancient inhabitants of the Balkans – descendants of the classical Illyrians – and certainly predating the in-migration of Slav groups to the region.

Straddling important trade routes and cultural fault lines, Albanian lands were incorporated into the western edge of the Islamic world through the conquests of the Ottoman Turks in the 15th century. The Strait of Otranto between Albania and Italy then became a cultural, political and technological divide for over 400 years (Ackerman, 1938). In 1913, when blunt pencil lines were drawn over the map of Europe in the wake of Turkey's disintegration, the new Albanian state was faced with as many Albanians left outside its borders as within them, bequeathing a Kosovo 'problem' to subsequent generations. For many in the West, Albania's size, language, location and politics have condemned the country to at best the psychological margins of Europe. The need to overcome a vacuum of understanding – filled in recent years with essentially negative images – remains a major task in Albania's attempts to join the common European home (Hall, 1999).

Following Italian and German wartime occupation – the Italians having invaded on Good Friday 1939 prior to the outbreak of war – Albania's low level of economic development was exacerbated in the second half of the 20th century by several decades of autarkic communist policies (1944–91). Irreversible ruptures in relations with political and economic patrons – Yugoslavia in 1948, the Soviet Union in 1961, China in 1978 – reinforced Albania's introspective position. The country's historic vulnerability to predatory neighbours nurtured a regime that encouraged xenophobic fears as a means of forging internal cohesion. In the vacuum of increasing isolation, economic and technological inertia from the mid- to late-1970s cemented

Figure 22.1: Albania

Europe's least developed country into a long-term spiral of social and financial impoverishment (Hall, 1994).

Although the country's post-war birth-rate declined from Europe's highest at over 35 per 1,000 in the mid-1960s to a 1988 figure of 25.3, a very explicit pro-natalist policy, with highly constrained access to contraceptive methods, remained until 1991. Although healthcare under communism was unimpressive, it was regarded as a state obligation. In the 1990s the healthcare system deteriorated, particularly in rural areas, as it became starved of funds. Most notably, there was an increase in both infant mortality and maternal death in childbirth. The latter was estimated by Albanian clinicians at 35 per 100,000 live births for 1996, and infant mortality at 49 per 1,000 live births, contrasting with much lower internationally recognised infant mortality levels (see Table 1.1) and a 1990 figure of 28 (Smeets *et al.*, 1997).

At 111 inhabitants per square kilometre in 1989 (compared to just 28 in 1923), Albania had the highest population density in the Balkans. The low average age of population (27 years), with 43 per cent of the total under 20 years old, built up pressures which by 1990 saw a large body of young people demanding change within the country. At the end of the communist period, Albania's population geography was unique in Europe: two-thirds of the total population lived in rural areas; the rural population was still growing in absolute terms; and most urban growth was derived from natural increase rather than from in-migration (Sjöberg, 1991).

The image of Albania and Albanians as Islamic has been manipulated by less friendly 'Christian' neighbours, as in Serb attempts to justify actions against 'fundamentalism' in Kosovo. Religion was subordinated to interests of nationalism during the period of national revival in the late 19th century and in the subsequent establishment of an Albanian state. But the perception that religion symbolised foreign (Italian, Greek and Turkish) predation was used to justify the communists' stance of state atheism (1967–91) in order to better develop a unifying 'Albanianness' (Trix, 1994; Liolin, 1997). Since 1991 Turkey and a number of Gulf states have provided development assistance, which in its turn has raised questions concerning the course of Albania's development path. Alongside EU, World Bank and other 'western' support, loans have been secured from the Islamic Development Bank; and significant levels of Middle Eastern support, particularly in the cultural sphere, have been viewed by some Albanians as a potential impediment to the country's acceptance by western supranational institutions. Indeed, in 1998 Albania withdrew from the Organisation of Islamic Conference (OIC), of which it had been a part – and the only European member – since 1993 (DPA, 1998). Socialist Prime Minister Fatos Nano declared that Albania had no other future than to be integrated in Europe.

First post-communist crisis, 1991–92

In 1991 one major and immediate impact of the country's exposure to global processes was the Albanians' realisation of the impoverishment and inadequacies of their country in comparison to its neighbours, prompting many to attempt to leave the country. Between 1990 and 1993 some 400,000 people – more than 10 per cent of Albania's total population, and 15 per cent of the country's labour force – succeeded in doing so (IMF, 1994).

The months of 1991–92 were also characterised by massive outbursts of collective frustration, which expressed itself in the wanton destruction and looting of property in any way associated with the state and the former regime: schools, factories, state farm glasshouses, irrigation systems and the country's vestigial railway system were just some of the victims of this anarchy. Disruption to the economy and particularly to distribution systems, already under strain, saw families falling back on their own resources for short-term survival, to the extent of felling roadside trees, protected forests and telegraph poles for winter fuel (Hall, 1994).

The economy had stagnated in the 1980s, and in the early 1990s the Albanian population of 3.3 million represented a very weak consumer society. The individual ownership of motor vehicles, for example, remained forbidden from the 1950s until 1991, at which time they numbered less than 10,000. Motor car numbers then grew rapidly, fuelled by the import of stolen vehicles – notably Mercedes – from other parts of Europe, and peaked in 1994 at 68,000 (EIU, 1999a). The combination of a volatile socio-political environment, large numbers of stolen high-powered vehicles and an absence of driver training presented a lethal cocktail which soon saw the countryside littered with the wrecked consequences of traffic accidents.

Although the restitution of private land and property confiscated by the communists posed problems for most CEE countries in the early 1990s, such processes were rarely accompanied by the level of migration and destruction that was experienced in Albania (Tarifa, 1995). Rural infrastructure was poor (Republic of Albania, 1996): water quality posed problems for a number of rural areas, many villages were only accessible by foot or mule, and provision of rural telephone lines was just 7 per 1,000 population (EIU, 1996: 66). The pent-up frustrations resulting from decades of repressive restrictions on mobility saw, in just three or four years, 350,000 spontaneous migrants, particularly from the country's remote north-eastern districts, moving south in search of better land and/or access to major urban areas (Hall, 1996). More than 3,000 homes were erected illegally on the outskirts of Tirana alone. Spontaneous movement to fertile areas on the coastal plain further hampered the redistribution of agrarian land (Anon, 1996). Unemployment and other social problems were exacerbated by such spontaneous migration and settlement, including a cholera outbreak in 1994 and a resurgence of polio in 1996 (Anon, 1997).

Second post-communist crisis, 1996–98

Much domestic investment had been channelled into nine pyramid 'investment' schemes, which collapsed at the end of 1996 and during the first months of 1997 (Elbirt, 1997; Korovilas, 1999). The very existence of, and popular support for, these schemes, and their aftermath, well encapsulated and symbolised the fragility of Albania's civil society. An estimated 70 per cent of all Albanian families had been willing to submit their savings to such schemes for returns of up to 50 per cent per month. Such savings had come from three major sources: (a) many families received their flats or houses virtually for free following the privatisation of state housing in 1992. This distortion of the perceived value of housing led many to sell their easily gained homes in order to acquire investment cash for the pyramid schemes. The pyramid failures rendered many homeless, placing greater strains on welfare provision and exacerbating the growth of apparently rootless subcultures within the country; (b) émigré remittances, which had become a vital source of income and consumer goods for many Albanian families during the 1990s; and (c) money accumulated in the south of the country, from both legal means and from such activities as smuggling and money laundering, which was rarely committed to formal banks. This was well positioned to be absorbed by the pyramids, and its loss stimulated cash-deprived criminal elements to resort to further, heightened, criminality.

The subsequent renewed social, economic and political instability revealed a vacuum in the processes and framework for sustaining civil society. The role of organised crime was strengthened and, partly as a result, there emerged alternative social networks, including the resurgence of clan-based loyalties in the north of the country (Lawson and Saltmarshe, 2000).

Economic development

Apart from war-ravaged Bosnia–Hercegovina, Albania endured the greatest post-communist contraction of industrial production in CEE. In 1998 industrial output was less than 30 per cent of that in 1989 (EIU, 1999b: 22). Albania remains Europe's poorest country (Table 22.1). Since the mid-1990s the IMF has been guiding the economy, but much depends upon a stable domestic security situation and the ability to sustain the rule of law and a civil society.

The grossly inefficient and outmoded industrial sector, based on processing Albanian minerals and other raw materials (ferrous-nickel, chrome, copper, petroleum lignite), quickly collapsed in the early 1990s. Lighter manufacturing industry based on traditional skills – carpet making, textiles and timber products – has been experiencing localised resurgence, although it faces stiff international competition. Construction has been the most explicit industrial activity, fuelled by waves of post-communist destruction and the continuing availability of overseas remittances – estimated at $421.3 mn in 1998, roughly twice the value of Albania's exports (EIU, 1999c: 9).

Table 22.1 Albania: key economic indicators, 1991–1999

	1991	1992	1993	1994	1995	1996	1997	1998[b]	1999[c]
Current account ($ mn)	−249.0	−434.0	−365.0	−279.0	−176.0	−245.0	−276.0	−186.0	−450.0
Trade balance ($ mn)	−208.0	−454.0	−490.0	−460.0	−474.0	−692.0	−518.0	−620.0	−1 151.0
Exports ($ mn)	73.0	70.0	112.0	141.0	205.0	229.0	167.0	206.0	234.0
Imports ($ mn)	281.0	524.0	602.0	601.0	697.0	921.0	685.0	826.0	1 385.0
Foreign direct investment, net ($ mn)	8.0	32.0	45.0	65.0	89.0	97.0	42.0	45.0	43.0
Population (mn, end-year)	3.3	3.2	3.2	3.2	3.2	3.3	3.3	3.2	na
Unemployment: annual average (% of labour force)[a]	8.9	27.9	29.0	19.6	16.9	12.4	14.9	17.7	na
GDP $ per capita	346.1	205.1	374.8	615.1	743.8	816.7	681.5	929.6	na
% share of industry in GDP	32.1	16.9	13.9	12.4	11.5	12.2	na	na	na
% share of agriculture in GDP	42.5	54.2	54.6	55.1	55.9	55.4	62.6	na	na
GDP (% change)	−27.7	−7.2	9.6	9.4	8.9	9.1	−7.0	8.0	8.0
Industrial gross output (% change)	−42.0	−51.2	−10.0	−2.0	1.0	15.8	−5.6	4.1	na
Agricultural gross output (% change)	−17.4	18.5	10.4	10.3	10.6	0.5	1.0	5.0	na

[a] Figures do not account for emigrant workers abroad who made up an estimated 18% of the total labour force in 1995.

[b] Estimates.

[c] Projections.

Source: *EBRD, 1999b: 185*

Early post-communist aspirations saw tourism as possibly the country's short-term salvation, and a number of joint-venture contracts were pursued for substantial developments along the coast and inland, following a plan drawn up with the European Bank for Reconstruction and Development to recognise tourism investment priority zones (Ministry of Tourism and EBRD, 1993). Subsequent bouts of civil unrest within the country have tended to inhibit both inward investment and international tourism development, such that most 'tourism' development has been driven either by the perceived needs of the international business and diplomatic communities or through the erratic development of a domestic market and a privatisation process that has seen the rise of a limited number of not always scrupulous entrepreneurs.

Small-scale privatisation proceeded rapidly in the earlier 1990s. By the turn of the century 98 per cent of Albanian enterprises consisted of ten or fewer employees, with the majority single-person or family organisations usually relying on savings or family remittances from abroad. To ameliorate this situation, the EBRD has invested in an institution specialising in micro-credit lending (the FEFAD Bank) (Table 22.2), to support the emergence of the private sector by ensuring that micro- and small entrepreneurs have permanent access to formal sector financing (EBRD, 1999a).

Table 22.2 Albania: EBRD-approved projects

Operation name	Sector	Total cost (€ mn)	EBRD Debt	EBRD Equity	EBRD Total
Public					
Albanian Telecom	Communications	39.22	9.41	na	9.41
Power sector reconstruction	Energy	61.60	30.00	na	30.00
Emergency road rehabilitation	Road infrastructure	16.10	10.00	na	10.00
Subtotal		116.92	49.41	na	49.41
Private					
Tirana Hotel	Tourism	18.37	10.04	0.83	10.87
Coca-Cola Tirana SRL	Food and beverages	14.94	na	2.37	2.37
Hotel Rogner	Tourism	19.60	11.18	2.04	13.22
Banca Italo–Albanese	Banking	11.95	na	1.96	1.96
FEFAD Bank	Financial	1.20	na	1.20	1.20
SME recovery credit line	Financial	5.81	5.81	na	5.81
Albania Reconstruction Equity Fund	Financial	16.26	na	6.69	6.69
Subtotal		88.13	27.03	15.09	42.12
Approved projects total, of which:		205.05	76.44	15.09	91.53
private					46%
public					54%

Situation as at 30 November 1999.

Source: *EBRD, 1999a*

For some time the government has been seeking strategic investors for the large state-owned enterprises that have remained in operation. In 1997 an Italian–British consortium signed a joint venture to rehabilitate the country's chrome mines with an initial investment of $41 mn, and Canadian investment of $4 mn was earmarked for upgrading copper production and processing (EIU, 1999a). A number of international ventures have been exploring the offshore potential for oil and gas, thus far with little success, although onshore petroleum production has recovered following UK and German investment. Turkish interests took a long lease on the Elbasan metallurgical complex, although subsequent labour problems have hampered development.

Albania has also been undertaking moves toward eligibility for membership of the World Trade Organization. During 1999 the reform of tariff rates and excise taxes and the adoption of a customs code were undertaken with this objective (EBRD, 1999b).

Agricultural production generates 60 per cent of GDP and continues to employ about half of the workforce. Albania had maintained the lowest level of urbanisation in Europe – just 35.5 per cent of the population were recorded as living in towns in 1989. This reflected an explicit rural-led development programme and the maintenance of a higher natural increase among the rural population (Sjöberg, 1991). New land and private property laws in 1991 dissolved all co-operatives but forbade the purchase or sale of land. In the consequent rush to regain lands held before the war, former rural landowning families were unilaterally claiming and fencing off territory, even destroying public buildings such as schools and installations such as oil wells in the process. Most farmland had been privatised by the mid-1990s (Giorgio, 1994). This structural change, coupled to international aid programmes and substantial remittances from Albanian émigrés, saw agriculture become a key motor for economic recovery. In the process of attempting to bring some equity to the redistribution of co-operative land, rural ownership became extremely fragmented. Almost 380,000 holdings of between 0.8 and 2 ha resulted from three-quarters of the country's arable acreage being given back to peasant families (Deslondes and Sivignon, 1995).

Only in August 1995 was legislation passed enabling the buying and selling of land, as one means of encouraging consolidation (Lemel, 1998). Credit was made available to farmers through an agricultural development fund, set up with support from the World Bank and other international donor agencies. The EU PHARE programme accorded ECU 6 mn to support the creation of a functioning market in agricultural land and other agricultural reforms. Ironically, consolidation was assisted by some farmers selling their land in order to invest in the country's pyramid 'investment' schemes.

With funding from the Soros Foundation and the UK government Know-How Fund (KHF), the Plunkett Foundation has been helping to develop self-supporting rural associations, including seed, sapling and flower growers, bee keepers and herb cultivators, with the aim of improving the quality and presentation of local upland products for niche marketing in Albania and abroad (Lucey, 1999). A major potential source of rural investment capital – émigré workers' remittances – was largely diverted to pyramid schemes in 1996 and lost in the schemes' subsequent collapse. Germany has made efforts to encourage emigrants to return to Albania by offering start-up credit for those wanting to open small businesses. However, the temporary influx of some 400,000 Kosovar refugees to Kukës and a number of other cities during 1999 further complicated ethnic Albanian mobility patterns as well as exacerbating local socio-economic problems.

The exclusion of Serbia from Balkan stabilisation and integration programmes developed in the wake of the Kosovo conflict provides Albania with a potentially key role in the region's political stability and commercial geography (EIU, 1999b). The country is at the intersection of two planned transport axes, one east–west the other north–south, although their construction is likely to be slow:

- Corridor 8: a road from Durrës across Albania, via Skopje to the Bulgarian Black Sea port of Varna, along the line of the old Roman *Via Egnatia*, together with rail links from Durrës via Pogradec across northern Greece to Florina and via Elbasan to Kičevo in FYR Macedonia;

- Corridor 10: a highway from Trieste, through Slovenia, Croatia, Montenegro and Albania to the Greek border at Igoumenitsa, and complemented by plans to re-open the Albania–Montenegro rail link.

The US Trade and Development Agency is also funding a $30 mn South Balkan Development Initiative (SBDI) to help develop and co-ordinate the transport systems of Albania, Bulgaria and FYR Macedonia and to promote regional co-operation (TDA, 1998).

The Albanian energy corporation (KESH) has required substantial assistance because of continued electricity distribution losses of almost 50 per cent. In November 1999 the EBRD approved a €30 mn loan to enable a reduction of such losses through more efficient management and to lower downstream costs to stimulate industrial activity. A pilot privatisation programme for regional distribution companies was launched in Shkodër, Elbasan and Vlorë (EBRD, 1999a, 1999b).

Environmental issues

In 1989 the country signed the World Heritage Convention. This was followed in 1990 by Albania becoming the last Mediterranean country to be a party to the United Nations Environment Programme (UNEP) Regional Seas Programme (Barcelona Convention), proposing the inclusion of six coastal sites under the convention. In October 1991 Albania gained access to the World Bank and the International Monetary Fund, as well as to the European Bank for Reconstruction and Development (EBRD). The country also became a signatory to the 1971 Convention on wetlands of international importance (Ramsar Convention), which has been important in supporting conservation measures and helped to secure PHARE programme funding. A coastal area management programme was also developed in conjunction with UNEP and the World Bank (CEP, 1998a), and Albania became a member of the Black Sea Economic Co-operation Council (BSECC) in 1994.

However, Albania entered its post-communist phase with a complete absence of sewage treatment plants, with obvious deleterious effects on water, land and human health. Subsequent PHARE and World Bank programmes have set about addressing this problem. In 1995 a PHARE programme was begun to examine urban and industrial waste management with a view to identifying appropriate disposal and treatment sites for eight major centres (CEP, 1998b).

Soil studies undertaken in 1993 in two important agricultural regions found significant heavy metal contamination and high concentrations of persistent organochlorine pesticide residues (Pilidis *et al.*, 1996). In February 1996 and April 1997 a total of four people died and 26 exhibited signs of lead intoxication in rural areas after eating flour contaminated from the repair of a mill's cracked grindstone using metallic lead (Tabaku and Panariti, 1996; Panariti and Bërxholi, 1998). Studies of children living in Berat, location of the country's battery plant, have also found high blood-lead concentrations (Tabaku *et al.*, 1998).

The impact of untreated urban domestic and industrial waste, offshore discharges, and pollution originating in Italy, Yugoslavia and Greece have begun to take their toll on Albania's marine environment. The polluted nature of water adjacent to the ports of Shëngjin, Durrës, Vlorë and Sarandë, where waste and spillages from vessels are locally problematic, has increasingly impacted upon nearby resorts. This is exacerbated by the discharge of polluted rivers reaching the Adriatic coast. At the latter, for example, high concentrations of heavy metals have been found (Babi *et al.*, 1998). Offshore oil and gas exploration has been taking place since the early 1990s; although no commercially exploitable deposits have been found, impacts from these activities need to be monitored carefully.

Albania–EU relations

Although a trade and economic co-operation agreement (TCA) came into force in December 1992, the European Commission concluded in 1995 that a classical Europe Agreement with Albania could not be envisaged, notably for economic reasons.

Albania received almost ECU 400 mn of EU grants for 1991–95 within the framework of the PHARE programme and is the CEE country that most benefited per capita from EU assistance. Albania has been a full member of the Council of Europe since July 1995 and has participated actively in NATO's Partnership for Peace programme (European Commission, 1996).

In the wake of the 1998–99 Kosovo conflict, a Stability Pact for south-eastern Europe was drawn up in Cologne in June 1999 between the western powers and international financial institutions,

Russia and the south-east European states, with the objective of establishing 'lasting peace, prosperity and stability' in the region. This looked to the co-ordination of international relations and confidence-building measures through such frameworks as the BSECC. Notably, the EU began formulating a common strategy toward the western Balkans with the longer-term prospect of Albania gaining EU membership on the basis of the Treaty of Amsterdam and the Copenhagen criteria. In October 1999 the European Commission recommended a strategy, which, in the wake of Kosovo, recognised the need 'to confirm the vocation for membership' of countries of former Yugoslavia and Albania but under strict conditions. In addition to the Copenhagen criteria, these countries would be required to mutually recognise each other's borders, settle all issues relating to the treatment of national minorities and pursue economic integration in a regional framework as a precondition for their integration within the EU.

As part of the stability pact, Albania's needs for external finance would be addressed by the IMF, the World Bank, the EBRD and the EIB, as well as by bilateral assistance programmes and project finance. The Albanian armed forces and police would be retrained with the support of the Western European Union and the south-east European defence ministers group. Although Albania's candidature for NATO could not be tabled before 2002, NATO personnel (AFOR–2) would remain stationed in Albania, principally to protect communications into Kosovo, while Albanian weapons systems would be aligned to NATO standards (EIU, 1999c: 16–17).

Albania should therefore benefit from the Stability Pact for south-eastern Europe. Whereas the country had made little progress toward EU membership prior to the Kosovo crisis, spurred on by a post-Kosovo President Prodi, the European Commission subsequently sought ways to accelerate the process and to offer interim arrangements that were previously unattainable. A component of the stability pact is a new form of contractual relationship which Albania will achieve, a Stabilisation and Association Agreement (EIU, 1999b: 6).

Conclusion

Entry into the world political and economic arena, transformation to elements of a market economy, and programmes for privatisation are familiar in much of central and eastern Europe. In Albania, however, these processes have followed some distance behind those of the rest of the region, reflecting the deeper ideological nature and inertia of the old Albanian regime, the country's hitherto relative isolation and its low level of economic development and technological sophistication. Periods of domestic disruption in 1991–92 and from 1997, together with the impacts of events in Kosovo and other neighbouring regions, have further constrained the efficacy of post-communist social, economic and political restructuring processes.

The integration of Albania within a relatively stable and diversified pan-European framework would appear vital. However, a necessary prerequisite for accepting Albania as a member of the common European home is the establishment of conditions for domestic stability and the democratic rule of law. While the Albanian authorities need to address the fundamental questions of establishing a rule of law and sustaining a civil society that can be embraced within the common European home, the West can assist that process, not only through technical assistance, training programmes and further injections of appropriately targeted capital, but also in sustaining more positive conceptions of Albania and the Albanian people.

Albania's enhanced Balkan role within the framework of stability pact should assist that process. Several questions remain unanswered, however. Will the EU countenance membership negotiations with Albania before both the Union's internal reforms and the embracing of the dozen candidates have taken place? Can the incentive of possible EU accession overcome historic hostilities in the Balkans? And particularly pertinent for Albania, how will the EU proceed with the candidature of that much larger Muslim country, Turkey, which historically has had such an influence on Albania?

References

Ackerman, E. A., 1938, Albania – a Balkan Switzerland. *Journal of Geography*, 38 (7), 253–262.

Anon, 1996, Albania. *Eastern Europe Newsletter*, 10 (2), 7.

Anon, 1997, Polio outbreak – Albania 1996. *European Journal of Pediatrics*, 156 (1), 77.

Babi, D., Celo, V., Cullaj, A., Pano, N., 1998, Evaluation of the heavy metals pollution of the sediments of Vlora Bay Adriatic Sea, Albania. *Fresenius Environmental Bulletin*, 7 (9–10), 577–84.

CEP (Committee for Environmental Protection), 1998a, *International cooperation*. Tirana: CEP.

CEP, 1998b, *The situation of forests and protected areas*. Tirana: CEP.

Deslondes, O., Sivignon, M., 1995, Albanian agriculture – from the cooperative to subsistence farming. *Revue d'Études Comparatives Est–Ouest*, 26 (3), 143–157.

DPA (Deutsche Presse Agenteur), 1998, Albania has quit the OIC, says Prime Minister. *The Indian Express*, 18 August. http://www.indian-express.com/ie/daily/19980818/23050664p.html.

EBRD, 1999a, *EBRD activities in Albania*. London: EBRD. http://www.ebrd.com/english/opera/COUNTRY/albaact.htm.

EBRD, 1999b, *Transition report 1999*. London: EBRD.

EIU, 1996, *Bulgaria, Albania: country profile 1995–96*. London: EIU.

EIU, 1999a, *Albania: country profile 1999–2000*. London: EIU.

EIU, 1999b, *Albania: country report 3rd quarter 1999*. London: EIU.

EIU, 1999c, *Albania: country report 4th quarter 1999*. London: EIU.

Elbirt, C., 1997, Albania under the shadow of the pyramids. *Transition*, 8 (5), 8–10.

European Commission, 1996, *EU–Albania relations*. Washington DC: European Commission. http://www.eurunion.org/legislat/extrel/cec/albania.htm.

Giorgio, S., 1994, *Farm survey*. Tirana: Republic of Albania Ministry of Agriculture and Food/FAO.

Hall, D. R., 1994, *Albania and the Albanians*. London: Frances Pinter.

Hall, D. R., 1996, Albania: rural development, migration and uncertainty. *GeoJournal*, 38 (2), 185–189.

Hall, D. R., 1999, Representations of place: Albania. *Geographical Journal*, 165 (3), 161–172.

IMF, 1994, *IMF economic reviews no. 5: Albania*. Washington DC: IMF.

Korovilas, J. P., 1999, The Albanian economy in transition: the role of remittances and pyramid investment schemes. *Post-Communist Economies*, 11 (3), 399–415.

Lawson, C., Saltmarshe, D., 2000, Security and economic transition: evidence from North Albania. *Europe–Asia Studies*, 52 (1), 133–148.

Lemel, H., 1998, Rural land privatisation and distribution in Albania: evidence from the field. *Europe–Asia Studies*, 50 (1), 121–140.

Liolin, A. E., 1997, The nature of faith in Albania toward the 21st century. *East European Quarterly*, 31 (2), 181–194.

Lucey, T., 1999, The Plunkett Foundation. *Besa*, 3 (2), 14.

Ministry of Tourism and EBRD, 1993, *Albania: investing in tourism*. Tirana/London: Albanian Ministry of Tourism/EBRD.

Panariti, E., Bërxholi, K., 1998, Lead toxicity in humans from contaminated flour in Albania. *Veterinary and Human Toxicology*, 40 (2), 91–92.

Pilidis, G., Ioannidou, A. G., Saraci, M., Stalikas, C., 1996, Determination of organochlorine pesticides and selected heavy metals in Albanian soils. *Fresenius Environmental Bulletin*, 5 (9–10), 551–556.

Republic of Albania, 1996, *Public investment programme 1996–1998*. Tirana: Council of Ministers Department of Economic Development and Aid Coordination.

Sjöberg, Ö., 1991, *Rural change and development in Albania*. Oxford: Westview.

Smeets, H., Caushi, N., Alikaj, E., 1997, Infant and maternal mortality in Albania. *European Journal of Public Health*, 7 (3), 279–283.

Tabaku, A., Panariti, E., 1996, Lead intoxication in rural Albania. *Veterinary and Human Toxicology*, 38 (6), 434–435.

Tabaku, A., Bizgha, V., Rahlenbeck, S. I., 1998, Biological monitoring of lead exposure in high risk groups in Berat, Albania. *Journal of Epidemiology and Community Health*, 52 (4), 234–236.

Tarifa, F., 1995, Albanian road from communism: political and social change, 1990–1993. *Development and Change*, 26 (1), 133–162.

TDA, 1998, *South Balkan Development Initiative*. Washington DC: TDA. http://www.tda.gov/region/sectoral/balkan.html.

Trix, F., 1994, The resurfacing of Islam in Albania. *East European Quarterly*, 28 (4), 533–549.

23

MOLDOVA

David Turnock

This chapter starts with a political summary tracing the origins of the state from the transfer of Bessarabia (the easternmost part of the Principality of Moldavia) from Ottoman suzerainty to Russian rule in 1812. After a parliamentary decision to join Romania after the First World War, Soviet rule was maintained from 1944 until 1990, since when Moldova has decided to go it alone. A review of Moldovan politics is dominated by the problem of the Transdniestria province where the Russian–Ukrainian majority insists on a degree of autonomy that is almost tantamount to independence. Economic problems arise from the high level of dependence on agriculture, following Soviet specialisation (though the situation is made worse by the location of much of the modest industrial capacity in Transdniestria), and the continued dependence on the Russian market gave Moldova little choice but to join the Commonwealth of Independent States (CIS). Finally there is a reference to severe social problems, underpinned by the deep economic recession, and a note on the trappings of international statehood, which provide some compensation for the problematic economic outlook.

A brief history

Moldova consists of part of the former territory of Bessarabia (between the Prut and Nistru/Dniester rivers) plus a strip of land on the eastern side of the Nistru known as Transdniestria (Figure 23.1). Bessarabia was an integral part of the medieval principality of Moldavia, which joined with Wallachia to form the independent state of Romania (proclaimed in 1877). But the province was ceded by the Ottoman Empire (then the suzerain power) to Russia in 1812 under the Treaty of Bucharest. After the collapse of the Russian Empire at the end of the First World War, Bessarabia declared itself an independent republic in 1918 and subsequently voted to became part of Greater Romania, a decision recognised in the Treaty of Paris (1920). But the Soviet Union (formed in 1922) did not accept the decision and demanded the return of the province in 1940. Romania almost immediately regained control in 1941, with German support, but the Soviets' will was again imposed in 1944 as the Second World War drew to a close. Meanwhile, Transdniestria was set up by the Soviets as the Moldavian Autonomous

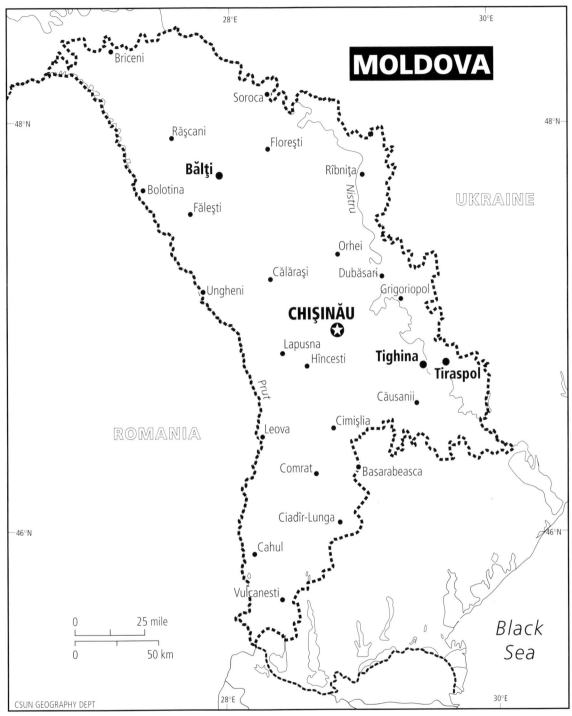

Figure 23.1: Moldova

Soviet Socialist Republic (within Ukraine) as part of an ideological offensive against Romania. But when the two territories were eventually brought together in 1940 and again in 1944 as the Moldavian Soviet Socialist Republic (SSR), now separate from Ukraine, the southernmost districts of Bessarabia, lying along the Danube's Chilia distributary, were allocated to Ukraine as compensation. The state comprises 33,900 sq km. The capital, Chișinău (Kishinev in Russian), had a population of 667,000 in 1989 and three cities have over 100,000 inhabitants: Tiraspol (186,000), Bălți (159,000) and Tighina (133,000).

Heavy 'Russification' took place in Bessarabia in the late 19th century and there was much immigration from Russia and Ukraine (Hamm, 1998). Russian became the official language and the Cyrillic script was used. Nevertheless, Romanians remained in a majority, and it was not surprising that they favoured union with Romania when the tsarist empire collapsed. However, cultural change was further accentuated after the Second World War. A total of 450,000 Russians moved in during the late 1940s and early 1950s, thus balancing deportations of 300,000 Romanians in the 1940s, mainly to central Asia. There was also a Soviet-inspired cultural policy that sought to protect the Romanians of Moldova as a distinct ethnic group, with cultural traits 'engineered' to suit the political concept of a border territory where Romanians, Russians and Ukrainians intermingled. This brought about a Slavicisation of the Romanian language, now designated 'Moldovan', with the Cyrillic script reinstated. Although the native language was still taught in the schools, Russian was the official language: it was widely seen as offering better career prospects and its importance for party business ensured that Russians and Ukrainians would be prominent in the professions. During the Stalin period even Romanian origins were played down, and separation from Romania was reinforced by strict frontier controls, while central planning emphasised the delivery of sugar, sunflower oil, tobacco and wine to other parts of the USSR.

The collapse of the USSR gave the Romanians of Moldova another historic opportunity, but the situation in the 1990s was very different from what it had been 70 years earlier and another union with Romania could not, therefore, be taken for granted. Moldovans now made up only 65 per cent (2.79 million) of the population of 4.33 million, while Slavs (essentially Russians – 562,000 or 13.0 per cent and Ukrainians – 600,000 or 13.8 per cent) made up just over a quarter; leaving 154,000 Gagauz (3.5 per cent), 88,000 Bulgarians (2 per cent), 66,000 Jews (1.5 per cent) and 71,000 others (1.6 per cent). Nevertheless, during the Gorbachev *glasnost* era the local Communist Party re-established Moldovan as the official language (the Soviet Union's only Romance language) in 1987. This prompted public pressure for restoration of the Latin alphabet, for Romanian being given the status of official language and for an end to immigration. Independent cultural and political groupings came together in 1989 to form the Popular Front of Moldova and demonstrations later in the year led to the replacement of first secretary Grossu by Petru Lucinschi. The elections of February 1990 for the Supreme Soviet did not allow for pluralism, but Communist Party candidates made their views clear on ethnic issues, and parliament was dominated by deputies with nationalist sympathies: Mircea Snegur of the Popular Front of Moldova (PFM) was elected chairman and the appointment of reformist prime ministers (Mircea Druc and later Andrei Sangheli) paved the way for rapid change. Declarations of sovereignty (June 1990) and independence (August 1991) marked the break-up of the USSR, and Snegur became the first president later in the year. There was a presumption that close ties would develop with Romania, with eventual unification as a distinct possibility. Romanian history and culture became part of the school curriculum, educational exchanges started with Romanian schools, and Russian language schools declined (King, 1994; Miller, 1994).

The politicising of education by 'Moldovanisation' (as if it were a distinct language, not even a Romanian dialect) led to protests in 1995 by students seeking recognition of an explicitly Romanian designation. But more significantly, the new political orientation was strongly opposed from the other side by minority groups: Bulgarians and Gagauz Turks in the southwest; Russians and Ukrainians in the east. In both areas there was a clear indication that independence would be sought if Chişinău were to persist with its pro-Romania policy. Indeed, Transdniestria did separate in 1992 after civil war (and after refusing to implement the language law), and re-establishing unity is the country's major problem. Policy has been reassessed and the dream of union with Romania is now effectively dead, with only a small fraction of the population still actively supporting this policy. As Batt (1997) has argued, it might seem that the Moldovan élite is seeking compromise after breakaways in response to national and linguistic self-assertion. Nevertheless, reappraisal cannot be seen as a victory for Soviet 'denationalisation', for Moldovans still assert their links with the Romanians even though they do not see closer cultural contact as the inevitable prelude to political unification. There is an appreciation of the benefits of having Chişinău as a national capital with the option of policy developments in different directions (King, 1998; van Meurs, 1998). The Iliescu presidency in Romania did not treat Moldovan independence seriously. This caused some offence to Moldovans defending the authenticity of Moldovan culture and helped to strengthen pride in Chişinău as the seat of a national government (Crowther, 1992). Moldova has a unicameral parliament. According to the 1994 constitution towns and villages function as autonomous units with directly elected local governments (but co-ordinated by directly elected councils for the 40 administrative districts). Foreign relations with Romania are conducted between two equal states.

Moldovan politics and problems of separatism

The record is quite confused, with shifting alliances based on clannish rivalries (Crowther, 1997, 1998). Although most of the communist members returned in the Supreme Soviet elections of 1990 were sympathetic to the PFM, the party (renamed the Christian Democratic Popular Front in 1992) did very badly in the first elections held in independent Moldova in 1994, and in 1998 only just cleared the 4 per cent threshold to qualify for parliamentary seats. Meanwhile, the Agrarian Democratic Party, which gained 56 of the 104 seats in 1994 (with 43.2 per cent of the vote) and led a new government of national accord, was eliminated from parliament in 1998 by failing to get the required 4 per cent: the party splintered over the language issue when the leadership refused to support a proposed change from 'Moldovan' to 'Romanian', while shortcomings in government created friction with President Snegur, despite the fact that he was a former member of the ruling party. Voronin's Moldovan Party of Communists became the largest party in 1998, with slightly more than 30 per cent of the vote. However, the apparent turnaround in public opinion from a desire for union with Romania to close association with Russia and the CIS, with reinforcement of state planning and a review of the results of privatisation (as advocated by the communists), is explained largely by the fragmentation of the reformist centre-right into groups, each led by an influential personality: the Democratic Convention (26 seats) is linked with the former president (Mircea Snegur); the Party for a Democratic and Prosperous Moldova (24 seats) is led by the present president, Petru Lucinschi, elected in 1996; and the Party of Democratic Forces (11 seats) is close to the Democratic Convention, though not supportive of union with Romania. However, despite the natural centre-right majority, parliament has not backed reform wholeheartedly. Following the resignation of prime minister Ciubuc in February 1999 (he replaced Sangheli in 1997 after the latter unsuccessfully ran for president the previous year), the reform-minded Urecheanu (mayor of Chişinău) failed to win parliamentary approval and a second reformist candidate, Deputy Prime Minister Sturza, was approved with the narrowest of margins. Meanwhile, President Lucinschi failed to get support in a referendum on a constitutional amendment giving him the right to form and lead the government.

In June 1992 Moldova introduced a coupon currency that circulated in parallel with the Russian rouble and became the sole legal tender in July 1993 when Russia froze pre-1993 roubles. The Moldovan leu was introduced in November 1993, backed by foreign exchange reserves and loans from the International Monetary Fund (IMF). It remained remarkably stable until 1998, appreciating against major currencies, which helped to control inflation although exports were hindered to some extent. However, the main problems have been in the political domain, with secession on two fronts (Forsberg, 1995). The Gagauz Turks in the Comrat area wanted cultural, linguistic and political autonomy, but following the draft 1994 constitution providing for autonomy in three southern districts – with Gagauz as an official language alongside Moldovan and Russian – they agreed to participate in the 1994 national elections, thus formally 'returning' to Moldova (Socor, 1994). Following the new parliament's approval of the constitution, an 'Autonomous Territorial Unit' was created for Gagauz Yeri (Gagauzia) in 1995, giving 153,000 Turkic Christians the right of self-determination (thus protecting the region should Moldova ever seek greater integration with Romania). Gagauz Yeri has its own Popular Assembly elected every four years. Executive authority rests with a directly elected 'bashkan' or governor, Gheorghe Tabunshchik, and an executive committee (Chinn and Roper, 1998; Socor, 1994).

But a much more intractable problem arose in Transdniestria (TD) where Russians and Ukrainians form a majority in the 700,000 community that declared itself an autonomous region in September 1990. They subsequently opted for independence when a separate 'Dniester SSR' was established at Tiraspol to safeguard their position in a Moscow-dominated world from the Romanianising policies of Chişinău (Grimm, 1997; Selivanova, 1996). After the failed *coup* in Moscow (which the Dniester SSR supported) the Dniester Republican Guard took over and even established a bridgehead at Tighina on the western side of the river. Civil war broke out in January 1992. Romania helped Moldova (for the Moldovan army was very small and the police and internal troops bore the brunt of the fighting), while remnants of the Russian 14th Army (led by Lt General Aleksandr Lebed) supplied arms to the separatists who controlled all the territory east of the Dniester plus the Tighina bridgehead on the western side. The 14th Army drew the Russians into the struggle, and they openly joined the separatists after the visit by Russian vice-president Aleksandr Rutskoi, who supported independence. But in July 1992 Yeltsin and Snegur signed a ceasefire agreement providing for a joint peacekeeping group of Russian, TD and Moldovan forces, with security zones on either side of the river. In October 1994, following the provision for autonomy in the Moldovan constitution and the failure of talks between Moldova and TD to resolve the issue of Russian troops, Russia and Moldova signed an agreement for Russian troop withdrawals to be effective within three years. But the Russian parliament has not yet ratified the agreement (despite downgrading of the 14th Army in 1995 to a level of 6,000 troops). Meanwhile, TD has gone its own way under the authoritarian control of its 'president' Igor Smirnov (re-elected 1996). Of the votes cast in a 1995 referendum 82.7 per cent endorsed independence (and 89.7 per cent supported membership of CIS as an independent state, though the CIS did not accept this). The territory remains an effective autonomous area and enjoys significant Russian support (which includes subsidised energy), although movement across the river for civilians is usually straightforward. The Cyrillic script is retained and there is a separate coupon currency and central bank. However, the value of the local rouble has fallen rapidly in the context of a command-style economy (Kolsto and Malgin, 1998; Socor, 1993).

Despite the agreement in 1997 providing for economic co-operation and reconciling autonomy for TD with the unity and territorial integrity of Moldova, people still seek a measure of autonomy barely indistinguishable from full sovereignty (Garnett and Lebenson, 1998). However, the momentum for NATO enlargement contributes to acceptance of a wider scope for conflict management, and there is now mediation by Ukraine as well as by Russia; there is even the possibility of Ukrainian peacekeeping forces supplementing Russian troops already on the ground (though this is opposed by the Russian military and parliament). Russia tolerates

Ukrainian involvement and also accepts a role for the Organization for Security and Co-operation in Europe (OSCE). Solving outstanding differences with Romania has strengthened Ukraine's position in TD negotiations. In January 1997 the newly elected Lucinschi made an unofficial visit to the Crimea and asked Ukraine's President Kuchma to take a more active role in the TD conflict. Soon afterwards a customs union between Moldova and Ukraine was set up, and Kuchma called for the withdrawal of Russian troops from TD. Ukrainian participation now seems assured in view of the wider context of Moldova–Romania and Ukraine–Romania friendship treaties (1997) and the formation of a GUAM group linking Georgia, Ukraine, Azerbaijan and Moldova ('seeking to integrate into transatlantic and European structures'), which could internationalise the TD issue to include the USA and the EU (Kaufman and Bowers, 1998).

The economy

Production collapsed in the early 1990s when the Moldovan economy had to cope with a bad balance of payments shock arising from very close interdependence with other parts of the former Soviet Union (FSU). This was compounded by adverse terms of trade: energy prices rose to world levels; farmers depended on imported fertilisers and feedstuffs. Armed conflict in TD provoked a budget deficit, as Moldova was deprived of its industrial heartland (some 40 per cent all industrial capacity) and this meant a high level of dependence on agriculture. This would have been dangerous in any case, given the adverse terms of trade, but bad weather had precipitated a series of disasters. A good harvest in 1997 was followed by frost, drought and flood in 1998 (a long cold winter preceded drought during much of the growing season and heavy rain in the autumn) and similar extremes were experienced in 1992 and 1994. In this context reform has been difficult, but the country has benefited from generally sound financial management. Most prices were liberalised by the end of 1992; though action over energy was delayed until 1997 when prices rose sharply as subsidies were removed. Currency stabilisation was achieved in late 1993 and there was a further financial agreement with the IMF in 1995. Economic restructuring in 1998 included privatisation in the energy sector: 50 per cent ownership of Moldova-Gaz – including the pipeline network – was assigned to Russia's Gazprom in order to pay off debts. There has been much delay due to parliamentary obstruction, but promising trends in 1997 (with low inflation and political risk, a steady exchange rate and projected GDP growth) were overtaken by the collapse of the leu in November 1998: the central bank was forced to give up defending the currency, which instantly lost half its value.

This acute crisis was due to weak public finances combined with energy difficulties and a fall in the Russian market. Capital has been taken out, exchange rates have worsened and international currency reserves are critically low following a big decline in trade, especially in exports to CIS. Despite a generally very good anti-inflation record, there has been an inflationary spiral linked with excessive budget deficits, increased indebtedness and incomplete structural reform. A predicted fall in GDP (despite a good harvest in 1998) will mean a cut in welfare and public works plus a boost in tax collection and a likely increase in VAT, though the falling leu will at least keep food exports competitive in Russia. But there is no money to spend on a post-1998 election programme in view of debt-servicing demands and IMF pressure. All this is bad news for the president, who in 1997 promised accelerated reform and industrial restructuring, including a free zone in Chişinău, tax changes and land reform. Over privatisation Moldova seems to be lagging behind much of the FSU: local entrepreneurs have limited funds and foreign investors have shown relatively little interest. The Dacia restaurant in Chişinău was put up for auction 14 times and sold twice, but it has not been transferred to new ownership because money was not deposited within the stipulated period (seven banking days). It is important that the Telecom tender is concluded successfully in order to reverse the damage arising from the botched tobacco privatisation of 1996. This will pave the way for privatisation of the three existing electricity generators and five distributors expected late in 1999. A new agency is proposed to provide for house building and introduce a system of construction by instalments, which may succeed in attracting private savings.

The employment structure is dominated by agriculture and manufacturing, although their shares have fallen between 1995 and 1998: this follows the problems on large farms and the growth of largely unrecorded private sector activities (Table 23.1). Falling output in manufacturing, as well as restructuring, means higher unemployment, although there has been some growth in chemicals, metal processing and medical equipment since independence. Many workers in the larger enterprises are on unpaid leave at any one time (a total of 215,000 in 1998). Meanwhile, health and education, which have seen investment decline, show an increase in their shares of employment on the basis of slower absolute decline. Only administration shows both absolute and relative increase. Industry (excluding food processing) accounts for a quarter of employment. Under the command system, output was maximised and subsidised, but following the change of regime demand collapsed, subsidies were reduced or eliminated and input prices rose. Restructuring is necessary, but market discipline has been slow to take effect because budget constraints have not been binding and arrears have mounted. However, there is little working capital, and barter is common because managers fear that any monetary payments received might be confiscated by creditors: it is thought that only a third to a fifth of transactions are in money.

Agriculture

There is a good basis for agriculture with long, warm summers and relatively mild winters (average temperatures in Chişinău range from 21 °C in July to -4 in January), though the fertile chernozem soils are considerably eroded after high-intensity farming and fertilisation.

Table 23.1 Moldova: employment, 1995–1998

Employment category	1995				1998			
	A	B	C	D	A	B	C	D
Agriculture and related	560.3	43.5	95.1	17.3	411.2	39.8	130.1	46.3
Manufacturing	185.5	14.4	42.0	23.8	125.1	12.1	37.1	42.1
Education	154.8	12.0	9.0	5.9	142.5	13.8	9.2	6.9
Health and social services	93.3	7.3	8.2	8.8	86.7	8.4	6.6	8.2
Construction	50.8	3.9	9.9	20.3	29.8	2.9	11.0	58.8
Wholesale and retail trade	49.0	3.8	30.3	37.1	40.6	3.9	6.0	17.4
Transport and communications	48.5	3.8	8.0	12.0	56.3	5.4	8.2	17.1
Real estate activity	33.2	2.6	2.8	8.4	27.9	2.7	2.1	8.3
Administration	26.8	2.1	0.7	2.6	52.0	5.0	1.0	1.9
Electricity/Gas/Water	20.9	1.6	0.7	3.3	22.7	2.2	1.3	6.0
Other	63.7	5.0	14.4	22.6	70.5	3.8	2.4	3.4
Total	1286.8	100.0	192.3	15.1	1065.3	100.0	215.0	26.3

These figures exclude Transdniestria.

A: Employees '000.

B: Employees as a percentage of national total.

C: Permanent workers ('000) not on the payroll (i.e. unpaid leave as well as people sick or on maternity leave).

D: C as a percentage of A.

Source: *Bobeica* et al., *1998*

Excluding TD, agriculture (with forestry and fishing) and processing accounted for 60 per cent of GDP in 1996 – and just under half the employment – compared with 25 per cent for industry. There has been a sharp decline in livestock numbers: cattle from 949,000 in 1990 to 483,000 in 1997 and pigs from 1.67 million to 728,000 (though sheep and goat numbers have remained stable). Although there is a dependence on imported feed, experts believe that livestock would be more efficiently used in the production of dairy products and that the tendency to sell off livestock needs to be revised.

In the crop sector there has been a sharp decline in area and yield for fruit, grapes and vegetables (the main resource-intensive crops) while output of low capital-intensive crops with a guaranteed market (wheat and sunflowers) peaked in 1996 or 1997 (Table 23.2). Some vineyards were uprooted during the Soviet anti-alcohol campaign in the 1980s, but new plantings are now being made as the wine industry has attracted investment. There are problems with tobacco because the huge loss of markets in the FSU gives farmer-producers little incentive to cultivate a 'strategic' crop when prices are falling. There is now a National Programme for Tobacco Sector Development 1998–2003, with investment in growing seedlings and in upgrading facilities for tobacco drying, sorting and packing (following concern expressed over insufficient infrastructure). Food accounts for 75 per cent of exports, but international competitiveness is constrained by lack of a low-inflation environment and by the need for restructuring of the agri-food sector and of rural credit for viable enterprises. In WTO (World Trade Organization) accession negotiations Moldova might expect some limited protection for agriculture with regard to fruit juice, vegetable and wine products (Hare, 1998).

Table 23.2 Moldova: production of main agricultural commodities, 1989–1998 ('000 tonnes)

	1989–91	1992	1993	1994	1995	1996	1997	1997[a]	1998[a]
Cereals[b]	2 989.2	2 099.8	3 340.2	1 753.8	2 668.9	2 010.0	3 519.0	3 180.0	2 488.0
Sunflowers	234.4	197.2	194.1	149.2	231.6	316.0	201.0	175.0	199.0
Sugar beet	2 749.3	1 973.4	2 248.7	1 526.7	2 083.6	1 917.0	1 873.0	1 748.0	1 455.0
Potatoes	349.9	310.8	725.9	474.7	400.7	383.0	441.0	391.2	412.0
Vegetables	na	787.5	777.2	598.5	604.7	393.0	419.0	355.0	500.0
Tobacco	65.7	45.0	50.2	42.0	27.2	19.0	na	24.0	25.0
Fruit	924.9	511.3	1 087.8	665.1	609.7	573.0	1 055.0	946.6	388.0
Grapes	917.3	823.8	927.8	670.2	875.5	189.0	310.0	300.8	339.0
Meat	na	334.4	262.1	225.7	198.9	189.0	na	147.0	148.0
Milk	na	1 135.0	976.0	908.7	837.0	744.0	666.0	597.4	583.0
Eggs (mn)	na	812.5	617.8	514.5	563.0	610.0	582.0	512.4	538.0

[a] Excluding Transdniestria.

[b] After purification.

Source: *Bobeica* et al., *1998*

With privatisation slow, the state continues to subsidise agriculture. This is very costly, especially in the case of *kolkhozes,* which are among the most indebted enterprises in the sector. 'The prevalence of soft-budget constraints, inter-enterprise arrears, debt write-offs and direct commodity credits to the agricultural sector are costly incentive-distorting interventions which are probably financially unsustainable in the medium term' (Davis, 1998: 89). Peasants are placed under heavy social pressure to remain within the *kolkhoz.* If they insist on leaving, they are allocated the worst land and machinery (even tractor parts!); yet the state does not seem to want to impose legislative order. From 1995 (when privatisation began) to the beginning of 1999 local administrations received requests from 310,000 people asking for private holdings. Of these, 241,000 have received land and 48 per cent have set up some 80,000 private farms with a combined area of 153,000 ha: 1.9 ha on average, consisting of 1.49 ha arable with 0.22 ha of vineyards and 0.19 ha of orchards. Meanwhile 52 per cent of the successful applicants have not yet registered agricultural enterprises. The business environment is not very supportive: private farmers do not have access to adequate financing on preferential terms and thus face high input supply costs, often operating in the least viable areas despite contributing 52 per cent of agricultural output in 1997 (67 per cent in the case of animal production).

Small farms give more attention to maize, due to the fodder value of the crop, and therefore grow less wheat. They also produce fewer industrial crops, although they appreciate profitability and intend to grow more. However, a problem may lie in poor access to the market network as well as in other barriers to competition with larger producers. New peasant farms face difficulties through lack of input (machinery/equipment), skills and reliable information. Continuing reduction in livestock numbers is being linked in part with privatisation and with the difficulty in distributing all relevant assets. It may be that any enterprises requiring indivisible assets will be abandoned no matter what their potential market demand may be. But all farms find difficulties with finance and marketing. World Bank credits (seeking to promote competition between commercial banks) are being allocated through the Rural Finance Corporation, linked with savings and credit associations (SCAs) which provide loans to farmers based on members' savings and other borrowed money. The SCAs were initiated in 1997 with the financial support of the Soros Foundation and the Dutch government. There is, however, increased competition over input supply through private commercial firms providing imported inputs. And progress is being made: there are now alternatives to the state procurement organisation, although this mainly benefits the large farms because private farms make much use of local markets.

Foreign affairs and trade

Moldova is running a trade deficit, especially with non-CIS countries, and must look to every opportunity to sell more abroad. Parliament was much preoccupied in 1998–99 with the merits of reform and the options for alignment: the CIS to the east or Romania to the west. But there is a realisation that Romania cannot provide an effective alternative to economic integration within the CIS, membership of which was negotiated in 1991 and finally ratified by the Chişinău parliament in 1994 (reversing the negative vote the previous year). Moldova believes that the CIS is a genuine commonwealth free of excessive Russian domination; it is also seen as a reliable source of energy and a market for agricultural produce and light manufactures though Moldova will not participate in CIS military structures or monetary union. At the same time, economic co-operation with Romania has grown rapidly following a free trade agreement signed in 1995. The Romanian link provides 'unconditional' support for membership of European structures: Moldova became a member of NATO's Partnership for Peace programme but has not applied to join the alliance itself (Dumbraveanu-Andone and Dumitrache, 1997). Moldova has also declined participation in the Cernavodă nuclear programme, preferring to generate capacity in Moldova itself: the main power station of Moldovaneasca is in TD territory, although it supplies a Moldovan grid reintegrated in 1992. Alsthom of France is now involved in a 300 MW electric power plant for the Budeşti suburb of Chişinău (125 MW by the end of 2000). The total cost is $70 mn and loans are being provided by the International Finance Corporation, the EBRD and western commercial banks. The aim is to support the energy-starved local market with a small margin for export. The 22 billion cubic metres of gas found in southern Moldova could make the country self-sufficient and eliminate part of the burden arising from the need to import 40 per cent of the electricity consumed. Moldova is keen to build an oil terminal on the Danube at Giurgiuleşti (between Galaţi and Reni) and work started in 1997. Ukraine pressed Moldova to invest in Reni, but it prefers to avoid transit costs and build a terminal on its own territory. Ukraine has now facilitated this by ceding a small area of land to provide the required river frontage. Hopefully this will mean cheaper energy and reduced dependence on Russia.

Moldova has pretensions as a regional trade and transit hub: a bridge between east and west. It could gain some benefit from Danubian trade (Schneidewind, 1997), also through the opening up of the 'Silk Route' using the Transport Corridor Europe–Caucasus–Central Asia (TRACECA) through Poti, Baku and Turkmenbashi to Uzbekistan and Kazakhstan (Celac, 1998), and the prospect of a substantial East–West trade in oil (Anon, 1998). Moldova is keen on the Euroregions, which integrate Moldovan, Romanian and Ukrainian border territories in the north (Upper Prut) and south (Lower Danube), and is interested in projects for the Galaţi and Iaşi free zones (1998) (Deică et al., 1998). A free-trade zone was also set up in Chişinău in 1996, and there were 62 resident companies by May 1998. Ukraine's customs deposit system (1998) severely impacted on Moldovan exports transiting to Russia, and Romania's ambitions to join the EU could undermine plans for a Danube delta free-trade area. But Ukraine has made concessions over the strategic railway junction of Basarabeasca and a 99-year lease has been granted in respect of eight kilometres of highway at Palanka in order to avoid a double customs examination.

Social problems

Moldova's population was 4.3 million in 1989, with females accounting for 52.4 per cent. More up-to-date figures are not available for TD, but information for the rest of the country shows a slight rise to just over 3.6 million in 1994, followed by a marginal decline to just 3.6 million in 1996. There is reduced life expectancy, a fall in natural increase and a high infant mortality linked with a deteriorating health infrastructure that has to cope with outbreaks of cholera and diphtheria. However, the younger age groups are increasing and more people are entering the labour market; hence the need for additional education and training and also for more employment opportunities. The welfare system is under strain with lower tax contributions and rising unemployment: the number of cars declined from 166,400 in 1993 to 163,900 in 1995 due to poverty and rising petrol prices (Shipley, 1999). Nominal wages only just outstrip inflation due to the large amount of labour employed in the former *kolkhozes*; many areas of industry are barely functioning. The workforce has to put up with arrears, payments in kind, unpaid leave and part-time employment. Agricultural work is low-paid and has become relatively poorer in terms of purchasing power. The exact situation is difficult to establish because there is both hidden unemployment through unpaid leave and hidden employment through a rising informal sector. However, the deep recession in the economy, with a widening gap between vacancies and unemployed, encourages people to seek work overseas: around 20,000 people are thought to be abroad at any one time, of which 15,000 are in Russia or other CIS countries.

Conclusion

When the Soviet Union broke up there seemed a good possibility that history might repeat itself through another reunion with Romania. But the Transdniestria problem – a throwback to the Soviet Union's ideological offensive against Romania in the inter-war years – stopped this movement in its tracks and Moldovans have now found the self-confidence to work out their own salvation. They remain frustrated over Transdniestria, where hardline politicians are able to take full advantage of somewhat lukewarm Russian support, and their economic policies reflect in full measure the ambivalence felt toward reform in countries that have not been favoured by foreign investors. There is no quick fix, but Moldova has built good relations with its neighbours and has found some satisfaction from membership of the international community to compensate for a somewhat bleak economic outlook.

It remains to be seen how Moldova will balance west European and Russian links in the future. Moldova is not an EU candidate country; although Romania is now within sight of accession negotiations, nobody east of the Prut will be getting excited about the notions of accelerated and broadened accession that emanated from the reconstituted European Commission during 1999.

References

Anon, 1998, The Pan-European zone of transport in the Black Sea region. *Romanian Business Journal*, 5 (36), 6.

Batt, J., 1997, Federalism versus nationalism in post-communist state-building: the case of Moldova. *Regional and Federal Studies*, 7 (3), 24–48.

Bobeica, V., Davis, J. R., Hare, P., eds, 1998 , *Moldova: economic trends – quarterly issue, Jan–Mar*. Brussels: European Expertise Service/Chişinău: Ministry of Economy and Reform.

Celac, S., 1998, Romania: a pivotal country along the Europe to Asia business route. *In* Erdeli, G., Dumbraveanu, D., eds, *Romanian–British geographical exchanges: proceedings of the third Romanian–British Colloquium*. Bucharest: Corint, pp. 13–18.

Chinn, J., Roper, S. D., 1998, Territorial autonomy in Gagauzia. *Nationalities Papers*, 26, 87–102.

Crowther, W., 1992, Romania and Moldavian political dynamics. *In* Nelson, D. N., ed., *Romania after tyranny*. Boulder CO: Westview, pp. 239–259.

Crowther, W., 1997, Moldova: caught between nation and empire. *In* Bremmer, I., Taras, R., eds, *New states, new politics*. New York: Cambridge University Press, pp. 316–349.

Crowther, W., 1998, Ethnic politics and the post-communist transition in Moldova. *Nationalities Papers*, 26, 147–164.

Davis, J. R., 1998, Restructuring Moldovan agriculture. *In* Bobeica, V., Davis, J. R., Hare, P., eds, *Moldova: economic trends – quarterly issue Jan–Mar*. Brussels: European Expertise Service/Chişinău: Ministry of Economy and Reform, pp. 89–94.

Deică, P., Alexandrescu, M., Dobraca, L., Nica-Guran, L., 1998, *Euroregiunile din Europa Centrala si de Est: zonele transfrontaliere de Romania*. Bucharest: Academia Romana, Institutul de Geografie.

Dumbraveanu-Andone, D., Dumitrache, L., 1997, Romania: a gateway to Europe. *In* Light, D., Dumbraveanu-Andone, D., eds, *Anglo–Romanian geographies: proceedings of the second Liverpool–Bucharest Geography Colloquium*. Liverpool: Liverpool Hope Press, pp. 89–98.

Forsberg, T., 1995, *Contested territory: border disputes on the edge of the former Soviet empire*. Aldershot: Edward Elgar.

Garnett, S. W., Lebenson, R., 1998, Ukraine joins the fray: will peace come to Trans-Dniestria? *Problems of Post-Communism*, 45 (6), 22–32.

Grimm, F. D., 1997, Transnistrien: ein postsowjetisches Relikt mit ungewissen Perspektiven. *Europa Regional*, 5 (2), 23–33.

Hamm, M. F., 1998, Kishinev: the character and development of a Tsarist frontier town. *Nationalities Papers*, 26, 19–38.

Hare, P. G., 1998, Trade regime and WTO accession. *In* Bobeica, V., Davis, J. R., Hare, P., eds, *Moldova: economic trends – quarterly issue Jan–Mar*. Brussels: European Expertise Service/Chişinău: Ministry of Economy and Reform, pp. 87–88.

Kaufman, S. J., Bowers, S. R., 1998, Transnational dimensions of the Transdniestrian conflict. *Nationalities Papers*, 26, 129–146.

King, C., 1994, Moldovan identity and the politics of Pan-Romanianism. *Slavic Review*, 53, 345–368.

King, C., 1998, Ethnicity and institutional reform: the dynamics of 'indigenization' in the Moldavian ASSR. *Nationalities Papers*, 26, 57–72.

Kolsto, P., Malgin, A., 1998, The Transnistrian Republic: a case of politicized regionalism. *Nationalities Papers*, 26, 103–128.

Miller, M. W., 1994, Moldova: a state-nation identity under post-communism. *Slovo*, 7 (1), 56–71.

Schneidewind, P., 1997, The Danube waterway as a key European transport resource. *In* Graute, U., ed., *Sustainable development for central and eastern Europe*. Berlin: Springer, pp. 127–144.

Selivanova, I. F., 1996, Trans-Dniestria. *In* Azrael, J. R., Pavin, E. A., eds, *US and Russian policymaking with respect to the use of force*. Santa Monica: RAND, pp. 57–73.

Shipley, G., 1999, Sink plus torches and toilet tissue: the rough guide to teaching in Moldova. *University of Warwick Open Studies Newsletter*, 30, 4.

Socor, V., 1993, Moldova's 'Dniester ulcer'. *Radio Free Europe/Radio Liberty Research*, 2 (1), 12–16.

Socor, V., 1994, Gagauz autonomy in Moldova: a precedent for Eastern Europe. *Radio Free Europe/Radio Liberty Research*, 3 (33), 20–28.

van Meurs, W., 1998, Carving a Moldovan identity out of history. *Nationalities Papers*, 26, 39–56.

24

BELARUS

David R. Marples

Belarus occupies a strategic position on the North European Plain between Russia and what is likely to become an eastern boundary of the EU (Figure 24.1). The country has a population of just over 10 million and its areal extent (207,600 sq km) is almost as great as Romania and nearly twice that of Bulgaria.

Although Belarus was hardly a developed nation-state at the time of its independence in 1991, there were some hopes that it would embark upon a programme of economic and democratic reforms. From 25 August 1991, when independence was declared, until January 1994 the *ipso facto* leader was Stanislau Shushkevich, the speaker of the parliament, a physicist by training and a man who appeared to have a good command of the issues of the day. Shushkevich, however, was never in a position of real authority. He faced constant opposition from a parliament made up of 85 per cent former Communist Party deputies and from Prime Minister Vyacheslau Kebich, an old Soviet-style leader. On the other hand, he was not popular among the opposition Belarusian Popular Front (BPF), which did not consider him sufficiently radical and willing to adhere to the stipulation that independent Belarus would be a neutral and nuclear-free nation.

Perhaps against his better judgement, Shushkevich was persuaded in January 1994 to agree to Belarus joining the CIS Collective Security Treaty that had been signed in Tashkent in May 1992. For several months he had resisted the notion of a military-security treaty with Russia. No sooner had this major compromise been reached than Shushkevich was removed from office on (trumped-up) charges of corruption. Subsequently, a new constitution was issued that stipulated the election of a president, and in June and July 1994 presidential elections took place. The winner was not Kebich, as widely predicted, but Alyaksandr Lukashenka, a former KGB border guard and state-farm chairman from the Mahileu region (some 240 km east of Minsk), although born in the Vitsebsk region. Lukashenka was chairman of a parliamentary commission on corruption, and at 39 was too young to be tainted either in this regard or through association with the Communist Party hierarchy.

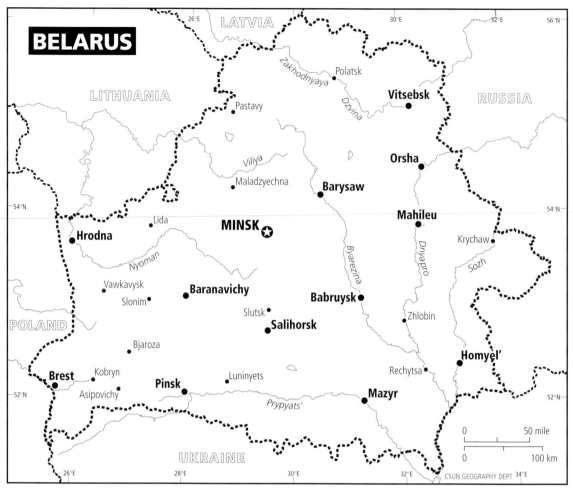

Figure 24.1: Belarus

To this point, Belarus had in truth taken few steps toward meaningful economic reforms. Nor was it very clear in which direction its foreign policy might lead. Also, under the new president it took some time for official policy to manifest itself. On 12 January 1995, for example, Foreign Minister Uladzimir Sianko signed an agreement with Brussels to join the NATO Partnership for Peace programme, by which Belarus agreed to remove its nuclear weapons to Russia for dismantling (Anon, 1995). One month later, Belarus signed a treaty of friendship and co-operation with the Russian Federation (Reuters, 1995a). Almost simultaneously, the EU Commission approved a proposal concerning the conclusion of a partnership and co-operation agreement between its member states and the Republic of Belarus. This followed a series of talks that had begun in 1993 and an initialled agreement after three sessions in December 1994. The agreement divided issues into Community and national control and began a political 'dialogue' with Belarus. It was indicated that the agreement would continue for an initial period of ten years, though with stipulations that it could be suspended if any of the clauses in the agreement (such as respect for human rights) were to be violated (European Commission, 1995).

The EU connection was fostered further in February 1995, when the two sides signed an agreement to promote trade relations and eventually develop an EU–Belarus customs union. The EU offered Lukashenka $97.5 mn in aid to assist reforms and the establishment of a market economy, though the Belarusian president appeared to indicate that the funds were needed mainly to offset environmental and health problems that had resulted from the 1986 disaster at the Chernobyl nuclear power plant (Reuters, 1995b). In April 1995 this agreement was ratified by the parliament of the 12th session in Minsk. In this year also, Belarus began to develop closer ties with its neighbours. These included, for example, visa-free travel between Belarus and Slovakia, and an agreement on co-operation in scientific and cultural matters between Belarus and Poland, which also included co-operation in customs procedures and the promotion of tourism (OMRI, 1995a, 1995b). Gradually, Belarus was paying more attention to its western neighbours. Thus, for approximately 20 months, the new Lukashenka administration appeared to be pursuing policies similar to those of its predecessor. They can be described as oriented toward Europe and Russia equally, with a gradualist approach to economic reforms and pedestrian privatisation. By comparison with what was to follow, however, this period can be regarded as the 'golden age' of pan-Europeanism in Belarus.

The Lukashenka administration was constantly frustrated by the limitations placed on the authority of the president through the constitution, and particularly the power of the constitutional court and the parliament (still known as the Supreme Soviet). In addition, the president personally declared himself to be a Russophile and a supporter of the now defunct Soviet Union. A myth was perpetuated that Lukashenka was the only deputy in the legislature to vote against the dissolution of the Soviet Union in December 1991. Through two referendums, the president significantly altered the *status quo* and in the process altered the 1994 constitution to provide himself with more powers. A referendum in the spring of 1995 raised Russian to the status of a state language (alongside Belarus), restored the Soviet flag (minus the hammer and sickle), gave the president the authority to dissolve parliament in certain instances and secured support for economic integration with Russia (see Marples, 1999: 73–74). The period 1995–96 also saw a crackdown on the opposition, the replacement of newspaper editors critical of or neutral toward the government, and the arrests of demonstrators.

In April 1996 Belarus and Russia formed a so-called Community of Sovereign Republics, by which the two countries agreed to co-ordinate their foreign policies, economy, transport and communication. The move seemed to signal that the Belarusian government was willing to give up its independence and merge with the Russian Federation. A year later this community was taken a step further when Russia and Belarus formed a union. Border controls were removed – indeed trains had not stopped at the border for some time, but now the border along the Minsk–Moscow highway was formally eliminated. (Further ramifications of this union are discussed below.) While purporting to give up independence, Belarus was enraging the Europeans with flagrant attacks on human rights and the usurpation of power by the presidency. A major conflict developed between the executive and the legislature (led by Speaker Semyon Sharetsky), which culminated in the referendum of November 1996. This referendum effectively changed the entire structure of government: reducing the parliament to a rump of 120 deputies (and thereby dissolving the parliament of the 13th session), creating a new upper assembly, revamping the constitutional court, and amending the constitution so that virtually all authority in the country rested with the president. Only token attention was paid to democratic procedures in the referendum.

As a result of these measures, Belarus began to be isolated from Europe. By mid-June 1996, for example, the EU Parliamentary Committee for Foreign Affairs asked the Union to suspend a provisional trade agreement with Belarus because of the assault on human rights (including the detention of protesters without trial) (Levshina, 1996). In mid-January 1997 the Council of Europe suspended Belarus's guest status, declaring that the new parliament had no legitimacy and that the new constitution (officially the amended constitution) issued in December 1996 did not respect the most minimal requirements of democracy. It was stated subsequently that a further reason for the suspension was the undemocratic way in which the November referendum had been undertaken (Reuters, 1997). Two months later, the North Atlantic Assembly (the inter-parliamentary organisation of NATO members) froze all links with Belarus, which up to that point had retained an associate membership. It noted that Lukashenka's tactics had ended the rule of law and dissolved the legitimate parliament (OMRI, 1997).

In October 1997 the new Belarusian foreign minister Ivan Antanovich (who was replaced in December 1998 by Ural Latypau), meeting with his Syrian counterpart, declared that Belarus had no interest in joining the European Union in the near future. Belarus was happy to establish equal relations with various European institutions, but essentially followed its own path (RFE/RL, 1997). What may be perceived as the final stage in the rift between Belarus and Europe occurred in the summer of 1998, when the ambassadors at the Drazdy complex just outside Minsk were evicted from their residences on the grounds that reconstruction was required to amend various problems there. Subsequently 11 ambassadors left Belarus: ten from the countries of the European Union plus the US ambassador. (German ambassador Horst Winkelmann was absent from Belarus at this time.) The reasons for this impasse remain unclear. The president portrayed himself as taking a strong stance against the West. At the same time, Belarus declared that the year 1997 had demonstrated an economic miracle: Belarus, in which only 20 per cent of enterprises had been privatised, had achieved a GDP growth rate of over 10 per cent, profits had risen by 11 per cent and the budget deficit amounted to only 2.2 per cent of the GDP. Thus the virtual separation from Europe occurred simultaneously with what appeared on paper to be a spectacular economic recovery, which gave credibility to the economic policy that could be termed 'the Lukashenka route'. Under these circumstances, the question is whether Belarus will really be affected by the expansion of the EU, or whether it can continue to maintain a command economy, monitored closely by the leadership, in union or partnership with Russia.

Impact of EU expansion

Economic and border issues

In the Soviet period Belarus played an important role within the Soviet economy. In the 1970s and 1980s its industrial output was significantly higher than the Union average. In the period of independence, however, its economy has contracted, and it has suffered because of the loss of immediate supplies and markets within the Soviet system. In addition, Belarus is dependent on imports for approximately 88 per cent of its energy needs. This fact alone has necessitated a reliance on Russia for imports of oil and gas, payment and prices for which have long remained the main item of dissension in Russian–Belarusian relations. Since 1995 Belarus has initiated a series of plans for closer coordination with Russia, from a customs union to a common currency. The latter was rejected by the Russian government late in 1995, but has been resurrected recently, though with no final date established for implementation. Belarus, however, has not begun a process of economic reform. The official parlance is that it is developing a 'socially oriented market economy', but in practice this resembles less one of the social democratic states of Europe, such as Germany or the United Kingdom, and more the old-style system reminiscent of the Soviet Union (e.g. see Nuti, 1999: 14–15).

Under Lukashenka, the system has grown closer to a command economy that remains reliant on former Soviet partners for trade. Of the present EU members, only Germany has any significant trade with Belarus (in 1996 representing 3.6 per cent of all Belarusian exports and 8.7 per cent of all imports). Russia still accounts for more than half of all Belarusian imports and exports, with Ukraine solidly in second place. In this respect, the expansion of the EU to the western border of Belarus will not in theory have a major impact on trade (see UNECE, 1999). The only exception is the case of Poland, where to the official figures (5.9 per cent of all Belarusian exports and 2.8 per cent of all imports) must be added black-market trading. Indeed, eastward movement of the EU boundary will curtail the unofficial or black-market trading that takes place on a wide scale between Belarus and Poland. In addition, Belarus's 'splendid isolation' can only succeed as long as the current rate of growth is maintained and relations with Russia continue on the basis of a barter relationship for the exchange of goods. In 1997 Russia accepted in barter form 70 per cent of the payments due for the supply of energy resources to Belarus (Bogdankevich and Romanchuk, 1998: 3). How authentic, then, is the Belarusian 'economic miracle' and how far can it be sustained?

Economists concur that the industrial growth of Belarus did take place as announced, but that growth is based on an 'unnatural' development of the economy. Industrial output had fallen in the period 1991–96 by 39 per cent, after which the president issued a series of decrees to 'persuade' enterprises to increase their output. In order to facilitate this, they were granted generous government subsidies, paid for not by foreign investment but by the simple process of credit allocation from the central bank and the fixing of prices for goods by presidential fiat. This, in turn, led to a rise in the inflation rate. In addition, it is clear that factories have been producing goods not for their quality and appeal to consumers, but to fulfil the demands of the government. As a result, inventories of goods are at peak levels and often the goods produced remain in storage for long periods (sometimes indefinitely). Thus market forces play little or no role in the development of the Belarusian economy. In 1997, it has been reported, about 30 per cent of Belarusian exports were in the form of barter, equal to some 35 per cent of industrial production. As noted, the total was significantly higher in the case of goods bartered for the import of energy products. The Russian giant company Gazprom became dissatisfied that only 10 per cent of the payment for supplies was in the form of cash and demanded that the figure be raised to 30 per cent (Biryuk *et al.*, 1998: 3).

The situation in foreign trade has proved similar. In the first half of 1999 Belarus achieved a more favourable trade balance than of late (-$144.2 mn) and exports exceeded imports by $21.5 mn. Its partners have remained the same, though there is some evidence that Belarus has been trying to export more products outside the CIS periphery, particularly to Latvia, Poland and Germany. However, as before, Russia is by far the major customer of Belarusian products ($1.22 bn), more than four times that of its nearest rivals taken together. Much of the trade is by barter, and barter deals are primarily responsible for the growth in Belarusian exports. The changes within the Belarusian economy remain baffling to most observers: thus GDP rose by 1 per cent in the first seven months of 1999, while real wages fell by 5 per cent; industrial output grew while purchases of raw materials abroad declined; production of foodstuffs rose by 11 per cent at the same time as agricultural production fell by 10 per cent (Zaiko, 1999). Clearly, the customs union with Russia has helped to finance the 'economic miracle'. Russia has also written off around $1.3 bn in debts, mainly for energy supplies (Marples, 1997). When Russia experienced a financial crisis in the autumn of 1998, the impact on Belarus was severe and almost instantaneous, though it was not of long duration.

It seems unlikely that Belarus can sustain its current rate of growth, and it is probable that the expansion of the EU will play a role in its slowdown. Though the presence of foreign companies in Belarus is meagre compared to the situation in neighbouring states, those that have established factories have fared relatively well, partly because of the cheapness of labour. None the less, the restrictions on trade with countries such as Poland and Latvia will have an impact and will serve to consolidate Belarusian reliance on its Russian partner. Moreover, the lack of economic reform in Belarus is in contrast to the situation in virtually all the states with which the country borders. The end of barter, of subsidies or of benign treatment from Russia, for whatever reason, would spell disaster in Belarus and isolate it economically. Under Lukashenka, Belarus has increasingly maintained a distance from the CIS. This was particularly the case during Boris Berezovsky's tenure as secretary general of the CIS (e.g. see Tomashevskaya, 1998). Indeed, Lukashenka has been so critical of this body that it seems evident the government is prepared to pursue a route of bilateral relations with the Russian Federation outside the CIS, in the hope that eventually other states – particularly Ukraine – may join the Russia–Belarus Union.

The question of borders has long been a sensitive one. Belarus has had grievances concerning the delineation of the border with Lithuania since 1939, but that border has remained visa-free until recently. Lithuania, however, has played a disproportionate role in serving as a refuge for Belarusian opposition leaders and as the home of a surrogate press. Two examples of this situation may suffice: until recently the only widely circulated opposition newspaper in Belarus, *Narodnaya Volya*, was printed and published in Lithuania because of the difficulties in Minsk. Second, when the speaker of the parliament of the 13th session, Semyon Sharetsky, became in the eyes of the opposition the *ipso facto* leader of the country with the expiry of President Lukashenka's mandate – he became the leader according to the stipulations of the original 1994 constitution – he fled to Vilnius, fearing that he was about to be arrested. In Vilnius he was provided with a bodyguard and a car, and generally given VIP treatment by the Lithuanian authorities.

Similarly Poland, which has a visa arrangement with Belarus, has also served as a refuge for Belarusians, including former speaker Shushkevich and the former BPF leader, Zyanon Paznyak. For three years Poland and Belarus have had consultations about a visa-free regime, and reports suggested that the two sides were close to an agreement (e.g. see Gulyakevich, 1998). Although relations between the two countries have generally been quite warm, no breakthrough took place on this question, and the extension of the EU is likely to end this discussion prematurely. From May 1999 Poland raised tariffs on Belarusian and Russian buses and trucks entering Poland from $11 to $100, much to the consternation of Belarus (Semenov, 1999). It is in the political dimension, however, that Belarus has become most isolated from Europe, and from Poland and Lithuania in particular. Let us turn, therefore, to the likely political impact of EU expansion.

Political impact

The political situation in Belarus is probably the most complex of all the post-Soviet states. On paper the situation appears self-evident. Belarus, under a would-be Soviet-style dictator, has turned the country back to its Russian neighbour, with the promotion of the Russian language and culture, the repression of national manifestations (the flag, culture, national symbols) and an apparent willingness to renounce independence in order to return to the Russian fold (e.g. see Goodspeed, 1999). Despite several versions of the union, however, and the potential signing of a final treaty in the near future, there is no indication that President Lukashenka has relinquished any of his powers, or for that matter the sovereignty of the country. At times he has grown irritated by what he perceives as the protraction by Russia of a final agreement. In addition, however, polls suggest that the union is far more popular among the public of the Russian Federation than among the citizens of Belarus. A poll published in the 3 May 1999 issue of *Naviny*, for example, indicates that 44.8 per cent of Belarusian residents support the union of Belarus and Russia in one state, while 43.6 per cent oppose it. In Minsk, the respective figures are 37.5 per cent and 49.7 per cent. Consequently, it is not surprising that the Belarusian president has emphasised repeatedly that within the planned union state, Belarus will retain its sovereignty and independence in full measure (e.g. see RFE/RL 1999).

The international community has not recognised the changes made by Lukashenka to the 1994 constitution. In general, it has supported the claims of the dissolved parliament – the parliament of the 13th session – to be the legitimate assembly in Belarus. Within the country also, the opposition declared that the mandate of the president had ended on 20 July 1999. (In the period 1988–97 the term opposition generally signified the BPF. By 1998–99 however, it signified the opposition united against Lukashenka, led by the United Civic Party, the Social Democratic Party, the BPF and sometimes even the communists.) Prior to that, the opposition had held an unofficial presidential election, a propaganda campaign to force the president to fulfil his democratic duties and authorise an official election. Lukashenka ignored the election, but its principal organiser, Viktar Hanchar, disappeared shortly afterwards and has not been seen since. Neither of the unofficial presidential candidates, Mykhail Chyhir and Zyanon Paznyak, actually did any campaigning. Chyhir was in jail on a trumped-up charge of embezzlement during his period as prime minister, while Paznyak (who withdrew during the final week of the campaign) remained in exile in Poland (see Padhol and Marples, 1999). Hanchar was one of four leading oppositionists to disappear during the year, illustrating the increasingly repressive nature of the regime. Under these circumstances, the Organization for Security and Co-operation in Europe (OSCE) decided to initiate a dialogue between the government and the opposition, using as the intermediary its advisory and monitoring group in Minsk, under the leadership of the German diplomat, Ambassador Hans Georg Wieck.

In the short term, therefore, the expanded EU is likely to stop at the Belarusian border; and in the present climate even the possibility of associate membership for Belarus seems remote. The coincidental expansion of the North Atlantic Treaty Organization (NATO) has long been a concern for Lukashenka. In April 1999, at the height of the NATO war in Yugoslavia, Lukashenka flew to Belgrade and appeared publicly with Serbian leader, Slobodan Milošević (Pecherskiy, 1999). Subsequently, both Yugoslavia and Russia appeared to favour the idea of Yugoslavia joining the Russia–Belarus Union. In Lukashenka's opinion, the inclusion of Yugoslavia – and possibly also other states (Ukraine was always foremost in his mind) – in the union could act as a counterweight to the all-embracing authority of NATO. However, the request to enlarge the union was rejected by the Russian side.

Conclusion

One economist (Zaiko, 1999: 7) has offered four possible models for Belarusian economic and social development in the future:

- post-socialist (the model currently in place);

- neo-Keynsian, with some state control along the lines of France and Italy;

- social-democratic, including a market economy but with significant social support institutions; and

- liberal (the Hong Kong model).

It is also posited that Belarus can follow a path toward Russia or toward the EU, though the two are not mutually exclusive. It was suggested by a TACIS official in Minsk in September 1999 that Belarus's task was if anything less burdensome than those faced in Russia and Ukraine, because Belarus does not have overwhelming debts to neighbouring states or institutions such as the International Monetary Fund or the World Bank. The relationship with Russia is also problematic because for all its political and social problems, Russia has taken significant steps toward privatisation and reform, and the Russian media have remained far more open and tolerant than their Belarusian counterparts.

To date, the Belarusian government is synonymous with the presidency of Alyaksandr Lukashenka, a man who has shown no compunction to offer any form of conciliation toward the opposition or toward a more open society. Of the EU countries, only Germany has seemed prepared to tolerate (although not accept) the actions of the president. Indeed, if Belarus is ever to choose the European route, it will be largely through its extensive links with that country. Germany has a significant presence in Belarus, including the embassy (led by a senior diplomat, Horst Winkelmann) and the OSCE (led by two Germans, Ambassador Wieck and Hans-Pieter

Kleiner). Germany has also offered significant aid to the Belarusian victims of Chernobyl, mainly through non-governmental organisations. On a more mundane level, international flights to and from Minsk operate only from Frankfurt and Munich (Lufthansa) and from the Austrian capital of Vienna (Austrian Airlines). It is posited that German interest in Belarus derives from preoccupation with the wartime period, when German troops remained on Belarusian territory for three years. This is not as far-fetched as it may seem. Belarus's national holiday of 3 July commemorates the day that Minsk was freed from German occupation.

Europe has not given up on Belarus, as illustrated by the presence in Minsk of the OSCE and TACIS offices, but plainly the Europeans face an uphill struggle to try to persuade the Belarusian government to construct a more open and tolerant society. Parliamentary elections were scheduled for 2000 (although at the time of writing it remained unclear whether parliament would be in its original or truncated form) and presidential elections are unlikely to be held until 2001. To date there are no indications that Belarus will change course, and its isolation from Europe will be solidified by the eastward growth of the EU. Whether or not Belarus proclaims its independence, it will of necessity become even more dependent on the whims and interests of its eastern neighbour.

References

Anon, 1995, *Press release of the Belarus Embassy in the United States*. Washington DC, 12 January.

Biryuk, V. G., Bakanova, M. V., Karyakina, O. A., Miroshichenko., A. V., 1998, *Is the growth in industrial production genuine?* Minsk: unpublished paper compiled for Belarusian Economic Trends.

Bogdankevich, S., Romanchuk, J., 1998, *Economic and social policy of the Republic of Belarus*. Minsk: unpublished paper, April.

European Commission, 1995, *Press Release*, 22 February.

Goodspeed, P., 1999, Mother Russia, Belarus to forge new union. *National Post* (Toronto), 7 July, p. A15.

Gulyakevich, L., 1998, Belorusskaya storona udovletvorena khodom konsul'tatsii s Pol'skim MID. *Narodnaya Volya*, 26 April, p. 1.

Levshina, I., 1996, Predstaviteli Evroparlamenta potrebovali ot ES priostanovit' vtsuplenie v silu vremennogo torgovogo soglasheniya mezhdu ES i Belarus'yu. *BelaPAN*, 13 June.

Marples, D., 1997, Belarus: borrowed boom. *Oxford Analytica*, unpublished paper, August.

Marples, D. R., 1999, *Belarus: a denationalized nation*. Amsterdam: Harwood Academic Publishers.

Nuti, D. M. 1999, The Belarusian alternative: transition or solely reform? *Belarusian Economic Trends, Quarterly Report*, April–June, 14–15. http://www.bettacis.by/q299/1.htm.

OMRI (Open Media Research Institute), 1995a, *OMRI Daily Digest*, 22 September.

OMRI, 1995b, *OMRI Daily Digest*, 28 November.

OMRI, 1997, *OMRI Daily Digest*, 14 March.

Padhol, U., Marples, D. R., 1999, Belarus: the president and the opposition. *The Harriman Review*, 12 (1), 11–18.

Pecherskiy, A., 1999, Mitrotvorets po vyvodu? *Belorusskaya Gazeta*, 17 April, pp. 1, 6.

Reuters, 1995a, News report, 21 February.

Reuters, 1995b, News report, 6 March.

Reuters, 1997, News report, 13 January.

RFE/RL, 1997, Belarus does not want to join EU. *RFE/RL Newsline*, 23 October.

RFE/RL, 1999, Lukashenko says Belarus to remain independent in union with Russia. *RFE/RL Newsline*, 17 November.

Semenov, A., 1999, Pochem pyl' pol'skikh dorog? *Sovetskaya Belorussiya*, 12 May, p. 1.

Tomashevskaya, O., 1998, Berezovskie vsekh stran, ob'edinyaytes'! *Belorusskaya Delovaya Gazeta*, 21 May, p. 1.

UNECE, 1999, *Trends in Europe and North America: Belarus*, 17 January. http://www.unece.org/stats/trend/blr/htm.

Zaiko, L., 1999, *National strategy of social and economic development*. Minsk: unpublished paper, September.

25

UKRAINE

David R. Marples

Ukraine has a population of just over 50 million in a land area larger than Poland and Romania combined (see Table 1.1). The country occupies an important position on the south-west of the former Soviet Union, sharing western borders with four EU candidate states – Poland, Slovakia, Hungary and Romania (Figure 25.1). Indeed, the configuration of the country was a direct result of the strategic need for Moscow to have direct land access from Soviet territory to its post-war satellites.

When Ukraine gained its independence in August 1991 it appeared to be in a better situation than most other former Soviet republics in terms of forging a path toward market reforms and closer links with Europe. In December 1991 Ukraine ratified its independence through a national referendum, in which over 90 per cent of the electorate supported the government's declaration. The following day, the EU issued a declaration about Ukraine, in which it welcomed the democratic nature of the Ukrainian referendum and appealed to Ukraine to open a constructive dialogue with the EU (Hudyma, 1998: 5).

The first years of independence, however, were a period of national consolidation. Under President Leonid Kravchuk, Ukraine concentrated first on the arduous programme of nation building, while responding to international pressure to dismantle the Soviet-era nuclear weapons and transport them to the Russian Federation. Economic decline and a difficult relationship with the Soviet Union, particularly on questions such as the future of the autonomous Crimean Republic and the disposal of the Black Sea Fleet, precluded progress in foreign relations. It is thus predominantly in the era of President Leonid Kuchma, who became Ukraine's second president in July 1994, that one can discern a definite policy of Ukraine toward the West. At the same time, no president of Ukraine has been able to operate independently of a parliament in which the forces of the left continue to play a significant role as the largest grouping, although not a majority.

Ukraine's foreign policy has been perceived as having four principal directions: the development of friendly relations with neighbours; the encouragement of an external view of Ukraine as a

Figure 25.1: Ukraine

potential member of the European Union; the forging of a new partnership with the Russian Federation that will allow Ukraine to preserve its political and economic interests; and, lastly, the promotion of a special relationship with the United States that includes Ukraine's integration into the Euro-Atlantic and other western structures (European Commission, 1999). Ukraine has succeeded in three out of the four spheres, the marked exception being the failure to cultivate an outside perception of the country as a viable candidate for membership of the EU. Among those states that are anxious ultimately to join the EU, Ukraine and Moldova are the only republics to remain outside the integration process. Although Ukrainian officials have often expressed a desire to see their country as part of the EU, no strategy is in place by which Ukraine may expedite this process.

Simply put, there are three basic alternatives for Ukraine: first, it can progress to full membership of the EU after a period as an associate member; second, it can conclude that associate membership for the indefinite future is the only realistic goal; or third, it can become simply a free-trade area in agreement with the EU, but without possessing any formal links (e.g. see Kanyshchenko and Pydlutskyi, 1999). However, the EU has always made clear that the principal catalyst in this process must be Ukraine itself. Since 1994 the republic has made progress in other, sometimes related, areas. In 1994 a partnership accord signed with the EU to promote trade between Ukraine and member countries (see below) was perceived as a first step in the process of membership. The following year Ukraine accepted an 'individual partnership programme' with NATO's Partnership for Peace, following which Ukrainian troops began to take part in a series of NATO exercises. In November 1995 Ukraine was admitted to the Council of Europe, a group of 39 nations that monitor democracy and human rights, and which expects its members to adhere to high standards in each of these areas (e.g. see de Weydenthal, 1996). Certainly Ukraine has given lip-service to its new role in the world, but there have been serious questions as to whether it takes seriously its commitment in a number of areas. In the summer of 1999, when EU officials and western experts visited Kyiv, they expressed concern about economic, legal and business restrictions in Ukraine. These included barriers to investment and trade, the inability of foreign companies to be treated equally with local ones, arbitrary laws and the lack of an adequate structure for conducting business, and the fact that there are too many laws in Ukraine that limit trade and business (Andersen, 1999).

While Ukraine under the Kuchma administration has failed to undertake major legal and economic reforms, its neighbours in eastern Europe have adopted such measures in spite of their unpopularity among the population. Politically, these nations are more united than Ukraine, with none of the pernicious disputes between left and right as to future political directions (Zamyatin, 1999). In part, the dilemma is related to the geographical situation of Ukraine, located directly between Poland and Russia and south of Belarus, meaning that two of the three neighbouring states have opted against the European direction. External events, such as NATO's war in Yugoslavia in the spring of 1999, also clouded issues for many Ukrainians who hitherto had welcomed the co-operation with the North Atlantic Treaty Organization. Whatever its failings, therefore, the Kuchma regime has had to walk a fine line between two increasingly intransigent military blocs: NATO and the Commonwealth of Independent States (CIS; or, for that matter, the emergent Russia–Belarus Union). From the European perspective, the country has had sufficient inducement and incentives. Between 1991 and 1998 the EU provided technical and financial assistance to Ukraine to the value of €3.9 bn, although, as will be discussed below, a significant portion of that aid was directed specifically to programmes related to nuclear safety.

The partnership and co-operation agreement (PCA)

The PCA has had a rather tortuous existence. Signed on 14 June 1994, it was not ratified by the EU member states until 1 March 1998, by which time all official formalities had been completed. It followed three rounds of discussions between Ukraine's foreign affairs ministry and EU officials. The final document signed by President Kuchma was a 'national strategy' for Ukraine's integration into the EU, which signified, as its ultimate goal, full membership in the organisation (Hudyma, 1998: 5). The established goals of the PCA, however, were to enhance ties between the parties in areas such as trade, energy, nuclear energy and nuclear safety, the environment and intellectual property. The EU agreed to help develop the automobile industry in Ukraine, in addition to improving trade in the coal and steel industries (Lyuta, 1999), two sectors of the economy that have been lagging badly in recent years. Ukraine has also been admonished for maintaining laws on capital punishment, in contravention of the agreement it signed when it joined the Council of Europe. Because of the number of concerns about the direction Ukraine has been taking, a request by the Ukrainian side for associate membership in the EU was promptly rebuffed at a meeting of the two sides in Luxembourg in what is termed the co-operation council (Carlsen, 1998a, 1998b). The latter body is itself a junior version of the associate membership arrangement, and thus a preliminary stage.

The rejection of the Ukrainian request was followed in the autumn of 1998 by a financial crisis in Russia, which spilled over into Ukraine. Shortly afterwards, Ukraine and the EU held their second summit in Vienna (the first was held in Kyiv in September 1997), with the participation of President Kuchma and Austrian Chancellor Klima. Although the focus of this summit was primarily on problems of external policies and security in Europe, and especially on the situation in the Balkans, Kuchma again took the opportunity to state his desire that Ukraine as a central European state was aiming ultimately for full EU membership (Anon, 1998). A third summit was held in July 1999 in Kyiv and, once again, the Ukrainian side began with high hopes that were to be dashed. It became clear that the EU was generally dissatisfied with the progress made in Ukraine on economic reform, human rights and the proposed (but delayed) closure of the Chernobyl plant. According to an account in *Den'* newspaper (24 July 1999), the EU was not seriously interested in developing closer relations with Ukraine.

The Council of Europe and NATO

The time was a difficult one for Ukraine. The summer of 1999 had already seen the start of political manoeuvring for the 31 October presidential election. Thus several political leaders, including President Kuchma, were prepared to take a strong stand on the question of relations with the EU. In addition, Ukraine was receiving warnings from a different direction, namely the Council of Europe. In January 1999 the Council's parliamentary assembly warned Ukraine that its membership in the Council could be suspended if it did not make significant progress on democratic and economic reforms (Hyde, 1999). In late May the threat was followed through when the Council's monitoring committee moved to suspend the credentials of Ukrainian parliamentary delegates. The Council maintained that Ukraine had failed to show that it was making progress on meeting its commitments to the body, especially on legal reform and the abolition of capital punishment. The Council, which accepted Ukraine as a member in 1995, had clearly grown impatient. Former minister of justice of Ukraine, Serhiy Holovatyi, savaged the Kuchma government for its lack of reforms, noting that if Ukraine were to be suspended, the next logical step would be its expulsion from the Council altogether. Capital punishment, however, was only one of several issues. Ukraine thus far had failed also to pass in final reading bills on the civil and criminal codes, and there had arisen serious concern about restrictions on freedom of the press. The limitations on the media were particularly evident at the beginning of the presidential election campaign, when newspapers focused almost exclusively on the speeches and policies of the president (Panchenko and Vikulina, 1999).

In late June the Council issued a final warning to Ukraine, noting that it would be expelled from membership if changes were not made within a six-month period. In particular, Ukraine must respect human rights, the freedom of the press, the rule of law and the decentralisation of authority. The differences were not assuaged by the attitude of the chairman of the Ukrainian delegation to the Council, Borys Oliynyk, who reportedly remarked that expulsion would be no great loss for Ukraine (Andersen, 1999). Ukraine has been further isolated on the European scene by its relations with NATO, which also threatened to come unhinged in the spring of 1999. In early April 1999, when the president of the parliamentary assembly of the Council of Europe came to Ukraine to lecture Ukraine's legislators on human rights, he was met by a barrage of criticism about NATO's bombing of Yugoslavia. Shortly thereafter the enraged leftist deputies walked out of the assembly, refusing to listen to a defence of NATO's actions by Lord Russell-Johnston (Hyde, 1999).

The NATO issue is closely related to that of EU expansion, as the same states, by and large, that are becoming or intend to become EU members are also prospective members of the NATO alliance. Ukraine's neighbour Poland is already a NATO member. Hungary and the Czech Republic, two states that had maintained close relations with Ukraine in the post-war period, are also full-fledged members. The other states that have applied to join NATO are Slovakia, Romania, Bulgaria, Macedonia, Slovenia, Albania and the three Baltic countries. Thus virtually all of central Europe is in the process of gaining NATO membership or has expressed an interest in joining the alliance. Under these circumstances the attitude of the Ukrainian deputies takes on a new hue. One analyst (Pidlutskiy, 1999) has noted that Ukraine has three options:

- a decisive turn to the West, making NATO membership, like EU membership, a priority of its foreign policy;

- the so-called Belarusian path, signifying a foreign policy that is oriented exclusively toward Russia and the formation of a military-political union with the giant neighbour; and

- a 'multi-vectored' foreign policy that maintains a balance between East and West, which gives rise to the problem that Ukraine could become a buffer zone between two hostile military alliances.

By nature, Kuchma has been a cautious president and, as a result, he has favoured precisely the third option. However, the decisions made by the states of central Europe signify that in the future Ukraine may be obliged to choose either the first or second options. The divisions in Ukrainian society were all too evident in the October presidential elections, in which pro-democratic and pro-market candidates were favoured by around 46 per cent of voters, and leftist candidates by around 54 per cent. The president's main support came significantly from Western Ukraine, the regions on the Polish and Romanian borders (P. B., 1999). It remained clear that a small majority of the electorate was generally opposed to the pro-European policies supported (at least in theory) by the current government.

EU expansion: specifics

Impact on trade and economic development

Since independence, Ukraine's trade with the EU has increased steadily. Ukraine has begun to reorient its trading practices from the countries of the former Soviet Union (principally Russia) toward the West. Thus the European share in the overall trade volume of Ukraine has doubled from 8.7 per cent in 1994 to 19 per cent in 1998 (exports 16.4 per cent; imports 21.6 per cent). The EU has become Ukraine's second largest trading partner after Russia, and much of this trade is conducted with Germany (Pavliuk, 1999). In addition, however, Ukraine has maintained important trading links with the countries of central Europe, both official and 'black market'. The Ukrainian government believes that this aspect of Ukrainian trade is threatened directly by the movement of ten new countries toward the EU. In November 1998 Ukraine called a meeting in Kyiv with three of those countries – Poland, Hungary and the Czech Republic – at which it expressed its fears. Ukraine's ambassador to the EU, Borys Hudyma, suggested that the EU instruct the 'candidate members' to have extensive discussions with Ukraine prior to officially joining the Union (Partridge, 1999).

Ukraine was concerned particularly with the loss of trade with two countries: Poland and Estonia. In the latter case, Ukraine would, under the rules of EU membership, be obliged to abandon its bilateral free-trade agreement with Estonia. Estonia would be included in the multilateral EU trading, at least in theory. Although Estonia expressed its willingness to continue its free trade with Ukraine (and Estonia has a healthy trade balance in this regard), the

EU response to that point had been (unofficially) negative (O'Rourke, 1999b). In the case of all ten countries, they would in effect be joining a trade circle from which Ukraine is excluded. Ukrainian goods imported into the EU, which are currently cheap, would become more expensive when they become liable to the EU's common external tariff. It is feared that Poland will cut off the well-known 'shuttle traders' from Ukraine (e.g. see Koublitsky, 1998), that is, those who come to Warsaw, in particular, to purchase Polish products that they can sell for a profit when they return to Ukraine. Both countries have become increasingly reliant on such traders since independence, although how much of each country's trade balance with the other this represents is a moot point. Ukraine's bilateral trade with Poland had already begun to decrease by 1998 (O'Rourke, 1999a).

In response, the EU has maintained that Ukraine's problem is less that of being cut off by an invisible barrier from the rest of Europe and more that of its own restrictive trade practices, which have impeded all EU attempts to develop better trading relations with Ukraine. The EU initially expressed interest in a number of facets of Ukrainian industry, particularly coal, steel, textiles and the manufacture of automobiles. In the latter sphere, it accuses Ukraine of policies that discriminate against European investors and violate an agreement made early in 1998. In 1997 Ukraine issued new laws that provided tax incentives for investors willing to expend over $150 mn on the Ukrainian car industry. The Korean firm Daewoo responded, agreeing to put $1.3 bn into that industry over a six-year period and demanding in return that Ukraine increase taxes on used cars and completely ban the import of cars over five years old. Regarding the coal and steel industries, the EU has begun several anti-dumping court cases against Ukraine. In short, therefore, the EU argument is that Ukrainian laws, and not the changing membership of the organisation, have placed Ukraine in a difficult situation.

Mutual accusations abound between the two sides on trade. The EU is concerned by the need for certification for goods, especially food and cosmetics. Tariff rates and registration charges have increased, seemingly at random. Excise duties are also applied. Ukraine has become a protectionist state, especially in such areas as the automobile industry and the production of colour televisions. Ukraine, in turn, has been furious at the anti-dumping cases, maintaining that by such measures the EU is cutting off exports of Ukraine's most valuable products, such as chemicals and steel, in addition to imposing quotas on textiles (Pavliuk, 1999). However, there have been criticisms of Ukraine's practices even from within the country. Writing in a Kyiv newspaper, Honcharuk, the minister of foreign connections and trade, writes that Ukraine lacks a system to stimulate exports, to finance export supplies and to provide guarantees of international risk. As a result, countries like Germany – Ukraine's main EU partner – are reluctant to trade with Ukraine. In 1998, for example, the volume of trade between Ukraine and Germany amounted to $2.1 bn, whereas the total for German–Polish trade was DM 18 bn and trade with the Czech Republic was DM 14 bn (Lyuta, 1999). Honcharuk implies that it is the restrictive practices being imposed by Ukraine that have proved the main impediment to enhanced trade with Germany and the other countries of the EU.

For the same reason, Ukraine has not yet been permitted to join the World Trade Organization (WTO), which many observers see as an essential prerequisite for EU membership. Discussions on this question have been under way for four years, and there were six meetings of working groups to discuss the question of Ukraine joining GATT/WTO in the period 1995–98. The key issue has always been the need to stabilise the trading regime in Ukraine. With reference to how Ukraine must improve in order to satisfy the requirements of WTO membership, the following main goals have been listed:

- end discriminatory taxes;

- observe GATT/WTO demands with regard to the creation of a favourable investment system;

- make consistent practices and laws in the sphere of technical regulation (standardisation and certification);

- attain sanitary standards at the level required by the WTO;

- respond to WTO demands in agriculture; and

- observe customs laws.

This discussion indicates that, thus far in its independent existence, Ukraine is not an attractive place for traders and potential investors. One source has noted also that if President Kuchma really wanted a better environment that would encourage foreign investment, then he should embark on a major public works programme to create modern highways and also an improved train service with neighbours. He should also begin to deal with some of the energy problems by establishing a conservation programme and harnessing some of the vast regions of natural gas (*Kyiv Post*, 1999).

Border restrictions

What will EU membership for Poland, Hungary and the Czech Republic mean for Ukrainians wishing to visit those countries? Clearly it is anticipated that these countries will be obliged to impose a visa system for visiting Ukrainian citizens. Kuchma visited Hungary in 1998, after which the two countries agreed to continue a visa-free system for the immediate future. Poland has also declared its intention to continue without visas for Ukrainians at least until the year 2002. The Czech Republic, however, is unlikely to wait so long because it does not share a border with Ukraine and bilateral Czech–Ukrainian relations are less important than Czech relations with the states of central and western Europe. The visa question is a complex one. During the second Ukraine–EU summit in the summer of 1998 the question of visas was discussed, including the continued visa requirements for citizens of the EU, Canada and the USA. Poland, for example, no longer requires visas from EU and American citizens, and most of the central European and Baltic countries have abandoned the visa system for westerners (e.g. see Koublitsky, 1998).

The Ukrainian authorities have argued that visa fees form an important source of hard currency that continues to benefit its economy. This argument, as a Ukrainian observer (Koublitsky, 1998) has pointed out, is short-sighted, in that the benefits to tourism of a non-visa system would surely outweigh the loss of hard-currency visa fees. The visa question affects Ukrainian–Polish relations first and foremost. A tempestuous relationship between these two countries in the past (particularly between the Ukrainian SSR and inter-war Poland, as well as during the Second World War) has been replaced in the 1990s by a new amicable relationship. In 1998, 4.8 million Ukrainians visited Poland. The official total of $1.7 bn worth of goods in trading each year is greatly underestimated, as black-market trade between Poland and western Ukraine raises the figure to around $2.5 bn. Thousands of Ukrainian agricultural workers cross the Polish border in search of employment and additional income for their families. Without this income, the future of these families would be much bleaker than at the present. Moreover, Poland and Ukraine have a number of bilateral projects in place, developed since independence, for free economic zones, shared water resources and the like (Andersen and Feuell, 1998; Pavliuk, 1999).

The concept of tight border controls and a visa regime between the two countries, albeit in 2002 rather than 2000, is simply unthinkable for many Ukrainians. In June 1999 President Kuchma went on a three-day visit to Poland where he met with President Aleksander Kwasniewski. The latter reportedly assured the Ukrainian visitor that a visa-free regime would remain in place even after Poland joins the EU, and that the border would remain 'friendly' for both business people and tourists (Turek, 1999). However, there are also reports that the volume of border traffic has already begun to fall in recent years. The number of Ukrainian citizens visiting the border town of Przemysl, for example, with which Ukraine has some historical and cultural links, fell from around 10,000 per day in 1995 to only 800 per day by the summer of 1999. This fall is in spite of the fact that the town of Przemysl began the construction of a modern customs control terminal in January 1998 (RFE/RL, 1999). However, the situation in Przemysl is not yet reflected in all areas on the Ukraine–Poland border.

Prevailing problems in Ukraine have been illegal immigration and the trafficking of both drugs and humans. Estimates of the number of illegal immigrants in or passing through Ukraine number as high as 500,000. Most of these immigrants enter Ukraine from Russia or Belarus. Ukraine has no border restrictions with Belarus for people travelling by train. There are some minimal inspections of documents at airports, but trains from Moscow, St Petersburg and other cities to Belarus do not stop at the border, and from the latter country migrants can travel without hindrance to Ukraine. To comply with EU requirements, therefore, Ukraine would first have to impose its own visa system and rigorous border checks on travellers entering the country from the north and the east. Ukraine, in short, has become a major smuggling route and holding tank for illegal immigrants, most of whom are from Asian and African countries for whom western Europe (or possibly the United States) is their final destination (Partridge, 1999; Pavliuk, 1999). Drug smuggling and the movement of humans (including young Ukrainian women taken for the purposes of prostitution in other countries) are reasons why the countries of the EU continue to impose a strict visa regime on Ukrainians. But the situation for the Ukrainian government is complex: without the prospect of an open border with the new EU members it cannot afford to close its borders with Russia and Belarus. To act otherwise would cut off vital trade for Ukraine: continued imports of essential oil and gas from Russia.

Political implications

Since independence Ukraine has pursued a tortuous political path, avoiding conflict with Russia while courting Europe and the United States. In recent times Ukraine's relations with Russia have improved significantly, particularly since the signing in 1997 of a treaty of friendship and co-operation. The treaty resolved – at least temporarily – the awkward questions of the division of the Black Sea Fleet and Russia's continued use of the port of Sevastopol (which was placed on a 10-year lease). Ukraine's relationship with the EU has not been affected by the existence of the CIS because Ukraine has never played more than a formalistic role in that organisation. Ukraine is not, however, opposed to a free-trade area between Ukraine, Russia and Belarus. Moreover, there are often significant differences in the perception of Ukrainian foreign policy between the president and the legislature. Members of the latter, including Speaker Oleksander Tkachenko, have often appeared to favour closer relations with its two former Soviet neighbours, even to the extent of joining the Russia–Belarus Union. For example, Tkachenko addressed the Belarusian Supreme Soviet in the spring of 1999, informing the truncated legislature in Minsk that Ukraine would be wise to adopt the economic practices and closer state control followed in Belarus.

Ukraine's foreign policy has been essentially flexible and far-reaching. In June 1998, in Yalta, the Black Sea Economic Co-operation Treaty was signed, with an initiation conference being held in the Crimea in the summer of 1999. Ukraine is also a member of GUAM (Georgia–Ukraine–Azerbaijan–Moldova), a grouping that has focused on the transport of natural resources between member states. The key question is whether the EU expansion will push Ukraine more firmly into the Russian or the Russia–Belarus camps, particularly with the simultaneous expansion of NATO into states bordering Ukraine. The short-term answer would appear to be yes, particularly given the current tension between Ukraine and the EU, and the seeming impossibility of Ukraine satisfying EU demands for a freer environment and less restrictive practices. One might ask this question in reverse, namely what can Ukraine do to improve its standing with the EU quickly enough to prompt a more positive dialogue? Is the EU in effect closed off to Ukraine for the next decade or so? Perhaps the best illustration of the critical differences between the two sides is the question of the future of the Chernobyl nuclear power plant.

Chernobyl: the continuing dilemma

The EU regards the Chernobyl plant as a potential danger to all citizens of Europe. In the first years after the 1986 accident, emphasis was placed on improving the technology of the graphite-moderated (RBMK) reactors there and to assisting those who had suffered from the radiation fall-out, particularly decontamination workers and evacuees. That situation changed with the dissolution of the Soviet Union in December 1991, after which control over the plant and the consequences of the accident devolved to the government of Ukraine. In April 1994 the International Atomic Energy Agency declared the station to be fundamentally unsafe. In December 1995, at a meeting of the Group of Seven (G-7) in Ottawa, a Memorandum of Understanding (MOU) was signed, according to which Ukraine agreed to close the station by the year 2000 in return for compensation (approximately $3.2 bn). The sum was intended to cover the closure and cost of decommissioning the plant, providing a new roof over the destroyed fourth reactor, and starting up two new reactors at the Ukrainian nuclear power stations at Rivne and Khmelnytskyy. Both these stations use pressurised-water reactors (PWRs – Russian designation VVERs) of 1,000 MW capacity. Because the reactors in question will be the fourth at Rivne and the second at Khmelnytskyy they have been abbreviated in international parlance to R4K2 (a more accurate transliteration would be R4Kh2). Although Ukraine had some reservations about the G-7 demand, the Ottawa meeting followed directly after Ukraine's acceptance into the Council of Europe (November 1995) and thus Ukraine was anxious to conciliate the European G-7 members in particular (see Marples, 1996).

At first Ukraine responded positively to the G-7 demands. In 1991 Chernobyl's unit 2 was taken off-line as a result of a fire, and the first unit is being decommissioned at the end of its life cycle. Unit 3, however, despite frequent shutdowns and both minor and less minor incidents has been kept in service, much to the consternation of the Europeans. In early March 1999 the third unit was once again in operation. According to the former director of the Chernobyl plant and now Ukraine's deputy minister of energy, Mykhailo Umanets', Ukraine is being ordered to close the station despite the failure of the EU and G-7 to come up with the funds promised to Ukraine. His comments have been echoed by the head of the information service at the Chernobyl station, Oleh Holoskokiv, who has noted that of the 5 bn *hryvnia* promised to Ukraine for the closure of Chernobyl 1 and 2, only 700 mn had actually been donated. Chernobyl's third unit has to be kept in operation to ensure stability at the plant. He also remarked on the apparent dual standards being imposed: strict demands being placed on Ukraine to close Chernobyl as opposed to the apparent lack of interest in other Soviet-built RBMK plants in Russia and Lithuania (Mikhalev, 1999).

Only on the question of the new roof for the fourth unit (the so-called *Ukryttya*, or covering) has the EU seemed likely to come up with promised funds. At the third Ukraine–EU summit in July 1999, the EU promised to provide $210 mn of the required $750 mn to complete this project. The Shelter Implementation Project (SIP) is being supervised by the European Bank for Reconstruction and Development, another entity with which Ukraine has had a difficult relationship, with mutual accusations being aired. The structure over the fourth reactor unit is collapsing and has a projected lifespan of 10–15 years (see Parashyn, 1998).

In July 1999 German chancellor Gerhard Schroeder came to Kyiv and – ostensibly under pressure from his coalition partners the Greens – urged Ukraine to scrap the construction of the two new reactors at Rivne and Khmelnytskyy and to replace them with non-nuclear sources. Kuchma responded that the West had promised approximately $1 bn to complete these reactors, which were 80 per cent completed when the Soviet Union collapsed in 1991. Regarding Germany's volte-face on the sort of energy industries required, Kuchma noted that nuclear power is by far the cheapest of the various alternatives (Anon, 1999). To the Ukrainians, the Germans appeared to be reneging on the original MOU of 1995. At the time of writing, there appeared to be little prospect of Ukraine's shutting down Chernobyl even by the end of 2000. Nuclear energy now comprises about 46 per cent of Ukraine's electricity output.

Why has the G-7 (and the EU) failed thus far to come up with the promised funds? Aside from the change of government in Germany, the main reason appears to be Europe's lack of faith in Ukraine. The Kuchma government has to date not adopted any form of energy policy for the future and appears intent on reliance on imported oil and gas from Russia, while leaning heavily on its nuclear power industry. The energy industry remains under control of the government, with authority being given to Kuchma's close associates in the various branches. The nuclear energy industry is currently in disarray, with changes of leadership at various levels (including the dismissal of Chernobyl boss Serhiy Parashyn, evidently for insubordination and refusal to accept the authority of a new leadership body called *Enerhoatom*) (Marples and Cerullo, 2000). There has been little indication that Ukraine has seriously investigated non-nuclear options or taken steps toward the final closure of Chernobyl.

Conclusion

The expansion of the EU into central and eastern Europe will force Ukraine to re-examine its trade, economic and energy policies. It will certainly lead the Ukrainian leadership to re-examine its post-independence trading policy, and eventually it is likely to cause a difficult situation for Ukraine with regard to visas, border crossing and international transportation. Finally, the expansion of the EU, when combined with the extension of NATO to the Ukrainian border, may put an end to Ukraine's policy of pursuing an ambivalent foreign policy. It forces the Kuchma administration to deal with the very real possibility that Ukraine may become the buffer state of central Europe.

The Kuchma presidency can be described as cautious and even negligent on the question of economic reform. Not all aspects of the period 1994–99 have been negative, but it has become increasingly difficult for foreign businesses and capital to operate in Ukraine. The country has pursued protectionist policies and measures that appear to be directed specifically against foreigners. One author has accurately described Ukraine–EU relations as being characterised by mutual misunderstanding and disappointment (Pavliuk, 1999: 4). According to Ukrainian foreign minister Borys Tarasyuk, speaking at the Royal Institute of International Affairs in London early in 1999, whereas Ukraine has stated clearly its long-term desire to be a full member of the EU, all it has received in response is 'delicate, small signals' (Partridge, 1999). These mutual recriminations between Ukraine and the EU are evident in virtually all aspects of the relationship: on trade, economic reform, energy reform, Chernobyl and EU membership. What Ukraine evidently has failed to see is that stating one's intentions alone is not enough. The demands must be matched by measures far more profound and fundamental than have occurred hitherto.

The alternative route – to respond to EU expansion by adopting a closer economic (if not political union) with Russia and Belarus – is not a very attractive option. The financial crisis in Russia in the autumn of 1998 made it obvious to Ukrainian leaders that the Russian regime was far from stable, a point exacerbated by the renewal of Russia's war with Chechnya and the partial breakdown of the federal system. Belarus represents the extreme example of a state that has moved in a different direction. At present, the Ukrainian president lacks the authority of his Belarusian (and Russian) counterpart, thus even if Kuchma or a future president wished to impose a presidential regime such as that of the northern neighbour, they do not have the means to do so. Any Ukrainian president must deal with parliament, and thus far Ukrainian parliaments have proven to be the most divisive and divided elements in society.

Ukraine is well endowed with natural resources. On the other hand, sophisticated technology, cell phones and Internet access are not readily available to a majority of the population. Its energy industry is becoming obsolete. Thermal power stations, which still provide a majority of electricity, are approaching or have reached the end of their natural lifespan. And yet there is no alternative energy system under consideration. The Chernobyl issue above all demonstrates the relative bankruptcy of ideas. As noted, Ukraine lacks a decent system of road networks that would facilitate trade and transportation to both the east and the west. Lastly, the country has a serious cash-flow problem outside the black market. Ukraine will be hard pressed in 2000 to meet the interest payments on its debts. Without credits and funds from the International Monetary Fund, the EU and other sources, the country faces financial collapse in the near future. Yet the government cannot come up with a strategy to convince its European supporters that it will put into practice the policies to which it continually gives lip-service. Ukraine, then, is being left behind in the process of reforms and European integration.

Perhaps the overriding problem in today's Ukraine is regionalism. Although there is no consensus as to whether one can identify particular politics with areas, there is little question that western Ukraine (the territories incorporated into Ukraine during or after the Second World War) remains far more market oriented and pro-democracy than the industrial regions of the east. It is the most nationally conscious part of Ukraine and, paradoxically, the most agrarian. It is also the area that will be most heavily affected by the new visa and trade laws that its neighbours are likely to impose once they become official members of the EU. The division of Ukraine was evident in the 1999 presidential election, just as it is manifested by the make-up of the current parliament, and it is perhaps the factor that has most limited the presidents of independent Ukraine in policy-making. The expansion of the EU will accelerate Ukraine's isolation from the rest of Europe and may catalyse reform in Ukraine. For the latter to occur, however, there must be a realistic possibility that Ukraine has reasonable long-term prospects of becoming, at least, an EU associate member. Were this possibility to disappear completely, the government may have little option but to turn eastward – and in more senses than one – backward in time.

Acknowledgement

The author is grateful to his research assistant Serhy Yekelchyk in ascertaining materials used in this paper.

References

Andersen, M., 1999, Kuchma has already turned away from the West. *Kyiv Post*, 29 July. http://www.thepost.kiev.ua.

Andersen, M., Feuell, W., 1998, Kuchma's desperate diplomacy. *Kyiv Post*, 11 December. http://www.thepost.kiev.ua.

Anon, 1998, Evropeyskiy vybir – nezminniy. *Polityka i Chas*, 11–12, 96–97.

Anon, 1999, Kantsler FRN – u Kievi. *Holos Ukrainy*, 9 July, p. 1.

Carlsen, T., 1998a, EU gives Ukraine abrupt brush off. *Kyiv Post*, 12 June. http://www. thepost.kiev.ua.

Carlsen, T., 1998b, Ukraine: EU rebuffs bid for association. *RFE/RL Newsline*, 16 June.

de Weydenthal, J., 1996, Ukraine aims to join the European Union. *RFE/RL Newsline*, 25 April.

European Commission, 1999, *The TACIS action programme 1999*. Brussels: European Commission.

Hudyma, B., 1998, Dorohoyu do spil'noho domu. *Polityka i chas*, 5, 3–6.

Hyde, L., 1999, European visitors defend NATO air strikes. *Kyiv Post*, 15 April. http://www. thepost.kiev.ua.

Kanyshchenko, O., Pydlutskyi, O., 1999, ES–Ukraine: pomogi sebe sama, togda i chlenstvo v ES stanet vozmozhnym. *Den'*, 20 May.

Koublitsky, D., 1998, The European club is closed to wafflers. *Kyiv Post*, 17 November. http://www.thepost.kiev.ua.

Kyiv Post, 1999, Editorial. *Kyiv Post*, 8 July. http://www.thepost.kiev.ua.

Lyuta, H., 1999, ES: Problemnye voprosy torgovykh otnosheniy. *Zerkalo nedeli*, 17 July. http://www.mirror.kiev.ua./paper/current/issue/1251/text/28-01-3.htm.

Marples, D. R., 1996, Chernobyl: the decade of despair. *The Bulletin of the Atomic Scientists*, 52 (3), 22–31.

Marples, D. R., Cerullo, T., 2000, International nuclear safety and the Chernobyl nuclear power station. *Vermont Legal Review*, Spring.

Mikhalev, V., 1999, Evrosoyuz prizyvaet uskorit' zakrytie Chernobyls'koy AES, no ne uvelichivaet finasovuyu pomoshch'. *Den'*, 11 March. http://www.day.kiev.ua/cjr/rus/text/0311r3.htm.

O'Rourke, B., 1999a, EU: negotiations with Easterners reaching tough point. *RFE/RL Newsline*, 22 March.

O'Rourke, B., 1999b, Ukraine: government concerned about isolation as EU expands. *RFE/RL Newsline*, 3 March.

Panchenko, O., Vikulina, N., 1999, Test na Evropu. *Den'*, 22 May, p. 1.

Parashyn, S., 1998, Cherez rik – dva CHAES mozhe zupynytysya sama po sobi. *Holos Ukrainy*, 25 April, p. 8.

Partridge, B., 1999, Ukraine: minister wants positive signal from EU on membership. *RFE/RL Newsline*, 3 February. http://www.rferl.org/newsline.

Pavliuk, O., 1999, *Ukraine and the European Union*. Kyiv: The East–West Institute.

P. B., 1999, Incumbent, communist leader to compete in runoff for Ukrainian presidency. *RFE/RL Newsline*, 1 November.

Pidlutskiy, O., 1999, Vid s'ohodni Ukraina mae kordony z NATO. *Den'*, 12 March, p. 3.

RFE/RL, 1999, Poland, Belarus and Ukraine report. *RFE/RL*, 1 (8), 20 July, pp. 1–2.

Turek, B., 1999, Poland/Ukraine: presidents discuss visa-free travel. *RFE/RL Newsline*, 24 June.

Zamyatin, V., 1999, Ukrainy v nayblyzhchykh planakh ES nemae. *Den'*, 3 March, pp. 1, 3.

Part IV

Forward Into History?

26

ENLARGEMENT

Derek Hall and Darrick Danta

Reprise

Although a widely held aspiration since the fall of communism in central and eastern Europe (CEE) in 1989, the current enlargement process, which now embraces 13 applicant countries – Bulgaria, Cyprus, the Czech Republic, Estonia, Hungary, Latvia, Lithuania, Malta, Poland, Romania, the Slovak Republic, Slovenia and Turkey – was formally launched by the EU in March 1998 through the approval of accession partnerships for all the applicant countries. In July 1997 the European Commission had released its *Opinions* on the membership applications, alongside documents outlining the *Agenda 2000* programme, in order to prepare the EU for the enlargement process (European Commission, 1997, 1998). At its summit in Luxembourg in December 1997 the European Council decided that, from March 1998, the enlargement process should encompass:

- the European Conference, a multilateral framework bringing together ten central European countries, Cyprus and Turkey;

- an accession process, covering ten central European countries and Cyprus;

- accession negotiations, which the European Council decided to open with six countries, as recommended by the European Commission: Cyprus, the Czech Republic, Estonia, Hungary, Poland and Slovenia.

Malta, which had 'frozen' its application for membership in 1996, reactivated it in October 1998.

The current enlargement process poses a unique challenge, since it is without precedent in terms of the scope and diversity of the number of candidates, their area (an increase of 34 per cent to EU territory), population (an increase of 105 million) and the wealth of histories and cultures. Further, if undertaken effectively, an enlarged Union should, theoretically, benefit third-party countries. A single set of trade rules, a single tariff and a single set of administrative procedures will apply not only just across the existing member states but across the single market of the enlarged Union. This will simplify dealings for third-party country operators within Europe and improve conditions for investment and trade (European Commission, 1999c).

In 1993, at the Copenhagen European Council, member states agreed that the associated CEE countries that so desired should become members of the European Union, and that accession would take place as soon as an applicant was able to assume the obligations of membership by satisfying the economic and political conditions required. These 'membership criteria' were set out and have been referred to subsequently as the 'Copenhagen criteria'. They require that each candidate country:

- has achieved stability of institutions, guaranteeing democracy, the rule of law, human rights and respect for and protection of minorities;

- has a functioning market economy, as well as the capacity to cope with competitive pressure and market forces within the Union;

- has the ability to take on the obligations of membership, including adherence to the aims of political, economic and monetary union; and

- has created the conditions for its integration through the adjustment of its administrative structures, so that European Community/Union legislation transposed into national legislation is implemented effectively through appropriate administrative and judicial structures.

The Luxembourg European Council (December 1997) also underlined that as a prerequisite for enlargement of the Union, the operation of the institutions must be strengthened and improved in keeping with the institutional provisions of the Amsterdam Treaty (1997), which modified the Treaty of Rome to accommodate the post-1989 era of political and economic change (Unwin, 1998; European Commission, 1999b).

Following the publication of the Commission's *Opinions* on the progress of the candidate countries in 1997, the Commission submits regular reports to the Council on further progress achieved by each country. The reports serve as a basis for the Council to take decisions on the conduct of negotiations or their extension to other candidates on the basis of the accession criteria. The Commission submitted the first set of these regular reports, covering the ten associated countries in central Europe plus Cyprus and Turkey, to the Council in November 1998.

On that basis, the analysis of progress made by candidate countries did not lead the Commission to modify its evaluation made in July 1997. Therefore, it did not feel it was necessary to make new recommendations on the conduct or extension of the negotiations. However, it did note:

- Particular progress had been made by Latvia (Chapter 12 in this volume), and indicated that if the momentum of change was maintained, it would be possible to confirm in the following year that Latvia had met the Copenhagen economic criteria and, before the end of 1999, to propose the opening of negotiations.

- Considerable progress had also been made by Lithuania (Chapter 13), although additional measures were required and recent decisions needed to be tested before the country could be considered to have met the Copenhagen criteria, which would then allow the Commission to propose the opening of negotiations.

- The new political situation created in Slovakia (Chapter 11), following the changes brought about by the general election, allowed for the prospect of opening negotiations on condition that the regular, stable and democratic functioning of the country's institutions were confirmed. It would also be necessary, before opening negotiations, to verify that Slovakia had undertaken measures to correct its economic situation and had introduced greater transparency in its operation.

- Bulgaria (Chapter 14) had made considerable progress in macroeconomic stabilisation and the reforms being implemented were helping to improve its international competitiveness.

- Romania (Chapter 15) had not made further progress since the *Opinion*, and its economic situation gave cause for concern. Sustained efforts were required, with the support of the EU and the international community, to accelerate reforms and put Romania back on track for accession negotiations.

The Vienna European Council (December 1998) welcomed and generally endorsed the European Commission's regular reports. Following the reactivation by Malta of its application for membership in October 1998 (Chapter 16), the Commission adopted, in February 1999, an update of its *Opinion*. The European Commission presented its next regular reports in October 1999, covering the ten associated countries in central Europe plus Cyprus, Malta and Turkey, and also a more general composite paper on the progress made by each of the candidate countries toward accession. These were available for the Helsinki European Council, held in December 1999.

The regular reports contain a detailed analysis of the progress made by these 13 candidate countries since November 1998. They showed that all countries except Turkey fulfilled the political criteria for accession, but that only Cyprus and Malta fully met the economic criteria.

Table 26.1 Enlargement: 1999 European Commission reports summary: the 10 CEE candidates

Country: overall ranking of readiness	Acquis: progress of adoption over past year	Acquis: areas not addressed	Requirements to meet political criteria	Requirements to meet economic criteria	BCE ranking[a] on key criteria
1 Hungary	Excellent	Regional development, steel restructuring, environment	Implement plans to address Roma rights and fight corruption	Give priority to health sector reform; current account and fiscal deficits problematic	A1 P1 E1
2 Poland	Very limited	Internal market reforms, state aids, steel restructuring, agriculture	Improve judiciary and fight corruption	Reform agriculture; restructure and privatise state companies	A3+ P1 E1
3 Slovenia	Good	State aids, insurance, border controls, public administration, judicial reform	Streamline parliamentary and judicial processes	Speed up structural reforms – privatisation and improved corporate governance	A2 P1 E2
4 Estonia	Mixed	State aids, agriculture, customs, regional policy, environment, financial control, social sector	Language law regressive and should be amended; fight corruption	Accelerate health and pension reform, financial supervision, land privatisation, restructuring of oil-shale sector	A2 P3+ E1
5= Czech Republic	Unsatisfactory	State aids, audio-visual, environment, transport, agriculture, employment laws, justice	Address Roma rights and end discrimination; fight economic crime and corruption	Priority for privatisation, liberalisation and corporate governance: reform of public finance urgent	A3+ P2 E2
5= Latvia	Good	Telecoms, agriculture, customs, taxation, maritime safety, financial control	Language law must meet international standards; strengthen judiciary and fight corruption	Focus on macroeconomic stability and complete structural reform	A3+ P2 E2
7 Slovakia	Good	Environment, asylum laws, justice, transport, regional development, agriculture, health and safety	Give judiciary legal independence; pay particular attention to Roma rights	Reform plans for privatisation and bank restructuring must be implemented; fiscal reform a medium-term priority	A3 P2 E3
8 Lithuania	Mixed	Piracy, state aids, standardisation, audio-visual, taxation, regional policy	Fight corruption and continue judicial reform	Complete bank privatisation and energy sector reform; current account and fiscal deficits may be unsustainable; progress not as strong as expected	A3 P1 E4+
9 Bulgaria	Good	Nuclear safety, state aids, social sector, corruption	Improve minority and Roma rights, fight corruption and improve judicial system	Give priority to privatisation, bankruptcy problems and financial discipline for state enterprises; clearly not a functioning market economy	A4 P2 E4

| 10 Romania Mixed | Environment, justice, public administration | Give priority to improving childcare institutions | Further progress with privatisation and banking reform; macroeconomic imbalances problematic; legal uncertainty deters foreign investment; clearly not a functioning market economy | A4 P3 E5 |

[a]*Business Central Europe* interpretation of EC reports and implicit ranking based on the Copenhagen criteria: 1: good; 2: OK; 3: borderline; 4: unsatisfactory; 5: terrible. A = *acquis*; P = political criteria; E = economic criteria.

Source: *O'Donnell, 1999a: 40–41*

Progress in adopting the *acquis* varied between countries: whilst good progress had been made by Hungary, Latvia and Bulgaria, the pace of transposition in Poland and the Czech Republic was slow (Table 26.1).

Spurred on by the Kosovo conflict of 1998–99 and its aftermath (Table 26.2), which re-emphasised the need to stabilise and eventually embrace the states of south-eastern Europe and to provide more effective and efficient means of pan-European co-ordination, new EU president Romano Prodi called for a speeding up of the enlargement process:

> *Under our enlargement strategy, the same accession rules will apply to all applicant countries – those already negotiating and those about to start. Each will move towards membership at its own pace over the next couple of decades. It is a fully flexible, multi-speed system which even allows countries in the second wave to overtake countries in the first wave. So a non-stop accession process is about to begin, and I no longer see any opportunity to pause for treaty review in the middle of this process or between waves.*

> *It is true that the Amsterdam protocol on the institutions and enlargement provided for a two-stage reform process: but these provisions have clearly been overtaken by events. The necessary changes to our institutions must be completed by the end of 2002, because negotiations with the most advanced candidate countries will by then be reaching their conclusion.*

> *This means the reform package must be agreed at the close of the Inter-Governmental Conference (IGC) in December 2000. This really is our last chance to put our house in order. I see nothing but risks and dangers in toying with the illusion that major reform can wait until a later conference ...*

> *With the Single Act, Maastricht and Amsterdam we have already had fifteen years of Treaty reviews, and I see no attraction in the idea of holding yet another conference after the forthcoming IGC. Our citizens will, I believe, react with boredom and incomprehension to a*

Europe which appears to spend all its time in a never-ending, inward-looking, institutional review. The very last thing we need right now is to further alienate our citizens!

(Prodi, 1999: 2; see also von Weizsäcker *et al.*, 1999)

Table 26.2 Enlargement: economic impact of the Kosovo crisis on neighbouring countries, 1999

	Humanitarian	Direct trade with FRY	Transit trade through FRY	Financial (access to capital market, FDI)	Tourism	GDP growth in 1999
Albania	4: over 450 000 refugees (14% of population)	1: exports to FRY were less than 3% in 1997	0: 70% of trade goes to Italy and Greece	1: private foreign investment negligible	0	Reduction in industrial production is offset by boost to service sector
Bosnia and Hercegovina	1: less than 1% of population (also from other parts of Serbia)	2/4: small impact for the Federation but large impact for Republic Srpska – FRY is a major export market	1	1: private foreign investment negligible	0	Lower growth is driven by decline in exports to FRY
Bulgaria	0	1: 2% of exports went to FRY in 1997	4: an estimated 50% of exports used to go through FRY	2: no decline in foreign investor interest, but municipal Eurobond issue was postponed	2: decline in tourists from FRY is offset by increase in tourists from EU	Lower growth forecast driven by poor export performance
Croatia	0	0	0: FRY was not a major transit route	1: no evidence of decline in foreign investor interest	3: tourism revenue is major source of foreign exchange	Lower growth forecast driven mainly by domestic factors
FYR Macedonia	4: 260 000 refugees (13% of population)	3: 10% of exports went to FRY in 1997	4: nearly 60% of exports were transited through FRY	2: some decline in foreign investor interest	0	Lower growth forecast due to difficulty in exporting and costs associated with refugees
Romania	0	1: less than 2% of exports go to FRY	2: curtailment of trade related to Danube traffic	1: low impact driven by domestic factors	0	Lower growth forecast driven by domestic factors

Impact rating – 0: negligible; 1: small; 2: moderate; 3: large; 4: very large.

Source: *EBRD, 1999: 86, adapted by the current authors*

Indeed, in a *Eurobarometer* survey in the EU15 countries during the last quarter of 1998 (European Commission, 1999f: 83), 72 per cent of respondents felt that the EU would be more important in the world if it included more countries, and 64 per cent regarded an expanded Union as a cultural enrichment and better guarantee for peace and security; but, negatively, 47 per cent believed that enlargement would cost their own country more money, 36 per cent felt that their country would become less important, and 35 per cent saw enlargement as leading to higher unemployment. Together with a further series of surveys undertaken in the spring of 1999, support for the membership of individual candidate countries varied considerably both between candidates and between the views of the individual EU15 countries (Tables 26.3 and 26.4). Notably, support for non-candidate (west European) countries Norway and Switzerland was far greater than for any actual (Mediterranean or CEE) candidate country.

What Table 26.3 appears to reveal is a comprehensive reduction in support for, and increase in opposition to, all of the candidate countries between the period of the two surveys (also compare this with Tables 1.2 and 1.3 in Chapter 1). In 1999 only Malta secured a support level of 50 per cent: in all other cases support was in the minority. From a slightly different perspective, however, Table 26.4 indicates that overall EU15 support appears to be relatively steady at just 42 per cent, with only the three Nordic countries, together with Greece, the Netherlands and Spain expressing an average support level of 50 per cent or above. The high percentage of 'don't knows' in a number of key member states is perhaps a matter of some reflection for EU leaders.

Commission recommendations

In conjunction with the publication of the 1999 regular reports on the candidate countries in preparation for the Helsinki European Council meeting, the European Commission recommended:

- opening negotiations with Malta, Latvia, Lithuania and Slovakia, and also with Bulgaria and Romania, but subject to certain conditions for the latter two;

- conducting accession negotiations through a 'differentiated' approach 'allowing each candidate to progress through the negotiations as quickly as is warranted by its own efforts to prepare for accession' (European Commission, 1999a: 2);

- considering Turkey as a candidate country, although with no question of opening negotiations at this stage – in order to allow Turkey to benefit from such candidate status, concrete actions were proposed as a means to stimulate in-depth reforms and to promote respect for the Copenhagen political criteria;

- a wider vision for the relations with countries of the former Yugoslavia and Albania on the one hand, and Russia, Ukraine, the Caucasus and Maghreb countries on the other; and

Table 26.3 Enlargement: EU15 survey – support for individual candidate countries' entry, 1998–1999

Candidate country	1998 Survey		1999 Survey	
	For (%)	Against (%)	For (%)	Against (%)
Bulgaria	**39**	36	35	**40**
Cyprus	**45**	31	**42**	33
Czech Republic	**45**	31	**40**	35
Estonia	**39**	36	36	**38**
Hungary	**50**	28	**46**	31
Latvia	**39**	36	35	**38**
Lithuania	**38**	36	35	**39**
Malta	**52**	25	**50**	26
Poland	**47**	32	**43**	35
Romania	37	**40**	33	**43**
Slovakia	**40**	36	35	**39**
Slovenia	36	**38**	32	42
Turkey	–	–	29	**47**
Norway	–	–	*70*	*12*
Switzerland	–	–	*70*	*13*

Sources: *European Commission, 1999f: 88, 1999g: 72*

- that EU institutional reform be in force by 2002 to allow accession of the first candidates who fulfilled the criteria.

The resolution of institutional matters not dealt with by the Treaty of Amsterdam, but which needed to be settled before enlargement, was assigned to the Inter-Governmental Conference (IGC); see below:

- the size and composition of the Commission;

- the weighting of votes in the Council (re-weighting, introduction of a dual majority and threshold for qualified-majority decision-making);

- the possible extension of qualified-majority voting in the Council;

- other necessary amendments to the treaties as regards the European institutions in connection with the above issues, and implementation of the Treaty of Amsterdam (European Commission, 1999h).

Table 26.4 Enlargement: EU15 survey – support for new countries joining the EU, 1998–1999

EU15 country	1998 Survey Average support (%)	Don't knows (%)	1999 Survey Average support (%)
Austria	30	19	29
Belgium	28	20	39
Denmark	**61**	**13**	**62**
Finland	**52**	**16**	**51**
France	35	20	33
Germany	34	22	38
Greece	**61**	**11**	**58**
Ireland	41	36	45
Italy	48	24	45
Luxembourg	36	23	45
Netherlands	**51**	**16**	**55**
Portugal	42	37	38
Spain	**51**	**34**	**51**
Sweden	**63**	**19**	**56**
United Kingdom	44	29	40
EU15	42	24	42

Sources: *European Commission, 1999f: 89, 1999g: 73*

Reform of decision-making structures, overhaul of regional policy, rationalisation of the CAP, the upgrading of co-operation in justice and home affairs and other aspects of *Agenda 2000* are urgently needed to cope with internal challenges. The CAP is a good example of the complex interdependence of eastward enlargement and the necessities of internal reform: it needs to be radically reformed for several reasons:

- In its present form it is in contradiction of the spirit, if not the letter, of commitments already made by the EU under the treaty on the World Trade Organization.

- Through the virtually complete absence of market mechanisms it is arguably, in the long term, incompatible with the interests of consumers as well as taxpayers.

- Through EU history, it has actively prevented development in less developed countries of the south (e.g. in Latin America).

An unreformed CAP would lead to financial collapse even if just Poland and Hungary joined the EU because of the vast subsidies to which these countries would be entitled (Freudenstein, 1998: 43–44).

Other elements of the Commission strategy included:

- *Accession partnerships* On the basis of the regular reports, revised accession partnerships were drawn up for each candidate country (with the exception of Turkey), proposing short- and medium-term priorities to be met in order to prepare for membership. They indicated the financial assistance available from the EU (over €3 bn a year from 2000) in support of these priorities and the conditionality attached to that assistance.

- *Nuclear safety* Ensuring high standards of nuclear safety throughout the European continent was a top priority for the EU. The Commission had been in discussion with each candidate country that had non-upgradeable nuclear reactors with the aim of securing agreement on closure dates for these reactors. Subsequently, the Lithuanian government decided to close Unit 1 at Ignalina before the end of 2005 and expected Unit 2 to be closed before 2009 (see Chapter 13). Similarly, the Slovak government was now to close Units 1–2 VI at Bohunice by, respectively, 2006 and 2008 (Chapter 11). Such decisions were viewed as constituting a significant step in preparation for EU membership. The Commission expressed its disappointment that the Bulgarian government had still not been prepared to commit itself to the closure of Units K1–4 at Kozloduy (Chapter 14).

- *PHARE guidelines for 2000–06* These confirmed the programme's focus on a limited number of pre-accession priorities, such as institution building and investment in the regulatory infrastructure needed to ensure compliance with the *acquis*. They also take account of the implementation, from 2000, of the two other pre-accession instruments, ISPA (co-financing of investment in environmental and transport infrastructure) and SAPARD (support for agriculture and rural development) (see below).

- *Strategy for neighbouring countries* The Commission proposed 'to confirm the vocation for membership' of countries of the former Yugoslavia and Albania, but under strict conditions. In addition to the Copenhagen criteria, these countries would be required to recognise each other's borders, settle all issues relating to the treatment of national minorities and pursue economic integration in a regional framework as a precondition for their integration in the EU. Relations with Russia, Ukraine, the Caucasus and Maghreb countries were recognised as being of strategic importance extending beyond trade and assistance programmes, and could be extended to the fight against organised crime and drug trafficking, migration or environmental policies.

Günter Verheugen, commissioner for enlargement, whose strong imprint lay on these recommendations, argued:

> *This strategy will help strike the right balance between two potentially conflicting objectives in the enlargement process: speed and quality. Speed is of the essence because there is a window of opportunity for enhanced momentum in the preparations for enlargement, in accordance with the expectations of the candidate countries. Quality is vital because the EU does not want partial membership, but new members exercising full rights and responsibilities.*

(European Commission, 1999a: 1)

Pre-accession strategy and support

The Europe Agreements

The Europe Agreements have provided the framework for bilateral relations between the EU and the partner countries and cover trade-related issues, political dialogue, legal approximation and other areas of co-operation, including industry, environment, transport and customs. They aim progressively to establish a free-trade area between the EU and the associated countries over a given period. The Association Agreements with Cyprus and Malta have covered similar fields (except political dialogue), while the agreement with Turkey was also aiming to achieve a customs union. A summary chronology of the ten Europe Agreements and three Association Agreements is shown in Table 26.5.

In addition to the liberalisation of trade, the Europe Agreements contain provisions regarding the free movement of services, payments and capital in respect of trade and investments, and the free movement of workers. The partner countries commit themselves to approximating their legislation to that of the European Union, particularly in the areas relevant to the internal market. This includes applying legislation favouring competition and applying state-aid rulings, which are compatible with comparable legislation in the EU. Legislation is required providing for similar levels of protection to intellectual, industrial and commercial property.

A question raised by a number of commentators (e.g. Blazyca, 2000) is related to the way in which trade relations may express a candidate country's capacity to meet the Copenhagen criteria. This arises from the fact that much of post-communist CEE witnessed a relatively rapid reorientation of trade from east to west Europe in the 1990s, in a number of cases generating significant trade deficits with the EU in the process. This might suggest that at least some countries' economies are not able to withstand EU competition and are, therefore, unable to meet one aspect of the Copenhagen criteria.

Table 26.5 Enlargement: chronology of Europe Agreements and Association Agreements for the candidate countries

Country	Europe Agreement signed	Europe Agreement into force	Official application for EU membership
Bulgaria	March 1993	February 1995	December 1995
Czech Republic	October 1993	February 1995	January 1996
Estonia	June 1995	–	November 1995
Hungary	December 1991	February 1994	March 1994
Latvia	June 1995	–	October 1995
Lithuania	June 1995	–	December 1995
Poland	December 1991	February 1994	April 1994
Romania	February 1993	February 1995	June 1995
Slovakia	October 1993	February 1995	June 1995
Slovenia	June 1996	February 1999	June 1996
Cyprus	December 1972	June 1973	3 July 1990
Malta	December 1970	April 1971	16 July 1990
Turkey	September 1963	December 1964	14 April 1987

Source: *European Commission, 1999e: 1*

Pre-accession assistance

PHARE was identified in the Europe Agreements as the financial instrument specifically aimed at helping achieve the objectives of the Europe Agreements. By providing the funding to enable the partner countries to prepare for membership of the EU, PHARE is fundamental to the process of integration and enlargement (European Commission, 1999e). In 1999 PHARE had a budget of €1.6 bn for projects emphasising education, training and institution capacity building.

Together with PHARE and aid for agricultural development *Agenda 2000* proposed structural aid for the applicant countries amounting to some €1.04 bn per year for the period 2000–06. This aid would be directed mainly toward aligning the applicant countries on Community infrastructure standards, particularly in the transport and environmental spheres. This became known as ISPA (Instrument for Structural Policies for Pre-Accession) and is the responsibility of former DGXVI, now DG Regional Policy. Over half of the total ISPA budget is allocated to Poland and Romania, by far the two largest countries of the region. However, as a percentage of GDP, Poland is receiving less than a third as much as Latvia. This suggests a commitment to encourage the former 'second six' candidates (Bowdler and O'Donnell, 1999).

SAPARD (the Special Accession Programme for Agriculture and Rural Development) aims to help candidate countries deal with the problems of the structural adjustment in their agricultural sectors and rural areas, as well as in the implementation of the *acquis communautaire* concerning the CAP and related legislation (European Commission, 1999d). Thus, with some anxiety already expressed about the size of the farming sector in CEE, SAPARD funds are not intended as production support subsidies, but are intended to encourage rural diversification away from agriculture. This is laying emphasis on:

- upgrading local infrastructure;

- supporting education and training;

- assisting the establishment of off-farm enterprise; and

- improving sales channels and quality controls for the food industry (Bowdler and O'Donnell, 1999).

SAPARD came into effect on 1 January 2000 and is budgeted until the end of 2006 at an annual rate of €520 mn from the former DGVI, now DG Agriculture. Candidate countries may benefit only up to the time they join the EU (European Commission, 1999d).

The Helsinki European Council

The Helsinki European Council meeting of December 1999 (EU leaders' summit) took the enlargement process forward (European Commission, 1999g):

- A formal decision was taken on the format and functions of the Inter-Governmental Conference which would begin its work in February 2000 and complete its task by the end of that year.

- The necessary changes in EU treaties, reforming the institutions to allow enlargement to proceed, would be in place by the end of 2002.

- The European Council confirmed that accession negotiations would start early in 2000 with a further six applicant countries – Latvia, Lithuania, Slovakia, Bulgaria, Romania and Malta – which would join the existing 'fast-track six' applicants: Poland, Hungary, the Czech Republic, Estonia, Slovenia and Cyprus.

- The European Council decided that Turkey should be granted the status of a candidate country.

This last decision was a reversal of the previously held position and marked a significant moderation in Greek opposition to Turkish membership. Barely 5 per cent of Turkey's territory falls within the geographical definition of Europe. It would be the EU's first large Muslim member (see Chapter 17), yet for more than a thousand years its largest city (Byzantium/Constantinople/Istanbul) was the seat of eastern Christianity. It would carry the EU's borders to Iran, Syria and Iraq. But together with Greece, with whom its history has been entwined for millennia, Turkey holds the key to the stability of the Union's south-eastern reaches. The granting of candidate status merely allows Europe more time, and it may be a generation before Turkey is ready for full EU membership. Indeed the Greek government did not accept the notion of eventual Turkish membership without imposing conditions. Turkey will have to agree to take any territorial disputes between the two countries in the Aegean to the International Court of Justice in The Hague. It also faces the prospect of Cyprus becoming an EU member, even if there is no internal political settlement for the divided island beforehand (see Chapter 10). Turkey would need to improve its human rights record and modernise sections of its economy before EU membership drew closer (e.g. see Jacobs, 1999). However, although candidate status for Turkey did not mean an immediate start to accession negotiations, it would permit Turkey to benefit from the type of accession agreement that would channel funding to the country in subsequent years.

A timetable?

In her opening address to the eighth meeting with presidents of parliaments of countries participating in the enlargement process, the president of the European Parliament, Nicole Fontaine, told the presidents of the parliaments of candidate countries that closer links between the European Parliament and their parliaments were an essential element in achieving greater mutual understanding and in ensuring that the enlargement process proceeded smoothly and on time. The Joint Parliamentary Committees had a special task of preparing public opinion both in the member states and in the candidate countries. At the meeting the parliamentary presidents adopted a series of conclusions in which they:

- emphasised that enlargement was the key to peace, stability and security in Europe;

- welcomed the opening, early in 2000, of accession negotiations with the six countries not yet participating in enlargement negotiations;

- supported maintaining the speed of negotiations already under way with the six central and eastern European countries;

- called on the EU to ensure that it was ready for enlargement by 2002, so that by 1 January 2003 those countries ready for accession could join the EU and their citizens would have an opportunity of voting in the European elections of 2004, and so that their MEPs could then take part in the procedure for appointing the new Commission, which would take office in January 2005;

- supported the establishment of the Stability Pact for South-eastern Europe and the EU's strategy for economic and social reconstruction in south-eastern Europe.

The presidents stressed that enlargement should be an open and inclusive process contributing to pan-European stability and co-operation with all countries committed to the EU's objective of achieving peace and security, democracy and the rule of law, economic growth and prosperity throughout Europe (European Parliament, 1999).

It is clear that, as the EU set a timetable for internal reform to be reached by the end of 2002, some candidate states interpreted this as an indication that they could attain membership in 2003. EU officials subsequently tried to emphasise that the process of establishing membership for new states – which each existing member nation must ratify – would in itself take a year. That meant new members would not be brought into the EU until 2004 at the earliest. Most existing EU member states appear opposed to the concept of target dates (O'Donnell, 1999b).

Regardless of apparent progress made, fundamental problems would appear to remain before enlargement can proceed:

- The proposed internal reforms are viewed by many commentators as insufficient for a union of 27/28 members, and Helsinki served to highlight the embryonic state of the enlargement debate.

- Current EU members have not recognised the fundamental way in which the Union will have to change if enlargement is to proceed on the scale outlined in Helsinki, perhaps reflecting a lack of enthusiasm for enlargement (see above and Chapter 4).

- Considerations of *Realpolitik* will probably thwart the hopes of some front-runners for early accession.

- Notably, there is recognised to be a lack of enthusiasm within the EU to have a first round of enlargement without Poland – the most important of all candidate countries; thus if Poland is not ready, the first round of accessions will be delayed. It is uncertain whether the complexity of the questions raised by the entry of a country the size of Poland, notably in relation to the role of agriculture (see Chapter 7), can be resolved in a few years (Lobjakas, 1999).

Indeed, the *Agenda 2000* arrangements agreed in Berlin failed to address comprehensively the key issues of accession such as agriculture, the free movement of people and market access for industrial goods. Poland illustrates the difficulties not only for the candidates but for the EU itself, for with its huge and inefficient farming sector, as noted above, it presents the prospect of bankrupting the CAP under present circumstances. While the *Agenda 2000* reforms capped farm spending for existing EU member states, they did not address the way new members would be financed under the CAP (O'Rourke, 1999).

It is likely that the enlargement process will mean the end of the European Union as we know it: the EU may become far less integrated than it is today. Ultimately, enlargement and the underlying principles of the present EU may be reconciled only if members are allowed to reach different levels of integration: a *multi-speed Europe*. Alternatively, the preferences of the existing 15 members may become increasingly hard to reconcile, with the result that lack of agreement and prevarication result in the threshold for the candidates' integration into the West becoming an ever-retreating mirage (Lobjakas, 1999). The consequences of this could see resentment expressing itself in political hostility and European fragmentation – perhaps along new fault lines – in mutual recrimination and economic protectionism. Alternatively, the process may proceed to a limited extent, but then the first new entrants may attempt to prevent further expansion in order to protect their own economic and political interests. Or existing EU15 members, particularly those on the less developed periphery, may attempt to block further expansion as, from the demonstration effects of the first new entrants, they see their own interests being eroded by enlargement to a greater extent than they had anticipated.

Certainly, as Europe goes East, the prospect of EU enlargement promises both diversity and uncertainty for the very institutions that have been developed and consolidated within an exclusively *western* European framework over almost half a century.

References

Blazyca, G., 2000, *Will Europe ever be 'round and whole'? Reflections on EU economic enlargement after the collapse of communism*. Paper presented at the conference, The Geography and Geopolitics of the New Eastern Europe. St Andrews: University of St Andrews Centre for Russian, Soviet, and Central and Eastern European Studies, 11 March.

Bowdler, N., O'Donnell, P., 1999, Semi-integration. *Business Central Europe*, 6 (64), 49.

EBRD, 1999, *Transition report 1999*. London: EBRD.

European Commission, 1997, *For a stronger and wider Union: Agenda 2000*. Strasbourg: European Commission (DOC 97/6).

European Commission, 1998, *EU–CEC relations*. Washington DC: European Commission. http://eurunion.org/legislat/extrel/cec/cec.htm.

European Commission, 1999a, *Commission sets out an ambitious accession strategy and proposes to open accession negotiations with six more candidate countries*. Brussels: European Commission. http://www.europa.eu.int/comm/enlargement/report_10-99/intro/index.htm.

European Commission, 1999b, *Enlargement: introduction. Accession criteria.* Brussels: European Commission. http://www.europa.eu.int/comm/enlargement/intro/criteria.htm.

European Commission, 1999c, *Enlargement: introduction. EU enlargement – a historic opportunity.* Brussels: European Commission. http://www.europa.eu.int/comm/enlargement/intro/index.htm.

European Commission, 1999d, *Enlargement: pre-accession strategy. Pre-accession assistance.* Brussels: European Commission. http://www.europa.eu.int/comm/enlargement/pas/envir_transp.htm.

European Commission, 1999e, *Enlargement: pre-accession strategy. The Europe Agreements.* Brussels: European Commission. http://www.europa.eu.int/comm/enlargement/pas/europe_agr.htm.

European Commission, 1999f, *Eurobarometer: public opinion in the European Union. Report number 50.* Brussels: European Commission. http://europa.eu.int/en/comm/dg10/infcom/epo/eb.htm.

European Commission, 1999g, *Helsinki European Council: presidency conclusions.* Brussels: European Commission. http://www.europa.eu.int/council/off/conclu/dec99/dec99_en.htm.

European Commission, 1999h, *Intergovernmental Conference.* Brussels: European Commission. http://www.europa.eu.int/igc2000/index_en.htm.

European Parliament, 1999, *Target is for first accessions to take place before next European elections.* Brussels: European Commission. http://www.europarl.eu.int/dg3/sdp/newsrp/en/n991201.htm.

Freudenstein, R., 1998, Poland, Germany and the EU. *International Affairs*, 74 (1), 41–54.

Jacobs, B., 1999, 1999 in review: Turkey's tumultuous year. *RFE/RL Report*, 22 December. http://www.rferl.orgnca/features/1999/12/F.RU991222134916.html.

Lobjakas, A., 1999, EU: doubts over expansion remain. *RFE/RL Report*, 15 December. http://www.rferl.org/nca/features/1999/12/F.RU.991215152348.html.

O'Donnell, P., 1999a, Gloves off. *Business Central Europe*, 6 (66), 39–41.

O'Donnell, P., 1999b, New agenda. *Business Central Europe*, 6 (65), 39–40.

O'Rourke, B., 1999, 1999 in review: genuine tests in EU enlargement still to come. *RFE/RL Report*, 17 December. http://www.rferl.org/nca/features/1999/12/F.RU.991217151938.html.

Prodi, R., 1999, *Speech to the European Parliament: Brussels, 10 November 1999.* Brussels: European Commission. http://europa.eu.int/rapid/start/cgi/guesten.ksh?p_action.gettxt=gt&doc=SPEECH/99/158.

Unwin, T., 1998, European futures. *In* Unwin, T., ed., *A European geography*. London: Longman, pp. 333–343.

von Weizsäcker, R., Dehaene, J.-L., Simon, D., 1999, *The institutional implications of enlargement: report to the European Commission. Brussels: 18 October.* Brussels: European Commission.

INDEX

Page numbers in italics refer to maps and tables